LYNCHBURG COLLEGE
SYMPOSIUM READINGS

CLASSICAL SELECTIONS ON GREAT ISSUES

SERIES ONE
VOLUME I

THE NATURE
OF MAN

Cicero

Mirandola

Lucretius

Aquinas

Johnson

Wordsworth

Darwin

Freud

Emerson

Sartre

Laotse

Tillich

NIVERSITY
RESS OF
MERICA

SERIES ONE

SYMPOSIUM READINGS

Lynchburg College in Virginia

Compiled and Edited by the
following faculty members of Lynchburg College:

Kenneth E. Alrutz, A.M., University of Pennsylvania; Assistant
Professor of English

Virginia B. Berger, M.A., Harvard University; Associate Professor
of Music

Anne Marshall Bippus, Ed.D., University of Virginia; Associate
Professor of Education

James L. Campbell, Ph.D., University of Virginia; Associate Professor of English

Robert L. Frey, Ph.D., University of Minnesota; Professor of
History

James A. Huston, Ph.D., New York University; Dean of the College,
Professor of History and International Relations

Shannon McIntyre Jordan, Ph.D., University of Georgia; Instructor
in Philosophy

Jan G. Linn, D.Min., Christian Theological Seminary; Assistant
Professor, College Chaplain

Peggy S. Pittas, M.A., Dalhousie University; Associate Professor
of Psychology

Clifton W. Potter, Jr., Ph.D., University of Virginia; Professor
of History

Julius A. Sigler, Ph.D., University of Virginia; Professor of
Physics

Phillip H. Stump, Ph.D., University of California at Los Angeles;
Assistant Professor of History

Thomas C. Tiller, Ph.D., Florida State University; Dean of Student
Affairs, Professor of Education

Copyright © 1982 by

University Press of America,™ Inc.

4720 Boston Way
Lanham, MD 20706

3 Henrietta Street
London WC2E 8LU England

Library of Congress Cataloging in Publication Data
Main entry under title:

The Nature of man.

    (Classical selections on great issues; series 1, v. 1)
    Compiled and edited by the faculty members of
Lynchburg College.
    1. Man–Addresses, essays, lectures. I. Cicero,
Marcus Tullius. II. Lynchburg College. III. Series.
BD450.N366   1982   128   82–45158
ISBN 0–8191–2462–1
ISBN 0–8191–2463–X (pbk.)

ACKNOWLEDGEMENTS

The following copyrighted materials have been used with the permission of the copyright holders:

From *The Wisdom of Laotse*, by Laotse. c.1948, Random House, Inc.

From *Existentialism and Human Emotions*, by Jean-Paul Sartre. c.1957, Philosophical Library, Inc.

From *The Courage To Be*, by Paul Tillich. c.1952,Yale University Press.

From *The Renaissance Philosophy of Man*, "Oration on the Dignity of Man" by Pico della Mirandola. c.1948, University of Chicago Press.

From *Totem and Taboo* by Sigmund Freud. Trans. by A.A. Brill. c.1918; c. renewed, 1946 by Gioia B. Bernheim and Edmund R. Brill. Reprinted by permission.

With appreciation:

From *The Complete Essays and Other Writings of Ralph Waldo Emerson*, "The Over-soul" by Ralph Waldo Emerson. c. 1940, Random House, Inc.

The authors acknowledge with appreciation the permissions granted by these holders of the respective copyrights.

INTRODUCTION TO THE SERIES

These reading selections are offered in support of the Senior Symposium at Lynchburg College.

The Symposium is intended to be a kind of capstone for the general education programs of the College. It has the general purpose of serving as a "bridge" between formal college courses and the continuing study and consideration of major issues by responsible college graduates. The objectives are to develop a sense of perspective in recognizing that mankind has faced similar issues through the ages and that no panaceas exist for settling human problems once for all; to bring together the thinking of people of broad experience, varying points of view, and diverse backgrounds in seeking ways to meet the questions which demand attention in public affairs, and to develop an awareness of unity in knowledge and of the inter-relationships of problems in various fields of activity and interest.

In a way, the course may be said to have had four major historic antecedents - "paternal and maternal grandparents" as it were. These were (1) the senior course in "Moral Philosophy" common in American colleges in the nineteenth century; (2) "Chapel" or "College Assembly" common in many American colleges until fairly recently; (3) the "Great Books" programs of Columbia, Chicago, and Harvard, and (4) the "Great Issues" course at Dartmouth, University of Denver, Purdue, and Michigan State.

In *A History of Curriculum* written for the Carnegie Council on Policy Studies in Higher Education, Frederick Rudolph describes the first of these as follows:

> The senior course in moral philosophy justi-
> fied the curriculum, it rationalized it. It
> asserted the unity of knowledge, sent the
> young graduates out into the world with a re-
> assuring sense of their own fitness to play
> a role in upholding the moral order; it
> treated them like men, they who had thus far
> been treated like boys. By the 19th Century
> the moral philosophy course, Aristotelian in
> origin and English and Scottish in modifica-
> tion, had become a remarkable excursion into
> social and individual ethics. Politics, eco-
> nomics, sociology, law, government, history,

esthetics, international law, and fine arts
were territories into which the moral philosophers ... roamed

     . . . . . .

In deed, the senior course in moral philosophy was the last moment when the idea of a
liberal education as an expression of the
unity of knowledge could be honestly held.

The traditional "chapel" evolved from an essentially
religious exercise to a series of lectures on a wide
range of topics in the arts and sciences for which the
attendance of all students commonly was required. At
Lynchburg College, this later became "assembly". At
first, attendance was required of all; then grades and
credit were assigned according to attendance. It survived in the catalogue as an assembly for which the
College might require attendance at certain meetings,
until 1972, though actually it had fallen into disuse
for want of a satisfactory meeting site.

The "Great Books" program at Columbia inspired the
one at the University of Chicago where it became a major element of the undergraduate curriculum, and then
reached the ultimate at St. John's, Annapolis, where
"Great Books" became the basis for the entire curriculum. Similar programs developed at Harvard, Notre
Dame, and other institutions across the country. As
a Harvard committee, reporting on the organization of
its course on "Selected Great Books", stated:

The aim of such a course would be the fullest understanding of the work read rather
than of men or periods represented, crafts-
manship evinced, historic or literary development shown, or anything else. These
other matters would be admitted only insofar as they are necessary to allow the work
to speak·for itself.

The treatment which is attempted by these
great themes can only do its best to be
worthy of them. They themselves are its
inspirations... The instructor can only
seek to be a means by which the authors
teach the course.

The distinguished jurist, Learned Hand, once wrote:

> I venture to believe that it is as important
> to a judge called upon to pass on a question
> of constitutional law, to have at least a
> bowing acquaintance with Thucydides, ...
> Shakespeare, with Machiavelli, Plato, and
> Bacon, as with the books which have been
> specifically written on the subject.
>
> For in such matters everything turns upon
> the spirit in which he approaches the ques-
> tions before him ... Men do not gather figs
> of thistles, nor supply institutions from
> judges whose outlook is limited by parish or
> class.

The Dartmouth course on "Great Issues" was a weekly assembly of seniors to hear visiting speakers on
current issues. But for background reading, the students depended on *The New York Times* and other period-
icals.

At least "first cousins" have been such programs
as the "Open Forum" which once flourished at Indiana
University to bring in outstanding speakers on major
current issues; the program of the Bell Telephone Company of Pennsylvania for its mid-career executives
which operated for several years at the University of
Pennsylvania, not for the study of engineering or fi-
nance, or management, but for study of "great books" -
in the humanities; and the activities and conferences
of the Aspen Institute for Humanistic Studies in Colo-
rado.

The Senior Symposium is an attempt to bring all
these elements together. The approach is to undertake
the discussion of major, continuing issues on the basis
of current ideas presented by visiting scholars, public
officials, artists, business and professional people,
and other leaders of thought and opinion with the perspective of ideas presented in "great books".

Theodore M. Greene of Yale University has written
that the four basic ingredients of a liberal education
- what the college should give to every student - are
the following:

1. Training in the accurate and felicitous
   use of *language* as the essential condi-

tion of all reflection, self-expression, and communication with others.

2. Training in the acquisition of *factual knowledge* of ourselves, our society, and other societies, the physical world, and ultimate reality so far as it is humanly knowable.

3. Training in mature and responsible *evaluation and decision* in the controversial areas of social policy, morality, art and religion.

4. Training in *synoptic comprehension,* i.e., in the escape from multiple provincialisms which bedevil mankind, and in the attainment of larger and more inclusive perspectives.

As conceived here, the purposes of the Senior Symposium fall precisely into the third and fourth of these categories.

Further, Lynchburg College shares the conviction of the Bell Company and the University of Pennsylvania, of the Aspen Institute, and of Cardinal Newman (in *The Idea of a University*) that studies in the liberal arts, including studies of the great classics, contribute not only to the development of a better person and a better citizen, but also to the development of a better business or professional person.

The "great issues" for consideration in the course are taken to be broad areas of great, continuing problems of mankind. Within each area certain questions are taken up for consideration in relation to the broader aspects of the problems.

Thus for the first semester the general themes are chosen from "The Nature of Man," "Education: Ends and Means," "Freedom and Tyranny," "Poverty and Wealth," and "War and Peace." Current questions taken up include such matters as individual freedom and internal security, the "new look" in United States foreign and military policies, economic stablization, and foreign aid and trade. In the second semester, the general themes are "Man and the Universe," "Science, Technology, and Society," "Man and the Imagination: The Fine Arts," "Faith and Morals," and "Man and Society."

The procedure includes assigned readings in selections from the "classics," lectures each week, usually by a visiting lecturer, on some related current question or to present contemporary views on broader issues, and then group discussions later in the week on the readings and lectures. Each student, then, has a weekly reading assignment, one lecture, and one discussion section.

Montaigne, himself a contributor to "great books," rather downgraded the study of books when he wrote, "The most fruitful and natural exercise of our mind, in my opinion, is discussion... Discussion teaches and excercises us at the same time."

The discussion gives an opportunity to compare reading selections, to counterbalance one-sided lectures, to place current issues in a humanities perspective. Thus students discover that when Thucydides, for example, writes on the causes of war, and appeasement, and alliances, and morality in war, and the over-extension of an expedition to Sicily, he is expressing concerns about the same questions that troubled Americans in World War II, or in Korea, or in Viet Nam. And they find food for thought in discussing the *Apology* and the *Crito* in relation to the lecture of a local judge who compared the trial of Socrates with that of Jesus, and then compared and contrasted both with modern-day trial procedures in the Soviet Union and the United States.

In the discussion sections, the students express and test their own views on the basis of what they have read and heard, no only in the course, but in their total experience. No effort is made to arrive at general conclusions of "final answers" for any of the questions. Each student is encouraged to develop his own ideas and to keep his mind open to modify his views whenever additional evidence demands it.

There is 'no assumption that the Symposium represents any thorough coverage of all the fields that it touches. As the capstone to a student's general education, it gains its depth by drawing upon all the educational experience of the student and by dwelling on particular questions. In discussions cutting across the lines of formal disciplines, students have a chance to learn a great deal from each other around a focus of concern common to all. It also is a demonstration for seniors that their education is far from complete, that much remains to be learned, and learning is a process which must continue through their lives.

While these readings are intended primarily for seniors, many of them, of course, would be appropriate for any level. Indeed, a common definition of a classic is a work which has such a quality of timelessness that it speaks to all ages of persons as well as to all ages of history. Still we have found that the discussion of these works is much more fruitful for seniors than for underclassmen. It is to be expected and hoped that students will have encountered many of these works earlier in their academic careers. But here they will be approaching them with a different perspective, and with the benefit of added experience and maturity which will make their reading and discussion all the more meaningful and all the more delightful.

The temptation in making such a collection as this is to include too much. A weakness of many anthologies which grows out of this is to select such small segments that the reader misses many of the significant points and especially the well reasoned argument of the masters. In this series some short selections have been included for a specific point, but for the most part selections comprise whole chapters or several chapters of the works. The plan has been deliberately to include substantially more selections than may be used in a semester. This allows flexibility in making assignments from year to year, and it provides additional material upon which students may draw for the preparation of special reports or simply to extend their reading.

Readings are grouped in units which are intended to correspond to assignments. For example, in one semester all five themes might be used with three units for each. In another, only three themes might be used with five assignments for each. Or there may be other combinations suitable for the purposes of the instructors. In further reading one might explore a particular theme in greater depth, or might search for relationships among readings which happen to be grouped under different themes.

It is to be hoped that study and reflection upon the reading selections presented here, and participation in the kind of symposium course which they support, will contribute something to a perspective with which, on the one hand, a person will resist falling prey to false prophets who promise quick and easy solutions for all the problems of the day, and on the other will be able to appreciate the remarkable achievements of man through the ages which have enabled him to deal with those problems in a way to find at least enough tentative answers to survive and to discover something of the "more abundant life."

This selection of readings is the result of the efforts of the group of Lynchburg College faculty members whose names appear on the title page. With the support of a National Endowment for the Humanities pilot grant, they worked individually, in small teams, and as a group to choose the readings and to prepare study questions and brief introductory statements. The questions, intended mainly to guide the reading, may also be useful for examinations and quizzes, but especially for discussion. Introductions have been left short that "the books may speak for themselves."

Dr. Jordan and Dr. Potter did further editing of materials; Dr. Potter did the final editing; and Shirley W. Moore prepared the materials for publication. George R. White, Jr., Assistant Librarian for Instructional Services, served as library consultant.

J.A.H.

INTRODUCTION

Throughout the ages, people of all cultures have concerned themselves with the nature of man. This volume contains writings, ancient and modern, which have been selected as representative of various views. These selections show the breadth and timelessness of the questions, ideas, and arguments raised by man about the nature and purpose of his existence. They represent differing emphases such as the rational and the romantic, the spiritual and the material, the classical and the Christian, and the individual and the communal.

CONTENTS

1

Cicero, ON THE LAWS (Trans. by Clinton W. Keyes)

Mirandola, "ORATION ON THE DIGNITY OF MAN"
(Trans. by Elizabeth L. Forbes)

1. What do laws have to do with human nature? Do people act justly because they fear punishment? If not, why do they? Why does Cicero feel that not all laws are just?

2. What evidence does Cicero offer to prove that all people share essentially the same nature? How does he explain evil tendencies in man? What is the origin of human nature?

3. What does Cicero mean when he criticizes those who separate utility from justice? Do you think Cicero's views are realistic?

4. Do you think that the human virtues which Cicero considers to be a part of man's essential nature would be considered to be virtues in every culture?

5. Do you think that Cicero and Mirandola give adequate attention to man's physical or material nature?

6. According to Mirandola, how do people become what they are? What evidence does Mirandola offer for his views?

7. What is Mirandola's view of human nature? How does it compare with traditional Judeo-Christian teachings?

In contrast to the philosophical concepts of
Lucretius, the writings of Marcus Tullius Cicero (106-
43 B.C.) on the nature of man reflect the broad main-
stream of classical thought. Based chiefly on the
teachings of Plato and the Stoics, the views of this
Roman orator, writer, and statesman have proved particularly amenable to synthesis with Christian concepts
of human nature. Over the centuries, the ideas of the
aristocratic Cicero have enriched the basic concepts of
democratic thought and enjoyed an enduring popularity.
This excerpt is from an imagined dialogue among Cicero
(Marcus) and his two brothers,(Quintus and Atticus).

ON THE LAWS

In our present
investigation we intend to cover the whole range of
universal Justice and Law in such a way that our
own civil law, as it is called, will be confined to a
small and narrow corner. For we must explain the
nature of Justice, and this must be sought for in the
nature of man; we must also consider the laws by
which States ought to be governed; then we must
deal with the enactments and decrees of nations
which are already formulated and put in writing;
and among these the civil law, as it is called, of the
Roman people will not fail to find a place.

VI. *Q.* You probe deep, and seek, as you should,
the very fountain-head, to find what we are after,
brother. And those who teach the civil law in any
other way are teaching not so much the path of
justice as of litigation.

M. There you are mistaken, Quintus, for it is rather
ignorance of the law than knowledge of it that leads to
litigation. But that will come later; now let us
investigate the origins of Justice.

Well then, the most learned men have determined
to begin with Law, and it would seem that they are
right, if, according to their definition, Law is the
highest reason, implanted in Nature, which commands
what ought to be done and forbids the opposite.
This reason, when firmly fixed and fully developed
in the human mind, is Law. And so they believe
that Law is intelligence, whose natural function it is
to command right conduct and forbid wrongdoing.
They think that this quality has derived its name in
Greek from the idea of granting to every man his
own, and in our language I believe it has been
named from the idea of choosing.[1] For as they have
attributed the idea of fairness to the word law, so we
have given it that of selection, though both ideas
properly belong to Law. Now if this is correct, as I
think it to be in general, then the origin of Justice
is to be found in Law, for Law is a natural force; it

is the mind and reason of the intelligent man, the standard by which Justice and Injustice are measured. But since our whole discussion has to do with the reasoning of the populace, it will sometimes be necessary to speak in the popular manner, and give the name of law to that which in written form decrees whatever it wishes, either by command or prohibition. For such is the crowd's definition of law. But in determining what Justice is, let us begin with that supreme Law which had its origin ages before any written law existed or any State had been established.

Q. Indeed that will be preferable and more suitable to the character of the conversation we have begun.

M. Well, then, shall we seek the origin of Justice itself at its fountain-head? For when that is discovered we shall undoubtedly have a standard by which the things we are seeking may be tested.

Q. I think that is certainly what we must do.

A. Put me down also as agreeing with your brother's opinion.

M. Since, then, we must retain and preserve that constitution of the State which Scipio proved to be the best in the six books [1] devoted to the subject, and all our laws must be fitted to that type of State, and since we must also inculcate good morals, and not prescribe everything in writing, I shall seek the root of Justice in Nature, under whose guidance our whole discussion must be conducted.

A. Quite right. Surely with her as our guide, it will be impossible for us to go astray.

VII. *M.* Do you grant us, then, Pomponius (for I am aware of what Quintus thinks), that it is by the might of the immortal gods, or by their nature, reason, power, mind, will, or any other term which may make my meaning clearer, that all Nature is governed? For if you do not admit it, we must begin our argument with this problem before taking up anything else.

A. Surely I will grant it, if you insist upon it, for the singing of the birds about us and the babbling of the streams relieve me from all fear that I may be overheard by any of my comrades in the School.[1]

M. Yet you must be careful; for it is their way to become very angry at times, as virtuous men will; and they will not tolerate your treason, if they hear of it, to the opening passage of that excellent book, in which the author [2] has written, " God troubles himself about nothing, neither his own concerns nor those of others."

A. Continue, if you please, for I am eager to learn what my admission will lead to.

M. I will not make the argument long. Your admission leads us to this : that animal which we call man, endowed with foresight and quick intelligence, complex, keen, possessing memory, full of reason and prudence, has been given a certain distinguished status by the supreme God who created him ; for he is the only one among so many different kinds and varieties of living beings who has a share in reason and thought, while all the rest are deprived of it. But what is more divine, I will not say in man only, but in all heaven and earth, than reason? And reason, when it is full grown and perfected, is rightly called wisdom. Therefore, since there is nothing better than reason, and since it exists both in man and God, the first common possession of man and God is reason. But those who have reason in common must also have right reason in common. And since right reason is Law, we must believe that men have Law also in common with the gods. Further, those who share Law must also share Justice; and those who share these are to be regarded as members of the same commonwealth. If indeed they obey the same authorities and powers, this is true in a far greater degree; but as a matter of fact they do obey this celestial system, the divine mind, and the God of transcendent power. Hence we must now conceive of this whole universe as one commonwealth of which both gods and men are members.

And just as in States distinctions in legal status are made on account of the blood relationships of families, according to a system which I shall take up in its proper place,[1] so in the universe the same thing holds true, but on a scale much vaster and more splendid, so that men are grouped with Gods on the basis of blood relationship and descent. VIII. For when the nature of man is examined, the theory is usually advanced (and in all probability it is correct) that through constant changes and revolutions in the heavens, a time came which was suitable for sowing the seed of the human race. And when this seed was scattered and sown over the earth, it was granted the divine gift of the soul. For while the other elements of which man consists were derived from what is mortal, and are therefore fragile and perishable, the soul was generated in us by God. Hence we are justified in saying that there is a blood relationship between ourselves and the celestial beings; or we may call it a common ancestry or origin. Therefore among all the varieties of living beings, there is no creature except man which has any knowledge of God, and among men themselves there is no race either so highly civilized or so savage as not to know that it must believe in a god, even if it does not know in what sort of god it ought to believe. Thus it is clear that man recognizes God because, in a way, he remembers and recognizes the source from which he sprang.

Moreover, virtue exists in man and God alike, but in no other creature besides; virtue, however, is nothing else than Nature perfected and developed to its highest point; therefore there is a likeness between man and God. As this is true, what relationship could be closer or clearer than this one? For this reason, Nature has lavishly yielded such a wealth of things adapted to man's convenience and use that what she produces seems intended as a gift to us, and not brought forth by chance; and this is true, not only of what the fertile earth bountifully bestows in the form of grain and fruit, but also of the animals; for it is clear that some of them have been created to be man's slaves, some to supply him with their products, and others to serve as his food. Moreover innumerable arts have been discovered through the teachings of Nature; for it is by a skilful imitation of her that reason has acquired the necessities of life. IX. Nature has likewise not only equipped man himself with nimbleness of thought, but has also given him the senses, to be, as it were, his attendants and messengers; she has laid bare the obscure and none too [obvious] meanings of a great many things, to serve as the foundations of knowledge, as we may call them; and she has granted us a bodily form which is convenient and well suited to the human mind. For while she has bent the other creatures down toward their food, she has made man alone erect, and has challenged him to look up toward heaven, as being, so to speak, akin to him, and his first home. In addition, she has so formed his features as to portray therein the character that lies hidden deep within him; for not only do the eyes declare with exceeding clearness the innermost feelings of our hearts, but also the countenance, as we Romans call it, which can be found in no living thing save man, reveals the character.[1] (The Greeks are familiar with the meaning which this word "countenance" conveys, though they have no name for it.) I will pass over the special faculties and aptitudes of the other parts of the body, such as the varying tones of the voice and the power of speech, which is the most effective promoter of human intercourse; for all these things are not in keeping with our present discussion or the time at our disposal; and besides, this topic has been adequately treated, as it seems to me, by Scipio in the books which you have read.[2] But, whereas God has begotten and equipped man, desiring him to be the chief of all created things, it should now be evident, without going into all the details, that Nature, alone and unaided, goes a step farther; for, with no guide to point the way, she starts with those things whose character she has learned through the rudimentary beginnings of intelligence, and, alone and unaided, strengthens and perfects the faculty of reason.

X. *A.* Ye immortal gods, how far back you go to find the origins of Justice! And you discourse so eloquently that I not only have no desire to hasten on to the consideration of the civil law, concerning

which I was expecting you to speak, but I should
have no objection to your spending even the entire
day on your present topic; for the matters which
you have taken up, no doubt, merely as preparatory
to another subject, are of greater import than the
subject itself to which they form an introduction.

M. The points which are now being briefly touched
upon are certainly important; but out of all the
material of the philosophers' discussions, surely there
comes nothing more valuable than the full realization that we are born for Justice, and that right is
based, not upon men's opinions, but upon Nature.
This fact will immediately be plain if you once get
a clear conception of man's fellowship and union
with his fellow-men. For no single thing is so like
another, so exactly its counterpart, as all of us are to
one another. Nay, if bad habits and false beliefs
did not twist the weaker minds and turn them in
whatever direction they are inclined, no one would
be so like his own self as all men would be like
all others.[1] And so, however we may define man,
a single definition will apply to all. This is a
sufficient proof that there is no difference in kind
between man and man; for if there were, one definition could not be applicable to all men; and indeed
reason, which alone raises us above the level of the
beasts and enables us to draw inferences, to prove
and disprove, to discuss and solve problems, and to
come to conclusions, is certainly common to us all,
and, though varying in what it learns, at least in the
capacity to learn it is invariable. For the same things
are invariably perceived by the senses, and those
things which stimulate the senses, stimulate them
in the same way in all men; and those rudimentary

beginnings of intelligence to which I have referred, which are imprinted on our minds, are imprinted on all minds alike ; and speech, the mind's interpreter, though differing in the choice of words, agrees in the sentiments expressed. In fact, there is no human being of any race who, if he finds a guide, cannot attain to virtue.

XI. The similarity of the human race is clearly marked in its evil tendencies as well as in its goodness. For pleasure also attracts all men ; and even though it is an enticement to vice, yet it has some likeness to what is naturally good. For it delights us by its lightness and agreeableness ; and for this reason, by an error of thought, it is embraced as something wholesome. It is through a similar misconception that we shun death as though it were a dissolution of nature, and cling to life because it keeps us in the sphere in which we were born ; and that we look upon pain as one of the greatest of evils, not only because of its cruelty, but also because it seems to lead to the destruction of nature. In the same way, on account of the similarity between moral worth and renown, those who are publicly honoured are considered happy, while those who do not attain fame are thought miserable. Troubles, joys, desires, and fears haunt the minds of all men without distinction, and even if different men have different beliefs, that does not prove, for example, that it is not the same quality of superstition that besets those races which worship dogs and cats as gods, as that which torments other races. But what nation does not love courtesy, kindliness, gratitude, and remembrance of favours bestowed ? What people does not hate and despise

10

the haughty, the wicked, the cruel, and the un-
grateful? Inasmuch as these considerations prove
to us that the whole human race is bound together
in unity, it follows, finally, that knowledge of the
principles of right living is what makes men better.

If you approve of what has been said, I will go on
to what follows. But if there is anything that you
care to have explained, we will take that up first.

A. We have no questions, if I may speak for both
of us.

XII. *M.* The next point, then, is that we are
so constituted by Nature as to share the sense of
Justice with one another and to pass it on to all
men. And in this whole discussion I want it understood that what I shall call Nature is [that which is
implanted in us by Nature]; that, however, the
corruption caused by bad habits is so great that the
sparks of fire, so to speak, which Nature has kindled
in us are extinguished by this corruption, and the
vices which are their opposites spring up and are
established. But if the judgments of men were in
agreement with Nature, so that, as the poet says,
they considered " nothing alien to them which
concerns mankind," [1] then Justice would be equally
observed by all. For those creatures who have received the gift of reason from Nature have also
received right reason, and therefore they have also
received the gift of Law, which is right reason
applied to command and prohibition. And if they
have received Law, they have received Justice also.
Now all men have received reason; therefore all
men have received Justice. Consequently Socrates
was right when he cursed, as he often did, the man
who first separated utility from Justice; for this

separation, he complained, is the source of all mischief.[1] For what gave rise to Pythagoras' famous words about friendship?[2] . . . From this it is clear that, when a wise man shows toward another endowed with equal virtue the kind of benevolence which is so widely diffused among men, that will then have come to pass which, unbelievable as it seems to some, is after all the inevitable result— namely, that he loves himself no whit more than he loves another. For what difference can there be among things which are all equal? But if the least distinction should be made in friendship, then the very name of friendship would perish forthwith ; for its essence is such that, as soon as either friend prefers anything for himself, friendship ceases to exist.

Now all this is really a preface to what remains to be said in our discussion, and its purpose is to make it more easily understood that Justice is inherent in Nature. After I have said a few words more on this topic, I shall go on to the civil law, the subject which gives rise to all this discourse.

XIII. Q. You certainly need to say very little more on that head, for from what you have already said, Atticus is convinced, and certainly I am, that Nature is the source of Justice.

A. How can I help being convinced, when it has just been proved to us, first, that we have been

---

[2] Whether the quotation from Pythagoras was given by Cicero or not we cannot tell, nor can we be sure what "famous words" are referred to. The well-known sayings, κοινὰ τὰ τῶν φίλων, "the possessions of friends are owned in common," and τὸν φίλον ἄλλον ἑαυτόν, "a friend is a second self," are credited to him, as well as several other aphorisms on the subject. (See Porphyrius, *De Vita Pythag.* § 33.)

provided and equipped with what we may call the
gifts of the gods; next, that there is only one
principle by which men may live with one another,
and that this is the same for all, and possessed
equally by all; and, finally, that all men are bound
together by a certain natural feeling of kindliness
and good-will, and also by a partnership in Justice?
Now that we have admitted the truth of these conclusions, and rightly, I think, how can we separate
Law and Justice from Nature?

M. Quite right; that is exactly the situation.
But we are following the method of the philosophers
—not those of former times, but those who have
built workshops, so to speak, for the production of
wisdom. Those problems which were formerly
argued loosely and at great length they now discuss
systematically, taking them up point by point;[1]
and they do not think that a treatment of the topic
which we are now considering is complete unless a
separate discussion is devoted to the particular point
that Justice springs from Nature.

A. And, of course, you have lost your independence
in discussion, or else you are the kind of man not to
follow your own judgment in a debate, but meekly
to accept the authority of others!

M. I do not always do that, Titus. But you see
the direction this conversation is to take; our whole
discourse is intended to promote the firm foundation
of States, the strengthening of cities, and the curing
of the ills of peoples. For that reason I want to be
especially careful not to lay down first principles
that have not been wisely considered and thoroughly
investigated. Of course I cannot expect that they
will be universally accepted, for that is impossible;

but I do look for the approval of all who believe
that everything which is right and honourable is to
be desired for its own sake, and that nothing
whatever is to be accounted a good unless it is
praiseworthy in itself, or at least that nothing should
be considered a great good unless it can rightly be
praised for its own sake.

But if it were a penalty and not Nature that
ought to keep men from injustice, what anxiety
would there be to trouble the wicked when the
danger of punishment was removed? But in fact
there has never been a villain so brazen as not to
deny that he had committed a crime, or else invent
some story of just anger to excuse its commission,
and seek justification for his crime in some natural
principle of right. Now if even the wicked dare
to appeal to such principles, how jealously should
they be guarded by the good! But if it is a
penalty, the fear of punishment, and not the

---

² Aeschylus' *Eumenides*, for example, where the Furies
pursue Orestes. The torches may possibly be referred to in
Eum. 1005 and 1021.

wickedness itself, that is to keep men from a life of wrongdoing and crime, then no one can be called unjust, and wicked men ought rather to be regarded as imprudent ; furthermore, those of us who are not influenced by virtue itself to be good men, but by some consideration of utility and profit, are merely shrewd, not good. For to what lengths will that man go in the dark who fears nothing but a witness and a judge ? What will he do if, in some desolate spot, he meets a helpless man, unattended, whom he can rob of a fortune ? Our virtuous man, who is just and good by nature, will talk with such a person, help him, and guide him on his way ; but the other, who does nothing for another's sake, and measures every act by the standard of his own advantage—it is clear enough, I think, what he will do ! If, however, the latter does deny that he would kill the man and rob him of his money, he will not deny it because he regards it as a naturally wicked thing to do, but because he is afraid that his crime may become known—that is, that he may get into trouble. Oh, what a motive, that might well bring a blush of shame to the cheek, not merely of the philosopher, but even of the simple rustic !

XV. But the most foolish notion of all is the belief that everything is just which is found in the customs or laws of nations. Would that be true, even if these laws had been enacted by tyrants? If the well-known Thirty [1] had desired to enact a set of laws at Athens, or if the Athenians without exception were delighted by the tyrants' laws, that would not entitle such laws to be regarded as just, would it ? No more, in my opinion, should that law be considered just which a Roman interrex [2]

proposed, to the effect that a dictator might put to
death with impunity any citizen he wished, even
without a trial. For Justice is one ; it binds all
human society, and is based on one Law, which is
right reason applied to command and prohibition.
Whoever knows not this Law, whether it has been
recorded in writing anywhere or not, is without
Justice.

But if Justice is conformity to written laws and
national customs, and if, as the same persons claim,
everything is to be tested by the standard of utility,
then anyone who thinks it will be profitable to him
will, if he is able, disregard and violate the laws.
It follows that Justice does not exist at all, if it
does not exist in Nature, and if that form of it
which is based on utility can be overthrown by
that very utility itself. And if Nature is not to
be considered the foundation of Justice, that will
mean the destruction [of the virtues on which
human society depends]. For where then will there
be a place for generosity, or love of country, or
loyalty, or the inclination to be of service to others
or to show gratitude for favours received ? For
these virtues originate in our natural inclination to
love our fellow-men, and this is the foundation of
Justice. Otherwise not merely consideration for
men but also rites and pious observances in honour
of the gods are done away with ; for I think that
these ought to be maintained, not through fear,
but on account of the close relationship which exists
between man and God. XVI. But if the principles
of Justice were founded on the decrees of peoples,
the edicts of princes, or the decisions of judges, then
Justice would sanction robbery and adultery and

forgery of wills, in case these acts were approved by the votes or decrees of the populace. But if so great a power belongs to the decisions and decrees of fools that the laws of Nature can be changed by their votes, then why do they not ordain that what is bad and baneful shall be considered good and salutary? Or, if a law can make Justice out of Injustice, can it not also make good out of bad? But in fact we can perceive the difference between good laws and bad by referring them to no other standard than Nature; indeed, it is not merely Justice and Injustice which are distinguished by Nature, but also and without exception things which are honourable and dishonourable. For since an intelligence common to us all makes things known to us and formulates them in our minds, honourable actions are ascribed by us to virtue, and dishonourable actions to vice; and only a madman would conclude that these judgments are matters of opinion, and not fixed by Nature. For even what we, by a misuse of the term, call the virtue[1] of a tree or of a horse, is not a matter of opinion, but is based on Nature. And if that is true, honourable and dishonourable actions must also be distinguished by Nature. For if virtue in general is to be tested by opinion, then its several parts must also be so tested; who, therefore, would judge a man of prudence and, if I may say so, hard common sense, not by his own character but by some external circumstance? For virtue is reason completely developed; and this certainly is natural; therefore everything honourable is likewise natural. XVII. For just as truth and falsehood, the logical and illogical, are judged by themselves and not by

anything else, so the steadfast and continuous use
of reason in the conduct of life, which is virtue, and
also inconstancy, which is vice, [are judged] by their
own nature.

[Or, when a farmer judges the quality of a tree
by nature,] shall we not use the same standard
in regard to the characters of young men? Then
shall we judge character by Nature, and judge virtue
and vice, which result from character, by some other
standard? But if we adopt the same standard for
them, must we not refer the honourable and the
base to Nature also? Whatever good thing is
praiseworthy must have within itself something
which deserves praise, for goodness itself is good
by reason not of opinion but of Nature. For, if
this were not true, men would also be happy by
reason of opinion; and what statement could be
more absurd than that? Wherefore since both good
and evil are judged by Nature and are natural
principles, surely honourable and base actions must
also be distinguished in a similar way and referred
to the standard of Nature. But we are confused
by the variety of men's beliefs and by their dis-
agreements, and because this same variation is not
found in the senses, we think that Nature has made
these accurate, and say that those things about
which different people have different opinions and
the same people not always identical opinions are
unreal. However, this is far from being the case.
For our senses are not perverted by parent, nurse,
teacher, poet, or the stage, nor led astray by popular
feeling; but against our minds all sorts of plots are
constantly being laid, either by those whom I have
just mentioned, who, taking possession of them

while still tender and unformed, colour and bend
them as they wish, or else by that enemy which
lurks deep within us, entwined in our every sense—
that counterfeit of good, which is, however, the
mother of all evils—pleasure. Corrupted by her
allurements, we fail to discern clearly what things
are by Nature good, because the same seductiveness
and itching does not attend them.

XVIII. To close now our discussion of this whole
subject, the conclusion, which stands clearly before
our eyes from what has already been said, is this:
Justice and all things honourable are to be sought
for their own sake. And indeed all good men love
fairness in itself and Justice in itself, and it is
unnatural for a good man to make such a mistake as
to love what does not deserve love for itself alone.
Therefore Justice must be sought and cultivated
for her own sake; and if this is true of Justice,
it is also true of equity; and if this is the case with
equity, then all the other virtues are also to be
cherished for their own sake. What of generosity?
Is it disinterested or does it look to a recompense?
If a man is kind without any reward, then it is
disinterested; but if he receives payment, then it is
hired. It cannot be doubted that he who is called
generous or kind answers the call of duty, not
of gain. Therefore equity also demands no reward
or price; consequently it is sought for its own sake.
And the same motive and purpose characterize all
the virtues.

In addition, if it be true that virtue is sought for
the sake of other benefits and not for its own sake,
there will be only one virtue, which will most properly be called a vice.[1] For in proportion as any one

makes his own advantage absolutely the sole standard
of all his actions, to that extent he is absolutely not
a good man; therefore those who measure virtue by
the reward it brings believe in the existence of no
virtue except vice. For where shall we find a kindly
man, if no one does a kindness for the sake of anyone
else than himself? Who can be considered grateful,
if even those who repay favours have no real consideration for those to whom they repay them?[1]
What becomes of that sacred thing, friendship, if
even the friend himself is not loved for his own sake,
"with the whole heart," as people say? Why,
according to this theory, a friend should even be
deserted and cast aside as soon as there is no longer
hope of benefit and profit from his friendship! But
what could be more inhuman than that? If, on the
other hand, friendship is to be sought for its own
sake, then the society of our fellow-men, fairness,
and Justice, are also to be sought for their own sake.
If this is not the case then there is no such thing as
Justice at all, for the very height of injustice is to
seek pay for Justice. XIX. But what shall we say
of sobriety, moderation, and self-restraint;[2] of
modesty, self-respect, and chastity? Is it for fear of
disgrace that we should not be wanton, or for fear of
the laws and the courts? In that case men are
innocent and modest in order to be well spoken of,
and they blush in order to gain a good reputation!
I am ashamed even to mention chastity! Or rather
I am ashamed of those philosophers who believe it
honourable to avoid condemnation for a crime without having avoided the crime itself.[3]

[3] The text is uncertain and the meaning doubtful.

And what shall we say of this? Is it possible for us to call those chaste who are kept from lewdness by the fear of disgrace, when the disgrace itself results from the inherent vileness of the deed? For what can properly be either praised or blamed, if you have disregarded the nature of the thing which in your opinion deserves praise or blame? Are bodily defects, if very conspicuous, to offend us, but not a deformity of character? And yet the baseness of this latter can easily be perceived from the very vices which result from it. For what can be thought of that is more loathsome than greed, what more inhuman than lust, what more contemptible than cowardice, what more degraded than stupidity and folly? Well, then, shall we say that those who are sunk deepest in a single vice, or in several, are wretched on account of any penalties or losses or tortures which they incur, or on account of the base nature of the vices themselves? And the same argument can be applied conversely to the praise accorded to virtue. Finally, if virtue is sought on account of other advantages, there must necessarily be something better than virtue. Is it money, then, or public office, or beauty, or health? But these things amount to very little when we possess them, and we can have no certain knowledge as to how long they will remain with us. Or is it—the very mention of such a thing is shameful—is it pleasure? But it is precisely in scorning and repudiating pleasure that virtue is most clearly discerned.

It is certainly true that, since Law ought to be a reformer of vice and an incentive to virtue, the guiding principles of life may be derived from it. It is therefore true that wisdom is the mother of all good things; and from the Greek expression meaning "the love of wisdom" philosophy has taken its name. And

philosophy is the richest, the most bounteous, and
the most exalted gift of the immortal gods to
humanity. For she alone has taught us, in addition
to all other wisdom, that most difficult of all things
—to know ourselves. This precept is so important
and significant that the credit for it is given, not to
any human being, but to the god of Delphi. For he
who knows himself will realize, in the first place,
that he has a divine element within him, and will
think of his own inner nature as a kind of consecrated image of God; and so he will always act and
think in a way worthy of so great a gift of the gods,
and, when he has examined and thoroughly tested
himself, he will understand how nobly equipped by
Nature he entered life, and what manifold means he
possesses for the attainment and acquisition of wisdom. For from the very first he began to form in
his mind and spirit shadowy concepts, as it were, of
all sorts, and when these have been illuminated
under the guidance of wisdom, he perceives that he
will be a good man, and, for that very reason, happy.
XXIII. For when the mind, having attained to a
knowledge and perception of the virtues, has
abandoned its subservience to the body and its
indulgence of it, has put down pleasure as if it were
a taint of dishonour, has escaped from all fear of
death or pain, has entered into a partnership of love
with its own, recognizing as its own all who are
joined to it by Nature; when it has taken up the
worship of the gods and pure religion, has sharpened
the vision both of the eye and of the mind so that
they can choose the good and reject the opposite—a
virtue which is called prudence because it foresees[1]
—then what greater degree of happiness can be
described or imagined? And further, when it has
examined the heavens, the earth, the seas, the nature
of the universe, and understands whence all these

things came and whither they must return, when and
how they are destined to perish, what part of them
is mortal and transient and what is divine and
eternal; and when it almost lays hold of the ruler
and governor of the universe, and when it realizes
that it is not shut in by [narrow] walls as a resident
of some fixed spot, but is a citizen of the whole
universe, as it were of a single city—then in the
midst of this universal grandeur, and with such a
view and comprehension of nature, ye immortal gods,
how well it will know itself, according to the precept
of the Pythian Apollo! How it will scorn and
despise and count as naught those things which the
crowd calls splendid! XXIV. And in defence of all
this, it will erect battlements of dialectic, of the
science of distinguishing the true from the false, and
of the art, so to speak, of understanding the consequences and opposites of every statement. And
when it realizes that it is born to take part in the life
of a State, it will think that it must employ not
merely the customary subtle method of debate, but
also the more copious continuous style,[1] considering,
for example, how to rule nations, establish laws,
punish the wicked, protect the good, honour those
who excel, publish to fellow-citizens precepts con-
ducive to their well-being and credit, so designed as
to win their acceptance; how to arouse them to
honourable actions, recall them from wrong-doing,
console the afflicted, and hand down to everlasting
memory the deeds and counsels of brave and wise
men, and the infamy of the wicked. So many and
so great are the powers which are perceived to exist

here seems to be that the latter is better suited for instruct-
ing and convincing one's fellow-citizens.

in man by those who desire to know themselves; and their parent and their nurse is wisdom.[1]

A. Your praise of wisdom is indeed impressive and true; but what is its purpose?

M. In the first place, Pomponius, it has to do with the subjects of which we are about to treat, which we desire shall assume an equally lofty character; for these matters cannot possess great dignity unless the sources from which they are derived possess it also. Secondly, I both take pleasure in praising wisdom, and do so, I believe, rightly, because, devoted as I am to its study, and since it has made me all I am, whatever that may be, I cannot pass over it in silence.

A. Indeed wisdom deserves this tribute from you, and it was your duty, as you say, to include it in your discussion.

Giovanni Pico della Mirandola (1463-1494) was one of the most creative scholars produced by the Italian Renaissance. At the age of twenty-three, seven years before his untimely death, he wrote the *Oration on the Dignity of Man*, from which this excerpt is taken. Intended as the keynote address for a great debate (which never took place) concerning the nature of man, this work is an impressive synthesis of classical and Christian ideas and reflects Mirandola's wide reading. But it also sets forth an original and provocative theory of its own concerning human nature, a theory which gives good expression to the Renaissance belief that "man can do all things if he will."

ORATION ON THE
DIGNITY OF MAN

I HAVE read in the records of the Arabians, reverend Fathers, that Abdala the Saracen, when questioned as to what on this stage of the world, as it were, could be seen most worthy of wonder, replied: "There is nothing to be seen more wonderful than man." In agreement with this opinion is the saying of Hermes Trismegistus: "A great miracle, Asclepius, is man." But when I weighed the reason for these maxims, the many grounds for the excellence of human nature reported by many men failed to satisfy me—that man is the intermediary between creatures, the intimate of the gods, the king of the lower beings, by the acuteness of his senses, by the discernment of his reason, and by the light of his intelligence the interpreter of nature, the interval between fixed eternity and fleeting time, and (as the Persians say) the bond, nay, rather, the marriage song of the world, on David's testimony but little lower than the angels. Admittedly great though these reasons be, they are not the principal grounds, that is, those which may rightfully claim for themselves the privilege of the highest admiration. For why should we not admire more the angels themselves and the blessed choirs of heaven? At last it seems to me I have come to understand why man is the most fortunate of creatures and consequently worthy of all admiration and what precisely is that rank which is his lot in the universal chain of Being—a rank to be envied not only by brutes but even by the stars and by minds beyond this world. It is a matter past faith and a wondrous one. Why should it not be? For it is on this very account that man is rightly called and judged a great miracle and a wonderful creature indeed.

2. But hear, Fathers, exactly what this rank is and, as friendly auditors, conformably to your kindness, do me this favor. God the Father, the supreme Architect, had already built this cosmic home we behold, the most sacred temple of His godhead, by the laws of His mysterious wisdom. The region above the heavens He had adorned with Intelligences, the heavenly spheres He had quickened with eternal souls, and the excrementary and filthy parts of the lower world He had filled with a multitude of animals of every kind. But, when the work was finished, the Craftsman kept wishing that there were someone to ponder the plan of so great a work, to love its beauty, and to wonder at its vastness. Therefore, when everything was done (as Moses and Timaeus bear witness), He finally took thought concerning the creation of man. But there was not among His archetypes that from which He could fashion a new offspring, nor was there in His treasure-houses anything which He might bestow on His new son as an inheritance, nor was there in the seats of all the world a place where the latter might sit to contemplate the universe. All was now complete; all things had been assigned to the highest, the middle, and the lowest orders. But in its final creation it was not the part of the Father's power to fail as though ex-

hausted. It was not the part of His wisdom to waver in a needful matter through poverty of counsel. It was not the part of His kindly love that he who was to praise God's divine generosity in regard to others should be compelled to condemn it in regard to himself.

3. At last the best of artisans ordained that that creature to whom He had been able to give nothing proper to himself should have joint possession of whatever had been peculiar to each of the different kinds of being. He therefore took man as a creature of indeterminate nature and, assigning him a place in the middle of the world, addressed him thus: "Neither a fixed abode nor a form that is thine alone nor any function peculiar to thyself have we given thee, Adam, to the end that according to thy longing and according to thy judgment thou mayest have and possess what abode, what form, and what functions thou thyself shalt desire. The nature of all other beings is limited and constrained within the bounds of laws prescribed by Us. Thou, constrained by no limits, in accordance with thine own free will, in whose hand We have placed thee, shalt ordain for thyself the limits of thy nature. We have set thee at the world's center that thou mayest from thence more easily observe whatever is in the world. We have made thee neither of heaven nor of earth, neither mortal nor immortal, so that with freedom of choice and with honor, as though the maker and molder of thyself, thou mayest fashion thyself in whatever shape thou shalt prefer. Thou shalt have the power to degenerate into the lower forms of life, which are brutish. Thou shalt have the power, out of thy soul's judgment, to be reborn into the higher forms, which are divine."

4. O supreme generosity of God the Father, O highest

and most marvelous felicity of man! To him it is granted to
have whatever he chooses, to be whatever he wills. Beasts
as soon as they are born (so says Lucilius) bring with them
from their mother's womb all they will ever possess.
Spiritual beings, either from the beginning or soon thereafter, become what they are to be for ever and ever. On
man when he came into life the Father conferred the seeds
of all kinds and the germs of every way of life. Whatever
seeds each man cultivates will grow to maturity and bear
in him their own fruit. If they be vegetative, he will be like
a plant. If sensitive, he will become brutish. If rational, he
will grow into a heavenly being. If intellectual, he will be
an angel and the son of God. And if, happy in the lot of no
created thing, he withdraws into the center of his own
unity, his spirit, made one with God, in the solitary darkness of God, who is set above all things, shall surpass them
all. Who would not admire this our chameleon? Or who
could more greatly admire aught else whatever? It is man
who Asclepius of Athens, arguing from his mutability of
character and from his self-transforming nature, on just
grounds says was symbolized by Proteus in the mysteries.
Hence those metamorphoses renowned among the Hebrews and the Pythagoreans.

5. For the occult theology of the Hebrews sometimes
transforms the holy Enoch into an angel of divinity whom
they call "Mal'akh Adonay Shebaoth," and sometimes
transforms others into other divinities. The Pythagoreans
degrade impious men into brutes and, if one is to believe
Empedocles, even into plants. Mohammed, in imitation,
often had this saying on his tongue: "They who have devi-
ated from divine law become beasts," and surely he spoke
justly. For it is not the bark that makes the plant but its

senseless and insentient nature; neither is it the hide that makes the beast of burden but its irrational, sensitive soul; neither is it the orbed form that makes the heavens but their undeviating order; nor is it the sundering from body but his spiritual intelligence that makes the angel. For if you see one abandoned to his appetites crawling on the ground, it is a plant and not a man you see; if you see one blinded by the vain illusions of imagery, as it were of Calypso, and, softened by their gnawing allurement, delivered over to his senses, it is a beast and not a man you see. If you see a philosopher determining all things by means of right reason, him you shall reverence: he is a heavenly being and not of this earth. If you see a pure contemplator, one unaware of the body and confined to the inner reaches of the mind, he is neither an earthly nor a heavenly being; he is a more reverend divinity vested with human flesh.

6. Are there any who would not admire man, who is, in the sacred writings of Moses and the Christians, not without reason described sometimes by the name of "all flesh," sometimes by that of "every creature," inasmuch as he himself molds, fashions, and changes himself into the form of all flesh and into the character of every creature? For this reason the Persian Euanthes, in describing the Chaldean theology, writes that man has no semblance that is inborn and his very own but many that are external and foreign to him; whence this saying of the Chaldeans: "Hanorish tharah sharinas," that is, "Man is a being of varied, manifold, and inconstant nature." But why do we emphasize this? To the end that after we have been born to this condition—that we can become what we will—we should understand that we ought to have especial care to this, that it should never be said against us that, although born to a

privileged position, we failed to recognize it and became like unto wild animals and senseless beasts of burden, but that rather the saying of Asaph the prophet should apply: "Ye are all angels and sons of the Most High," and that we may not, by abusing the most indulgent generosity of the Father, make for ourselves that freedom of choice He has given into something harmful instead of salutary. Let a certain holy ambition invade our souls, so that, not content with the mediocre, we shall pant after the highest and (since we may if we wish) toil with all our strength to obtain it.

7. Let us disdain earthly things, despise heavenly things, and, finally, esteeming less whatever is of the world, hasten to that court which is beyond the world and nearest to the Godhead. There, as the sacred mysteries relate, Seraphim, Cherubim, and Thrones hold the first places; let us, incapable of yielding to them, and intolerant of a lower place, emulate their dignity and their glory. If we have willed it, we shall be second to them in nothing.

8. But how shall we go about it, and what in the end shall we do? Let us consider what they do, what sort of life they lead. If we also come to lead that life (for we have the power), we shall then equal their good fortune. The Seraph burns with the fire of love. The Cherub glows with the splendor of intelligence. The Throne stands by the steadfastness of judgment. Therefore if, in giving ourselves over to the active life, we have after due consideration undertaken the care of the lower beings, we shall be strengthened with the firm stability of Thrones. If, unoccupied by deeds, we pass our time in the leisure of contemplation, considering the Creator in the creature and the creature in the Creator, we shall be all ablaze with Cherubic light. If

we long with love for the Creator himself alone, we shall speedily flame up with His consuming fire into a Seraphic likeness. Above the Throne, that is, above the just judge, God sits as Judge of the ages. Above the Cherub, that is, above him who contemplates, God flies, and cherishes him, as it were, in watching over him. For the spirit of the Lord moves upon the waters, the waters, I say, which are above the firmament and which in Job praise the Lord with hymns before dawn. Whoso is a Seraph, that is, a lover, is in God and God in him, nay, rather, God and himself are one. Great is the power of Thrones, which we attain in using judgment, and most high the exaltation of Seraphs, which we attain in loving.

9. But by what means is one able either to judge or to love things unknown? Moses loved a God whom he saw and, as judge, administered among the people what he had first beheld in contemplation upon the mountain. Therefore, the Cherub as intermediary by his own light makes us ready for the Seraphic fire and equally lights the way to the judgment of the Thrones. This is the bond of the first minds, the Palladian order, the chief of contemplative philosophy. This is the one for us first to emulate, to court, and to understand; the one from whence we may be rapt to the heights of love and descend, well taught and well prepared, to the functions of active life. But truly it is worth while, if our life is to be modeled on the example of the Cherubic life, to have before our eyes and clearly understood both its nature and its quality and those things which are the deeds and the labor of Cherubs. But since it is not permitted us to attain this through our own efforts, we who are but flesh and know of the things of earth, let us go to the ancient fathers who, inasmuch as they were familiar

and conversant with these matters, can give sure and altogether trustworthy testimony. Let us consult the Apostle
Paul, the chosen vessel, as to what he saw the hosts of
Cherubim doing when he was himself exalted to the third
heaven. He will answer, according to the interpretation of
Dionysius, that he saw them being purified, then being
illuminated, and at last being made perfect. Let us also,
therefore, by emulating the Cherubic way of life on earth,
by taming the impulses of our passions with moral science,
by dispelling the darkness of reason with dialectic, and by,
so to speak, washing away the filth of ignorance and vice,
cleanse our soul, so that her passions may not rave at random nor her reason through heedlessness ever be deranged.

10. Then let us fill our well-prepared and purified soul
with the light of natural philosophy, so that we may at last
perfect her in the knowledge of things divine. And lest we
be satisfied with those of our faith, let us consult the pat-
riarch Jacob, whose form gleams carved on the throne of
glory. Sleeping in the lower world but keeping watch in
the upper, the wisest of fathers will advise us. But he will
advise us through a figure (in this way everything was
wont to come to those men) that there is a ladder extending
from the lowest earth to the highest heaven, divided in a
series of many steps, with the Lord seated at the top, and
angels in contemplation ascending and descending over
them alternately by turns.

11. If this is what we must practice in our aspiration to
the angelic way of life, I ask: "Who will touch the ladder
of the Lord either with fouled foot or with unclean
hands?" As the sacred mysteries have it, it is impious for the
impure to touch the pure. But what are these feet? What
these hands? Surely the foot of the soul is that most con-

temptible part by which the soul rests on matter as on the soil of the earth, I mean the nourishing and feeding power, the tinder of lust, and the teacher of pleasurable weakness. Why should we not call the hands of the soul its irascible power, which struggles on its behalf as the champion of desire and as plunderer seizes in the dust and sun what desire will devour slumbering in the shade? These hands, these feet, that is, all the sentient part whereon resides the attraction of the body which, as they say, by wrenching the neck holds the soul in check, lest we be hurled down from the ladder as impious and unclean, let us bathe in moral philosophy as if in a living river. Yet this will not be enough if we wish to be companions of the angels going up and down on Jacob's ladder, unless we have first been well fitted and instructed to be promoted duly from step to step, to stray nowhere from the stairway, and to engage in the alternate comings and goings. Once we have achieved this by the art of discourse or reasoning, then, inspired by the Cherubic spirit, using philosophy through the steps of the ladder, that is, of nature, and penetrating all things from center to center, we shall sometimes descend, with titanic force rending the unity like Osiris into many parts, and we shall sometimes ascend, with the force of Phoebus collecting the parts like the limbs of Osiris into a unity, until, resting at last in the bosom of the Father who is above the ladder, we shall be made perfect with the felicity of theology.

12. Let us also inquire of the just Job, who entered into a life-covenant with God before he himself was brought forth into life, what the most high God requires above all in those tens of hundreds of thousands who attend him. He will answer that it is peace, in accord with what we read

in him: "He maketh peace in his high places." And since the middle order expounds to the lower orders the counsel of the highest order, let Empedocles the philospoher expound to us the words of Job the theologian. He indicates to us a twofold nature present in our souls, by one side of which we are raised on high to the heavenly regions, and by the other side plunged downward into the lower, through strife and friendship or through war and peace, as he witnesses in the verses in which he makes complaint that he is being driven into the sea, himself goaded by strife and discord into the semblance of a madman and a fugitive from the gods.

13. Surely, Fathers, there is in us a discord many times as great; we have at hand wars grievous and more than civil, wars of the spirit which, if we dislike them, if we aspire to that peace which may so raise us to the sublime that we shall be established among the exalted of the Lord, only philosophy will entirely allay and subdue in us. In the first place, if our man but ask a truce of his enemies, moral philosophy will check the unbridled inroads of the many-sided beast and the leonine passions of wrath and violence. If we then take wiser counsel with ourselves and learn to desire the security of everlasting peace, it will be at hand and will generously fulfil our prayers. After both beasts are felled like a sacrificed sow, it will confirm an inviolable compact of holiest peace between flesh and spirit. Dialectic will appease the tumults of reason made confused and anxious by inconsistencies of statement and sophisms of syllogisms. Natural philosophy will allay the strife and differences of opinion which vex, distract, and wound the spirit from all sides. But she will so assuage them as to compel us to remember that, according to Heraclitus, nature was begotten

from war, that it was on this account repeatedly called "strife" by Homer, and that it is not, therefore, in the power of natural philosophy to give us in nature a true quiet and unshaken peace but that this is the function and privilege of her mistress, that is, of holiest theology. She will show us the way and as comrade lead us to her who, seeing us hastening from afar, will exclaim "Come to me, ye who have labored. Come and I will restore you. Come to me, and I will give you peace, which the world and nature cannot give you."

14. When we have been so soothingly called, so kindly urged, we shall fly up with winged feet, like earthly Mercuries, to the embraces of our blessed mother and enjoy that wished-for peace, most holy peace, indivisible bond, of one accord in the friendship through which all rational souls not only shall come into harmony in the one mind which is above all minds but shall in some ineffable way become altogether one. This is that friendship which the Pythagoreans say is the end of all philosophy. This is that peace which God creates in his heavens, which the angels descending to earth proclaimed to men of good will, that through it men might ascend to heaven and become angels. Let us wish this peace for our friends, for our century. Let us wish it for every home into which we go; let us wish it for our own soul, that through it she shall herself be made the house of God, and to the end that as soon as she has cast out her uncleanness through moral philosophy and dialectic, adorned herself with manifold philosophy as with the splendor of a courtier, and crowned the pediments of her doors with the garlands of theology, the King of Glory may descend and, coming with his Father, make his stay with her. If she show herself worthy of so great a guest, she

shall, by the boundless mercy which is his, in golden rai-
ment like a wedding gown, and surrounded by a varied
throng of sciences, receive her beautiful guest not merely
as a guest but as a spouse from whom she will never be
parted. She will desire rather to be parted from her own
people and, forgetting her father's house and herself, will
desire to die in herself in order to live in her spouse, in
whose sight surely the death of his saints is precious—death,
I say, if we must call death that fulness of life, the consideration of which wise men have asserted to be the aim of
philosophy.

15. Let us also cite Moses himself, but little removed from
the springing abundance of the holy and unspeakable wisdom by whose nectar the angels are made drunk. Let us
hearken to the venerable judge in these words proclaiming
laws to us who are dwellers in the desert loneliness of this
body: "Let those who, as yet unclean, still need moral
philosophy, live with the people outside the tabernacle
under the sky, meanwhile purifying themselves like the
priests of Thessaly. Let those who have already ordered
their conduct be received into the sanctuary but not quite
yet touch the holy vessels; let them first like zealous Levites
in the service of dialectic minister to the holy things of
philosophy. Then when they have been admitted even to
these, let them now behold the many-colored robe of the
higher palace of the Lord, that is to say, the stars; let them
now behold the heavenly candlestick divided into seven
lights; let them now behold the fur tent, that is, the elements, in the priesthood of philosophy, so that when they
are in the end, through the favor of theological sublimity,
granted entrance into the inner part of the temple, they
may rejoice in the glory of the Godhead with no veil be-

fore his image." This of a surety Moses commands us and, in commanding, summons, urges, and encourages us by means of philosophy to prepare ourselves a way, while we can, to the heavenly glory to come.

16. But indeed not only the Mosaic and Christian mysteries but also the theology of the ancients show us the benefits and value of the liberal arts, the discussion of which I am about to undertake. For what else did the degrees of the initiates observed in the mysteries of the Greeks mean? For they arrived at a perception of the mysteries when they had first been purified through those expiatory sciences, as it were, moral philosophy and dialectic. What else can that perception possibly be than an interpretation of occult nature by means of philosophy? Then at length to those who were so disposed came that ΕΠΟΠΤΕΙΑ, that is to say, the observation of things divine by the light of theology. Who would not long to be initiated into such sacred rites? Who would not desire, by neglecting all human concerns, by despising the goods of fortune, and by disregarding those of the body, to become the guest of the gods while yet living on earth, and, made drunk by the nectar of eternity, to be endowed with the gifts of immortality though still a mortal being? Who would not wish to be so inflamed with those Socratic frenzies sung by Plato in the *Phaedrus*, that, by the oarage of feet and wings escaping speedily from hence, that is, from a world set on evil, he might be borne on the fastest of courses to the heavenly Jerusalem? Let us be driven, Fathers, let us be driven by the frenzies of Socrates, that they may so throw us into ecstasy as to put our mind and ourselves in God. Let us be driven by them, if we have first done what is in our power. For if through moral philoso-

phy the forces of our passions have by a fitting agreement become so intent on harmony that they can sing together in undisturbed concord, and if through dialectic our reason has moved progressively in a rhythmical measure, then we shall be stirred by the frenzy of the Muses and drink the heavenly harmony with our inmost hearing. Thereupon Bacchus, the leader of the Muses, by showing in his mysteries, that is, in the visible signs of nature, the invisible things of God to us who study philosophy, will intoxicate us with the fulness of God's house, in which, if we prove faithful, like Moses, hallowed theology shall come and inspire us with a doubled frenzy. For, exalted to her lofty height, we shall measure therefrom all things that are and shall be and have been in indivisible eternity; and, admiring their original beauty, like the seers of Phoebus, we shall become her own winged lovers. And at last, roused by ineffable love as by a sting, like burning Seraphim rapt from ourselves, full of divine power we shall no longer be ourselves but shall become He Himself Who made us.

17. If anyone investigates the holy names of Apollo, their meanings and hidden mysteries, these amply show that that god is no less a philosopher than a seer; but, since Ammonius has sufficiently examined this subject, there is no reason why I should now treat it otherwise. But, Fathers, three Delphic precepts may suggest themselves to your minds, which are very necessary to those who are to go into the most sacred and revered temple, not of the false but of the true Apollo, who lights every soul as it enters this world. You will see that they give us no other advice than that we should with all our strength embrace this threefold philosophy which is the concern of our present debate. For the saying μηδὲν ἄγαν, that is, "Nothing too

much," prescribes a standard and rule for all the virtues through the doctrine of the Mean, with which moral philosophy duly deals. Then the saying γνῶθι σεαυτὸν, that is, "Know thyself," urges and encourages us to the investigation of all nature, of which the nature of man is both the connecting link and, so to speak, the "mixed bowl." For he who knows himself in himself knows all things, as Zoroaster first wrote, and then Plato in his *Alcibiades*. When we are finally lighted in this knowledge by natural philosophy, and nearest to God are uttering the theological greeting, εἶ, that is, "Thou art," we shall likewise in bliss be addressing the true Apollo on intimate terms.

18. Let us also consult the wise Pythagoras, especially wise in that he never deemed himself worthy the name of a wise man. He will first enjoin us not to sit on a bushel, that is, not by unoccupied sloth to lose our rational faculty, by which the soul measures, judges, and considers all things; but we must direct and stimulate it unremittingly by the discipline and rule of dialectic. Then he will point out to us two things particularly to beware of: that we should not make water facing the sun or cut our nails while offering sacrifice. But after we have, through the agency of moral philosophy, both voided the lax desires of our too abundant pleasures and pared away like nail-cuttings the sharp corners of anger and the stings of wrath, only then may we begin to take part in the holy rites, that is, the mysteries of Bacchus we have mentioned, and to be free for our contemplation, whose father and leader the Sun is rightly named. Finally, Pythagoras will enjoin us to feed the cock, that is, to feast the divine part of our soul on the knowledge of things divine as if on substantial food and heavenly ambrosia. This is the cock at whose sight the lion, that is, all

earthly power, trembles and is filled with awe. This is that
cock to whom, we read in Job, intelligence was given.
When this cock crows, erring man comes to his senses. This
cock in the twilight of morning daily sings with the morning stars as they praise God. The dying Socrates, when he
hoped to join the divinity of his spirit with the divinity of
a greater world, said that he owed this cock to Aesculapius,
that is, to the physician of souls, now that he had passed
beyond all danger of illness.

19. Let us review also the records of the Chaldeans, and
we shall see (if they are to be trusted) the road to felicity
laid open to mortals through the same sciences. His Chaldean interpreters write that it was a saying of Zoroaster
that the soul is winged and that, when the wings drop off,
she falls headlong into the body; and then, after her wings
have grown again sufficiently, she flies back to heaven.
When his followers asked him in what manner they could
obtain souls winged with well-feathered wings, he replied:
"Refresh ye your wings in the waters of life." Again when
they asked where they should seek those waters, he answered them thus by a parable (as was the custom of the
man): "God's paradise is laved and watered by four rivers,
from whose same source ye may draw the waters of your
salvation. The name of that in the north is Pischon, which
meaneth the right. The name of that in the west is Dichon,
which signifieth expiation. The name of that in the east is
Chiddikel, which expresseth light, and of that in the south,
Perath, which we may interpret as piety."

20. Turn your attention, Fathers, to the diligent consideration of what these doctrines of Zoroaster mean. Surely
nothing else than that we should wash away the uncleanness from our eyes by moral science as if by the western

waves; that we should align their keen vision toward the right by the rule of dialectic as if by the northern line; that we should then accustom them to endure in the contemplation of nature the still feeble light of truth as if it were the first rays of the rising sun, so that at last, through the agency of the theological piety and the most holy worship of God, we may like heavenly eagles boldly endure the most brilliant splendor of the meridian sun. These are, perhaps, those ideas proper to morning, midday, and evening first sung by David and given a broader interpretation by Augustine. This is that noonday light which incites the Seraphs to their goal and equally sheds light on the Cherubs. This is that country toward which Abraham, our father of old, was ever journeying. This is that place where, as the doctrines of Cabalists and Moors have handed down to posterity, there is no room for unclean spirits. And, if it is right to bring into the open anything at all of the occult mysteries, even in the guise of a riddle, since a sudden fall from heaven has condemned the head of man to dizziness, and, in the words of Jeremiah, death has come in through our windows and smitten our vitals and our heart, let us summon Raphael, celestial physician, that he may set us free by moral philosophy and by dialectic as though by wholesome drugs. Then, when we are restored to health, Gabriel, "the strength of God," shall abide in us, leading us through the miracles of nature and showing us on every side the merit and the might of God. He will at last consign us to the high priest Michael, who will distinguish those who have completed their term in the service of philosophy with the holy office of theology as if with a crown of precious stones.

21. These, reverend Fathers, are the considerations that

have not only inspired but compelled me to the study of philosophy. I should certainly not set them forth were I not answering those who are wont to condemn the study of philosophy, especially among men of rank or even of a mediocre station in life. For this whole study of philosophy has now (and it is the misfortune of our age) come to despite and contumely rather than to honor and glory. Thus this deadly and monstrous conviction has come to pervade the minds of well-nigh all—that philosophy either must be studied not at all or by few persons, as if it were absolutely nothing to have clearly ascertained, before our eyes and before our hands, the causes of things, the ways of nature, the plan of the universe, the purposes of God, and the mysteries of heaven and earth; unless one may obtain some favor, or make money for one's self. Rather, it has come to the point where none is now deemed wise, alas, save those who make the study of wisdom a mercenary profession, and where it is possible to see the chaste Pallas, who was sent among men as the gift of the gods, hooted, hissed, and whistled off the stage; and not having anyone to love or to befriend her, unless by selling herself, as it were, she repays into the treasury of her "lover" even the ill-gained money received as the poor price of her tarnished virginity.

22. I speak all these accusations (not without the deepest grief and indignation) not against the princes of this time but against the philosophers, who both believe and openly declare that there should be no study of philosophy for the reason that no fee and no compensation have been fixed for philosophers, just as if they did not show by this one sign that they are no philosophers, that since their whole life is set either on profit or on ambition they do not embrace the very discovery of truth for its own sake. I shall grant my-

self this and blush not at all to praise myself to this extent that I have never studied philosophy for any other reason than that I might be a philosopher; and that I have neither hoped for any pay from my studies, from my labors by lamplight, nor sought any other reward than the cultivation of my mind and the knowledge of the truth I have ever longed for above all things. I have always been so desirous, so enamored of this, that I have relinquished all interest in affairs private and public and given myself over entirely to leisure for contemplation, from which no disparagements of those who hate me, no curses of the enemies of wisdom, have been able in the past or will be able in the future to discourage me. Philosophy herself has taught me to rely on my own conscience rather than on the opinions of others, and always to take thought not so much that people may speak no evil of me, as, rather, that I myself may neither say nor do aught that is evil.

23. For my part, reverend Fathers, I was not unaware that this very disputation of mine would be as grateful and pleasing to you who favor all good sciences, and have been willing to honor it with your most august presence, as it would be offensive and annoying to many others. And I know there is no lack of those who have heretofore condemned my project, and who condemn it at present on a number of grounds. Enterprises that are well and conscientiously directed toward virtue have been wont to find no fewer—not to say more—detractors than those that are wickedly and falsely directed toward vice. There are, indeed, those who do not approve of this whole method of disputation and of this institution of publicly debating on learning, maintaining that it tends rather to the parade of talent and the display of erudition than to the increase of

learning. There are those who do not indeed disapprove this kind of practice, but who in no wise approve it in me because I, born I admit but twenty-four years ago, should have dared at my age to offer a disputation concerning the lofty mysteries of Christian theology, the highest topics of philosophy and unfamiliar branches of knowledge, in so famous a city, before so great an assembly of very learned men, in the presence of the apostolic senate. Others, who give me leave to offer this disputation, are unwilling to allow me to debate nine hundred theses, and misrepresent it as being a work as unnecessary and as ostentatious as it is beyond my powers. I would have yielded to their objections and given in immediately if the philosophy I profess had so instructed me; and I should not now be answering them, even with philosophy as my preceptress, if I believed that this debate between us had been undertaken for the purpose of quarreling and scolding. Therefore, let the whole intention to disparage and to exasperate depart from our minds, and malice also, which Plato writes is ever absent from the heavenly choir. Let us in friendly wise try both questions: whether I am to debate and whether I am to debate about this great number of theses.

24. First, as to those who revile this custom of debating in public I shall certainly not say a great deal, since this crime, if it is held a crime, is shared with me not only by all of you, excellent doctors, who have rather frequently engaged in this office not without the highest praise and glory, but also by Plato, also by Aristotle, and also by the most worthy philosophers of every age. For them it was certain that, for the attainment of the knowledge of truth they were always seeking for themselves, nothing is better than to attend as often as possible the exercise of debate.

For just as bodily energy is strengthened by gymnastic exercise, so beyond doubt in this wrestling-place of letters, as it were, energy of mind becomes far stronger and more vigorous. And I could not believe, either that the poets, by the arms of Pallas which they sang, or that the Hebrews, when they called the sword the symbol of wise men, were indicating to us anything else than that such honorable contests are surely a necessary way of attaining wisdom. For this reason it is, perchance, that the Chaldeans desired in the horoscope of one who was to be a philosopher that Mars should be to Mercury in the trinal aspect, as much as to say, "If these assemblies, these disputations, should be given up, all philosophy would become sluggish and drowsy."

25. But truly with those who say I am unequal to this commission, my method of defense is more difficult. For if I say that I am equal to it, it seems that I shall take on myself the reproach of being immodest and of thinking too well of myself, and, if I admit that I am not equal to it, the reproach of being imprudent and thoughtless. See into what straits I have fallen, in what a position I am placed, since I cannot without blame promise about myself what I cannot then fail to fulfil without blame. Perhaps I could refer to that saying of Job: "The spirit is in all men," and be told with Timothy, "Let no man despise thy youth." But out of my own conscience I shall with more truth say this: that there is nothing either great or extraordinary about me. I do not deny that I am, if you will, studious and eager for the good sciences, but nevertheless I neither assume nor arrogate to myself the title of learned. However great the burden I may have taken on my shoulders, therefore, it was not because I was not perfectly aware of my own want of

strength but because I knew that it is a distinction of contests of this kind, that is, literary ones, that there is a profit
in being defeated. Whence it is that even the most feeble
are by right able and bound not only not to decline but
even more to court them, seeing that he who yields receives
no injury but a benefit from the victor, in that through him
he returns home even richer, that is, wiser and better
equipped for future contests. Inspired by this hope, I, who
am but a feeble soldier, have feared not at all to wage so
burdensome a war with the strongest and most vigorous
men of all. Whether this action be ill considered or not may
be judged from the outcome of the battle and not from
my age.

26. It remains in the third place to answer those who
take offense at the great number of my propositions, as if
the weight of these lay on their shoulders, and as if the burden, such as it is, were not rather to be borne by me alone.
It is surely unbecoming and beyond measure captious to
wish to set bounds to another's effort and, as Cicero says, to
desire moderation in a matter which is the better as it is on a
larger scale. In so great a venture it was necessary for me
either to give complete satisfaction or to fail utterly.
Should I succeed, I do not see why what is laudable to do
in an affair of ten theses should be deemed culpable to have
done also in an affair of nine hundred. Should I fail, they
will have the wherewithal to accuse me if they hate me and
to forgive me if they love me. For the failure of a young
man with but slender talent and little learning in so grave
and so great a matter will be more deserving of pardon than
of blame. Nay, according to the poet: "If strength fails,
there shall surely be praise for daring; and to have wished
for great things is enough." And if many in our time, in imi-

tation of Gorgias of Leontini, have been wont, not without praise, to propose debates not concerning nine hundred questions only, but also concerning all questions in all branches of knowledge, why should I not be allowed, and that without criticism, to discuss questions admittedly numerous but at least fixed and limited? Yet they say it is unnecessary and ostentatious. I contend that this enterprise of mine is in no way superfluous but necessary indeed; and if they will ponder with me the purpose of studying philosophy, they must, even against their wills, admit that it is plainly needful. Those who have devoted themselves to any one of the schools of philosophy, favoring, for instance, Thomas or Scotus, who are now most in fashion, are, to be sure, quite capable of making trial of their particular doctrines in the discussion of but a few questions. I, on the other hand, have so prepared myself that, pledged to the doctrines of no man, I have ranged through all the masters of philosophy, investigated all books, and come to know all schools. Therefore, since I had to speak of them all in order that, as champion of the beliefs of one, I might not seem fettered to it and appear to place less value on the rest, even while proposing a few theses concerning individual schools I could not help proposing a great number concerning all the schools together. And let no man condemn me for coming as a friend whithersoever the tempest bear me. For it was a custom observed by all the ancients in studying every kind of writer to pass over none of the learned works they were able to read, and especially by Aristotle, who for this reason was called by Plato ἀναγνώστης, that is, "reader." And surely it is the part of a narrow mind to have confined itself within a single Porch or Academy. Nor can one rightly choose what suits one's

self from all of them who has not first come to be familiar
with them all. Consider, in addition, that there is in each
school something distinctive that is not common to the
others.

27. And now, to begin with the men of our faith, to
whom philosophy came last: There is in John Scotus something lively and subtle; in Thomas, sound and consistent; in
Aegidius, terse and exact; in Francis, acute and penetrating;
in Albert, venerable, copious, and grand; in Henry, as it
always seems to me, something sublime and to be revered.
Among the Arabs, there is in Averroes something stable
and unshaken; in Avempace . . . ; in Alfarabi, serious and
thoughtful; in Avicenna, divine and Platonic. Among the
Greeks philosophy as a whole is certainly brilliant and
above all chaste. With Simplicius it is rich and abundant;
with Themistius, graceful and compendious; with Alex-
ander, harmonious and learned; with Theophrastus,
weightily worked out; with Ammonius, smooth and
agreeable. And if you turn your attention to the Platonists,
to examine a few: in Porphyry you will rejoice in the
abundance of his material and in the complexity of his
religion; in Jamblichus you will revere an occult philosophy and the mysteries of the East. In Plotinus there is no
isolated aspect you will admire; he shows himself admirable
on every side. The toiling Platonists themselves scarcely
understand him when he speaks divinely of things divine
and, with learned obliquity of speech, far more than humanly of human things. I prefer to pass over the later Platonists: Proclus abounding in Asiatic richness, and those
stemming from him, Hermias, Damascius, Olympiodorus,
and several others, in all of whom there ever gleams that τò

θεῖον, that is, "the Divine," which is the distinctive mark of the Platonists.

28. Add to this that any sect which assails the truer doctrines, and makes game of good causes by clever slander, strengthens rather than weakens the truth and, like flames stirred by agitation, fans rather than extinguishes it. This has been my reason for wishing to bring before the public the opinions not of a single school alone (which satisfied some I could name) but rather of every school, to the end that that light of truth Plato mentions in his *Epistles* through this comparison of several sects and this discussion of manifold philosophies might dawn more brightly on our minds, like the sun rising from the deep. What were the gain if only the philosophy of the Latins were investigated, that is, that of Albert, Thomas, Scotus, Aegidius, Francis, and Henry, if the Greek and Arabian philosophers were left out—since all wisdom has flowed from the East to the Greeks and from the Greeks to us? In their way of philosophizing, our Latins have always found it sufficient to stand on the discoveries of foreigners and to perfect the work of others. Of what use were it to treat with the Peripatetics on natural philosophy, unless the Platonic Academy were also invited? Their teaching in regard to divinity besides has always (as Augustine witnesses) been thought most hallowed of all philosophies, and now for the first time, so far as I know (may no one grudge me the word), it has after many centuries been brought by me to the test of public disputation. What were it to have dealt with the opinions of others, no matter how many, if we are come to a gathering of wise men with no contribution of our own and are supplying nothing from our own store, brought forth and

worked out by our own genius? It is surely an ignoble part
to be wise only from a notebook (as Seneca says) and, as if
the discoveries of our predecessors had closed the way to
our own industry and the power of nature were exhausted
in us, to produce from ourselves nothing which, if it does
not actually demonstrate the truth, at least intimates it from
afar. For if a tiller of the soil hates sterility in his field, and a
husband in his wife, surely the Divine mind joined to and
associated with an infertile soul will hate it the more in that
a far nobler offspring is desired.

29. For this reason I have not been content to add to the
tenets held in common many teachings taken from the ancient theology of Hermes Trismegistus, many from the
doctrines of the Chaldeans and of Pythagoras, and many
from the occult mysteries of the Hebrews. I have proposed
also as subjects for discussion several theses in natural
philosophy and in divinity, discovered and studied by me. I
have proposed, first of all, a harmony between Plato and
Aristotle, believed to exist by many ere this but adequately
proved by no one. Boethius among the Latins promised
that he would do it, but there is no trace of his having done
what he always wished to do. Among the Greeks, Simplicius made the same declaration, and would that he had
been as good as his word! Augustine also writes, in the
Contra Academicos, that there were not lacking several
who tried with their keenest arguments to prove the same
thing, that the philosophies of Plato and Aristotle are identical. John the Grammarian likewise, although he did say
that Plato differs from Aristotle only in the minds of those
who do not understand Plato's words, nevertheless left it
to posterity to prove. I have, moreover, brought to bear
several passages in which I maintain that the opinions of

Scotus and Thomas, and several in which I hold that those of Averroes and Avicenna, which are considered to be contradictory, are in agreement.

30. In the second place, I have next arranged the fruit of my thinking on both the Platonic and the Aristotelian philosophy, and then seventy-two new physical and metaphysical theses by means of which whoever holds them will be able (unless I am mistaken—which will soon be made manifest to me) to answer any question whatever proposed in natural philosophy or divinity, by a system far other than we are taught in that philosophy which is studied in the schools and practiced by the doctors of this age. Nor ought anyone, Fathers, to be so amazed that I, in my first years, at my tender age, at which it was hardly legitimate for me (as some have taunted) to read the books of others, should wish to introduce a new philosophy; but rather one should praise it if it is sustained or condemn it if it does not find favor, and finally, when these my discoveries and my scholarship come to be judged, number not their author's years so much as their own merits or faults.

31. There is, furthermore, still another method of philosophizing through numbers, which I have introduced as new, but which is in fact old, and was observed by the earliest theologians, principally by Pythagoras, by Aglaophamos, Philolaus, and Plato, and by the first Platonists, but which in this present era, like many other illustrious things, has perished through the carelessness of posterity, so that hardly any traces of it can be found. Plato writes in the *Epinomis* that, of all the liberal arts and theoretical sciences, the science of computation is the chief and the most divine. Likewise, inquiring, "Why is man the wisest of animals?" he concludes, "Because he knows how to

count," an opinion which Aristotle also mentions in his *Problems*. Abumasar writes that it was a saying of Avenzoar of Babylon that he knows all things who knows how to count. These statements cannot possibly be true if by the science of computation they mean that science in which, at present, merchants in particular are most skilled. To this also Plato bears witness, warning us with raised voice not to think that this divine arithmetic is the arithmetic of traders. I therefore promised, when I seemed after much nocturnal labor to have discovered that arithmetic which is so highly extolled, that I myself would (in order to make trial of this matter) reply in public through the art of number to seventy-four questions considered of chief importance in physics and metaphysics.

32. I have also proposed theorems dealing with magic, in which I have indicated that magic has two forms, one of which depends entirely on the work and authority of demons, a thing to be abhorred, so help me the God of truth, and a monstrous thing. The other, when it is rightly pursued, is nothing else than the utter perfection of natural philosophy. While the Greeks make mention of both of them, they call the former γοητεία, in no wise honoring it with the name of magic; the latter they call by the characteristic and fitting name of μαγεία, as if it were a perfect and most high wisdom. For, as Porphyry says, in the Persian tongue *magus* expresses the same idea as "interpreter" and "worshiper of the divine" with us. Moreover, Fathers, the disparity and unlikeness between these arts is great, nay, rather, the greatest possible. The former not only the Christian religion but all religions and every well-constituted state condemn and abhor. The latter all wise men, all peoples devoted to the study of heavenly and divine things,

approve and embrace. The former is the most deceitful of arts; the latter a higher and more holy philosophy. The former is vain and empty; the latter, sure, trustworthy, and sound. Whoso has cherished the former has ever dissembled, because it is a shame and a reproach to an author; but from the latter the highest renown and glory of letters was derived in ancient days, and almost always has been. No man who was a philosopher and eager to study the good arts has ever been a student of the former; but Pythagoras, Empedocles, Democritus, and Plato all traveled to study the latter, taught it when they returned, and esteemed it before all others in their mysteries. As the former is approved by no reasonable arguments, so is it not by established authors; the latter, honored by the most celebrated fathers, as it were, has in particular two authors: Zamolxis, whom Abaris the Hyperborean copied, and Zoroaster, not him of whom perhaps you are thinking but him who is the son of Oromasius.

33. If we ask Plato what the magic of both these men was, he will reply, in his *Alcibiades*, that the magic of Zoroaster was none other than the science of the Divine in which the kings of the Persians instructed their sons, to the end that they might be taught to rule their own commonwealth by the example of the commonwealth of the world. He will answer, in the *Charmides*, that the magic of Zamolxis was that medicine of the soul through which temperance is brought to the soul as through temperance health is brought to the body. In their footsteps Charondas, Damigeron, Apollonius, Osthanes, and Dardanus thereafter persevered. Homer persevered, whom I shall sometime prove, in my *Poetic Theology*, to have concealed this philosophy beneath the wanderings of his Ulysses, just as

he has concealed all others. Eudoxus and Hermippus persevered. Almost all who have searched through the Pythago-
rean and Platonic mysteries have persevered. Furthermore,
from among the later philosophers I find three who have
scented it out—the Arabian al-Kindi, Roger Bacon, and
William of Paris. Plotinus also mentions it when he demonstrates that a *magus* is the servant of nature and not a
contriver. This very wise man approves and maintains this
magic, so hating the other that, when he was summoned to
the rites of evil spirits, he said that they should come to him
rather than that he should go to them; and surely he was
right. For even as the former makes man the bound slave of
wicked powers, so does the latter make him their ruler and
their lord. In conclusion, the former can claim for itself the
name of neither art nor science, while the latter, abounding
in the loftiest mysteries, embraces the deepest contemplation of the most secret things, and at last the knowledge of
all nature. The latter, in calling forth into the light as if
from their hiding-places the powers scattered and sown in
the world by the loving-kindness of God, does not so much
work wonders as diligently serve a wonder-working nature. The latter, having more searchingly examined into
the harmony of the universe, which the Greeks with
greater significance call συμπάθεια, and having clearly perceived the reciprocal affinity of natures, and applying to
each single thing the suitable and peculiar inducements
(which are called the ἴυγγες of the magicians) brings forth
into the open the miracles concealed in the recesses of the
world, in the depths of nature, and in the storehouses and
mysteries of God, just as if she herself were their maker;
and, as the farmer weds his elms to vines, even so does the
magus wed earth to heaven, that is, he weds lower things to

the endowments and powers of higher things. Whence it comes about that the latter is as divine and as salutary as the former is unnatural and harmful; for this reason especially, that in subjecting man to the enemies of God, the former calls him away from God, but the latter rouses him to the admiration of God's works which is the most certain condition of a willing faith, hope, and love. For nothing moves one to religion and to the worship of God more than the diligent contemplation of the wonders of God; if we have thoroughly examined them by this natural magic we are considering, we shall be compelled to sing, more ardently inspired to the worship and love of the Creator: "The heavens and all the earth are full of the majesty of thy glory." And this is enough about magic. I have said these things about it, for I know there are many who, just as dogs always bark at strangers, in the same way often condemn and hate what they do not understand.

34. I come now to the things I have elicited from the ancient mysteries of the Hebrews and have cited for the confirmation of the inviolable Catholic faith. Lest perchance they should be deemed fabrications, trifles, or the tales of jugglers by those to whom they are unfamiliar, I wish all to understand what they are and of what sort, whence they come, by what and by how illustrious authors supported, and how mysterious, how divine, and how necessary they are to the men of our faith for defending our religion against the grievous misrepresentations of the Hebrews. Not only the famous doctors of the Hebrews, but also from among men of our opinion Esdras, Hilary, and Origen write that Moses on the mount received from God not only the Law, which he left to posterity written down in five books, but also a true and more occult expla-

nation of the Law. It was, moreover, commanded him of
God by all means to proclaim the Law to the people but
not to commit the interpretation of the Law to writing or
to make it a matter of common knowledge. He himself
should reveal it only to Iesu Nave, who in his turn should
unveil it to the other high priests to come after him, under a
strict obligation of silence. It was enough through guileless
story to recognize now the power of God, now his wrath
against the wicked, his mercy to the righteous, his justice to
all; and through divine and beneficial precepts to be
brought to a good and happy way of life and the worship
of true religion. But to make public the occult mysteries,
the secrets of the supreme Godhead hidden beneath the
shell of the Law and under a clumsy show of words—what
else were this than to give a holy thing to dogs and to cast
pearls before swine? Therefore to keep hidden from the
people the things to be shared by the initiate, among whom
alone, Paul says, he spoke wisdom, was not the part of human deliberation but of divine command. This custom the
ancient philosophers most reverently observed, for
Pythagoras wrote nothing except a few trifles, which he
intrusted on his deathbed to his daughter Dama. The
Sphinxes carved on the temples of the Egyptians reminded
them that mystic doctrines should be kept inviolable from
the common herd by means of the knots of riddles. Plato,
writing certain things to Dion concerning the highest substances, said: "It must be stated in riddles, lest the letter
should fall by chance into the hands of others and what I
am writing to you should be apprehended by others."
Aristotle used to say that his books of *Metaphysics*, in
which he treated of things divine, were both published and
not published. What further? Origen asserts that Jesus

Christ, the Teacher of life, made many revelations to his disciples, which they were unwilling to write down lest they should become commonplaces to the rabble. This is in the highest degree confirmed by Dionysius the Areopagite, who says that the occult mysteries were conveyed by the founders of our religion ἐκ νοῦ εἰς νοῦν διὰ μέσον λόγον, from mind to mind, without writing, through the medium of speech.

35. In exactly the same way, when the true interpretation of the Law according to the command of God, divinely handed down to Moses, was revealed, it was called the Cabala, a word which is the same among the Hebrews as "reception" among ourselves; for this reason, of course, that one man from another, by a sort of hereditary right, received that doctrine not through written records but through a regular succession of revelations. But after the Hebrews were restored by Cyrus from the Babylonian captivity, and after the temple had been established anew under Zorobabel, they brought their attention to the restoration of the Law. Esdras, then the head of the church, after the book of Moses had been amended, when he plainly recognized that, because of the exiles, the massacres, the flights, and the captivity of the children of Israel, the custom instituted by their forefathers of transmitting the doctrine from mouth to mouth could not be preserved, and that it would come to pass that the mysteries of the heavenly teachings divinely bestowed on them would be lost, since the memory of them could not long endure without the aid of written records, decided that those of the elders then surviving should be called together and that each one should impart to the gathering whatever he possessed by personal recollection concerning the mysteries of

the Law and that scribes should be employed to collect them into seventy volumes (about the number of elders in the Sanhedrin). That you may not have to rely on me alone in this matter, Fathers, hear Esdras himself speak thus: "And it came to pass, when the forty days were fulfilled, that the Most High spake unto me, saying, The first that thou has written publish openly, and let the worthy and the unworthy read it: but keep the seventy last books, that thou mayst deliver them to such as be wise among thy people: for in them is the spring of understanding, the fountain of wisdom, and the stream of knowledge. And I did so." And these are the words of Esdras to the letter. These are the books of cabalistic lore. In these books principally resides, as Esdras with a clear voice justly declared, the spring of understanding, that is, the ineffable theology of the supersubstantial deity; the fountain of wisdom, that is, the exact metaphysic of the intellectual and angelic forms; and the stream of knowledge, that is, the most steadfast philosophy of natural things. Pope Sixtus the Fourth who last preceded the pope under whom we are now fortunate to be living, Innocent the Eighth, took the greatest pains and interest in seeing that these books should be translated into the Latin tongue for a public service to our faith, and, when he died, three of them had been done into Latin. Among the Hebrews of the present day these books are cherished with such devotion that it is permitted no man to touch them unless he be forty years of age.

36. When I had purchased these books at no small cost to myself, when I had read them through with the greatest diligence and with unwearying toil, I saw in them (as God is my witness) not so much the Mosaic as the Christian religion. There is the mystery of the Trinity, there the

Incarnation of the Word, there the divinity of the Messiah; there I have read about original sin, its expiation through Christ, the heavenly Jerusalem, the fall of the devils, the orders of the angels, purgatory, and the punishments of hell, the same things we read daily in Paul and Dionysius, in Jerome and Augustine. But in those parts which concern philosophy you really seem to hear Pythagoras and Plato, whose principles are so closely related to the Christian faith that our Augustine gives immeasurable thanks to God that the books of the Platonists have come into his hands. Taken altogether, there is absolutely no controversy between ourselves and the Hebrews on any matter, with regard to which they cannot be refuted and gainsaid out of the cabalistic books, so that there will not be even a corner left in which they may hide themselves. I have as a most weighty witness of this fact that very learned man Antonius Chronicus who, when I was with him at a banquet, with his own ears heard Dactylus, a Hebrew trained in this lore, with all his heart agree entirely to the Christian idea of the Trinity.

37. But let me return to surveying the chapters of my disputation. I have introduced also my own idea of the interpretation of the prophetic verses of Orpheus and Zoroaster. Orpheus is read among the Greeks in a nearly complete text, Zoroaster only in part, though, among the Chaldeans, in a more complete text, and both are believed to be the fathers and authors of ancient wisdom. Now, to pass over Zoroaster, the frequent mention of whom among the Platonists is never without the greatest respect, Jamblichus of Chalcis writes that Pythagoras followed the Orphic theology as the model on which he fashioned and built his own philosophy. Nay, furthermore, they say that

the maxims of Pythagoras are alone called holy, because he proceeded from the principles of Orpheus; and that the secret doctrine of numbers and whatever Greek philosophy has of the great or the sublime has flowed from thence as its first font. But as was the practice of the ancient theologians, even so did Orpheus protect the mysteries of his dogmas with the coverings of fables, and conceal them with a poetic veil, so that whoever should read his hymns would suppose there was nothing beneath them beyond idle tales and perfectly unadulterated trifles. I have wished to say this so that it might be known what a task it was for me, how difficult it was to draw out the hidden meaning of the secrets of philosophy from the intentional tangles of riddles and from the obscurity of fables, especially since I have been aided, in a matter so serious, so abstruse, and so little known, by no toil, no application on the part of other interpreters. And yet like dogs they have barked that I have made a kind of heap of inconsequential nothings for a vain display of mere quantity, as if these were not all questions in the highest degree disputed and controversial, in which the main schools are at swords' points, and as if I had not contributed many things utterly unknown and untried to these very men who are even now tearing at my reputation and who consider that they are the leaders in philosophy. Nay, I am so far from this fault that I have taken great pains to reduce my argument to as few chapters as I could. If I myself had (after the wont of others) wished to divide it into parts and to cut it to pieces, it would undoubtedly have grown to a countless number.

38. And, to hold my peace about the rest, who is there who does not know that a single proposition of the nine hundred, the one that treats of reconciling the philosophies

of Plato and Aristotle, I could have developed, beyond all suspicion of my having wooed mere quantity, into six hundred, nay, more chapters, by enumerating one after the other all those points in which others consider those philosophers to differ and I, to agree? But I must certainly speak (for I shall speak, albeit neither modestly nor in conformity with my own character), since my enviers and detractors compel me to: I have wished to give assurance by this contest of mine, not so much that I know many things, as that I know things of which many are ignorant. And now, in order that this, reverend Fathers, may become manifest to you by the facts and that my oration may no longer stand in the way of your desire, excellent doctors, whom I perceive to be prepared and girded up in the expectation of the dispute, not without great delight: let us now—and may the outcome be fortunate and favorable— join battle as to the sound of a trumpet of war.

Titus Carus Lucretius,   ON THE NATURE OF THINGS

Thomas Aquinas,   SUMMA THEOLOGICA: ON MAN
        (Trans. by Fathers of the English Dominican Province)

1. Lucretius speaks of the spirit of the wine and the spirit of man; how are these alike? What is the lesson of this comparison?

2. Medicine can alter the mind as well as the body. How does Lucretius use this fact to support his claim about the nature of the soul?

3. What does the amputation metaphor tell us about the nature of the soul?

4. If reincarnation were possible, what difference would it make to the nature of the soul?

5. Does Lucretius' materialism necessarily lead to theory of determinism? What does this say about human freedom?

6. How does Cicero's position contrast with that of Lucretius? How do these two compare with the Christian view of human nature?

7. Aquinas' view of the soul differs from that of Lucretius in several ways. Discuss the principal differences and tell how these men would respond to each other.

8. Aquinas says that man is free, but what does he mean by freedom? What is his justification?

9. What does Aquinas mean when he says that man is the image of God? How is man's intellectual nature a likeness of God?

10. How is the image of the Trinity found in the acts of man's soul?

11. For Aquinas, man's nature imposes limitations on him. How does this compare with Lucretius' theory of determinism and with Mirandola's belief that man has the capacity to be whatever he wills to be?

Adopting a poetic framework for his presentation of the theory of materialism, Titus Carus Lucretius (99-55 B.C.) confronted his fellow Romans with a philosophical alternative to the ideas of Cicero.

On the Nature of Things

BOOK III

THEE, WHO FIRST WAST ABLE FROM AMID SUCH THICK darkness to raise on high so bright a beacon and shed a light on the true interests of life, thee I follow, glory of the Greek race, and plant now my footsteps firmly fixed in thy imprinted marks, not so much from a desire to rival thee as that from the love I bear thee I yearn to imitate thee; for why need the swallow contend with swans, or what likeness is there between the feats of racing performed by kids with tottering limbs and by the powerful strength of the horse? Thou, father, art discoverer of things, thou furnishest us with fatherly precepts, and like as bees sip of all things in the flowery lawns, we, O glorious being, in like manner feed from out thy pages upon all the golden maxims, golden I say, most worthy ever of endless life. For soon as thy philosophy issuing from a godlike intellect has begun with loud voice to proclaim the nature of things, the terrors of the mind are dispelled, the walls of the world part asunder, I see things in operation throughout the whole void: the divinity of the gods is revealed and their tranquil abodes which neither winds do shake nor clouds drench with rains nor snow congealed by sharp frost harms with hoary fall: an ever cloudless ether o'ercanopies them, and they laugh with light shed largely round. Nature too supplies all their wants and nothing ever impairs their peace of mind. But on the other hand the Acherusian quarters are nowhere to be seen, though earth is no bar to all things being descried, which are in operation underneath our feet throughout the void. At all this a kind of godlike delight mixed with shuddering awe comes over me to think that nature by thy power is laid thus visibly open, is thus unveiled on every side.

And now since I have shewn what-like the beginnings of all things are and how diverse with varied shapes as they fly spontaneously driven on in everlasting motion, and how all things can be severally produced out of these, next after these questions the nature of the mind and soul should methinks be cleared up by my verses and that dread of Acheron be driven headlong forth, troubling as it does the life of man from its inmost depths and over-spreading all things with the blackness of death, allowing no pleasure to be pure and unalloyed. For as to what men often give out that diseases and a life of shame, are more to be feared than Tartarus, place of death, and that they know the soul to be of blood or it may be of wind, if haply their choice so direct, and that they have no need at all of our philosophy, you may perceive for the following reasons that all these boasts are thrown out more for glory's sake than because the thing is really believed. These very men, exiles from their country and banished far from the sight of men, live degraded by foul charge of guilt, sunk in a word in every kind of misery, and whithersoever the poor wretches have come, they yet do offer sacrifices to the dead and slaughter black sheep and make libations to the gods' manes and in times of distress turn their thoughts to religion much more earnestly. Wherefore you can better test the man in doubts and dangers and mid adversity learn what he is; for then and not till then the words of truth are forced out from the bottom of his heart: the mask is torn off, the reality is left. Avarice again and blind lust of honours which constrain unhappy men to overstep the bounds of right and sometimes as partners and agents of crimes to strive night and day with surpassing effort to struggle up to the summit of power—these sores of life are in no small measure fostered by the dread of death. For foul scorn and pinching want in every case are seen to be far removed from a life of pleasure and security and to be a loitering so to say before the gates of death. And while men driven on by an unreal dread wish to escape far away from these and keep them far from them, they amass wealth by civil bloodshed and greedily double their riches piling up murder on murder; cruelly triumph in the sad death of a brother and hate and fear the tables of kinsfolk. Often likewise from the same fear envy causes them to pine: they make moan that before their very eyes he is powerful, he attracts attention, who walks arrayed in gorgeous dignity, while they are wallowing in darkness and dirt. Some wear themselves to death for the sake of statues and a name. And often to such a degree through dread of death does hate of life and of the sight of daylight seize upon mortals, that they commit self-murder with a sorrowing heart, quite forgetting that this fear is the source of their cares, puts shame to rout, bursts asunder the bonds of friendship and in fine overturns duty from its very base; since often ere now men have betrayed country and dear parents in seeking to shun the Acherusian quarters. For even as children are flurried and dread all things in the thick darkness, thus we in the daylight fear at times things not a whit more to be dreaded than what children shudder at in the dark and fancy sure to be. This terror therefore and darkness of mind must be dispelled not by the rays of the sun and glittering shafts of day, but by the aspect and law of nature.

First then I say that the mind which we often call the understanding, in which dwells the directing and governing principle of life, is no less part of the man, than hand and foot and eyes are parts of the whole living creature. [Some however affirm] that the sense of the mind does not dwell in a distinct part, but is a certain vital state of the body, which the Greeks call harmonia, because by it, they say, we live with sense, though the understanding is in no one part; just as when good health is said to belong to the body, though yet it is not any one part of the man in health. In this way they do not assign a distinct part to the sense of the mind; in all which they appear to me to be grievously at fault in more ways than one. Oftentimes the body which is visible to sight, is sick, while yet we have pleasure in another hidden part; and oftentimes the case is the very reverse, the man who is unhappy in mind feeling pleasure in his whole body, just as if, while a sick man's foot is pained, the head meanwhile should be in no pain at all. Moreover when the limbs are consigned to soft sleep and the burdened body lies diffused without sense, there is yet a something else in us which during that time is moved in many ways and admits into it all the motions of joy and unreal cares of the heart. Now that you may know that the soul as well is in the limbs and that the body is not wont to have sense by any harmony, this is a main proof: when much of the body has been taken away, still life often stays in the limbs; and yet the same life, when a few bodies of heat have been dispersed abroad and some air has been forced out through the mouth, abandons at once the veins and quits the bones: by this you may perceive that all bodies have not functions of like importance nor alike uphold existence, but rather that those seeds which constitute wind and heat, cause life to stay in the limbs. Therefore

vital heat and wind are within the body, and abandon
our frame at death. Since then the nature of the mind
and of the soul have been proved to be a part as it
were of the man, surrender the name of harmony,
whether brought down to musicians from high Helicon,
or whether rather they have themselves taken it from
something else and transferred it to that thing which
then was in need of a distinctive name; whatever it be,
let them keep it: do you take in the rest of my precepts.

Now I assert that the mind and the soul are kept
together in close union and make up a single nature, but
that the directing principle which we call mind and
understanding, is the head so to speak and reigns paramount in the whole body. It has a fixed seat in the middle regions of the breast: here throb fear and apprehension, about these spots dwell soothing joys; therefore here is the understanding or mind. All the rest of
the soul disseminated through the whole body obeys
and moves at the will and inclination of the mind. It by
itself alone knows for itself, rejoices for itself, at times
when the impression does not move either soul or body
together with it. And as when some part of us, the head
or the eye, suffers from an attack of pain, we do not
feel the anguish at the same time over the whole body,
thus the mind sometimes suffers pain by itself or is in-
spirited with joy, when all the rest of the soul throughout the limbs and frame is stirred by no novel sensation.
But when the mind is excited by some more vehement
apprehension, we see the whole soul feel in unison
through all the limbs, and thus sweats and paleness
spread over the whole body, the tongue falter, the voice
die away, a mist cover the eyes, the ears ring, the limbs
sink under one; in short we often see men drop down
from terror of mind; so that anybody may easily perceive from this that the soul is closely united with the

mind, and, when it has been smitten by the influence of the mind, forthwith pushes and strikes the body.

This same principle teaches that the nature of the mind and soul is bodily; for when it is seen to push the limbs, rouse the body from sleep, and alter the countenance and guide and turn about the whole man, and when we see that none of these effects can take place without touch nor touch without body, must we not admit that the mind and the soul are of a bodily nature? Again you perceive that our mind in our body suffers together with the body and feels in unison with it. When a weapon with a shudder-causing force has been driven in and has laid bare bones and sinews within the body, if it does not take life, yet there ensues a faintness and a lazy sinking to the ground and on the ground the turmoil of mind which arises, and sometimes a kind of undecided inclination to get up. Therefore the nature of the mind must be bodily, since it suffers from bodily weapons and blows.

I will now go on to explain in my verses of what kind of body the mind consists and out of what it has been formed. First of all I say that it is extremely fine and formed of exceedingly minute bodies. That this is so you may, if you please to attend, clearly perceive from what follows: nothing that is seen takes place with a velocity equal to that of the mind when it starts some suggestion and actually sets it agoing; the mind therefore is stirred with greater rapidity than any of the things whose nature stands out visible to sight. But that which is so passing nimble, must consist of seeds exceedingly round and exceedingly minute, in order to be stirred and set in motion by a small moving power. Thus water is moved and heaves by ever so small a force, formed as it is of small particles apt to roll. But on the other hand the nature of honey is more sticky, its liquid more

sluggish and its movement more dilatory; for the whole
mass of matter coheres more closely, because sure enough
it is made of bodies not so smooth, fine, and round. A
breeze however gentle and light can force, as you may see,
a high heap of poppy seed to be blown away from the
top downwards; but on the other hand Eurus itself cannot move a heap of stones. Therefore bodies possess a
power of moving in proportion to their smallness and
smoothness; and on the other hand the greater weight
and roughness bodies prove to have, the more stable
they are. Since then the nature of the mind has been
found to be eminently easy to move, it must consist of
bodies exceedingly small, smooth, and round. The knowledge of which fact, my good friend, will on many accounts prove useful and be serviceable to you. The
following fact too likewise demonstrates how fine the
texture is of which its nature is composed, and how small
the room is in which it can be contained, could it only
be collected into one mass: soon as the untroubled sleep
of death has gotten hold of a man and the nature of the
mind and soul has withdrawn, you can perceive then no
diminution of the entire body either in appearance or
weight: death makes all good save the vital sense and
heat. Therefore the whole soul must consist of very
small seeds and be inwoven through veins, flesh, sinews;
inasmuch as, after it has withdrawn from the whole body,
the exterior contour of the limbs preserves itself entire
and not a tittle of the weight is lost. Just in the same
way when the flavour of wine is gone or when the de-
licious aroma of a perfume has been dispersed into the
air or when the savour has left some body, yet the thing
does not look smaller to the eye, nor does aught seem to
have been taken from the weight, because sure enough
many minute seeds make up the savours and the odour
in the whole body of the several things. Therefore, again

and again I say, you are to know that the nature of the mind and the soul has been formed of exceedingly minute seeds, since at its departure it takes away none of the weight.

We are not however to suppose that this nature is single. For a certain subtle spirit mixed with heat quits men at death, and then the heat draws air along with it; there being no heat which has not air too mixed with it: for since its nature is rare, many first-beginnings of air must move about through it. Thus then the nature of the mind is proved to be threefold; and yet these things all together are not sufficient to produce sense; since the fact of the case does not admit that any of these can produce sense-giving motions and the thoughts which a man turns over in mind. Thus some fourth nature too must be added to these: it is altogether without name; than it nothing exists more nimble or more fine, or of smaller or smoother elements: it first transmits the sense-giving motions through the frame; for it is first stirred, made up as it is of small particles; next the heat and the unseen force of the spirit receive the motions, then the air; then all things are set in action, the blood is stirred, every part of the flesh is filled with sensation; last of all the feeling is transmitted to the bones and marrow, whether it be one of pleasure or an opposite excitement. No pain however can lightly pierce thus far nor any sharp malady make its way in, without all things being so thoroughly disordered that no room is left for life and the parts of the soul fly abroad through all the pores of the body. But commonly a stop is put to these motions on the surface as it were of the body: for this reason we are able to retain life.

Now though I would fain explain in what way these are mixed up together and what is the method of their arrangement when they exert their powers, the poverty of my native speech deters me sorely against my will: yet will I touch upon them and in summary fashion to the best of my ability: the first-beginnings by their mutual motions are interlaced in such a way that none of them can be separated by itself, nor can the function of any go on divided from the rest by any interval; but they are so to say the several qualities of one body. Even so in any flesh of living creature you please without exception there is a smell and a heat and savour, and yet out of all these is made up one single bulk of body. Thus the heat and the air and the unseen power of the spirit mixed together produce a single nature, together with that nimble force which transmits to them from itself the origin of motion; by which means sense-giving motion first takes its rise through the fleshly frame. For this nature lurks secreted in its inmost depths, and nothing in our body is farther beneath all ken than it, and more than this it is the very soul of the whole soul. Just in the same way as the power of the mind and the function of the soul are latent in our limbs and throughout our body, because they are each formed of small and few bodies: even so, you are to know, this nameless power made of minute bodies is concealed and is moreover the very soul so to say of the whole soul, and reigns supreme in the whole body. On a like principle the spirit and air and heat must, as they exert their powers, be mixed up together through the frame, and one must ever be more out of view or more prominent than another, that one substance may be seen to be formed from the union of all, lest the heat and spirit apart by themselves and the power of the air apart by itself should destroy sense and dissipate it by their disunion. Thus the mind possesses that heat which it displays when it boils up in anger and fire flashes from the keen eyes; there is too much cold spirit, comrade of fear, which spreads a shivering over the limbs and stirs the whole frame; yes, and there is also that condition of still air which has place when the breast is calm and the looks cheerful. But they have more of the hot whose keen heart and passionate mind lightly boils up in anger. Foremost in this class comes the fierce violence of lions who often as they chafe break their hearts with their roaring and cannot contain within their breast the billows of their rage. Then the chilly mind of stags is fuller of the spirit and more quickly rouses through all the flesh its icy currents which spread over the limbs a shivering motion. But the nature of oxen has its life rather from the still air, and never does the smoky torch of anger applied to it stimulate it too much, shedding over it the shadow of murky gloom, nor is it transfixed and stiffened by the icy shafts of fear: it lies between the other two, stags and cruel lions. And thus it is with mankind: however much teaching renders some equally refined, it yet leaves behind the earliest traces of the nature of each mind; and we are not to suppose that evil habits can be so thoroughly plucked up by the roots, that one man shall not be more prone than another to keen anger, a second shall not be somewhat more quickly assailed by fear, a third shall not take some things more meekly than is right. In many other points there must be differences between the varied natures of men and the tempers which follow upon these; though at present I am unable to set forth the hidden causes of these or to find names enough for the different shapes which belong to the first-beginnings from which arises this diversity of things. What herein I think I may affirm is this: traces of the different natures left behind, which reason is unable to expel from us are so exceedingly slight that there is nothing to hinder us from living a life worthy of gods.

Well, this nature is contained by the whole body and

is in turn the body's guardian and the cause of its existence; for the two adhere together with common roots and cannot, it is plain, be riven asunder without destruction. Even as it is not easy to pluck the perfume out of lumps of frankincense without quite destroying its nature as well; so it is not easy to withdraw from the whole body the nature of the mind and soul without dissolving all alike. With principles so interlaced from the beginning of their existence are they formed and gifted with a life of joint partnership, and it is plain that the faculty of the body and of the mind cannot feel separately, each alone without the other's power, but sense is kindled throughout our flesh and blown into flame between the two by the joint motions of these two natures. Moreover the body by itself is never either begotten or grows or, it is plain, continues to exist after death. For not in the way that the liquid of water often loses the heat which has been given to it, yet is not for that reason itself riven in pieces, but remains unimpaired —not in this way, I say, can the abandoned frame endure the separation of the soul, but riven in pieces it utterly perishes and rots away. Thus the mutual connexions of body and soul from the first moment of their existence learn the vital motions even while hid in the body and womb of the mother, so that no separation can take place without mischief and ruin. Thus you may see that, since the cause of existence lies in their joint action, their nature too must be a joint nature.

Furthermore if any one tries to disprove that the body feels and believes that the soul mixed through the whole body takes upon it this motion which we name sense, he combats even manifest and undoubted facts. For who will ever bring forward any explanation of what the body's feeling is, except that which the plain fact of the case has itself given and taught to us? But when the soul it is said has departed, the body throughout is without sense; yes, for it loses what was not its own peculiar property in life.

Again to say that the eyes can see no object, but that the soul discerns through them as through an open door, is far from easy, since their sense contradicts this; and the more so that often we are unable to perceive bright things, because our eyes are embarrassed by the lights. But this is not the case with doors; for, because we ourselves see, the open doors do not therefore undergo any fatigue. Again if our eyes are in the place of doors, in that case when the eyes are removed the mind ought to have more power of seeing things after doors, jambs and all have been taken out of the way.

And herein you must by no means adopt the opinion which the revered judgment of the worthy man Democritus lays down, that the first-beginnings of body and mind placed together in successive layers come in alternate order and so weave the tissue of our limbs. For not only are the elements of the soul much smaller than those of which our body and flesh are formed, but they are also much fewer in number and are disseminated merely in scanty number through the frame, so that you can warrant no more than this: the several first-beginnings of the soul keep at distances from each other exactly coresponding to the smallest possible number of bodies which being severally infused into us have the power of exciting in our body the sense-giving motions. Thus at times we do not feel the adhesion of dust when it settles on our body, nor the impact of chalk when it settles on our limbs, nor do we feel a mist at night nor a spider's slender threads as they come against us, when we are caught in its meshes in moving along, nor the same insect's flimsy web when it has fallen on our head, nor the feathers of birds and down of plants as it flies about, which commonly from exceeding lightness does not lightly fall, nor do we feel the tread of every creeping creature whatsoever nor each particular foot-print which gnats and the like stamp on our body. So invariably must many seeds mixed up in our bodies throughout our frames be set in motion ere the first-beginnings of the soul are roused to feel, and ere by thumping with such spaces between, they can clash, unite, and in turn recoil.

The mind has more to do with holding the fastnesses of life and has more sovereign sway over it than the power of the soul. For without the understanding and the mind no part of the soul can maintain itself in the frame the smallest fraction of time, but follows at once in the other's train and passes away into the air and leaves the cold limbs in the chill of death. But he abides in life whose mind and understanding continue to stay with him: though the trunk is mangled with its limbs shorn all round it, after the soul has been taken away on all sides and been severed from the limbs, the trunk yet lives and inhales the ethereal airs of life. When robbed, if not of the whole, yet of a large portion of the soul, it still lingers in and cleaves to life; just as, after the eye has been lacerated all round if the pupil has continued uninjured, the living power of sight remains, provided always you do not destroy the whole ball of the eye and pare close round the pupil and leave only it; for that will not be done without destroying the eyes. But if that middle portion of the eye, small as it is, is eaten into, the sight is gone at once and darkness ensues, though a man have the bright ball quite unimpaired. On such terms of union soul and mind are ever bound to each other.

Now mark me: that you may know that the minds and light souls of living creatures have birth and are mortal, I will go on to set forth verses worthy of your attention got together by long study and invented with welcome effort. Do you mind to attach to either of the two either name, and when for instance I shall choose to speak of the soul, showing it to be mortal, believe that I speak of the mind as well, inasmuch as both make up one thing and are one united substance. First of all then since I have shewn the soul to be fine and to be formed of minute bodies and made up of much smaller first-beginnings than is the liquid of water or mist or smoke:—for it far surpasses these in nimbleness and moves if struck by a far slenderer cause; inasmuch as it moves by images of smoke and mist; as when for instance sunk in sleep we see altars steam forth their heat and send up their smoke on high; for beyond a doubt images are begotten for us from these things:—well then since you see on the vessels being shattered the water flow away on all sides, and since mist and smoke pass away into air, believe that the soul too is shed abroad and perishes much more quickly and dissolves sooner into its first bodies, when once it has been taken out of the limbs of a man and has withdrawn. For how can you believe that this soul which the body that serves for its vessel, cannot hold, if shattered from any cause and rarefied by the withdrawal of blood from the veins, how can you believe I say that this soul can be held by any air? How can that air which is rarer than our body hold it in?

Again we perceive that the mind is begotten along with the body and grows up together with it and becomes old along with it. For even as children go about with a tottering and weakly body, so slender sagacity of mind follows along with it; then when their life has reached the maturity of confirmed strength, the judgment too is greater and the power of the mind more developed.

Afterwards when the body has been shattered by the mastering might of time and the frame has drooped with its forces dulled, then the intellect halts, the tongue dotes, the mind gives away, all faculties fail and are found wanting at the same time. It naturally follows then that the whole nature of the soul is dissolved, like smoke, into the high air; since we see it is begotten along with the body and grows up along with it and, as I have shown, breaks down at the same time worn out with age.

Moreover we see that even as the body is liable to violent diseases and severe pain, so is the mind to sharp cares and grief and fear; it naturally follows therefore that it is its partner in death as well. Again in diseases of the body the mind often wanders and goes astray; for it loses its reason and drivels in its speech and often in a profound lethargy is carried into deep and never-ending sleep with drooping eyes and head; out of which it neither hears the voices nor can recognize the faces of those who stand round calling it back to life and be-dewing with tears face and cheeks. Therefore you must admit that the mind too dissolves, since the infection of disease reaches to it; for pain and disease are both forgers of death: a truth we have fully learned ere now by the death of many. Again, when the pungent strength of wine has entered into a man and its spirit has been in-fused into and transmitted through his veins, why is it that a heaviness of the limbs follows along with it, his legs are hampered as he reels about, his tongue falters, his mind is besotted, his eyes swim, shouting, hiccough-ing, wranglings are rife, together with all the other usual concomitants, why is all this, if not because the over-powering violence of the wine is wont to disorder the soul within the body? But whenever things can be dis-ordered and hampered, they give token that if a some-what more potent cause gained an entrance, they would perish and be robbed of all further existence. Moreover it often happens that some one constrained by the violence of disease suddenly drops down before our eyes, as by a stroke of lightning, and foams at the mouth, moans and shivers through his frame, stiffens his muscles, is racked, gasps for breath fitfully, and wearies his limbs with tossing. Sure enough, because the violence of the disease spreads itself through his frame and disorders him, he foams as he tries to eject his soul, just as in the salt sea the waters boil with the mastering might of the winds. A moan too is forced out, because the limbs are seized with pain, and mainly because seeds of voice are driven forth and are carried in a close mass out by the mouth, the road which they are accustomed to take and where they have a well-paved way. Loss of reason follows, because the powers of the mind and soul are disordered and, as I have shewn, are riven and forced asunder, torn to pieces by the same baneful malady. Then after the cause of the disease has bent its course back and the acrid humours of the distempered body return to their hiding-places, then he first gets up like one reeling, and by little and little comes back into full possession of his senses and regains his soul. Since therefore even within the body, mind and soul are harassed by such violent distempers and so miserably racked by sufferings, why believe that they without the body in the open air can continue existence battling with fierce winds? And since we perceive that the mind is healed, like the sick body, and we see that it can be altered by medicine, this too gives warning that the mind has a mortal existence. For it is natural that whosoever essays and attempts to change the mind or seeks to alter any other nature you like, should add new parts or change the arrangement of the present, or at least withdraw some small fraction from the whole sum. But that which is immortal wills not to have its parts transposed nor any addition to be made nor one tittle to ebb away; for whenever a thing changes and quits its proper limits, this change is at once the death of that which was before. Therefore the mind, whether it is sick or whether it is altered by medicine, alike, as I have shewn, gives forth mortal symptoms. So invariably is truth found to make head against false reason and to cut off all retreat from the assailant and by a two-edged refutation to put falsehood to rout.

Again we often see a man pass gradually away and limb by limb lose vital sense; first the toes of his feet and the nails turn livid, then the feet and shanks die, then next the steps of chilly death creep with slow pace over the other members. Since in this way the nature of the soul is rent and passes away and comes not forth all at once in its entireness, it must be reckoned mortal. But if haply you suppose that it can draw itself in through the whole frame and mass its parts together and in this way withdraw sense from all the limbs, yet then that spot into which so great a store of soul is gathered, ought to shew itself in possession of a greater amount of sense. But as this is nowhere found, sure enough as we said before, it is torn in pieces and scattered abroad, and therefore dies. Moreover if I were pleased for the moment to grant what is false and admit that the soul might be collected in one mass in the body of those who leave the light dying piecemeal, even then you must admit the soul to be mortal; and it makes no difference whether it perish dispersed in air, or gathered into one lump out of all its parts lose all feeling, since sense ever more and more fails the whole man throughout and less and less of life remains throughout.

And since the mind is one part of a man which remains fixed in a particular spot, just as are the ears and eyes and the other senses which guide and direct life; and just as the hand or eye or nose when separated from us cannot feel and exist apart, but in however short a time waste away in putrefaction, thus the mind cannot exist by itself without the body and the man's self which as you see serves for the mind's vessel or any thing else you choose to imagine which implies a yet closer union with it, since the body is attached to it by the nearest ties.

Again the quickened power of body and mind by their joint partnership enjoy health and life; for the nature of the mind cannot by itself alone without the body give forth vital motions nor can the body again bereft of the soul continue to exist and make use of its senses: just, you are to know, as the eye itself torn away from its roots cannot see anything when apart from the whole body, thus the soul and mind cannot it is plain do anything by themselves. Sure enough, because mixed up through veins and flesh, sinews and bones, their first-beginnings are confined by all the body and are not free to bound away leaving great spaces between, therefore thus shut in they make those sense-giving motions which they cannot make after death when forced out of the body into the air by reason that they are not then confined in a like manner; for the air will be a body and a living thing, if the soul shall be able to keep itself together and to enclose in it those motions which it used before to perform in the sinews and within the body. Therefore, again and again I say, when the enveloping body has been all broken up and the vital airs have been forced out, you must admit that the senses of the mind and the soul are dissolved, since the cause of destruction is one and inseparable for both body and soul.

Again since the body is unable to bear the separation of

the soul without rotting away in a noisome stench, why doubt that the power of the soul gathering itself up from the inmost depths of body has oozed out and dispersed like smoke, and that the crumbling body has changed and tumbled in with so total a ruin for this reason because its foundations are stirred throughout their place, the soul oozing out abroad through the frame, through all the winding passages which are in the body, and all openings? So that in ways manifold you may learn that the nature of the soul has been divided piecemeal and gone forth throughout the frame, and that it has been first torn to shreds within the body, ere it glided forth and swam out into the air. Moreover even while it yet moves within the confines of life, often the soul shaken from some cause or other is seen to wish to pass out and be loosed from the whole body, the features are seen to droop as at the last hour and all the limbs to sink flaccid over the bloodless trunk: just as happens, when the phrase is used, the mind is in a bad way, or the soul is quite gone; when all is hurry and every one is anxious to keep from parting the last tie of life; for then the mind and the power of the soul are shaken throughout and both are quite loosened together with the body; so that a cause somewhat more powerful can quite break them up. Why doubt, I would ask, that the soul when driven forth out of the body, when in the open air, feeble as it is, stript of its covering, not only cannot continue through eternity, but is unable to hold together the smallest fraction of time? No one when dying appears to feel the soul go forth entire from his whole body or first mount up to the throat and gullet, but all feel it fail in that part which lies in a particular quarter; just as they know that other senses suffer dissolution each in its own place. But if our mind were immortal, it would not when dying complain so much of its dissolution, as of passing abroad and quitting its vesture, like a snake.

Again why are the mind's understanding and judgment never begotten in the head or feet or hands, but cling to one spot and fixed quarter of the man, if it be not that particular places are assigned for the birth of each part, and for the abode of each after it is born, that thus the members may be distributed with such a manifold organisation of parts, that no perverted arrangement of them shall ever show itself? so invariably effect follows cause, nor is flame wont to be born in rivers nor cold in fire.

Again if the nature of the soul is immortal and can feel when separated from our body, methinks we must suppose it to be provided with five senses; and in no other way can we picture to ourselves souls below flitting about Acheron. Painters therefore and former generations of writers have thus represented souls provided with senses. But neither eyes nor nose nor hand can exist for the soul apart from the body nor can tongue, nor can ears perceive by the sense of hearing or exist for the soul by themselves apart from the body.

And since we perceive that vital sense is in the whole body and we see that it is all endowed with life, if on a sudden any force with swift blow shall have cut it in twain so as quite to dissever the two halves, the power of the soul will without doubt at the same time be cleft and cut asunder and dashed in twain together with the body. But that which is cut and divides into any parts, you are to know renounces for itself an everlasting nature. Stories are told how scythed chariots reeking with indiscriminate slaughter often lop off limbs so instantaneously that that which has fallen down lopped off from the frame is seen to quiver on the ground, while yet the mind and faculty of the man from the suddenness of the mischief cannot feel the pain; and because his mind once for all is wholly given to the business of fighting, with what remains of his body he mingles in the fray and carnage, and often perceives not that the wheels and devouring scythes have carried off among the horses' feet his left arm, shield and all; another sees not that his right arm has dropped from him, while he mounts and presses forward. Another tries to get up after he has lost his leg, while the dying foot quivers with its toes on the ground close by. The head too when cut off from the warm and living trunk retains on the ground the expression of life and open eyes, until it has delivered up all the remnants of soul. To take another case, if, as a serpent's tongue is quivering, as its tail is darting out from its long body, you choose to chop with an axe into many pieces both tail and body, you will see all the separate portions thus cut off writhing under the fresh wound and bespattering the earth with gore, the fore part with the mouth making for its own hinder part, to allay with burning bite the pain of the wound with which it has been smitten. Shall we say then that there are entire souls in all those pieces? Why from that argument it will follow that one living creature had many souls in its body; and this being absurd, therefore the soul which was one has been divided together with the body; therefore each alike must be reckoned mortal, since each is alike chopped up into many pieces.

Again if the nature of the soul is immortal and makes its way into our body at the time of birth, why are we unable to remember besides the time already gone, and why do we retain no traces of past actions? If the power of the mind has been so completely changed, that all remembrance of past things is lost, that methinks differs not widely from death; therefore you must admit that the soul which was before has perished and that which now is has now been formed.

Again if the quickened power of the mind is wont to be put into us after our body is fully formed, at the instant of our birth and our crossing the threshold of life, it ought agreeably to this to live not in such a way as to seem to have grown with the body and together with its members within the blood, but in a den apart by and to itself: the very contrary to what undoubted fact teaches; for it is so closely united with the body throughout the veins, flesh, sinews, and bones, that the very teeth have a share of sense; as the act of biting proves and the sharp twinge of cold water and the crunching of a rough stone, when it has got into them out of bread. Wherefore, again and again I say, we must believe souls to be neither without a birth nor exempted from the law of death; for we must not believe that they could have been so completely united with our bodies, if they found their way into them from without, nor, since they are so closely inwoven with them, does it appear that they can get out unharmed and unloose themselves without destruction from all the sinews and bones and joints. But if haply you believe that the soul finds its way in from without and is wont to ooze through all our limbs, so much the more it will perish thus blended with the body; for what oozes through another is dissolved, and therefore dies. As food distributed through all the cavities of the body, while it is transmitted into the limbs and the whole frame, is destroyed and furnishes out of itself the matter of another nature, thus the soul and mind, though they pass entire into a fresh body, yet in oozing through it are dissolved, whilst there are transmitted so to say into the frame through all the cavities those particles of which this nature of mind is formed, which now is sovereign in our body, being born out of that soul which then perished when dispersed through the frame. Wherefore the nature of the soul is seen to be neither without a birthday nor exempt from death.

Again are seeds of the soul left in the dead body or not? If they are left and remain in it, the soul cannot fairly be deemed immortal, since it has withdrawn lessened by the loss of some parts; but if when taken away it has fled forth with its members so entire that it has left in the body no parts of itself, whence do carcasses exude worms from the now rank flesh and whence does such a swarm of living things, boneless and bloodless, surge through the heaving frame? But if haply you believe that souls find their way into worms from without and can severally pass each into a body and you make no account of why many thousands of souls meet together in a place from which one has withdrawn, this question at least must, it seems, be raised and brought to a decisive test, whether souls hunt out the several seeds of worms and build for themselves a place to dwell in, or find their way into bodies fully formed, so to say. But why they should on their part make a body or take such trouble, cannot be explained; since being without a body they are not plagued as they flit about with diseases and cold and hunger: the body indeed is more akin to, more troubled by such infirmities, and by its contact with it the mind suffers many ills. Nevertheless be it ever so expedient for them to make a body, when they are going to enter, yet clearly there is no way by which they can so do. Therefore souls do not make for themselves bodies and limbs; no, nor is there any mode by which they can find their way into bodies after they are fully formed; for they will neither be able to unite themselves with a nice precision nor will any connexion of mutual sensation be formed between them.

Again why does untamed fierceness go along with the

sullen brood of lions, cunning with foxes and proneness to flight with stags? And to take any other instance of the kind, why are all qualities engendered in the limbs and temper from the very commencement of life, if not because a fixed power of mind derived from its proper seed and breed grows up together with the whole body? If it were immortal and wont to pass into different bodies, living creatures would be of interchangeable dispositions; a dog of Hyrcanian breed would often fly before the attack of an antlered stag, a hawk would cower in mid air as it fled at the approach of a dove, men would be without reason, the savage races of wild-beasts would have reason. For the assertion that an immortal soul is altered by a change of body is advanced on a false principle. What is changed, is dissolved, and therefore dies: the parts are transposed and quit their former order; therefore they must admit of being dissolved throughout the frame, in order at last to die one and all together with the body. But if they shall say that souls of men always go into human bodies, I yet will ask how it is a soul can change from wise to foolish, and no child has discretion, and why the mare's foal is not so well trained as the powerful strength of the horse. You may be sure they will fly to the subterfuge that the mind grows weakly in a weakly body. But granting this is so, you must admit the soul to be mortal, since changed so completely throughout the frame it loses its former life and sense. Then too, in what way will it be able to grow in strength uniformly with its allotted body and reach the coveted flower of age, unless it shall be its partner at its first beginning? Or what means it by passing out from the limbs when decayed with age? Does it fear to remain shut up in a crumbling body, fear that its tenement, worn out by protracted length of days, bury it in its ruins? Why an immortal being incurs no risks.

Again for souls to stand by at the unions of Venus and the birth-throes of beasts seems to be passing absurd, for them the immortals to wait for mortal limbs in number numberless and struggle with one another in forward rivalry, which shall first and by preference have entrance in; unlesss haply bargains are struck among the souls on these terms, that whichever in its flight shall first come up, shall first have right of entry, and that they shall make no trial at all of each other's strength.

Again a tree cannot exist in the ether, nor clouds in the deep sea nor can fishes live in the fields nor blood exist in woods nor sap in stones. Where each thing can grow and abide is fixed and ordained. Thus the nature of the mind cannot come into being alone without the body nor exist far away from the sinews and blood. But if (for this would be much more likely to happen than that) the force itself of the mind might be in the head or shoulders or heels or might be born in any other part of the body, it would after all be wont to abide in one and the same man or vessel. But since in our body even it is fixed and seen to be ordained where the soul and the mind can severally be and grow, it must still more strenuously be denied that it can abide and be born out of the body altogether. Therefore when the body has died, we must admit that the soul has perished, wrenched away throughout the body. To link forsooth a mortal thing with an everlasting and suppose that they can have sense in common and can be reciprocally acted upon, is sheer folly; for what can be conceived more incongruous, more discordant and inconsistent with itself, than a thing which is mortal, linked with an immortal and everlasting thing, trying in such union to weather

furious storms? But if the soul is to be accounted immortal for this reason rather, because it is kept sheltered
from death-bringing things, either because things hostile
to its existence do not approach at all, or because those
which do approach, in some way or other retreat dis-
comfited before we can feel the harm they do, [manifest
experience proves that this can not be true]. For besides
that it sickens in sympathy with the maladies of the
body, it is often attacked by that which frets it on the
score of the future and keeps it on the rack of suspense
and wears it out with cares, remorse for sins gnawing it
on account of past misdeeds: then there is madness
peculiar to the mind and forgetfulness of all things;
then too it often sinks into the black waters of lethargy.

Death therefore is nothing and concerns us not a
jot, since the nature of the mind is proved to be
mortal. And as in time gone by we felt no distress, when
the Poeni from all sides came together to do battle, and
all things shaken by war's troublous uproar shuddered
and quaked beneath high heaven, and mortal men were
in doubt which of the two peoples it should be to whose
empire all must fall by sea and land alike, thus when we
shall be no more, when there shall have been a separation
of body and soul, out of both of which we are each
formed into a single being, to us, you may be sure,
who then shall be no more, nothing whatever can happen
to excite sensation, not if earth shall be mingled with sea
and sea with heaven. And even supposing the nature of
the mind and power of the soul do feel, after they have
been severed from our body, yet that is nothing to us who
by the binding tie of marriage between body and soul
are formed each into one single being. And if time
should gather up our matter after our death and bring
it once more into the condition in which it now is, and
the light of life be given to us again, this result even

would concern us not at all, when the chain of our self-consciousness has once been snapped asunder. So now we give ourself no concern about any self which we have been before, nor do we feel any distress on the score of that self. For when you look back on the whole past course of immeasurable time and think how manifold are the shapes which the motions of matter take, you may easily credit this too, that these very same seeds of which we now are formed, have often before been placed in the same order in which they now are; and yet we cannot recover this in memory: a break in our existence has been interposed, and all the motions have wandered to and fro far astray from the sensations they produced. For he whom evil is to befall, must in his own person exist at the very time it comes, if the misery and suffering are haply to have any place at all; but since death precludes this, and forbids him to be, upon whom the ills can be brought, you may be sure that we have nothing to fear after death, and that he who exists not, cannot become miserable, and that it matters not a whit whether he has been born into life at any other time, when immortal death has taken away his mortal life.

Therefore when you see a man bemoaning his hard case, that after death he shall either rot with his body laid in the grave or be devoured by flames or the jaws of wild-beasts, you may be sure that his ring betrays a flaw and that there lurks in his heart a secret goad, though he himself declare that he does not believe that any sense will remain to him after death. He does not me-thinks really grant the conclusion which he professes to grant nor the principle on which he so professes, nor does he take and force himself root and branch out of life, but all unconsciously imagines something of self to survive. For when any one in life suggests to himself that birds and beasts will rend his body after death, he makes moan for himself: he does not separate himself from that self, nor withdraw himself fully from the body so thrown out, and fancies himself that other self and stands by and impregnates it with his own sense. Hence he makes much moan that he has been born mortal, and sees not that after real death there will be no other self to remain in life and lament to self that his own self has met death, and there to stand and grieve that his own self there lying is mangled or burnt. For if it is an evil after death to be pulled about by the devouring jaws of wild-beasts, I cannot see why it should not be a cruel pain to be laid on fires and burn in hot flames, or to be placed in honey and stifled, or to stiffen with cold, stretched on the smooth surface of a cold slab of stone, or to be pressed down and crushed by a load of earth from above.

'Now no more shall thy house admit thee with glad welcome, nor a most virtuous wife and sweet children run to be the first to snatch kisses and touch thy heart with a silent joy. No more mayst thou be properous in thy doings, a safeguard to thine own. One disastrous day has taken from thee luckless man in luckless wise all the many prizes of life.' This do men say; but add not thereto 'and now no longer does any craving for these things beset thee withal.' For if they could rightly perceive this in thought and follow up the thought in words, they would release themselves from great distress and apprehension of mind. 'Thou, even as now thou art, sunk in the sleep of death, shalt continue so to be all time to come, freed from all distressful pains; but we with a sorrow that would not be sated wept for thee, when close by thou didst turn to an ashen hue on thy appalling funeral pile, and no length of days shall pluck from our hearts our ever-during grief.' This question therefore should be asked of this speaker, what there is in it so passing bitter, if it come in the end to sleep and rest, that any one should pine in never-ending sorrow.

This too men often, when they have reclined at table and shade their brows with crowns, love to say from the heart, 'short is this enjoyment for poor weak men; presently it will have been and never after may it be called back.' As if after their death it is to be one of their chiefest afflictions that thirst and parching drought is to burn them up hapless wretches, or a craving for any thing else is to beset them. What folly! for no one feels the want of himself and life at the time when mind and body are together sunk in sleep; for all we care this sleep might be everlasting, no craving whatever for ourselves then moves us. And yet by no means do those first-beginnings throughout our frame wander at that time far away from their sense-producing motions, when a man starts up from sleep and collects himself at once. Death therefore must be supposed to concern us much less, if less there can be than what we see to be nothing; for a greater dispersion of the mass of matter follows in the train of death, and no one wakes up, upon whom the chill cessation of life has once come.

Once more, if the nature of things could suddenly utter a voice and in person could rally any of us in such words as these, 'what hast thou, O mortal, so much at heart, that thou goest such lengths in sickly sorrows? why bemoan and bewail death? For if thy life past and gone has been welcome to thee and thy blessings have not all, as if they were poured into a perforated vessel, run through and been lost without avail; why not take thy departure like a guest filled with life, and with resignation, thou fool, enter upcn untroubled rest? But if all that thou hast enjoyed, has been squandered and lost and life is a grievance, why seek to make any addition to be wasted perversely in its turn and lost utterly without avail? Why not rather make an end of life and travail? For there is nothing more which I can contrive and discover for thee to give pleasure: all things are ever the same. Though thy body is not yet decayed with years nor thy frame worn out and exhausted, yet all things remain the same, ay and would remain, though in length of life thou shouldst out-last all races of things now living, nay even more if thou shouldst never die,' what answer do we make save this, that nature sets up against us a well-founded claim and puts forth in her pleading a true indictment? If however one of greater age and more advanced in years should complain and lament, poor wretch, his death more than is right, would she not with greater cause raise her voice and rally him in sharp accents, 'away from this time forth with your tears, rascal; a truce to your complainings: thou decayest after full enjoyment of all the prizes of life. But because thou ever yearnest for what is not present, and despisest what is, life has slipped from thy grasp unfinished and unsatisfying, and or ever thou thoughtest, death has taken his stand at thy pillow, before thou canst take thy departure sated and filled with good things. Now however give up all things unsuited to thy age, and come give place to thy children; for it must be so.' With good reason methinks she would bring her charge, with reason rally and reproach; for old things give way and are supplanted by new without fail, and one thing must ever be replenished out of other things; and no one is delivered over to the pit and black Tartarus: matter is needed for after generations to grow; all of which though will follow thee when they have finished their term of life; and it follows that all these no less than thou have before this come to an end and hereafter will come to an end. Thus one thing never ceases to rise out of another, and life is granted to none in fee-simple, to all in usufruct. Think too how the bygone antiquity of everlasting time before our birth was nothing to us. Nature therefore holds this up to us as a mirror of the time yet to come after our death. Is there aught in this that looks appalling, aught that wears an aspect of gloom? Is it not more untroubled than any sleep?

And those things sure enough, which are fabled to be in the deep of Acheron, do all exist for us in this life. No Tantalus, numbed by groundless terror, as the story is, fears, poor wretch, a huge stone hanging in air; but in life rather a baseless dread of the gods vexes mortals: the fall they fear is such fall of luck as chance brings to each. Nor do birds eat a way into Tityos laid in Acheron, nor can they sooth to say find during eternity food to peck under his large breast. However huge the bulk of body he extends, though such as to take up with out-spread limbs not nine acres merely, but the whole earth, yet will he not be able to endure everlasting pain and supply food from his own body for ever. But he is for us a Tityos, whom as he grovels in love vultures rend and bitter, bitter anguish eats up or troubled thoughts from any other passion do rive. In life too we have a Sisyphus before our eyes who is bent on asking from the people the rods and cruel axes, and always retires defeated and disappointed. For to ask for power, which empty as it is, is never given, and always to undergo in the pursuit severe toil, this is forcing up-hill with much effort a stone which after all rolls back again from the summit and seeks in headlong haste the levels of the plain. Then to be ever feeding the thankless nature of the mind, and never to fill it full and sate it with good things, as the seasons of the year do for us, when they come round and bring their fruits and varied delights, though after all we are never filled with the enjoyments of life, this

methinks is to do what is told of the maidens in the
flower of their age, to keep pouring water into a perforated vessel which in spite of all can never be filled full.
Moreover Cerberus and the furies and yon privation of
light [are idle tales, as well as all the rest, Ixion's wheel
and black] Tartarus belching forth hideous fires from
his throat: things which nowhere are nor sooth to say
can be. But there is in life a dread of punishment for
evil deeds, signal as the deeds are signal, and as atone-
ment of guilt, the prison and the frightful hurling down
from the rock, scourgings, executioners, the dungeon of
the doomed, the pitch, the metal plate, torches; and even
though these are wanting, yet the conscience-stricken
mind through boding fears applies to itself goads and
frightens itself with whips, and sees not meanwhile what
end there can be of ills or what limit at last is to be set
to punishments, and fears lest these very evils be aggravat-
ed after death. The life of fools at length becomes a hell
here on earth.

This too you may sometimes say to yourself: even
worthy Ancus has quitted the light with his eyes, who
was far far better than thou, unconscionable man. And
since then many other kings and kesars have been laid
low, who lorded it over mighty nations. He too, even he
who erst paved a way over the great sea and made a path
for his legions to march over the deep and taught them
to pass on foot over the salt pools and set at naught the
roarings of the sea, trampling on them with his horses,
had the light taken from him and shed forth his soul
from his dying body. The son of the Scipios, thunderbolt
of war, terror of Carthage, yielded his bones to earth
just as if he were the lowest menial. Think too of the
inventors of all sciences and graceful arts, think of the
companions of the Heliconian maids; among whom
Homer bore the sceptre without a peer, and he now sleeps

the same sleep as others. Then there is Democritus who, when a ripe old age had warned him that the memory-waking motions of his mind were waning, by his own spontaneous act offered up his head to death. Even Epicurus passed away, when his light of life had run its course, he who surpassed in intellect the race of man and quenched the light of all, as the ethereal sun arisen quenches the stars. Wilt thou then hesitate and think it a hardship to die? thou for whom life is well nigh dead whilst yet thou livest and seest the light, who wastest the greater part of thy time in sleep and snorest wide awake and ceasest not to see visions and hast a mind troubled with groundless terror and canst not discover often what it is that ails thee, when, besotted man, thou art sore pressed on all sides with a multitude of cares and goest astray tumbling about in a maze of mental error.

If, just as they are seen to feel that a load is on their mind which wears them out with its pressure, men might apprehend from what causes too it is produced and whence such a pile, if I may say so, of ill lies on their breast, they would not spend their life as we see them now for the most part do, not knowing any one of them what he means and wanting ever change of place as though he might lay down his burden. The man who is sick of home often issues forth from his large mansion, and as suddenly comes back to it, finding as he does that he is no better off abroad. He races to his country-house, driving his jennets in headlong haste, as if hurrying to bring help to a house on fire: he yawns the moment he has reached the door of his house, or sinks heavily into sleep and seeks forgetfulness, or even in haste goes back again to town. In this way each man flies from himself (but self from whom, as you may be sure is commonly the case, he cannot escape, clings to him in his own despite) and hates himself, because he is sick and knows not the cause of the malady; for if he could rightly see into this, relinquishing all else, each man would study to learn the nature of things, since the point at stake is the condition for eternity, not for one hour, in which mortals have to pass all the time which remains for them to expect after death.

Once more what evil lust of life is this which constrains us with such force to be so mightily troubled in doubts and dangers? A sure term of life is fixed for mortals, and death cannot be shunned, but meet it we must. Moreover we are ever engaged, ever involved in the same pursuits, and no new pleasure is struck out by living on; but whilst what we crave is wanting, it seems to transcend all the rest; then, when it has been gotten, we crave something else, and ever does the same thirst of life possess us, as we gape for it open-mouthed. Quite doubtful it is what fortune the future will carry with it or what chance will bring us or what end is at hand. Nor by prolonging life do we take one tittle from the time past in death nor can we fret anything away, whereby we may haply be a less long time in the condition of the dead. Therefore you may complete as many generations as you please during your life; none the less however will that everlasting death await you; and for no less long a time will he be no more in being, who beginning with today has ended his life, than the man who has died many months and years ago.

Thomas Aquinas (1224-1274) was a Dominican friar whose cloister was the world of scholarship. His masterful examination of Aristotle and his synthesis of that philosopher's ideas with the tenets of Christianity still exert a powerful influence on the intellectual climate of Roman Catholocism. These selections are from *Summa Theologica*, which is widely regarded as the classic statement of Christian belief.

TREATISE ON MAN

QUESTION LXXV
Of man, who is composed of a
spiritual and a corporeal
substance; and first, what pertains
to the essence of the soul
(In Seven Articles)

HAVING treated of the spiritual and of the corporeal creature, we now proceed to treat of man, who is composed of a spiritual and of a corporeal substance. We shall treat first of the nature of man, and secondly of his origin. (Q. xc). Now the theologian considers the nature of man in relation to the soul, but not in relation to the body, except in so far as the body has relation to the soul. Hence the first object of our consideration will be the soul. And since Dionysius (*Ang. Hier.* xi)[1] says that three things are to be found in spiritual substances—essence, power, and operation—we shall treat first of what belongs to the essence of the soul; secondly, of what belongs to its power (Q. LXXVII); thirdly, of what belongs to its operation (Q. LXXXIV).

Concerning the first, two points have to be considered: the first is the nature of the soul considered in itself; the second is the union of the soul with the body. (Q. LXXVI). Under the first head there are seven points of inquiry.

(1) Whether the soul is a body? (2) Whether the human soul is something subsistent? (3) Whether the souls of brute animals are subsistent? (4) Whether the soul is man, or whether man is composed of soul and body? (5) Whether the soul is composed of matter and form? (6) Whether the soul is incorruptible? (7) Whether the soul is of the same species as an angel?

ARTICLE 1. *Whether the Soul Is a Body?*

We proceed thus to the First Article: It would seem that the soul is a body.

Objection 1. For the soul is the mover of the body. Nor does it move unless moved. First, because it seems that nothing can move unless it is itself moved, since nothing gives what it has not; for instance, what is not hot does not give heat. Secondly, because if there is anything that moves and is not moved, "it is the cause of eternal, unvarying movement," as we find proved in the *Physics*;[2] and this does not appear to be the case in the movement of an animal, which is caused by the soul. Therefore the soul is a mover moved. But every mover moved is a body. Therefore the soul is a body.

Obj. 2. Further, all knowledge is caused by means of some likeness. But there can be no likeness of a body to an incorporeal thing. If, therefore, the soul were not a body, it could not have knowledge of corporeal things.

Obj. 3. Further, between the mover and the moved there must be contact. But contact is only between bodies. Since, therefore, the soul moves the body, it seems that the soul must be a body.

On the contrary, Augustine says (*De Trin.* vi, 6)[3] that the soul "is simple in comparison with the body, because it does not occupy space by its bulk."

I answer that, To seek the nature of the soul, we must lay down first that the soul is defined as the first principle of life in those things which in our judgment live; for we call living things "animate," and those things which have no life, "inanimate." Now life is shown principally by two actions, knowledge and movement. The philosophers of old,[4] not being able to rise above their imagination, supposed that the principle of these actions was something corporeal; for they asserted that only bodies were real things and that what is not a body is nothing.[5] Hence they maintained that the soul is a kind of body.[6] Although this opinion can be proved to be false in many ways, we shall make use of only one proof, which shows clearly in a general and certain way that the soul is not a body.

It is manifest that not every principle of vital action is a soul, for then the eye would be a soul, as it is a principle of vision, and the same might be applied to the other instruments of the soul; but it is the *first* principle of life which we call the soul. Now, though a body may be a principle of life, as the heart is a principle of life in an animal, yet no body can be the first principle of life. For it is clear that to be a principle of life, or to be a living thing, does not pertain to a body as such; since, if that were the case, every body would be a living thing, or a principle of life. Therefore a body is suited to be a living thing or even a principle of life, from the fact that it is this kind of body. Now that it is actually such a kind of body it owes to some principle which is called its act. Therefore the soul, which is the first principle of life, is not a body, but the act of a body; thus heat, which is the principle of making hot, is not a body, but an act of a body.

Reply Obj. 1. As everything which is in motion must be moved by something else, a process which cannot proceed to infinity, we must allow that not every mover is moved. For, since to be moved is to pass from potency to act, the mover gives what it has to the thing moved, in so far as it causes it to be in act. But, as is shown in the *Physics*,[1] "there is a mover which is altogether immovable, and not moved either per se, or accidentally; and such a mover can cause an invariable movement." There is, however, another kind of mover, which, though not moved *per se,* is moved accidentally, and for this reason it does not cause an invariable movement; such a mover is the soul. There is, again, another mover, which is moved per se—namely, the body. And because the philosophers of old believed that nothing existed but bodies,[2] they maintained that every mover is moved, and that the soul is moved per se, and is a body.

Reply Obj. 2. The likeness of the thing known is not of necessity actually in the nature of the knower; but given a thing which knows in potency, and afterwards knows in act, the likeness of the thing known must be in the nature of the knower not actually, but only in potency; thus colour is not actually in the pupil of the eye, but only in potency. Hence it is necessary not that the likeness of corporeal things should be actually in the nature of the soul, but that it be in potency to such a likeness. But the ancient naturalists[3] did not know how to distinguish between act and potency; and so they held that the soul must be a body, and that it must be composed of the principles of which all bodies are formed in order to know all bodies.

Reply Obj. 3. There are two kinds of contact: of quantity, and of power. By the former a body can be touched only by a body; by the latter a body can be touched by an incorporeal thing, which moves that body.

ARTICLE 2. *Whether the Human Soul Is Something Subsistent?*

We proceed thus to the Second Article: It would seem that the human soul is not something subsistent.

Objection 1. For that which subsists is said to be "this particular thing." Now "this particular thing" is said not of the soul, but of that which is composed of soul and body. Therefore the soul is not something subsistent.

Obj. 2. Further, everything subsistent operates. But the soul does not operate; for, as the Philosopher says,[4] "to say that the soul feels or understands is like saying that the soul weaves or builds." Therefore the soul is not subsistent.

Obj. 3. Further, if the soul were subsistent, it would have some operation apart from the body. But it has no operation apart from the body, not even that of understanding, for the act of understanding does not take place without a phantasm, which cannot exist apart from the body. Therefore the human soul is not something subsistent.

On the contrary, Augustine says (*De Trin.* x, 7):[5] "Whoever understands that the nature of the soul is that of a substance and not that of a body, will see that those who maintain the corporeal nature of the soul are led astray through associating with the soul those things without which they are unable to think of any nature" that is, imaginary pictures of corporeal things. Therefore the nature of the human intellect is not only incorporeal, but it is also a substance, that is, something subsistent.

I answer that, It must necessarily be allowed that the principle of intellectual operation which we call the soul is a principle both incorporeal and subsistent. For it is clear that by means of the intellect man can know the natures of all corporeal things. Now whatever knows certain things cannot have any of them in its own nature because that which is in it naturally would impede the knowledge of anything else. Thus we observe that a sick man's tongue being vitiated by a feverish and bitter humour, cannot perceive anything sweet, and everything seems

103

bitter to it. Therefore, if the intellectual principle contained the nature of any body it would be unable to know all bodies. Now every body has some determinate nature. Therefore it is impossible for the intellectual principle to be a body. It is likewise impossible for it to understand by means of a bodily organ, since the determinate nature of that bodily organ would prevent the knowledge of all bodies; as when a certain determinate colour is not only in the pupil of the eye, but also in a glass vase, the liquid in the vase seems to be of that same colour.

Therefore the intellectual principle which we call the mind or the intellect has an operation *per se* apart from the body. Now only that which subsists can have an operation *per se.* For nothing can operate except a being in act; hence a thing operates according as it is. For this reason we do not say that heat imparts heat, but that what is hot gives heat. We must conclude, therefore, that the human soul, which is called the intellect or the mind, is something incorporeal and subsistent.

Reply Obj. 1. "This particular thing" can be taken in two senses. Firstly, for anything subsistent; secondly, for that which subsists, and is complete in a specific nature. The former sense excludes the inherence of an accident or of a material form; the latter excludes also the imperfection of the part, so that a hand can be called "this particular thing" in the first sense, but not in the second. Therefore, as the human soul is a part of the human species, it can be called "this particular thing" in the first sense, as being something subsistent; but not in the second, for in this sense what is composed of body and soul is said to be "this particular thing."

Reply Obj. 2. Aristotle wrote those words as expressing not his own opinion, but the opinion of those who said that to understand is to be moved, as is clear from the context.

Or we may reply that to act *per se* belongs to what exists *per se.* But for a thing to exist *per se,* it suffices sometimes that it be not inherent, as an accident or a material form, even though it be part of something. Nevertheless, that is rightly said to subsist *per se* which is neither inherent in the above sense nor part of anything else. In this sense, the eye or the hand cannot be said to subsist *per se;* nor can it for that reason be said to operate *per se.* Hence the operation of the parts is through each part attributed to the whole. For we say that man sees with the eye, and feels with the hand, and not in the same sense as when we say that what is hot gives heat by its heat; for heat, strictly speaking, does not give heat. We may therefore say that the soul understands, as the eye sees; but it is more correct to say that man understands through the soul.

Reply Obj. 3. The body is necessary for the action of the intellect not as its organ of action, but by reason of the object; for the phantasm is to the intellect what colour is to the sight. Neither does such a dependence on the body prove the intellect to be non-subsistent; otherwise it would follow that an animal is non-subsistent, since it requires external senible things in order to sense.

QUESTION LXXXIII
OF FREE CHOICE
(*In Four Articles*)

WE now inquire concerning free choice. Under this head there are four points of inquiry: (1) Whether man has free choice? (2) What is free choice—a power, an act, or a habit? (3) If it is a power, is it appetitive or cognitive? (4) If it is appetitive, is it the same power as the will, or distinct?

ARTICLE 1. *Whether Man Has Free Choice?*

We proceed thus to the First Article: It would seem that man has not free choice.

Objection 1. For whoever has free choice does what he wills. But man does not what he wills, for it is written (Rom. 7. 19): *For the good which I will I do not, but the evil which I will not, that I do.* Therefore man has not free choice.

Obj. 2. Further, whoever has free choice has in his power to will or not to will, to do or not to do. But this is not in man's power, for it is written (Rom. 9. 16): *It is not of him that willeth* —namely, to will—*nor of him that runneth*— namely, to run. Therefore man has not free choice.

Obj. 3. Further "what is free is cause of itself," as the Philosopher says.[4] Therefore what is moved by another is not free. But God moves the will, for it is written (Prov. 21. 1): *The heart of the king is in the hand of the Lord; whithersoever He will He shall turn it;* and (Phil. 2. 13): *It is God Who worketh in you both to will and to accomplish.* Therefore man has not free choice.

Obj. 4. Further, whoever has free choice is master of his own actions. But man is not master of his own actions: for it is written (Jer. 10. 23): *The way of a man is not his: neither is it in a man to walk.* Therefore man has not free choice.

Obj. 5. Further, the Philosopher says,[1] "According as each one is, such does the end seem to him." But it is not in our power to be of one quality or another, for this comes to us from nature. Therefore it is natural to us to follow some particular end, and therefore we do not do so from free choice.

On the contrary, It is written (Ecclus. 15. 14): *God made man from the beginning, and left him in the hand of his own counsel;* and the gloss adds[2]: That is "of his free choice."

I answer that, Man has free choice. Otherwise counsels, exhortations, commands, prohibitions, rewards and punishments would be in vain. In order to make this evident, we must observe that some things act without judgment, as a stone moves downwards; and in like manner all things which lack knowledge. And some act from judgment, but not a free judgment; as brute animals. For the sheep, seeing the wolf, judges it a thing to be shunned, from a natural and not a free judgment, because it judges, not from an act of comparison, but from natural instinct. And the same thing is to be said of any judgment of brute animals. But man acts from judgment because by his knowing power he judges that something should be avoided or sought. But because this judgment, in the case of some particular act, is not from a natural instinct, but from some act of comparison in the reason, therefore he acts from free judgment and retains the power of being inclined to various things. For reason in contingent matters may follow opposite courses, as we see in dialectic syllogisms and rhetorical arguments. Now particular operations are contingent, and therefore in such matters the judgment of reason may follow opposite courses, and is not determined to one. And since man is rational man must have free choice.

Reply Obj. 1. As we have said above (Q. LXXXI. A. 3, ANS. 2), the sensitive appetite, though it obeys the reason, yet in a given case can resist by desiring what the reason forbids. This is therefore the good which man does not when he wishes—namely, not to desire against reason, as Augustine says.[3]

Reply Obj. 2. Those words of the Apostle are not to be taken as though man does not wish or does not run of his free choice, but because the free choice is not sufficient for this unless it be moved and helped by God.

Reply Obj. 3. Free choice is the cause of its own movement, because by his free choice man moves himself to act. But it does not of necessity belong to liberty that what is free should be the first cause of itself, as neither for one thing to be cause of another need it be the first cause. God, therefore. is the first cause, Who moves causes both natural and voluntary. And just as by moving natural causes He does not prevent their acts being natural, so by moving voluntary causes He does not deprive their actions of being voluntary. but rather is He the cause of this very thing in them; for He operates in each thing according to its own nature.

Reply Obj. 4. "Man's way" is said "not to be his" in the execution of his choice, in which he may be impeded, whether he will or not. The choice itself, however, is in us, but presupposes the help of God.

Reply Obj. 5. Quality in man is of two kinds: natural and coming from without. Now the natural quality may be in the intellectual part or in the body and its powers. From the very fact, therefore, that man is such by virtue of a natural quality which is in the intellectual part. he naturally desires his last end. which is happiness. Which, indeed, is a natural desire, and is not subject to free choice, as is clear from what we have said above (Q. LXXXII, AA. 1, 2). But on the part of the body and its powers man may be such by virtue of a natural quality, in so far as he is of such a temperament or disposition due to any impression whatever produced by corporeal causes. which cannot affect the intellectual part. since it is not the act of a corporeal organ. And such as a man is by virtue of a corporeal quality. such also does his end seem to

him, because from such a disposition a man is
inclined to choose or reject something. But these
inclinations are subject to the judgment of reason, which the lower appetite obeys, as we have
said (Q. LXXXI, A 3). And so this is in no way
prejudicial to free choice.

The qualities that come from without are habits and passions, by virtue of which a man is inclined to one thing rather than to another. And
yet even these inclinations are subject to the
judgment of reason. Such qualities, too, are subject to reason, as it is in our power either to acquire them, whether by causing them or dispos-
ing ourselves to them, or to reject them. And so
there is nothing in this that is contrary to the
freedom of choice.

QUESTION LXXXIX
OF THE KNOWLEDGE OF THE
SEPARATED SOUL
(*In Eight Articles*)

WE must now consider the knowledge of the
separated soul. Under this head there are eight
points of inquiry: (1) Whether the soul separated from the body can understand? (2)
Whether it understands separate substances?
(3) Whether it understands all natural things?
(4) Whether it understands singulars? (5)
Whether the habits of knowledge acquired in
this life remain? (6) Whether the soul can use
the habit of knowledge acquired in this life?
(7) Whether local distance impedes the separated soul's knowledge? (8) Whether souls
separated from the body know what happens
here?

ARTICLE 1. *Whether the Separated Soul Can
Understand Anything?*

We Proceed thus to the First Article: It
would seem that the soul separated from the
body can understand nothing at all.

Objection 1. For the Philosopher says[1] that
"the understanding is corrupted together with
its interior principle." But by death all human
interior principles are corrupted. Therefore also
the intellect itself is corrupted.

Obj. 2. Further, the human soul is hindered
from understanding when the senses are bound,

and by a disordered imagination, as explained above (Q. LXXXIV, AA. 7, 8). But death destroys the senses and imagination, as we have shown above (Q. LXXVII, A. 8). Therefore after death the soul understands nothing.

Obj. 3. Further, if the separated soul can understand, this must be by means of some species. But it does not understand by means of innate species, because from the first, it is like a tablet on which nothing is written. Nor does it understand by species abstracted from things, for it does not then possess organs of sense and imagination which are necessary for the abstraction of species. Nor does it understand by means of species formerly abstracted and retained in the soul, for if that were so, a child's soul after death would have no means of understanding at all. Nor does it understand by means of intelligible species divinely infused, for such knowledge would not be natural, such as we treat of now, but the effect of grace. Therefore the soul apart from the body understands nothing.

On the contrary, The Philosopher says,[2] "If the soul had no proper operation, it could not be separated from the body." But the soul is separated from the body. Therefore it has a proper operation, and above all, that which consists in understanding. Therefore the soul can understand when it is apart from the body.

I answer that, The difficulty in solving this question arises from the fact that the soul united to the body can understand only by turning to the phantasms, as experience shows. If this did not proceed from the soul's very nature, but accidentally through its being bound up with the body, as the Platonists said,[3] the difficulty would vanish, for in that case when the hindrance of the body was once removed,[4] the soul would return to its own nature, and would understand intelligible things simply, without turning to the phantasms, as is the case with other separate substances. In that case, however, the union of soul and body would not be for the soul's good, for evidently it would understand worse in the body than out of it, but for the good of the body, which would be unreasonable, since matter exists on account of the form, and not the form for the sake of the matter. But if we admit that the nature of the soul requires it to understand by turning to the phantasms. it will seem, since the death of the body does not change its nature, that it can then naturally understand nothing. as the phantasms are wanting to which it may turn.

To solve this difficulty we must consider that as nothing acts except so far as it is actual. the mode of action in every agent follows from its mode of being. Now the soul has one mode of being when joined to the body, and another when separated from it. its nature remaining always the same. But this does not mean that its union with the body is an accidental thing. for, on the contrary. such a union belongs to it by reason of its nature. just as the nature of a light object is not changed whether it is in its proper place, which is natural to it, or outside its proper place. which is foreign to its nature. The soul, therefore. when united to the body, appropriately to that mode of existence has a mode of understanding by turning to corporeal phantasms. which are in corporeal organs; but when it is separated from the body, it is fitting to it to have a mode of understanding by turning to absolutely intelligible objects, as is proper to other separate substances. Hence it is as natural for the soul to understand by turning to the phantasms as it is for it to be joined to the body. But to be separated from the body is not in accordance with its nature, and likewise to understand without turning to the phantasms is not natural to it, and hence it is united to the body in order that it may have an existence and an operation suitable to its nature. But here again a difficulty arises. For since a thing is always ordered to what is best, and since it is better to understand by turning to absolutely intelligible things than by turning to the phantasms, God should have made the soul's nature so that the nobler way of understanding would have been natural to it. and it would not have needed the body for that purpose.

In order to resolve this difficulty we must consider that while it is true that it is nobler in itself to understand by turning to something higher than to understand by turning to phantasms, nevertheless such a mode of understanding was not so perfect as regards what was possible to the soul. This will appear if we consider that every intellectual substance possesses the power of understanding by the influx of the

110

Divine light, which is one and simple in its first principle, and the further off intellectual creatures are from the first principle so much the more is the light divided and diversified, as is the case with lines radiating from the centre of a circle. Hence it is that God by His own Essence understands all things, while the superior intellectual substances understand by means of many forms, which nevertheless are fewer and more universal and bestow a deeper comprehension of things, because of the efficaciousness of the intellectual power of such natures. But the inferior intellectual natures possess a greater number of forms, which are less universal, and bestow a lower degree of comprehension in proportion as they recede from the intellectual power of the higher natures. If, therefore, the inferior substances received forms in the same degree of universality as the superior substances, since they are not so strong in understanding, the knowledge which they would derive through them would be imperfect and of a general and confused nature. We can see this to a certain extent in man, for those who are of weaker intellect fail to acquire perfect knowledge through the universal conceptions of those who have a better understanding, unless things are explained to them singly and in detail. Now it is clear that in the natural order human souls hold the lowest place among intellectual substances. But the perfection of the universe required various grades of being. If, therefore, God had willed human souls to understand in the same way as separate substances, it would follow that human knowledge, so far from being perfect, would be confused and general. Therefore to make it possible for human souls to possess perfect and proper knowledge, they were so made that their nature required them to be joined to bodies, and thus to receive a proper knowledge of sensible things from the sensible things themselves; thus we see in the case of uneducated men that they have to be taught by sensible examples.

It is clear then that it was for the soul's good that it was united to a body, and that it understands by turning to the phantasms. Nevertheless it is possible for it to exist apart from the body, and also to understand in another way.

Reply Obj. 1. The Philosopher's words carefully examined will show that he said this on the previous supposition[1] that understanding is a movement of body and soul as united, just as sensation is, for he had not as yet explained the difference between intellect and sense. We may also say that he is referring to the way of understanding by turning to phantasms. This is also the meaning of the second objection.

Reply Obj. 3. The separated soul does not understand by way of innate species, nor by species abstracted in that state, nor only by retained species, and this the objection proves; but the soul in that state understands by means of participated species arising from the influx of the Divine light, shared by the soul as by other separate substances though, in a lesser degree. Hence as soon as it ceases to act by turning to the body, the soul turns at once to the superior things; nor is this way of knowledge unnatural, for God is the author of the influx both of the light of grace and of the light of nature.

QUESTION XCIII

The end or term of the production of man

(In Nine Articles)

We now treat of the end of term of man's production, according as he is said to be made to the image and likeness of God. There are under this head nine points of inquiry: (1) Whether the image of God is in man? (2) Whether the image of God is in irrational creatures? (3) Whether the image of God is in the angels more than in man? (4) Whether the image of God is in every man? (5) Whether the image of God is in man by comparison with the Essence, or with all the Divine Persons, or with one of them? (6) Whether the image of God is in man, as to his mind only? (7) Whether the image of God is in man's power or in his habits and acts? (8) Whether the image of God is in man by comparison with every object? (9) Of the difference between image and likeness.

ARTICLE 1. *Whether the Image of God Is in Man?*

We proceed thus to the First Article: It would seem that the image of God is not in man.

Objection 1. For it is written (Isa. 40. 18): *To whom have you likened God? or what image will you make for Him?*

Obj 2. Further, to be the image of God is the property of the First-Begotten, of Whom the Apostle says (Col. 1. 15): *Who is the image of the invisible God, the First-Born of every creature.* Therefore the image of God is not to be found in man.

Obj. 3. Further, Hilary says (*De Synod.*)[1] that "an image is of the same species as that which it represents"; and he also says[2] that "an image is the undivided and united likeness of one thing adequately representing another." But there is no species common to both God and man, nor can there be an equality between God and man. Therefore there can be no image of God in man.

On the contrary, It is written (Gen. 1. 26): *Let Us make man to Our own image and likeness.*

I answer that, As Augustine says (QQ. LXXXIII, *qu.* 74):[3] "Where an image exists, there immediately is likeness; but where there is likeness, there is not necessarily an image." Hence it is clear that likeness pertains to the notion of image, and that an image adds something to the notion of likeness—namely, that it is copied from something else. For an image is called so because it is produced as an imitation of something else; and so, for instance, an egg, however much like and equal to another egg, is not called an image; for, as Augustine says (*ibid.*); copied from it.

But equality does not belong to the notion of an image; for, as Augustine says (*ibid.*): "Where there is an image there is not necessarily equality," as we see in a person's image reflected in a glass. Yet this pertains to the notion of a perfect image, for in a perfect image nothing is wanting that is to be found in that of which it is a copy. Now it is manifest that in man there is some likeness to God, copied from God as from an exemplar. Yet this likeness is not one of equality, for such an exemplar infinitely excels its copy. Therefore there is in man a likeness to God; not, indeed, a perfect likeness, but imperfect. And Scripture implies the same when it says that man was made "to" God's likeness, for the preposition "to" signifies a certain approach, as of something at a distance.

Reply Obj. 1. The Prophet speaks of bodily images made by man. Therefore he says pointedly: *What image will you make for Him?* But God made a spiritual image to Himself in man.

Reply Obj. 2. The First-Born of creatures is the perfect Image of God, reflecting perfectly that of which He is the Image, and so He is said to be the Image, and never to the Image. But man is said to be both image by reason of the likeness, and to the image by reason of the imperfect likeness. And since the perfect likeness to God cannot be except in identity of nature, the Image of God exists in His first-born Son; as the image of the king is in his son, who is of the same nature as himself; but it exists in man as in an alien nature, as the image of the king is in a silver coin, as Augustine explains in *De decem Chordis (Serm.* ix).[1]

Reply Obj. 3. As unity means absence of division, a species is said to be the same in so far as it is one. Now a thing is said to be one not only numerically, specifically, or generically, but also according to a certain analogy or proportion. In this sense a creature is one with God, or like to Him; but when Hilary says "of a thing which adequately represents another," this pertains to the notion of a perfect image.

ARTICLE 7. *Whether the Image of God Is to Be Found in the Acts of the Soul?*

We proceed thus to the Seventh Article: It would seem that the image of God is not found in the acts of the soul.

Objection 1. For Augustine says[1] that "man was made to God's image, inasmuch as we are and know that we are, and love this being and knowledge." But to be does not signify an act. Therefore the image of God is not to be found in the soul's acts.

Obj. 2. Further, Augustine (*De Trin.* ix, 12)[2] assigns God's image in the soul to these three things—"mind, knowledge, and love." But mind does not signify an act, but rather the power or the essence of the intellectual soul. Therefore the image of God does not extend to the acts of the soul.

Obj. 3. Further, Augustine (*De Trin.* x, 12)[3] assigns the image of the Trinity in the soul to "memory, understanding, and will." But these three are "natural powers of the soul," as the Master of the Sentences says (1 *Sent.* D. iii).[4] Therefore the image of God is in the powers, and does not extend to the acts of the soul.

Obj. 4. Further, the image of the Trinity always remains in the soul. But an act does not always remain. Therefore the image of God does not extend to the acts.

On the contrary, Augustine (*De Trin.* xi, 2 *seqq.*)[5] assigns the trinity in the lower part of the soul, in relation to the actual vision, whether sensible or imaginative. Therefore, also, the trinity in the mind, by reason of which man is like God's image, must be referred to actual vision.

I answer that, As above explained (A. 2), a certain representation of the species belongs to the notion of an image. Hence, if the image of the Divine Trinity is to be found in the soul, we must look for it where the soul approaches the nearest (so far as this is possible) to a representation of the species of the Divine Persons. Now the Divine Persons are distinct from each other by reason of the procession of the Word from the Speaker, and the procession of Love joining Both. But in our soul word "cannot exist without actual thought," as Augustine says (*De Trin.* xiv, 7).[6] Therefore, first and chiefly, the image of the Trinity is to be found in the acts of the mind, that is, namely, as from the knowledge which we possess, by thinking we form an internal word, and thence break forth into love. But, since the principles of acts are the habits and powers, and everything exists virtually in its principle, therefore, secondarily and as though consequently, the image of the Trinity may be considered as existing in the powers, and still more in the habits, according as the acts exist virtually in them.

Reply Obj. 1. Our being bears the image of God so far as it is proper to us, and excels that of the other animals, in so far as we are endowed with a mind. Therefore, this trinity is the same as that which Augustine mentions (*De Trin.* ix, 12),[7] and which consists in "mind, knowledge, and love."

Reply Obj. 2. Augustine observed this trinity first in the mind. But because the mind, though it knows itself entirely in a certain degree, yet also in a way does not know itself—namely, as

115

being distinct from others (and thus also it seeks itself, as Augustine subsequently proves —*De Trin.* x);[8] therefore, since knowledge is not wholly equal to the mind. he takes three things in the soul which are proper to the mind, namely, memory, understanding, and will, which everyone knows he has, and assigns the image of the Trinity preeminently to these three, as though the first ascription were in part deficient.

Reply Obj. 3. As Augustine proves (*De Trin.* xiv, 7),[9] we may be said to understand, will, or to love certain things, both when we actually think of them, and when we do not think of them. When they are not under our actual consideration, they belong to memory only, which, in his opinion, is nothing else than habitual retention of knowledge and love.[1] "But since," as he says.[2] "a word cannot be there without actual thought (for we think everything that we say, even if we speak with that interior word belonging to no nation's tongue), this image chiefly consists in these three things. memory, understanding, and will. And by understanding I mean here that whereby we understand with actual thought; and by will, love, or dilection I mean that which unites this child with its parent." From which it is clear that he places the image of the Divine Trinity more in actual understanding and will than in these as existing in the habitual retention of the memory, although even thus the image of the Trinity exists in the soul in a certain degree, as he says in the same place. Thus it is clear that memory, understanding, and will are not three powers as stated in the *Sentences.*

Reply Obj. 4. Someone might answer by referring to Augustine's statement (*De Trin.* xiv, 6),[3] that "the mind ever remembers itself, ever understands itself, ever loves itself," which some take to mean that the soul ever actually understands, and loves itself.[4] But he excludes this interpretation by adding that "it does not always think of itself as actually distinct from other things." Thus it is clear that the soul always understands and loves itself, not actually but habitually, though we might say that by perceiving its own act, it understands itself whenever it understands anything. But since it is not always actually understanding, as in the case of sleep, we must say that these acts, although not always actually existing in themselves, yet always exist in their principles, the habits and powers. And so, Augustine says (*De Trin.* xiv, 4):[5] "If the rational soul is made to the image of God in the sense that it can make use of reason and intellect to understand and consider God, then the image of God was in the soul from the beginning of its existence."

3

Samuel Johnson,   THE HISTORY OF RASSELAS PRINCE OF
ABYSSINIA

William Wordsworth,   "TINTERN ABBEY"
"ODE: INTIMATIONS OF IMMORTALITY"

1. This philosophical fable employs the route metaphor,
    that is, a character's actual journey leads to an
    understanding of life. Trace Rasselas' growing dis-
    illusionment with the world. What particular aspects
    of life prove false during the course of his travels?

2. Discuss the role of Imlac in the book.

3. While *Rasselas* contains much gloom, elements of
    humor also appear.   Give some examples and com-
    ment on their effects.

4. How is this work a model of eighteenth-century
    rationalism?

5. Discuss the importance of memory to the narrator of
    Tintern Abbey.

6. After examining the way Wordsworth defines nature,
    comment on the narrator's changing response to it
    during the course of his life. Have your percep-
    tions of various things changed as you have grown
    older? How do you explain this phenomenon?

7. According to M. H. Abrams, Wordsworth held the Neo-
    Platonic doctrine "that the soul is immortal and
    exists separately from the body both before birth
    and after death," and that "the glory of the unborn
    soul is gradually quenched by its descent into the
    darkness of matter." How is this belief important
    to an understanding of the *Ode: Intimations of Immor-
    tality*?

8. Why is childhood a desirable time in the eye of
    the *Ode's* narrator? In what sense is the child
    the "best Philosopher" and an "Eye among the
    blind"?

Londoner, lexicographer, poet, essayist, critic, and especially a conversationalist, Samuel Johnson (1709-1784) was one of the dominant figures of his age. Indeed, if he had never written a word, accounts of his life written by Boswell and many others, would be a source of instruction and delight for later readers. He did write, however, and his work represents the enlightenment and cynicism of the eighteenth-century.

Rasselas

PRINCE OF ABYSSINIA

Description of a Palace in a Valley

I   YE who listen with credulity to the whispers of fancy and pursue with eagerness the phantoms of hope, who expect that age will perform the promises of youth and that the deficiencies of the present day will be supplied by the morrow, — attend to the history of Rasselas, prince of Abyssinia.

Rasselas was the fourth son of the mighty emperor, in whose dominions the Father of Waters begins his course; whose bounty pours down the streams of plenty and scatters over half the world the harvests of Egypt.

According to the custom which has descended from age to age among the monarchs of the torrid zone, Rasselas was confined in a private palace with the other sons and daughters of Abyssinian royalty, till the order of succession should call him to the throne.

The place which the wisdom or policy of antiquity had destined for the residence of the Abyssinian princes was a spacious valley in the kindom of Amhara, surrounded on every side by mountains, of which the summits overhang the middle part. The only passage by which it could be entered was a cavern that passed under a rock, of which it has long been disputed whether it was the work of nature or of human industry. The outlet of the cavern was concealed by a thick wood, and the mouth which opened into the valley was closed with gates of iron, forged by the artificers of ancient days, so massy that no man could without the help of engines open or shut them.

From the mountains on every side, rivulets descended that filled all the valley with verdure and fertility, and formed a lake in the middle, inhabited by fish of every species and frequented by every fowl whom nature has taught to dip the wing in water. This lake discharged its superfluities by a stream which entered a dark cleft of the mountain on the northern side and fell with dreadful noise from precipice to precipice, till it was heard no more.

The sides of the mountains were covered with trees; the banks of the brooks were diversified with flowers; every blast shook spices from the rocks, and every month dropped fruits upon the ground. All animals that bite the grass or browse the shrub, whether wild or tame, wandered in this extensive circuit, secured from beasts of prey by the mountains which confined them. On one part were flocks and herds feeding in the pastures, on another all the beasts of chase frisking in the lawns; the sprightly kid was bounding on the rocks, the subtle monkey frolicking in the trees, and the solemn elephant reposing in the shade. All the diversities of the world were brought together; the blessings of nature were collected, and its evils extracted and excluded.

The valley, wide and fruitful, supplied its inhabitants with the necessaries of life, and all delights and superfluities were added at the annual visit which the emperor paid his children, when the iron gate was opened to the sound of music; and, during eight days, everyone that resided in the valley was required to propose whatever might contribute to make seclusion pleasant, to fill up the vacancies of attention and lessen the tediousness of time. Every desire was immediately granted. All the artificers of pleasure were called to gladden the festivity; the musicians exerted the power of harmony, and the dancers showed their activity before the princes, in hope that they should pass their lives in this blissful captivity, to which those only were admitted whose performance was thought able to add novelty to luxury. Such was the appearance of security and delight which this retirement afforded that they to whom it was new always desired that it might be perpetual; and, as those on whom the iron gate had once closed were never suffered to return, the effect of longer experience could not be known. Thus every year produced new schemes of delight and new competitors for imprisonment.

The palace stood on an eminence raised about thirty paces above the surface of the lake. It was divided into many squares or courts, built with greater or less magnificence according to the rank of those for whom they were designed. The roofs were turned into arches of massy stone, joined by a cement that grew harder by time, and the building stood from century to century, deriding the solstitial rains and equinoctial hurricanes, without need of reparation.

This house, which was so large as to be fully known to none but some ancient officers who successively inherited the secrets of the place, was built as if suspicion herself had dictated the plan. To every room there was an open and secret passage; every square had a communication with the rest, either from the upper stories by private galleries or by subterranean passages from the lower apartments. Many of the columns had unsuspected cavities, in which a long race of monarchs had deposited their treasures. They then closed up the opening with marble, which was never to be removed but in the utmost exigencies of the kingdom, and recorded their accumulations in a book, which was itself concealed in a tower, not entered but by the emperor attended by the prince who stood next in succession.

The Discontent of Rasselas in the Happy Valley

2   HERE the sons and daughters of Abyssinia lived only to know the soft vicissitudes of pleasure and repose, attended by all that were skilful to delight, and gratified with whatever the senses can enjoy. They wandered in gardens of fragrance and slept in the fortresses of security. Every art was practiced to make them pleased with their own condition. The sages who instructed them told them of nothing but the miseries of public life, and described all beyond the mountains as regions of calamity, where discord was always raging and where man preyed upon man.

To heighten their opinion of their own felicity, they were daily entertained with songs, the subject of which was *the happy valley*. Their appetites were excited by frequent enumerations of different enjoyments, and revelry and merriment was the business of every hour, from the dawn of morning to the close of even.

These methods were generally successful: few of the princes had ever wished to enlarge their bounds, but passed their lives in full conviction that they had all within their reach that art or nature could bestow, and pitied those whom fate had excluded from this seat of tranquillity as the sport of chance and the slaves of misery.

Thus they rose in the morning and lay down at night, pleased with each other and with themselves, — all but Rasselas, who, in the twenty-sixth year of his age, began to withdraw himself from their pastimes and assemblies, and to delight in solitary walks and silent meditation. He often sat before tables covered with luxury, and forgot to taste the dainties that were placed before him; he rose abruptly in the midst of the song, and hastily retired beyond the sound of music. His attendants observed the change and endeavored to renew his love of pleasure; he neglected their officiousness, repulsed their invitations, and spent day after day on the banks of rivulets sheltered with trees, where he sometimes listened to the birds in the branches, sometimes observed the fish playing in the stream, and anon cast his eyes upon the pastures and mountains filled with animals, of which some were biting the herbage and some sleeping among the bushes.

This singularity of his humor made him much observed. One of the sages, in whose conversation he had formerly delighted, followed him secretly in hope of discovering the cause of his disquiet. Rasselas, who knew not that anyone was near him, having for some time fixed his eyes upon the goats that were browsing among the rocks, began to compare their condition with his own.

"What," said he, "makes the difference between man and all the rest of the animal creation? Every beast that strays beside me has the same corporeal necessities with myself: he is hungry and crops the grass; he is thirsty and drinks the stream; his thirst and hunger are appeased; he is satisfied and sleeps; he arises again and is hungry; he is again fed and is at rest. I am hungry and thirsty like him, but when thirst and hunger cease, I am not at rest; I am like him pained with want, but am not like him satisfied with fullness. The intermediate hours are tedious and gloomy; I long again to be hungry that I may again quicken my attention. The birds peck the berries or the corn, and fly away to the groves, where they sit in seeming happiness on the branches and waste their lives in tuning one unvaried series of sounds. I likewise can call the lutanist and the singer; but the sounds that pleased me yesterday weary me today, and will grow yet more wearisome tomorrow. I can discover within me no power of perception which is not glutted with its proper pleasure; yet I do not feel myself delighted. Man surely has some latent sense for which this place affords no gratification, or he has some desires distinct from sense, which must be satisfied before he can be happy."

After this he lifted up his head and, seeing the moon rising, walked towards the palace. As he passed through the fields and saw the animals around him, "Ye," said he, "are happy, and need not envy me that walk thus among you, burdened with myself; nor do I, ye gentle beings, envy your felicity, for it is not the felicity of man. I have many distresses from which ye are free; I fear pain when I do not feel it; I sometimes shrink at evils recollected and sometimes start at evils anticipated. Surely the equity of Providence has balanced peculiar sufferings with peculiar enjoyments."

With observations like these the prince amused himself as he returned, uttering them with a plaintive voice, yet with a look that discovered him to feel some complacence in his own perspicacity and to receive some solace of the miseries of life from consciousness of the delicacy with which he felt and the eloquence with which he bewailed them. He mingled cheerfully in the diversions of the evening, and all rejoiced to find that his heart was lightened.

The Wants of Him
That Wants Nothing

3 ❦ ON the next day, his old instructor, imagining that he had now made himself acquainted with his disease of mind, was in hope of curing it by counsel, and officiously sought an opportunity of conference, which the prince, having long considered him as one whose intellects were exhausted, was not very willing to afford. "Why," said he, "does this man thus intrude upon me? Shall I be never suffered to forget those lectures which pleased only while they were new and, to become new again, must be forgotten?" He then walked into the wood and composed himself to his usual meditations, when, before his thoughts had taken any settled form, he perceived his pursuer at his side, and was at first prompted by his impatience to go hastily away; but, being unwilling to offend a man whom he had once reverenced and still loved, he invited him to sit down with him on the bank.

The old man, thus encouraged, began to lament the change which had been lately observed in the prince, and to inquire why he so often retired from the pleasures of the palace to loneliness and silence. "I fly from pleasure," said the prince, "because pleasure has ceased to please; I am lonely, because I am miserable and am unwilling to cloud with my presence the happiness of others." "You, sir," said the sage, "are the first who has complained of misery in the *happy valley*. I hope to convince you that your complaints have no real cause. You are here in full possession of all that the emperor of Abyssinia can bestow; here is neither labor to be endured, nor danger to be dreaded, yet here is all that labor or danger can procure or purchase. Look round, and tell me which of your wants is without supply. If you want nothing, how are you unhappy?"

"That I want nothing," said the prince, "or that I know not what I want, is the cause of my complaint. If I had any known want, I should have a certain wish; that wish would excite endeavor, and I should not then repine to see the sun move so slowly towards the western mountain, or lament when the day breaks and sleep will no longer hide me from myself. When I see the kids and the lambs chasing one another, I fancy that I should be happy if I had something to pursue. But, possessing all that I can want, I find one day and one hour exactly like another, except that the latter is still more tedious than the former. Let your experience inform me how the day may now seem as short as in my childhood, while nature was yet fresh and every moment showed me what I never had observed before. I have already enjoyed too much; give me something to desire."

The old man was surprised at this new species of affliction, and knew not what to reply, yet was unwilling to be silent. "Sir," said he, "if you had seen the miseries of the world, you would know how to value your present state." "Now," said the prince, "you have given me something to desire; I shall long to see the miseries of the world, since the sight of them is necessary to happiness."

The Prince Continues to Grieve and Muse

4 AT this time the sound of music proclaimed the hour of repast, and the conversation was concluded. The old man went away sufficiently discontented, to find that his reasonings had produced the only conclusion which they were intended to prevent. But in the decline of life shame and grief are of short duration, whether it be that we bear easily what we have borne long; or that, finding ourselves in age less regarded, we less regard others; or that we look with slight regard upon afflictions to which we know that the hand of death is about to put an end.

The prince, whose views were extended to a wider space, could not speedily quiet his emotions. He had been before terrified at the length of life which nature promised him, because he considered that in a long time much must be endured; he now rejoiced in his youth, because in many years much might be done.

The first beam of hope, that had been ever darted into his mind, rekindled youth in his cheeks and doubled the lustre of his eyes. He was fired with the desire of doing something, though he knew not yet with distinctness either end or means.

He was now no longer gloomy and unsocial; but, considering himself as master of a secret stock of happiness, which he could enjoy only by concealing it, he affected to be busy in all schemes of diversion, and endeavored to make others pleased with the state of which he himself was weary. But pleasures never can be so multiplied or continued as not to leave much of life unemployed; there were many hours, both of the night and day, which he could spend without suspicion in solitary thought. The load of life was much lightened; he went eagerly into the assemblies, because he supposed the frequency of his presence necessary to the success of his purposes; he retired gladly to privacy, because he had now a subject of thought.

His chief amusement was to picture to himself that world which he had never seen; to place himself in various conditions, to be entangled in imaginary difficulties, and to be engaged in wild adventures; but his benevolence always terminated his projects in the relief of distress, the detection of fraud, the defeat of oppression, and the diffusion of happiness.

Thus passed twenty months of the life of Rasselas. He busied himself so intensely in visionary bustle that he forgot his real solitude, and, amidst hourly preparations for the various incidents of human affairs, neglected to consider by what means he should mingle with mankind.

One day, as he was sitting on a bank, he feigned to himself an orphan virgin robbed of her little portion by a treacherous lover and crying after him for restitution and redress. So strongly was the image impressed upon his mind that he started up in the maid's defense, and ran forward to seize the plunderer, with all the eagerness of real pursuit. Fear naturally quickens the flight of guilt. Rasselas could not catch the fugitive with his utmost efforts; but, resolving to weary by perseverance him whom he could not surpass in speed, he pressed on till the foot of the mountain stopped his course.

Here he recollected himself and smiled at his own useless impetuosity. Then raising his eyes to the mountain, "This," said he, "is the fatal obstacle that hinders at once the enjoyment of pleasure and the exercise of virtue. How long is it that my hopes and wishes have flown beyond this boundary of my life, which yet I never have attempted to surmount!"

Struck with this reflection, he sat down to muse; and remembered that, since he first resolved to escape from his confinement, the sun had passed twice over him in his annual course. He now felt a degree of regret with which he had never been before acquainted. He considered how much might have been done in the time which had passed and left nothing real behind it. He compared twenty months with the life of man. "In life," said he, "is not to be counted the ignorance of infancy or imbecility of age. We are long before we are able to think, and we soon cease from the power of acting. The true period of human existence may be reasonably estimated at forty years, of which I have mused away the four and twentieth part. What I have lost was certain, for I have certainly possessed it; but of twenty months to come, who can assure me?''

The consciousness of his own folly pierced him deeply, and he was long before he could be reconciled to himself. ''The rest of my time,'' said he, ''has been lost by the crime or folly of my ancestors and the absurd institutions of my country; I remember it with disgust, yet without remorse; but the months that have passed since new light darted into my soul, since I formed a scheme of reasonable felicity, have been squandered by my own fault. I have lost that which can never be restored; I have seen the sun rise and set for twenty months, an idle gazer on the light of heaven. In this time the birds have left the nest of their mother and committed themselves to the woods and to the skies; the kid has forsaken the teat and learned by degrees to climb the rocks in quest of independent sustenance. I only have made no advances, but am still helpless and ignorant. The moon, by more than twenty changes, admonished me of the flux of life; the stream that rolled before my feet upbraided my inactivity. I sat feasting on intellectual luxury, regardless alike of the examples of the earth and the instructions of the planets. Twenty months are passed. Who shall restore them?''

These sorrowful meditations fastened upon his

mind; he passed four months in resolving to lose no more time in idle resolves, and was awakened to more vigorous exertion by hearing a maid, who had broken a porcelain cup, remark that what cannot be repaired is not to be regretted.

This was obvious, and Rasselas reproached himself that he had not discovered it, having not known, or not considered how many useful hints are obtained by chance and how often the mind, hurried by her own ardor to distant views, neglects the truths that lie open before her. He for a few hours regretted his regret, and from that time bent his whole mind upon the means of escaping from the valley of happiness.

The Prince Meditates His Escape

HE now found that it would be very difficult to effect that which it was very easy to suppose effected. When he looked round about him, he saw himself confined by the bars of nature, which had never yet been broken, and by the gate, through which none that once had passed it were ever able to return. He was now impatient as an eagle in a grate. He passed week after week in clambering the mountains to see if there was any aperture which the bushes might conceal, but found all the summits inaccessible by their prominence. The iron gate he despaired to open, for it was not only secured with all the power of art, but was always watched by successive sentinels, and was by its position exposed to the perpetual observation of all the inhabitants.

He then examined the cavern through which the waters of the lake were discharged, and, looking down at a time when the sun shone strongly upon its mouth, he discovered it to be full of broken rocks which, though they permitted the stream to flow through many narrow passages, would stop any body of solid bulk. He returned discouraged and dejected, but, having now known the blessing of hope, resolved never to despair.

In these fruitless researches he spent ten months. The time, however, passed cheerfully away; in the morning he rose with new hope, in the evening applauded his own diligence, and in the night slept sound after his fatigue. He met a thousand amusements which beguiled his labor and diversified his thoughts. He discerned the various instincts of animals and properties of plants, and found the place replete with wonders of which he purposed to solace himself with the contemplation, if he should never be able to accomplish his flight; rejoicing that his endeavors, though yet unsuccessful, had supplied him with a source of inexhaustible inquiry.

But his original curiosity was not yet abated; he resolved to obtain some knowledge of the ways of men. His wish still continued, but his hope grew less. He ceased to survey any longer the walls of his prison, and spared to search by new toils for interstices which he knew could not be found, yet determined to keep his design always in view and lay hold on any expedient that time should offer.

Imlac's History Continued.
A Dissertation upon Poetry

10 "WHEREVER I went, I found that poetry was considered as the highest learning and regarded with a veneration somewhat approaching to that which man would pay to the angelic nature. And yet it fills me with wonder that, in almost all countries, the most ancient poets are considered as the best, whether it be that every other kind of knowledge is an acquisition gradually attained and poetry is a gift conferred at once; or that the first poetry of every nation surprised them as a novelty and retained the credit by consent, which it received by accident at first; or whether, as the province of poetry is to describe nature and passion, which are always the same, the first writers took possession of the most striking objects for description and the most probable occurrences for fiction, and left nothing to those that followed them but transcription of the same events and new combinations of the same im-

ages. Whatever be the reason, it is commonly observed that the early writers are in possession of nature, and their followers of art; that the first excel in strength and invention, and the latter in elegance and refinement.

"I was desirous to add my name to this illustrious fraternity. I read all the poets of Persia and Arabia, and was able to repeat by memory the volumes that are suspended in the mosque of Mecca. But I soon found that no man was ever great by imitation. My desire of excellence impelled me to transfer my attention to nature and to life. Nature was to be my subject, and men to be my auditors. I could never describe what I had not seen; I could not hope to move those with delight or terror, whose interests and opinions I did not understand.

"Being now resolved to be a poet, I saw everything with a new purpose; my sphere of attention was suddenly magnified; no kind of knowledge was to be overlooked. I ranged mountains and deserts for images and resemblances, and pictured upon my mind every tree of the forest and flower of the valley. I observed with equal care the crags of the rock and the pinnacles of the palace. Sometimes I wandered along the mazes of the rivulet, and sometimes watched the changes of the summer clouds. To a poet nothing can be useless. Whatever is beautiful, and whatever is dreadful, must be familiar to his imagination; he must be conversant with all that is awfully vast or elegantly little. The plants of the garden, the animals of the wood, the minerals of the earth, and meteors of the sky, must all concur to store his mind with inexhaustible variety, for every idea is useful for the enforcement or decoration of moral or religious truth; and he who knows most will have most power of diversifying his scenes and of gratifying his reader with remote allusions and unexpected instruction.

"All the appearances of nature I was therefore careful to study, and every country which I have surveyed has contributed something to my political powers."

"In so wide a survey," said the prince, "you must surely have left much unobserved. I have lived, till now, within the circuit of these mountains, and yet cannot walk abroad without the sight of something which I had never beheld before or never heeded."

"The business of a poet," said Imlac, "is to examine not the individual, but the species; to remark general properties and large appearances. He does not number the streaks of the tulip, or describe the different shades in the verdure of the forest; he is to exhibit in his portraits of nature such prominent and striking features as recall the original to every mind, and must neglect the minuter discriminations, which one may have remarked and another have neglected, for those characteristics which are alike obvious to vigilance and carelessness.

"But the knowledge of nature is only half the task of a poet; he must be acquainted likewise with all the modes of life. His character requires that he estimate the happiness and misery of every condition, and trace the changes of the human mind as they are modified by various institutions and accidental influences of climate or custom, from the sprightliness of infancy to the despondence of decrepitude. He must divest himself of the prejudices of his age and country; he must consider right and wrong in present laws and opinions, and rise to general and transcendental truths, which will always be the same. He must therefore content himself with the slow progress of his name, contemn the applause of his own time, and commit his claims to the justice of posterity. He must write as the interpreter of nature, and the legislator of mankind, and consider himself as presiding over the thoughts and manners of future generations, as a being superior to time and place.

"His labor is not yet at an end; he must know many languages and many sciences; and, that his style may be worthy of his thoughts, must, by incessant practice, familiarize to himself every delicacy of speech and grace of harmony."

Imlac's Narrative Continued.
A Hint on Pilgrimage

11 IMLAC now felt the enthusiastic fit, and was proceeding to aggrandize his own profession, when the prince cried out, "Enough! Thou hast convinced me that no human being can ever be a poet. Proceed with thy narration."

"To be a poet," said Imlac, "is indeed very difficult."

"So difficult," returned the prince, "that I will at present hear no more of his labors. Tell me whither you went when you had seen Persia."

"From Persia," said the poet, "I travelled through Syria, and for three years resided in Palestine, where I conversed with great numbers of the northern and western nations of Europe, the nations which are now in possession of all power and all knowledge, whose armies are irresistible and whose fleets command the remotest parts of the globe. When I compared these men with the natives of our own kingdom and those

that surround us, they appeared almost another
order of beings. In their countries it is difficult
to wish for anything that may not be obtained.
A thousand arts, of which we never heard, are
continually laboring for their convenience and
pleasure, and whatever their own climate has
denied them is supplied by their commerce."

"By what means," said the prince, "are the
Europeans thus powerful, or why, since they can
so easily visit Asia and Africa for trade or conquest,
cannot the Asiatics and Africans invade their
coasts, plant colonies in their ports, and give laws
to their natural princes? The same wind that carries
them back would bring us thither."

"They are more powerful, sir, than we," answered Imlac, "because they are wiser. Knowledge
will always predominate over ignorance, as man
governs the other animals. But why their knowledge is more than ours, I know not what reason
can be given, but the unsearchable will of the
Supreme Being."

"When," said the prince with a sigh, "shall I
be able to visit Palestine and mingle with this
mighty confluence of nations? Till that happy moment shall arrive, let me fill up the time with such
representations as thou canst give me. I am not
ignorant of the motive that assembles such numbers in that place, and cannot but consider it as
the center of wisdom and piety, to which the best
and wisest men of every land must be continually
resorting."

"There are some nations," said Imlac, "that send
few visitants to Palestine, for many numerous and

learned sects in Europe concur to censure pilgrimage as superstitious or deride it as ridiculous."

"You know," said the prince, "how little my
life has made me acquainted with diversity of
opinions; it will be too long to hear the arguments
on both sides; you, that have considered them,
tell me the result."

"Pilgrimage," said Imlac, "like many other acts
of piety, may be reasonable or superstitious, according to the principles upon which it is performed. Long journeys in search of truth are not
commanded. Truth, such as is necessary to the
regulation of life, is always found where it is
honestly sought. Change of place is no natural
cause of the increase of piety, for it inevitably
produces dissipation of mind. Yet, since men go
every day to view the fields where great actions
have been performed and return with stronger impressions of the event, curiosity of the same kind
may naturally dispose us to view that country
whence our religion had its beginning; and I believe
no man surveys those awful scenes without some
confirmation of holy resolutions. That the Supreme
Being may be more easily propitiated in one place
than in another, is the dream of idle superstition;
but that some places may operate upon our own
minds in an uncommon manner, is an opinion
which hourly experience will justify. He who supposes that his vices may be more successfully com-
bated in Palestine will, perhaps, find himself
mistaken; yet he may go thither without folly.
He who thinks they will be more freely pardoned
dishonors at once his reason and religion."

"These," said the prince, "are European distinctions. I will consider them another time. What have you found to be the effect of knowledge? Are those nations happier than we?"

"There is so much infelicity," said the poet, "in the world, that scarce any man has leisure from his own distresses to estimate the comparative happiness of others. Knowledge is certainly one of the means of pleasure, as is confessed by the natural desire which every mind feels of increasing its ideas. Ignorance is mere privation, by which nothing can be produced; it is a vacuity in which the soul sits motionless and torpid for want of attraction, and, without knowing why, we always rejoice when we learn and grieve when we forget. I am therefore inclined to conclude that, if nothing counteracts the natural consequence of learning, we grow more happy as our minds take a wider range.

"In enumerating the particular comforts of life, we shall find many advantages on the side of the Europeans. They cure wounds and diseases with which we languish and perish. We suffer inclemencies of weather which they can obviate. They have engines for the dispatch of many laborious works which we must perform by manual industry. There is such communication between distant places that one friend can hardly be said to be absent from another. Their policy removes all public inconveniences; they have roads cut through their mountains and bridges laid upon their rivers. And, if we descend to the privacies of life, their habitations are more commodious, and their possessions are more secure."

"They are surely happy," said the prince, "who have all these conveniences, of which I envy none so much as the facility with which separated friends interchange their thoughts."

"The Europeans," answered Imlac, "are less unhappy than we; but they are not happy. Human life is everywhere a state in which much is to be endured, and little to be enjoyed."

They Enter Cairo and Find Every Man Happy

16 AS they approached the city, which filled the strangers with astonishment, "This," said Imlac to the prince, "is the place where travellers and merchants assemble from all the corners of the earth. You will here find men of every character, and every occupation. Commerce is here honorable; I will act as a merchant, and you shall live as strangers who have no other end of travel than curiosity. It will soon be observed that we are rich; our reputation will procure us access to all whom we shall desire to know; you will see all the conditions of humanity, and enable yourself at leisure to make your *choice of life*."

They now entered the town, stunned by the noise and offended by the crowds. Instruction had not yet so prevailed over habit but that they wondered to see themselves pass undistinguished along the street and met by the lowest of the people without reverence or notice. The princess could not at first bear the thought of being levelled with the vulgar, and for some days continued in her chamber, where she was served by her favorite Pekuah as in the palace of the valley.

Imlac, who understood traffic, sold part of the jewels the next day and hired a house, which he adorned with such magnificence that he was immediately considered as a merchant of great wealth. His politeness attracted many acquaintance, and his generosity made him courted by many dependents. His table was crowded by men of every nation, who all admired his knowledge and solicited his favor. His companions, not being able to mix in the conversation, could make no discovery of their ignorance or surprise, and were gradually initiated in the world as they gained knowledge of the language.

The prince had, by frequent lectures, been taught the use and nature of money; but the ladies could not, for a long time, comprehend what the merchants did with small pieces of gold and silver, or why things of so little use should be received as equivalent to the necessaries of life.

They studied the language two years, while Imlac was preparing to set before them the various ranks and conditions of mankind. He grew acquainted with all who had anything uncommon in their fortune or conduct. He frequented the voluptuous and the frugal, the idle and the busy, the merchants and the men of learning.

The prince, being now able to converse with fluency and having learned the caution necessary to be observed in his intercourse with strangers, began to accompany Imlac to places of resort and to enter into all assemblies, that he might make his *choice of life*.

For some time he thought choice needless, because all appeared to him equally happy. Whereever he went, he met gaiety and kindness, and heard the song of joy or the laugh of carelessness. He began to believe that the world overflowed with universal plenty and that nothing was withheld either from want or merit, that every hand showered liberality and every heart melted with benevolence. "And who then," says he, " will be suffered to be wretched?"

Imlac permitted the pleasing delusion and was unwilling to crush the hope of inexperience, till, one day, having sat a while silent, "I know not," said the prince, "what can be the reason that I am more unhappy than any of our friends. I see them perpetually and unalterably cheerful, but feel my own mind restless and uneasy. I am unsatisfied with those pleasures which I seem most to court. I live in the crowds of jollity, not so much to enjoy company as to shun myself, and am only loud and merry to conceal my sadness."

"Every man," said Imlac, "may, by examining his own mind, guess what passes in the minds of others. When you feel that your own gaiety is counterfeit, it may justly lead you to suspect that of your companions not to be sincere. Envy is commonly reciprocal. We are long before we are convinced that happiness is never to be found, and each believes it possessed by others, to keep alive the hope of obtaining it for himself. In the assembly where you passed the last night, there appeared such sprightliness of air and volatility of fancy as might have suited beings of a higher order, formed to inhabit serener regions inaccessible to care or sorrow. Yet, believe me, prince, there was not one who did not dread the moment when solitude should deliver him to the tyranny of reflection."

"This," said the prince, "may be true of others, since it is true of me; yet, whatever be the general infelicity of man, one condition is more happy than another, and wisdom surely directs us to take the least evil in the *choice of life*."

"The causes of good and evil," answered Imlac, "are so various and uncertain, so often entangled with each other, so diversified by various relations, and so much subject to accidents which cannot be foreseen, that he who would fix his condition upon incontestable reasons of preference must live and die inquiring and deliberating."

"But surely," said Rasselas, "the wise men, to whom we listen with reverence and wonder, chose that mode of life for themselves which they thought most likely to make them happy."

"Very few," said the poet, "live by choice. Every man is placed in his present condition by causes which acted without his foresight and with which he did not always willingly cooperate; and therefore you will rarely meet one who does not think the lot of his neighbor better than his own."

"I am pleased to think," said the prince, "that my birth has given me at least one advantage over others, by enabling me to determine for myself. I have here the world before me; I will review it at leisure. Surely happiness is somewhere to be found."

The Prince Associates with Young Men of Spirit and Gaiety

17 RASSELAS rose next day and resolved to begin his experiments upon life. "Youth," cried he, "is the time of gladness. I will join myself to the young men whose only business is to gratify their desires and whose time is all spent in a succession of enjoyments."

To such societies he was readily admitted, but a few days brought him back weary and disgusted. Their mirth was without images, their laughter without motive; their pleasures were gross and sensual, in which the mind had no part. Their conduct was at once wild and mean. They laughed at order and at law, but the frown of power dejected, and the eye of wisdom abashed them.

The prince soon concluded that he should never be happy in a course of life of which he was ashamed. He thought it unsuitable to a reasonable being to act without a plan, and to be sad or cheerful only by chance. "Happiness," said he, "must be something solid and permanent, without fear and without uncertainty."

But his young companions had gained so much of his regard by their frankness and courtesy that he could not leave them without warning and remonstrance. "My friends," said he, "I have seriously considered our manners and our prospects, and find that we have mistaken our own interest. The first years of man must make provision for the last. He that never thinks never can be wise. Perpetual levity must end in ignorance, and intemperance, though it may fire the spirits for an hour, will make life short or miserable. Let us consider that youth is of no long duration and that in maturer age, when the enchantments of fancy shall cease and phantoms of delight dance no more about us, we shall have no comforts but the esteem of wise men and the means of doing good. Let us, therefore, stop, while to stop is in our power. Let us live as men who are some time to grow old and to whom it will be the most dreadful of all evils to count their past years by follies and to be reminded of their former luxuriance of health only by the maladies which riot has produced."

They stared a while in silence one upon another, and at last drove him away by a general chorus of continued laughter.

The consciousness that his sentiments were just, and his intentions kind, was scarcely sufficient to support him against the horror of derision. But he recovered his tranquillity and pursued his search.

The Prince finds a Wise and Happy Man

18 As he was one day walking in the street, he saw a spacious building, which all were, by the open doors, invited to enter. He followed the stream of people, and found it a hall or school of declamation, in which professors read lectures to their auditory. He fixed his eye upon a sage raised above the rest, who discoursed with great energy on the government of the passions. His look was venerable, his action graceful, his pronunciation clear, and his diction elegant. He showed, with great strength of sentiment and variety of illustration, that human nature is degraded and debased when the lower faculties predominate over the higher; that when fancy, the parent of passion, usurps the dominion of the mind, nothing ensues but the natural effect of unlawful government — perturbation and confusion; that she betrays the fortresses of the intellect to rebels and excites her children to sedition against reason, their lawful

sovereign. He compared reason to the sun, of which light is constant, uniform, and lasting; and fancy to a meteor, of bright but transitory lustre, irregular in its motion and delusive in its direction.

He then communicated the various precepts given from time to time for the conquest of passion, and displayed the happiness of those who had obtained the important victory, after which man is no longer the slave of fear, nor the fool of hope; is no more emaciated by envy, inflamed by anger, emasculated by tenderness, or depressed by grief, but walks on calmly through the tumults or privacies of life, as the sun pursues alike his course through the calm of the stormy sky.

He enumerated many examples of heroes immovable by pain or pleasure, who looked with indifference on those modes or accidents to which the vulgar give the names of good and evil. He exhorted his hearers to lay aside their prejudices, and arm themselves against the shafts of malice or misfortune, by invulnerable patience; concluding that this state only was happiness and that this happiness was in everyone's power.

Rasselas listened to him with the veneration due to the instructions of a superior being, and, waiting for him at the door, humbly implored the liberty of visiting so great a master of true wisdom. The lecturer hesitated a moment, when Rasselas put a purse of gold into his hand, which he received with a mixture of joy and wonder.

"I have found," said the prince at his return to Imlac, "a man who can teach all that is necessary to be known; who, from the unshaken throne of rational fortitude, looks down on the scenes of life changing beneath him. He speaks, and attention watches his lips; he reasons, and conviction closes his periods. This man shall be my future guide. I will learn his doctrines, and imitate his life."

"Be not too hasty," said Imlac, "to trust or to admire the teachers of morality. They discourse like angels, but they live like men."

Rasselas, who could not conceive how any man could reason so forcibly without feeling the cogency of his own arguments, paid his visit in a few days, and was denied admission. He had now learned the power of money, and made his way by a piece of gold to the inner apartment, where he found the philosopher, in a room half darkened, with his eyes misty and his face pale. "Sir," said he, "you are come at a time when all human friendship is useless. What I suffer cannot be remedied; what I have lost cannot be supplied. My daughter, my only daughter, from whose tenderness I expected all the comforts of my age, died last night of a fever. My views, my purposes, my hopes are at an end. I am now a lonely being, disunited from society."

"Sir," said the prince, "mortality is an event by which a wise man can never be surprised. We know that death is always near, and it should therefore always be expected."

"Young man," answered the philosopher, "you speak like one that has never felt the pangs of separation." "Have you then forgot the precepts," said Rasselas, "which you so powerfully enforced? Has wisdom no strength to arm the heart against calamity? Consider that external things are naturally variable, but truth and reason are always the same." "What comfort," said the mourner, "can truth and reason afford me? Of what effect are they now, but to tell me that my daughter will not be restored?"

The prince, whose humanity would not suffer him to insult misery with reproof, went away convinced of the emptiness of rhetorical sound, and the inefficacy of polished periods and studied sentences.

A Glimpse of Pastoral Life

19 HE was still eager upon the same inquiry; and having heard of a hermit that lived near the lowest cataract of the Nile and filled the whole country with the fame of his sanctity, resolved to visit his retreat and inquire whether that felicity, which public life could not afford, was to be found in solitude, and whether a man, whose age and virtue made him venerable, could teach any peculiar art of shunning evils or enduring them.

Imlac and the princess agreed to accompany him; and, after the necessary preparations, they began their journey. Their way lay through the fields, where shepherds tended their flocks, and the lambs were playing upon the pasture. "This," said the poet, "is the life which has been often celebrated for its innocence and quiet; let us pass the heat of the day among the shepherds' tents, and know whether all our searches are not to terminate in pastoral simplicity."

The proposal pleased them, and they induced the shepherds, by small presents and familiar questions, to tell their opinion of their own state. They were so rude and ignorant, so little able to compare the good with the evil of the occupation, and so indistinct in their narratives and descriptions, that very little could be learned from them. But it was evident that their hearts were cankered with discontent, that they considered themselves as condemned to labor for the luxury of the rich, and looked up with stupid malevolence toward those that were placed above them.

The princess pronounced with vehemence that she would never suffer these envious savages to be her companions and that she should not soon be desirous of seeing any more speciments of rustic happiness; but could not believe that all the accounts of primeval pleasures were fabulous, and was yet in doubt whether life had anything that could be justly preferred to the placid gratifications of fields and woods. She hoped that the time would come when, with a few virtuous and elegant companions, she should gather flowers planted by her own hand, fondle the lambs of her own ewe, and listen without care, among brooks and breezes, to one of her maidens reading in the shade.

The Danger of Prosperity

20 ON the next day they continued their journey, till the heat compelled them to look round for shelter. At a small distance they saw a thick wood, which they no sooner entered than they perceived that they were approaching the habitations of men. The shrubs were diligently cut away to open walks where the shades were darkest; the boughs of opposite trees were artificially interwoven; seats of flowery turf were raised in vacant spaces; and a rivulet, that wantoned along the side of a winding path, had its banks sometimes opened into small basins and its stream sometimes obstructed by little mounds of stone, heaped together to increase its murmurs.

They passed slowly through the wood, delighted with such unexpected accommodations, and entertained each other with conjecturing what or who he could be that, in those rude and unfrequented regions, had leisure and art for such harmless luxury.

As they advanced, they heard the sound of music,

and saw youths and virgins dancing in the grove, and, going still further, beheld a stately palace built upon a hill, surrounded with woods. The laws of eastern hospitality allowed them to enter, and the master welcomed them like a man liberal and wealthy.

He was skilful enough in appearances soon to discern that they were no common guests, and spread his table with magnificance. The eloquence of Imlac caught his attention, and the lofty courtesy of the princess excited his respect. When they offered to depart, he entreated their stay, and was the next day still more unwilling to dismiss them than before. They were easily persuaded to stop, and civility grew up in time to freedom and confidence.

The prince now saw all the domestics cheerful and all the face of nature smiling round the place, and could not forbear to hope he should find here what he was seeking; but, when he was congratulating the master upon his possessions, he answered with a sigh: "My condition has indeed the appearance of happiness, but appearances are delusive. My prosperity puts my life in danger; the Bassa of Egypt is my enemy, incensed only by my wealth and popularity. I have been hitherto protected against him by the princes of the country, but, as favor of the great is uncertain, I know not how soon my defenders may be persuaded to share the plunder with the Bassa. I have sent my treasures into a distant country, and, upon the first alarm, am prepared to follow them. Then will my enemies riot in my mansion, and enjoy the gardens which I have planted.''

They all joined in lamenting his danger and deprecating his exile; and the princess was so much disturbed with the tumult of grief and indignation that she retired to her apartment.

They continued with their kind inviter a few days longer, and then went forward to find the hermit.

The Happiness of a Life
Led According to Nature

22 RASSELAS went often to an assembly of learned men who met at stated times to unbend their minds and compare their opinions. Their manners were somewhat coarse, but their conversation was instructive, and their disputations acute, though sometimes too violent and often continued till neither controvertist remembered upon what question they began. Some faults were almost general among them: everyone was desirous to dictate to the rest, and everyone was pleased to hear the genius or knowledge of another depreciated.

In this assembly Rasselas was relating his interview with the hermit and the wonder with which he heard him censure a course of life which he had so deliberately chosen and so laudably followed. The sentiments of the hearers were various. Some were of opinion that the folly of his choice had been justly punished by condemnation to perpetual perseverance. One of the youngest among them, with great vehemence, pronounced him a hypocrite. Some talked of the right of society to the labor of individuals, and considered retirement as a desertion of duty. Others readily allowed that there was a time when the claims of the public were satisfied and when a man might properly sequester himself, to review his life and purify his heart.

One, who appeared more affected with the narrative than the rest, thought it likely that the hermit would, in a few years, go back to his retreat, and, perhaps, if shame did not restrain or death intercept him, return once more from this retreat into the world: "For the hope of happiness," said he, "is so strongly impressed that the longest experience is not able to efface it. Of the present state, whatever it be, we feel and are forced to confess the misery; yet, when the same state is again at a distance, imagination paints it as desirable. But the time will surely come when desire will be no longer our torment, and no man shall be wretched but by his own fault."

"This," said a philosopher who had heard him with tokens of great impatience, "is the present condition of a wise man. The time is already come when none are wretched but by their own fault. Nothing is more idle than to inquire after happiness, which nature has kindly placed within our reach. The way to be happy is to live according to nature, in obedience to that universal and unalterable law with which every heart is originally impressed; which is not written on it by precept, but engraven by destiny; not instilled by education, but infused at our nativity. He that lives according to nature will suffer nothing from the delusions of hope or importunities of desire; he will receive and reject with equability of temper, and act or suffer as the reason of things shall alternately prescribe. Other men may amuse themselves with subtle definitions or intricate ratiocinations. Let them learn to be wise by easier means. Let them observe the hind of the forest and the linnet of the grove; let them consider the life of animals, whose motions are regulated by instinct; they obey their guide, and are happy. Let us therefore, at length, cease to dispute, and learn to live; throw away the encumbrance of precepts, which they who utter them with so much pride and pomp do not understand, and carry with us this simple and intelligible maxim — that deviation from nature is deviation from happiness.''

When he had spoken, he looked round him with a placid air, and enjoyed the consciousness of his own beneficence. ''Sir,'' said the prince with great modesty, ''as I, like all the rest of mankind, am desirous of felicity, my closest attention has been fixed upon your discourse; I doubt not the truth of a position which a man so learned has so confidently advanced. Let me only know what it is to live according to nature.''

''When I find young men so humble and so docile,'' said the philosopher, ''I can deny them no information which my studies have enabled me to afford. To live according to nature is to act always with due regard to the fitness arising from the relations and qualities of causes and effects; to concur with the great and unchangeable scheme of universal felicity; to cooperate with the general disposition and tendency of the present system of things."

The prince soon found that this was one of the sages whom he should understand less as he heard him longer. He therefore bowed and was silent, and the philosopher, supposing him satisfied and the rest vanquished, rose up and departed with the air of a man that had cooperated with the present system.

The Prince Examines the Happiness of High Stations

24 &&& RASSELAS applauded the design, and appeared next day with a splendid retinue at the court of the Bassa. He was soon distinguished for his magnificence, and admitted, as a prince whose curiosity had brought him from distant countries, to an intimacy with the great officers and frequent conversation with the Bassa himself.

He was at first inclined to believe that the man must be pleased with his own condition, whom all approached with reverence and heard with obedience, and who had the power to extend his edicts to a whole kingdom. "There can be no pleasure," said he, "equal to that of feeling at once the joy of thousands, all made happy by wise administration. Yet, since by the law of subordination this sublime delight can be in one nation but the lot of one, it is surely reasonable to think that there is some satisfaction more popular and accessible, and that millions can hardly be subjected to the will of a single man, only to fill his particular breast with incommunicable content.

These thoughts were often in his mind, and he found no solution of the difficulty. But, as presents and civilities gained him more familiarity, he found that almost every man who stood high in employment hated all the rest, and was hated by them, and that their lives were a continual succession of plots and detections, stratagems and escapes, faction and treachery. Many of those who surrounded the Bassa were sent only to watch and report his conduct; every tongue was muttering censure, and every eye was searching for a fault.

At last the letters of revocation arrived; the Bassa was carried in chains to Constantinople, and his name was mentioned no more.

"What are we now to think of the prerogatives of power?" said Rasselas to his sister. "Is it without any efficacy to good? Or is the subordinate degree only dangerous, and the supreme safe and glorious? Is the Sultan the only happy man in his dominions? Or is the Sultan himself subject to the torments of suspicion and the dread of enemies?"

In a short time the second Bassa was deposed; the Sultan that had advanced him was murdered by the Janizaries, and his successor had other views and different favorites.

Most modern literary critics agree that William
Wordsworth (1770-1850) was a serious philosopher-poet
rather than a single-minded observer of nature. Nevertheless it is clear that this great English Romantic
used the natural world as a vehicle, in Geoffrey Hart-
man's words, "to the borders of vision." *Tintern Abbey*
and the *Ode: Intimations* exemplify Wordsworth's poetry,
and indicate much about the Romantic conception of man.

LINES COMPOSED A FEW MILES ABOVE TINTERN ABBEY, ON RE-VISITING THE BANKS OF THE WYE DURING A TOUR

JULY 13, 1798

Five years have past; five summers, with
  the length
Of five long winters! and again I hear
These waters, rolling from their mountain-
  springs
With a soft inland murmur.—Once again
Do I behold these steep and lofty cliffs, 5
That on a wild secluded scene impress
Thoughts of more deep seclusion; and con-
  nect
The landscape with the quiet of the
  sky.
The day is come when I again repose
Here, under this dark sycamore, and view
These plots of cottage-ground, these
  orchard-tufts,   11
Which at this season, with their unripe
  fruits,
Are clad in one green hue, and lose them-
  selves
'Mid groves and copses. Once again I see
These hedgerows, hardly hedgerows, little
  lines   15
Of sportive wood run wild: these pastoral
  farms,
Green to the very door; and wreaths of
  smoke
Sent up, in silence, from among the trees!
With some uncertain notice, as might
  seem

One impulse from a vernal wood
May teach you more of man,
Of moral evil and of good,
Than all the sages can.

Sweet is the lore which Nature brings; 25
Our meddling intellect
Misshapes the beauteous forms of things:—
We murder to dissect.

Enough of Science and of Art;
Close up those barren leaves;   30
Come forth, and bring with you a heart
That watches and receives.

Of vagrant dwellers in the houseless woods,
Or of some hermit's cave, where by his
    fire   21
The hermit sits alone.
                        These beauteous forms,
Through a long absence, have not been
    to me
As is a landscape to a blind man's eye:
But oft, in lonely rooms, and 'mid the din 25
Of towns and cities, I have owed to them
In hours of weariness, sensations sweet,
Felt in the blood, and felt along the
    heart;
And passing even into my purer mind,
With tranquil restoration:—feelings too 30
Of unremembered pleasure: such, perhaps,
As have no slight or trivial influence
On that best portion of a good man's life,
His little, nameless, unremembered acts
Of kindness and of love. Nor less, I trust,
To them I may have owed another gift, 36
Of aspect more sublime; that blessed
    mood,
In which the burthen of the mystery,
In which the heavy and the weary weight
Of all this unintelligible world,   40
Is lightened:—that serene and blessed
    mood
In which the affections gently lead us on,—
Until, the breath of this corporeal frame
And even the motion of our human blood
Almost suspended, we are laid asleep 45
In body, and become a living soul:
While with an eye made quiet by the
    power
Of harmony, and the deep power of joy,
We see into the life of things.
                        If this
Be but a vain belief, yet, oh! how oft— 50
In darkness and amid the many shapes
Of joyless daylight; when the fretful stir
Unprofitable, and the fever of the world,
Have hung upon the beatings of my
    heart—
How oft, in spirit, have I turned to thee, 55
O sylvan Wye! thou wanderer through the
    woods,

170

How often has my spirit turned to thee!
  And now, with gleams of half-extin-
    guished thought,
With many recognitions dim and faint,
And somewhat of a sad perplexity,   60
The picture of the mind revives again:
While here I stand, not only with the sense
Of present pleasure, but with pleasing
    thoughts
That in this moment there is life and food
For future years. And so I dare to hope, 65
Though changed, no doubt, from what
    I was when first
I came among these hills; when like a roe
I bounded o'er the mountains, by the
    sides
Of the deep rivers, and the lonely streams,
Wherever nature led: more like a man 70
Flying from something that he dreads,
    than one
Who sought the thing he loved.   For
    nature then
(The coarser pleasures of my boyish days,
And their glad animal movements all gone
    by)
To me was all in all.—I cannot paint   75
What then I was. The sounding cataract
Haunted me like a passion; the tall rock,
The mountain, and the deep and gloomy
    wood,
Their colors and their forms, were then to
    me
An appetite; a feeling and a love,   80
That had no need of a remoter charm,
By thought supplied, nor any interest
Unborrowed from the eye.—That time is
    past,
And all its aching joys are now no more,
And all its dizzy raptures. Not for this 85
Faint I, nor mourn, nor murmur; other
    gifts
Have followed; for such loss, I would
    believe,
Abundant recompense.   For I have
    learned
To look on nature, not as in the hour
Of thoughtless youth; but hearing often-
    times   90
The still, sad music of humanity,
Nor harsh nor grating, though of ample
    power
To chasten and subdue. And I have
    felt

A presence that disturbs me with the
        joy
Of elevated thoughts; a sense sublime, 95
Of something far more deeply interfused,
Whose dwelling is the light of setting
        suns,
And the round ocean and the living air,
And the blue sky, and in the mind of man;
A motion and a spirit, that impels   100
All thinking things, all objects of all
        thought,
And rolls through all things. Therefore
        am I still
A lover of the meadows and the woods,
And mountains; and of all that we be-
        hold
From this green earth; of all the mighty
        world   105
Of eye, and ear,—both what they half
        create,
And what perceive; well pleased to recog-
        nize
In nature and the language of the sense,
The anchor of my purest thoughts, the
        nurse,
The guide, the guardian of my heart, and
        soul   110
Of all my moral being.
                        Nor perchance,
If I were not thus taught, should I the
        more
Suffer my genial spirits to decay:
For thou art with me here upon the banks
Of this fair river; thou my dearest friend,
My dear, dear friend; and in thy voice I
        catch   116
The language of my former heart, and
        read
My former pleasures in the shooting lights
Of thy wild eyes. Oh! yet a little while
May I behold in thee what I was once, 120
My dear, dear sister! and this prayer I
        make,
Knowing that Nature never did betray
The heart that loved her; 'tis her privilege,
Through all the years of this our life, to
        lead
From joy to joy: for she can so inform 125
The mind that is within us, so impress
With quietness and beauty, and so feed
With lofty thoughts, that neither evil
        tongues,

Rash judgments, nor the sneers of selfish
    men,
Nor greetings where no kindness is, nor
    all   130
The dreary intercourse of daily life,
Shall e'er prevail against us, or disturb
Our cheerful faith, that all which we be-
    hold
Is full of blessings. Therefore let the
    moon
Shine on thee in thy solitary walk;   135
And let the misty mountain-winds be
    free
To blow against thee: and, in after years,
When these wild ecstasies shall be matured
Into a sober pleasure; when thy mind
Shall be a mansion for all lovely forms, 140
Thy memory be as a dwelling-place
For all sweet sounds and harmonies; oh!
    then,
If solitude, or fear, or pain, or grief,
Should be thy portion, with what healing
    thoughts
Of tender joy wilt thou remember me, 145
And these my exhortations! Nor, per-
    chance—
If I should be where I no more can hear

Thy voice, nor catch from thy wild eyes
    these gleams
Of past existence—wilt thou then forget
That on the banks of this delightful
    stream   150
We stood together; and that I, so long
A worshipper of Nature, hither came
Unwearied in that service: rather say
With warmer love—oh! with far deeper
    zeal

Of holier love. Nor wilt thou then forget,
That after many wanderings, many years
Of absence, these steep woods and lofty
    cliffs,   157
And this green pastoral landscape, were
    to me
More dear, both for themselves and for
    thy sake!

ODE

INTIMATIONS OF IMMORTALITY FROM RECOLLECTIONS OF EARLY CHILDHOOD

" The child is father of the man;
And I could wish my days to be
Bound each to each by natural piety."

I

There was a time when meadow, grove
and stream,
The earth, and every common sight,
To me did seem
Apparelled in celestial light,
The glory and the freshness of a dream. 5
It is not now as it hath been of yore;—
Turn wheresoe'er I may,
By night or day,
The things which I have seen I now can
see no more.

II

The Rainbow comes and goes, 10
And lovely is the Rose;
The Moon doth with delight
Look round her when the heavens are
bare;
Waters on a starry night
Are beautiful and fair;   15
The sunshine is a glorious birth;
But yet I know, where'er I go,
That there hath passed away a glory from
the earth.

III

Now, while the birds thus sing a joyous
song,
And while the young lambs bound   20
As to the tabor's sound,
To me alone there came a thought of
grief;
A timely utterance gave that thought re-
lief,
And I again am strong:

The cataracts blow their trumpets from
                    the steep;   25
No more shall grief of mine the season
                    wrong;
I hear the echoes through the mountains
                    throng,
The winds come to me from the fields of
                    sleep,
          And all the earth is gay;
               Land and sea   30
          Give themselves up to jollity,
               And with the heart of May
Doth every beast keep holiday;—
               Thou child of joy,
Shout round me, let me hear thy shouts,
                    thou happy shepherd-boy!35

                         IV

Ye blessèd creatures, I have heard the call
     Ye to each other make; I see
The heavens laugh with you in your jubi-
                    lee:
          My heart is at your festival,
          My head hath its coronal,   40
The fullness of your bliss, I feel—I feel it
                    all.
          Oh evil day! if I were sullen
          While Earth herself is adorning,
               This sweet May-morning,
          And the children are culling   45
               On every side,
          In a thousand valleys far and wide,
          Fresh flowers; while the sun shines
                    warm,
And the babe leaps up on his mother's
                    arm:—
          I hear, I hear, with joy I hear!   50
     —But there's a tree, of many, one,
A single field which I have looked upon,
Both of them speak of something that is
                    gone:
          The pansy at my feet
          Doth the same tale repeat: 55
Whither is fled the visionary gleam?
Where is it now, the glory and the dream?

V

Our birth is but a sleep and a forgetting:
The Soul that rises with us, our life's Star,
    Hath had elsewhere its setting,   60
    And cometh from afar:
    Not in entire forgetfulness,
    And not in utter nakedness,
But trailing clouds of glory do we come
    From God, who is our home: 65
Heaven lies about us in our infancy!
Shades of the prison-house begin to close
  Upon the growing boy,

But he beholds the light, and whence it
    flows,
    He sees it in his joy;   70
The youth, who daily farther from the
    east
    Must travel, still is Nature's priest.
    And by the vision splendid
    Is on his way attended;
At length the man perceives it die away, 75
And fade into the light of common day.

VI

Earth fills her lap with pleasures of her
    own;
Yearnings she hath in her own natural
    kind,
And, even with something of a mother's
    mind,
    And no unworthy aim,   80
    The homely nurse doth all she can
To make her foster-child, her inmate Man,
    Forget the glories he hath known,
And that imperial palace whence he
    came.

VII

Behold the Child among his new-born
    blisses,   85
A six years' darling of a pigmy size!
See, where 'mid work of his own hand he
    lies,
Fretted by sallies of his mother's kisses,
With light upon him from his father's
    eyes!

See, at his feet, some little plan or chart, 90
Some fragment from his dream of human
life,
Shaped by himself with newly-learnèd art;
A wedding or a festival,
A mourning or a funeral;
And this hath now his heart, 95
And unto this he frames his song:
Then will he fit his tongue
To dialogues of business, love, or strife;
But it will not be long
Ere this be thrown aside, 100
And with new joy and pride
The little actor cons another part;
Filling from time to time his "humorous
stage"
With all the persons, down to palsied Age,
That Life brings with her in her equipage;
As if his whole vocation 106
Were endless imitation.

VIII

Thou, whose exterior semblance doth belie
Thy soul's immensity;
Thou best philosopher, who yet dost
keep 110
Thy heritage, thou eye among the blind,
That, deaf and silent, read'st the eternal
deep,
Haunted forever by the eternal mind,—
Mighty prophet! Seer blest!
On whom those truths do rest, 115
Which we are toiling all our lives to find,
In darkness lost, the darkness of the
grave;
Thou, over whom thy immortality
Broods like the day, a master o'er a slave,
A presence which is not to be put by; 120
Thou little child, yet glorious in the might
Of heaven-born freedom on thy being's
height,
Why with such earnest pains dost thou
provoke
The years to bring the inevitable yoke,
Thus blindly with thy blessedness at
strife? 125

Full soon thy Soul shall have her earthly
freight,
And custom lie upon thee with a weight,
Heavy as frost, and deep almost as life!

IX

O joy! that in our embers
Is something that doth live,   130
That nature yet remembers
What was so fugitive!
The thought of our past years in me doth
breed
Perpetual benediction: not indeed
For that which is most worthy to be
blest—   135
Delight and liberty, the simple creed
Of childhood, whether busy or at rest,
With new-fledged hope still fluttering in his
breast:—

Not for these I raise
The song of thanks and praise;   140
But for those obstinate questionings
Of sense and outward things,
Fallings from us, vanishings;
Blank misgivings of a creature
Moving about in worlds not realised,   145
High instincts before which our mortal
nature

Did tremble like a guilty thing surprised:
But for those first affections,
Those shadowy recollections,
Which, be they what they may,   150
Are yet the fountain light of all our day,
Are yet a master light of all our seeing;
Uphold us, cherish, and have power to
make
Our noisy years seem moments in the being
Of the eternal Silence: truths that wake,
To perish never;   156
Which neither listlessness, nor mad en-
deavor,
Nor man nor boy,
Nor all that is at enmity with joy,
Can utterly abolish or destroy!   160
Hence in a season of calm weather
Though inland far we be,
Our souls have sight of that immortal sea
Which brought us hither,

178

Can in a moment travel thither, 165
And see the children sport upon the shore,
And hear the mighty waters rolling ever-
    more.

X

Then sing, ye birds, sing, sing a joyous
    song!
    And let the young lambs bound
    As to the tabor's sound! 170
We in thought will join your throng,
    Ye that pipe and ye that play,
    Ye that through your hearts to-day
    Feel the gladness of the May!

What though the radiance which was once
    so bright 175
Be now forever taken from my sight,
    Though nothing can bring back the
    hour
Of splendor in the grass, of glory in the
    flower;
    We will grieve not, rather find
    Strength in what remains behind; 180
    In the primal sympathy
    Which having been must ever be;
    In the soothing thoughts that spring
    Out of human suffering; 184
    In the faith that looks through death,
In years that bring the philosophic mind.

XI

And O ye fountains, meadows, hills, and
    groves,
Forebode not any severing of our loves!
Yet in my heart of hearts I feel your might;
I only have relinquished one delight 190
To live beneath your more habitual sway.
I love the brooks which down their chan-
    nels fret,
Even more than when I tripped lightly as
    they;
The innocent brightness of a new-born day
    Is lovely yet; 195
The clouds that gather round the setting
    sun
Do take a sober coloring from an eye
That hath kept watch o'er man's mor-
    tality;

Another race hath been, and other palms
    are won.
Thanks to the human heart by which we
    live,   200
Thanks to its tenderness, its joys, and fears,
To me the meanest flower that blows can
    give
Thoughts that do often lie too deep for
    tears.

Charles Darwin, THE ORIGIN OF SPECIES

THE DESCENT OF MAN

1. Darwin writes of natural selection, the struggle for existence, and the geometric rate of increase which is curtailed by the environment. What are each of these and how are they related?

2. Darwin compares his inability to determine the exact moment of man's separation from other higher primates with our inability to pinpoint the moment at which an infant becomes self-conscious and reflective. Does this presuppose the old adage that "ontogeny recapitulates phylogeny"? If so, is this a valid assumption?

3. Darwin holds that the moral sense is the best and highest distinction between man and the lower animals. What is the moral sense?

4. How has recent scientific work affected Darwin's theories?

5. Does Darwin's theory of evolution undercut the biblical account of creation? What does Darwin himself say in this regard?

6. How might Darwin's investigation of nature affect traditional moral theories?

7. What are the dangers of applying scientific theories like Darwin's to society and social life?

The theory of evolution which Charles Darwin (1809-1882) presented in his book *On the Origin of Species by Means of Natural Selection, or The Preservation of Favoured Races in the Struggle for Life* (published in 1859), initiated a revolution in biological science. Although others had proposed similar theories, Darwin's impact was greatest because he was the first to base his theory upon factual evidence through experimentation and observation.

Educated at the University of Edinburgh and at Cambridge, Darwin, soon after graduation, sailed as a naturalist with an expedition on H.M.S. *Beagle* on a five-year voyage along the coast of South America and to various Pacific Islands. This gave him the opportunity to collect much of the data on which he based his theory.

The publication of his *The Descent of Man* (1871) only added fuel to the fires of controversy which he had lighted with his earlier publication.

The Origin of Species

CHAPTER IV

Natural Selection; or the Survival of the Fittest

Natural Selection—its power compared with man's selection—its power
on characters of trifling importance—its power at all ages and on
both sexes—Sexual selection—On the generality of intercrosses
between individuals of the same species—Circumstances favourable
and unfavourable to the results of Natural Selection, namely, intercrossing, isolation, number of individuals—Slow action—Extinction
caused by Natural Selection—Divergence of Character, related to the
diversity of inhabitants of any small area, and to naturalisation—
Action of Natural Selection, through divergence of Character and
Extinction, on the descendants from a common parent—Explains the
grouping of all organic beings—Advance in organisation—Low
forms preserved—Convergence of Character—Indefinite multipli-
cation of species—Summary.

HOW will the struggle for existence, briefly discussed in the
last chapter, act in regard to variation? Can the principle
of selection, which we have seen is so potent in the hands
of man, apply under nature? I think we shall see that it can act
most efficiently. Let the endless number of slight variations and
individual differences occurring in our domestic productions, and,
in a lesser degree, in those under nature, be borne in mind; as well
as the strength of the hereditary tendency. Under domestication, it
may be truly said that the whole organisation becomes in some degree plastic. But the variability, which we almost universally meet
with in our domestic productions, is not directly produced, as
Hooker and Asa Gray have well remarked, by man; he can neither
originate varieties, nor prevent their occurrence; he can only preserve and accumulate such as do occur. Unintentionally he exposes
organic beings to new and changing conditions of life, and variability ensues; but similar changes of conditions might and do occur
under nature. Let it also be borne in mind how infinitely complex
and close-fitting are the mutual relations of all organic beings to
each other and to their physical conditions of life; and consequently

what infinitely varied diversities of structure might be of use to each being under changing conditions of life. Can it, then, be thought improbable, seeing that variations useful to man have undoubtedly occurred, that other variations useful in some way to each being in the great and complex battle of life, should occur in the course of many successive generations? If such do occur, can we doubt (remembering that many more individuals are born than can possibly survive) that individuals having any advantage, however slight, over others, would have the best chance of surviving and of procreating their kind? On the other hand, we may feel sure that any variation in the least degree injurious would be rigidly destroyed. This preservation of favourable individual differences and variations, and the destruction of those which are injurious, I have called Natural Selection, or the Survival of the Fittest. Variations neither useful nor injurious would not be affected by natural selection, and would be left either a fluctuating element, as perhaps we see in certain polymorphic species, or would ultimately become fixed, owing to the nature of the organism and the nature of the conditions.

Several writers have misapprehended or objected to the term Natural Selection. Some have even imagined that natural selection induces variability, whereas it implies only the preservation of such variations as arise and are beneficial to the being under its conditions of life. No one objects to agriculturists speaking of the potent effects of man's selection; and in this case the individual differences given by nature, which man for some object selects, must of necessity first occur. Others have objected that the term selection implies conscious choice in the animals which become modified; and it has even been urged that, as plants have no volition, natural selection is not applicable to them! In the literal sense of the word, no doubt, natural selection is a false term; but who ever objected to chemists speaking of the elective affinities of the various elements?—and yet an acid cannot strictly be said to elect the base with which it in preference combines. It has been said that I speak of natural selection as an active power or deity; but who objects to an author speaking of the attraction of gravity as ruling the movements of the planets? Every one knows what is meant and is implied by such metaphorical expressions; and they are almost necessary for brevity. So again it is difficult to avoid personifying the word Nature; but I mean by Nature, only the aggregate action and product of many natural laws, and by laws the sequence of events as ascertained by us. With a little familiarity such superficial objections will be forgotten.

We shall best understand the probable course of natural selection by taking the case of a country undergoing some slight physical change, for instance, of climate. The proportional numbers of its inhabitants will almost immediately undergo a change, and some species will probably become extinct. We may conclude, from what we have seen of the intimate and complex manner in which the inhabitants of each country are bound together, that any change in the numerical proportions of the inhabitants, independently of the change of climate itself, would seriously affect the others. If the country were open on its borders, new forms would certainly immigrate, and this would likewise seriously disturb the relations of some of the former inhabitants. Let it be remembered how powerful the influence of a single introduced tree or mammal has been shown to be. But in the case of an island, or of a country partly surrounded by barriers, into which new and better adapted forms could not freely enter, we should then have places in the economy of nature which would assuredly be better filled up, if some of the original inhabitants were in some manner modified; for, had the area been open to immigration, these same places would have been seized on by intruders. In such cases, slight modifications, which in any way favoured the individuals of any species, by better adapting them to their altered conditions, would tend to be preserved; and natural selection would have free scope for the work of improvement.

We have good reason to believe, as shown in the first chapter, that changes in the conditions of life give a tendency to increased variability; and in the foregoing cases the conditions have changed, and this would manifestly be favourable to natural selection, by affording a better chance of the occurrence of profitable variations. Unless such occur, natural selection can do nothing. Under the term of "variations," it must never be forgotten that mere individual differences are included. As man can produce a great result with his domestic animals and plants by adding up in any given direction individual differences, so could natural selection, but far more easily from having incomparably longer time for action. Nor do I believe that any great physical change, as of climate, or any unusual degree of isolation, to check immigration, is necessary in order that new and unoccupied places should be left, for natural selection to fill up by improving some of the varying inhabitants. For as all the inhabitants of each country are struggling together with nicely balanced forces, extremely slight modifications in the structure or habits of one species would often give it an advantage over others; and still further modifications of the same kind would often still further increase the advantage, as long as the species continued under the same conditions of life and profited by similar means of subsistence and defence. No country can be named in which all the native inhabitants are now so perfectly adapted to each other and to the physical conditions under which they live, that none of them could be still better adapted or improved; for in all countries, the natives have been so far conquered by naturalised productions, that they have allowed some foreigners to take firm possession of the land. And as foreigners have thus in every country beaten some of the natives, we may safely conclude that the natives might have been modified with advantage, so as to have better resisted the intruders.

As man can produce, and certainly has produced, a great result by his methodical and unconscious means of selection, what may not natural selection effect? Man can act only on external and visible characters: Nature, if I may be allowed to personify the natural preservation or survival of the fittest, cares nothing for appearances, except in so far as they are useful to any being. She can act on every internal organ, on every shade of constitutional difference, on the whole machinery of life. Man selects only for his own good: Nature only for that of the being which she tends. Every selected character is fully exercised by her, as is implied by the fact of their selection. Man keeps the natives of many climates in the same country; he seldom exercises each selected character in some peculiar and fitting manner; he feeds a long and a short beaked pigeon on the same food; he does not exercise a long-backed or long-legged quadruped in any peculiar manner; he exposes sheep with long and short wool to the same climate. He does not allow the most vigorous males to struggle for the females. He does not rigidly destroy all inferior animals, but protects during each varying season, as far as lies in his power, all his productions. He often begins his selection by some half-monstrous form; or at least by some modification prominent enough to catch the eye or to be plainly useful to him. Under nature, the slightest differences of structure or constitution may well turn the nicely balanced scale in the struggle for life, and so be preserved. How fleeting are the wishes and efforts of man! how short his time! and consequently how poor will be his results, compared with those accumulated by Nature during whole geological periods? Can we wonder, then, that Nature's productions should be far "truer" in character than man's productions; that they should be infinitely better adapted to the most complex conditions of life, and should plainly bear the stamp of far higher workmanship?

It may metaphorically be said that natural selection is daily and hourly scrutinising, throughout the world, the slightest variations; rejecting those that are bad, preserving and adding up all that are good; silently and insensibly working, *whenever and wherever opportunity offers,* at the improvement of each organic being in relation to its organic and inorganic conditions of life. We see nothing of these slow changes in progress, until the hand of time has marked the lapse of ages, and then so imperfect is our view into long-past geological ages, that we see only that the forms of life are now different from what they formerly were.

In order that any great amount of modification should be effected in a species, a variety, when once formed, must again, perhaps after a long interval of time, vary or present individual differences of the same favourable nature as before; and these must be again preserved, and so onwards step by step. Seeing that individual differences of the same kind perpetually recur, this can hardly be considered as an unwarrantable assumption. But whether it is true, we can judge only by seeing how far the hypothesis accords with and explains the general phenomena of nature. On the other hand, the ordinary belief that the amount of possible variation is a strictly limited quantity is likewise a simple assumption.

Although natural selection can act only through and for the good of each being, yet characters and structures, which we are apt to consider as of very trifling importance, may thus be acted on. When we see leaf-eating insects green, and bark-feeders mottled-grey; the alpine ptarmigan white in winter, the red grouse the colour of heather, we must believe that these tints are of service to these birds and insects in preserving them from danger. Grouse, if not destroyed at some period of their lives, would increase in countless numbers; they are known to suffer largely from birds of prey; and hawks are guided by eyesight to their prey—so much so, that on parts of the Continent persons are warned not to keep white pigeons, as being the most liable to destruction. Hence natural selection might be effective in giving the proper colour to each kind of grouse, and in keeping that colour, when once acquired, true and constant. Nor ought we to think that the occasional destruction of an animal of any particular colour would produce little effect: we should remember how essential it is in a flock of white sheep to destroy a lamb with the faintest trace of black. We have seen how the colour of the hogs, which feed on the "paint root" in Virginia, determines whether they shall live or die. In plants, the down on the fruit and the colour of the flesh are considered by botanists as characters of the most trifling importance: yet we hear from an excellent horti-culturist, Downing, that in the United States smooth-skinned fruits suffer far more from a beetle, a Curculio, than those with down; that purple plums suffer far more from a certain disease than yellow plums, whereas another disease attacks yellow-fleshed peaches far more than those with other coloured flesh. If, with all the aids of art, these slight differences make a great difference in cultivating the several varieties, assuredly, in a state of nature, where the trees would have to struggle with other trees and with a host of enemies, such differences would effectually settle which variety, whether a smooth or downy, a yellow or purple fleshed fruit, should succeed.

In looking at many small points of difference between species, which, as far as our ignorance permits us to judge, seem quite un-important, we must not forget that climate, food, etc., have no doubt produced some direct effect. It is also necessary to bear in mind that, owing to the law of correlation, when one part varies, and the variations are accumulated through natural selection, other modifi-cations, often of the most unexpected nature, will ensue.

As we see that those variations which, under domestication, appear at any particular period of life, tend to reappear in the offspring at the same period; for instance, in the shape, size, and flavour of the seeds of the many varieties of our culinary and agricultural plants; in the caterpillar and cocoon stages of the varieties of the silkworm; in the eggs of poultry, and in the colour of the down of their chickens; in the horns of our sheep and cattle when nearly adult; so in a state of nature natural selection will be enabled to act on and modify organic beings at any age, by the accumulation of variations profitable at that age, and by their inheritance at a corresponding age. If it profit a plant to have its seeds more and more widely disseminated by the wind, I can see no greater difficulty in this being effected through natural selection, than in the cotton planter increasing and improving by selection the down in the pods on his cotton trees. Natural selection may modify and adapt the larva of an insect to a score of contingencies, wholly different from those which concern the mature insect; and these modifications may effect, through correlation, the structure of the adult. So, conversely, modifications in the adult may affect the structure of the larva; but in all cases natural selection will ensure that they shall not be injurious: for if they were so, the species would become extinct.

Natural selection will modify the structure of the young in relation to the parent, and of the parent in relation to the young. In social animals it will adapt the structure of each individual for the benefit of the whole community; if the community profits by the selected change. What natural selection cannot do, is to modify the structure of one species, without giving it any advantage, for the good of another species; and though statements to this effect may be found in works of natural history, I cannot find one case which will bear investigation. A structure used only once in an animal's life, if of high importance to it, might be modified to any extent by natural selection; for instance, the great jaws possessed by certain insects, used exclusively for opening the cocoon—or the hard tip to the beak of unhatched birds, used for breaking the egg. It has been asserted, that of the best short-beaked tumbler pigeons a greater number perish in the egg than are able to get out of it; so that fanciers assist in the act of hatching. Now, if nature had to make the beak of a full-grown pigeon very short for the bird's own advantage, the process of modification would be very slow, and there would be simultaneously the most rigorous selection of all the young birds within the egg, which had the most powerful and hardest beaks, for all with weak beaks would inevitably perish; or, more delicate and more easily broken shells might be selected, the thickness of the shell being known to vary like every other structure.

It may be well here to remark that with all beings there must be much fortuitous destruction, which can have little or no influence on the course of natural selection. For instance a vast number of eggs or seeds are annually devoured, and these could be modified through natural selection only if they varied in some manner which protected them from their enemies. Yet many of these eggs or seeds would perhaps, if not destroyed, have yielded individuals better adapted to their conditions of life than any of those which happened to survive. So again a vast number of mature animals and plants, whether or not they be the best adapted to their conditions, must be annually destroyed by accidental causes, which would not be in the least degree mitigated by certain changes of structure or constitution which would in other ways be beneficial to the species. But let the destruction of the adults be ever so heavy, if the number which can exist in any district be not wholly kept down by such causes,—or again let the destruction of eggs or seeds be so great that only a hundredth or a thousandth part are developed,—yet of those which do survive, the best adapted individuals, supposing that there is any variability in a favourable direction, will tend to propagate their kind in larger numbers than the less well adapted. If the numbers be wholly kept down by the causes just indicated, as will often have been the case, natural selection will be powerless in certain beneficial directions; but this is no valid objection to its efficiency at other times and in other ways; for we are far from having any reason to suppose that many species ever undergo modification and improvement at the same time in the same area.

SEXUAL SELECTION

Inasmuch as peculiarities often appear under domestication in one sex and become hereditarily attached to that sex, so no doubt it will be under nature. Thus it is rendered possible for the two sexes to be modified through natural selection in relation to different habits of life, as is sometimes the case; or for one sex to be modified in relation to the other sex, as commonly occurs. This leads me to say a few words on what I have called Sexual Selection. This form of selection depends, not on a struggle for existence in relation to other organic beings or to external conditions, but on a struggle between the individuals of one sex, generally the males, for the possession of the other sex. The result is not death to the unsuccessful competitor, but few or no offspring. Sexual selection is, therefore, less rigorous than natural selection. Generally, the most vigorous males, those which are best fitted for their places in nature, will leave most progeny. But in many cases, victory depends not so much on general vigour, as on having special weapons, confined to the male sex. A hornless stag or spurless cock would have a poor chance of leaving numerous offspring. Sexual selection, by always allowing the victor to breed, might surely give indomitable courage, length to the spur, and strength to the wing to strike in the spurred leg, in nearly the same manner as does the brutal cockfighter by the careful selection of his best cocks. How low in the scale of nature the law of battle descends, I know not; male alligators have been described as fighting, bellowing, and whirling round, like Indians in a war dance, for the possession of the females; male salmons have been observed fighting all day long; male stag beetles sometimes bear wounds from the huge mandibles of other males; the males of certain hymenopterous insects have been frequently seen by that inimitable observer M. Fabre, fighting for a particular female who sits by, an apparently unconcerned beholder of the struggle, and then retires with the conqueror. The war is, perhaps, severest between the males of polygamous animals, and these seem oftenest provided with special weapons. The males of carnivorous animals are already well armed; though to them and to others, special means of defence may be given through means of sexual selection, as the mane of the lion, and the hooked jaw to the male salmon; for the shield may be as important for victory, as the sword or spear.

Amongst birds, the contest is often of a more peaceful character. All those who have attended to the subject, believe that there is the severest rivalry between the males of many species to attract, by singing, the females. The rock thrush of Guiana, birds of paradise, and some others, congregate; and successive males display with the most elaborate care, and show off in the best manner, their gorgeous plumage; they likewise perform strange antics before the females, which, standing by as spectators, at last choose the most attractive partner. Those who have closely attended to birds in confinement well know that they often take individual preferences and dislikes; thus Sir R. Heron has described how a pied peacock was eminently attractive to all his hen birds. I cannot here enter on the necessary details; but if man can in a short time give beauty and an elegant carriage to his bantams, according to his standard of beauty, I can see no good reason to doubt that female birds, by selecting, during thousands of generations, the most melodious or beautiful males, according to their standard of beauty, might produce a marked effect. Some well-known laws, with respect to the plumage of male and female birds, in comparison with the plumage of the young, can partly be explained through the action of sexual selection on variations occurring at different ages, and transmitted to the males alone or to both sexes at corresponding ages; but I have not space here to enter on this subject.

Thus it is, as I believe, that when the males and females of any animal have the same general habits of life, but differ in structure, colour, or ornament, such differences have been mainly caused by sexual selection: that is, by individual males having had, in successive generations, some slight advantage over other males, in their weapons, means of defence, or charms, which they have transmitted to their male offspring alone. Yet, I would not wish to attribute all sexual differences to this agency: for we see in our domestic animals peculiarities arising and becoming attached to the male sex, which apparently have not been augmented through selection by man. The tuft of hair on the breast of the wild turkey cock cannot be of any use, and it is doubtful whether it can be ornamental in the eyes of the female bird; indeed, had the tuft appeared under domestication, it would have been called a monstrosity.

ACTION OF NATURAL SELECTION

ILLUSTRATIONS OF THE ACTION OF NATURAL SELECTION, OR THE SURVIVAL OF THE FITTEST

In order to make it clear how, as I believe, natural selection acts, I must beg permission to give one or two imaginary illustrations. Let us take the case of a wolf, which preys on various animals, securing some by craft, some by strength, and some by fleetness; and let us suppose that the fleetest prey, a deer for instance, had from any change in the country increased in numbers, or that other prey had decreased in numbers, during that season of the year when the wolf was hardest pressed for food. Under such circumstances the swiftest and slimmest wolves would have the best chance of surviving and so be preserved or selected,—provided always that they retained strength to master their prey at this or some other period of the year, when they were compelled to prey on other animals. I can see no more reason to doubt that this would be the result, than that man should be able to improve the fleetness of his greyhounds by careful and methodical selection, or by that kind of unconscious selection which follows from each man trying to keep the best dogs without any thought of modifying the breed. I may add, that, according to Mr. Pierce, there are two varieties of the wolf inhabiting the Catskill Mountains, in the United States, one with a light greyhound-like form, which pursues deer, and the other more bulky, with shorter legs, which more frequently attacks the shepherd's flocks.

It should be observed that, in the above illustration, I speak of the slimmest individual wolves, and not of any single strongly-marked variation having been preserved. In former editions of this work I sometimes spoke as if this latter alternative had frequently occurred. I saw the great importance of individual differences, and this led me fully to discuss the results of unconscious selection by man, which depends on the preservation of all the more or less valuable individuals, and on the destruction of the worst. I saw, also, that the preservation in a state of nature of any occasional deviation of structure, such as a monstrosity, would be a rare event; and that, if at first preserved, it would generally be lost by subsequent intercrossing with ordinary individuals. Nevertheless, until reading an able and valuable article in the 'North British Review' (1867), I did not appreciate how rarely single variations, whether slight or strongly-marked, could be perpetuated. The author takes the case of a pair of animals, producing during their lifetime two hundred offspring, of which, from various causes of destruction, only two on an average survive to procreate their kind. This is rather an extreme estimate for most of the higher animals, but by no means so for many of the lower organisms. He then shows that if a single individual were born, which varied in some manner, giving it twice as good a chance of life as that of the other individuals, yet the chances would be strongly against its survival. Supposing it to survive and to breed, and that half its young inherited the favourable variation; still, as the reviewer goes on to show, the young would have only a slightly better chance of surviving and breeding; and this chance would go on decreasing in the succeeding generations. The justice of these remarks cannot, I think, be disputed. If, for instance, a bird of some kind could procure its food more easily by having its beak curved, and if one were born with its beak strongly curved, and which consequently flourished, nevertheless there would be a very poor chance of this one individual perpetuating its kind to the exclusion of the common form; but there can hardly be a doubt, judging by what we see taking place under domestication, that this result would follow from the preservation during many generations of a large number of individuals with more or less strongly curved beaks, and from the destruction of a still larger number with the straightest beaks.

It should not, however, be overlooked that certain rather strongly marked variations, which no one would rank as mere individual differences, frequently recur owing to a similar organisation being similarly acted on—of which fact numerous instances could be given with our domestic productions. In such cases, if the varying individual did not actually transmit to its offspring its newly acquired character, it would undoubtedly transmit to them, as long as the existing conditions remained the same, a still stronger tendency to vary in the same manner. There can also be little doubt that the tendency to vary in the same manner has often been so strong that all the individuals of the same species have been similarly modified without the aid of any form of selection. Or only a third, fifth, or tenth part of the individuals may have been thus affected, of which fact several instances could be given. Thus Graba estimates that about one-fifth of the guillemots in the Faroe Islands consist of a variety so well marked, that it was formerly ranked as a distinct species under the name of Uria lacrymans. In cases of this kind, if the variation were of a beneficial nature, the original form would soon be supplanted by the modified form, through the survival of the fittest.

To the effects of intercrossing in eliminating variations of all kinds, I shall have to recur; but it may be here remarked that most animals and plants keep to their proper homes, and do not needlessly wander about; we see this even with migratory birds, which almost always return to the same spot. Consequently each newly-formed variety would generally be at first local, as seems to be the common rule with varieties in a state of nature; so that similarly modified individuals would soon exist in a small body together, and would often breed together. If the new variety were successful in its battle for life, it would slowly spread from a central district, competing with and conquering the unchanged individuals on the margins of an ever-increasing circle.

It may be worth while to give another and more complex illustration of the action of natural selection. Certain plants excrete sweet juice, apparently for the sake of eliminating something injurious from the sap: this is effected, for instance, by glands at the base of the stipules in some Leguminosæ, and at the backs of the leaves of the common laurel. This juice, though small in quantity, is greedily sought by insects; but their visits do not in any way benefit the plant. Now, let us suppose that the juice or nectar was excreted from the inside of the flowers of a certain number of plants of any species. Insects in seeking the nectar would get dusted with pollen, and would often transport it from one flower to another. The flowers of two distinct individuals of the same species would thus get crossed; and the act of crossing, as can be fully proved, gives rise to vigorous seedlings, which consequently would have the best chance of flourishing and surviving. The plants which produced flowers with the largest glands or nectaries, excreting most nectar, would oftenest be visited by insects, and would oftenest be crossed; and so in the long run would gain the upper hand and form a local variety. The flowers, also, which had their stamens and pistils placed, in relation to the size and habits of the particular insect which visited them, so as to favour in any degree the transportal of the pollen, would likewise be favoured. We might have taken the case of insects visiting flowers for the sake of collecting pollen instead of nectar; and as pollen is formed for the sole purpose of fertilisation, its destruction appears to be a simple loss to the plant; yet if a little pollen were carried, at first occasionally and then habitually, by the pollen-devouring insects from flower to flower, and a cross thus effected, although nine-tenths of the pollen were destroyed, it might still be a great gain to the plant to be thus robbed; and the individuals which produced more and more pollen, and had larger anthers, would be selected.

When our plant, by the above process long continued, had been rendered highly attractive to insects, they would, unintentionally on their part, regularly carry pollen from flower to flower; and that they do this effectually, I could easily show by many striking facts. I will give only one, as likewise illustrating one step in the separation of the sexes of plants. Some holly trees bear only male flowers, which have four stamens producing a rather small quantity of pollen, and a rudimentary pistil; other holly trees bear only female flowers; these have a full-sized pistil, and four stamens with shrivelled anthers, in which not a grain of pollen can be detected. Having found a female tree exactly sixty yards from a male tree, I put the stigmas of twenty flowers, taken from different branches, under the microscope, and on all, without exception, there were a few pollen grains, and on some a profusion. As the wind had set for several days from the female to the male tree, the pollen could not thus have been carried. The weather had been cold and boisterous, and therefore not favourable to bees, nevertheless every female flower which I examined had been effectually fertilised by the bees, which had flown from tree to tree in search of nectar. But to return to our imaginary case: as soon as the plant had been rendered so highly attractive to insects that pollen was regularly carried from flower to flower, another process might commence. No naturalist doubts the advantage of what has been called the "physiological division of labour"; hence we may believe that it would be advantageous to a plant to produce stamens alone in one flower or on one whole plant, and pistils alone in another flower or on another plant. In plants under culture and placed under new conditions of life, sometimes the male organs and sometimes the female organs become more or less impotent; now if we suppose this to occur in ever so slight a degree under nature, then, as pollen is already carried regularly from flower to flower, and as a more complete separation of the sexes of our plant would be advantageous on the principle of the division of labour, individuals with this tendency more and more increased, would be continually favoured or selected, until at last a complete separation of the sexes might be effected. It would take up too much space to show the various steps, through dimorphism and other means, by which the separation of the sexes in plants of various kinds is apparently now in progress; but I may add that some of the species of holly in North America, are, according to Asa Gray, in an exactly intermediate condition, or, as he expresses it, are more or less diœciously polygamous.

Let us now turn to the nectar-feeding insects; we may suppose the plant, of which we have been slowly increasing the nectar by continued selection, to be a common plant; and that certain insects depended in main part on its nectar for food. I could give many facts showing how anxious bees are to save time: for instance, their habit of cutting holes and sucking the nectar at the bases of certain flowers, which with a very little more trouble, they can enter by the mouth. Bearing such facts in mind, it may be believed that under certain circumstances individual differences in the curvature or length of the proboscis, etc., too slight to be appreciated by us, might profit a bee or other insect, so that certain individuals would be able to obtain their food more quickly than others; and thus the communities to which they belonged would flourish and throw off many swarms inheriting the same peculiarities. The tubes of the corolla of the common red and incarnate clovers (Trifolium pratense and incarnatum) do not on a hasty glance appear to differ in length; yet the hive bee can easily suck the nectar out of the incarnate clover, but not out of the common red clover, which is visited by humble bees alone; so that whole fields of the red clover offer in vain an abundant supply of precious nectar to the hive bee. That this nectar is much liked by the hive bee is certain; for I have repeatedly seen, but only in the autumn, many hive bees sucking the flowers through holes bitten in the base of the tube by humble bees. The difference in the length of the corolla in the two kinds of clover, which determines the visits of the hive bee, must be very trifling; for I have been assured that when red clover has been mown, the flowers of the second crop are somewhat smaller, and that these are visited by many hive bees. I do not know whether this statement is accurate; nor whether another published statement can be trusted, namely, that the Ligurian bee, which is generally considered a mere variety of the common hive bee, and which freely crosses with it, is able to reach and suck the nectar of the red clover. Thus, in a country where this kind of clover abounded, it might be a great advantage to the hive bee to have a slightly longer or differently constructed proboscis. On the other hand, as the fertility of this clover absolutely depends on bees visiting the flowers, if humble bees were to become rare in any country, it might be a great advantage to the plant to have a shorter or more deeply divided corolla, so that the hive bees should be enabled to suck its flowers. Thus I can understand how a flower and a bee might slowly become, either simultaneously or one after the other, modified and adapted to each other in the most perfect manner, by the continued preservation of all the individuals which presented slight deviations of structure mutually favourable to each other.

I am well aware that this doctrine of natural selection, exemplified in the above imaginary instances, is open to the same objections which were first urged against Sir Charles Lyell's noble views on "the modern changes of the earth, as illustrative of geology"; but we now seldom hear the agencies which we see still at work, spoken of as trifling or insignificant, when used in explaining the excavation of the deepest valleys or the formation of long lines of inland cliffs. Natural selection acts only by the preservation and accumulation of small inherited modifications, each profitable to the preserved being; and as modern geology has almost banished such views as the excavation of a great valley by a single diluvial wave, so will natural selection banish the belief of the continued creation of new organic beings, or of any great and sudden modification in their structure.

I must here introduce a short digression. In the case of animals and plants with separated sexes, it is of course obvious that two individuals must always (with the exception of the curious and not well understood cases of parthenogenesis) unite for each birth; but in the case of hermaphrodites this is far from obvious. Nevertheless there is reason to believe that with all hermaphrodites two individuals, either occasionally or habitually, concur for the reproduction of their kind. This view was long ago doubtfully suggested by Sprengel, Knight, and Kölreuter. We shall presently see its importance; but I must here treat the subject with extreme brevity, though I have the materials prepared for an ample discussion. All vertebrate animals, all insects, and some other large groups of animals, pair for each birth. Modern research has much diminished the number of supposed hermaphrodites, and of real hermaphrodites a large number pair; that is, two individuals regularly unite for reproduction, which is all that concerns us. But still there are many hermaphrodite animals which certainly do not habitually pair, and a vast majority of plants are hermaphrodites. What reason, it may be asked, is there for supposing in these cases that two individuals ever concur in reproduction? As it is impossible here to enter on details, I must trust to some general considerations alone.

In the first place, I have collected so large a body of facts, and made so many experiments, showing, in accordance with the almost universal belief of breeders, that with animals and plants a cross between different varieties, or between individuals of the same variety but of another strain, gives vigour and fertility to the offspring; and on the other hand, that *close* interbreeding diminishes vigour and fertility; that these facts alone incline me to believe that it is a general law of nature that no organic being fertilises itself for a perpetuity of generations; but that a cross with another individual is occasionally—perhaps at long intervals of time—indispensable.

On the belief that this is a law of nature, we can, I think, understand several large classes of facts, such as the following, which on any other view are inexplicable. Every hybridizer knows how un-favourable exposure to wet is to the fertilisation of a flower, yet what a multitude of flowers have their anthers and stigmas fully exposed to the weather! If an occasional cross be indispensable, notwithstanding that the plant's own anthers and pistil stand so near each other as almost to insure self-fertilisation, the fullest freedom for the entrance of pollen from another individual will explain the above state of exposure of the organs. Many flowers, on the other hand, have their organs of fructification closely enclosed, as in the great papilionaceous or pea-family; but these almost invariably present beautiful and curious adaptations in relation to the visits of insects. So necessary are the visits of bees to many papilionaceous flowers, that their fertility is greatly diminished if these visits be prevented. Now, it is scarcely possible for insects to fly from flower to flower, and not to carry pollen from one to the other, to the great good of the plant. Insects act like a camel-hair pencil, and it is sufficient, to ensure fertilisation, just to touch with the same brush the anthers of one flower and then the stigma of another; but it must not be supposed that bees would thus produce a multitude of hybrids between distinct species; for if a plant's own pollen and that from another species are placed on the same stigma, the former is so prepotent that it invariably and completely destroys, as has been shown by Gärtner, the influence of the foreign pollen.

When the stamens of a flower suddenly spring towards the pistil, or slowly move one after the other towards it, the contrivance seems adapted solely to ensure self-fertilisation; and no doubt it is useful for this end: but the agency of insects is often required to cause the stamens to spring forward, as Kölreuter has shown to be the case with the barberry; and in this very genus, which seems to have a special contrivance for self-fertilisation, it is well known that, if closely-allied forms or varieties are planted near each other, it is hardly possible to raise pure seedlings, so largely do they naturally cross. In numerous other cases, far from self-fertilisation being favoured, there are special contrivances which effectually prevent the stigma receiving pollen from its own flower, as I could show from the works of Sprengel and others, as well as from my own observations: for instance, in Lobelia fulgens, there is a really beautiful and elaborate contrivance by which all the infinitely numerous pollen-granules are swept out of the conjoined anthers of each flower, before the stigma of that individual flower is ready to receive them; and as this flower is never visited, at least in my garden, by insects, it never sets a seed, though by placing pollen from one flower on the stigma of another, I raise plenty of seedlings. Another species of Lobelia, which is visited by bees, seeds freely in my garden. In very many other cases, though there is no special mechanical contrivance to prevent the stigma receiving pollen from the same flower, yet, as Sprengel, and more recently Hildebrand, and others, have shown, and as I can confirm, either the anthers burst before the stigma is ready for fertilisation, or the stigma is ready before the pollen of that flower is ready, so that these so-named dichogamous plants have in fact separated sexes, and must habitually be crossed. So it is with the reciprocally dimorphic and trimorphic plants previously alluded to. How strange are these facts! How strange that the pollen and stigmatic surface of the same flower, though placed so close together, as if for the very purpose of self-fertilisation, should be in so many cases mutually useless to each other? How simply are these facts explained on the view of an occasional cross with a distinct individual being advantageous or indispensable!

If several varieties of the cabbage, radish, onion, and of some other plants, be allowed to seed near each other, a large majority of the seedlings thus raised turn out, as I have found, mongrels: for instance, I raised 233 seedling cabbages from some plants of different varieties growing near each other, and of these only seventy-eight were true to their kind, and some even of these were not perfectly true. Yet the pistil of each cabbage-flower is surrounded not only by its own six stamens but by those of the many other flowers on the same plant; and the pollen of each flower readily gets on its own stigma without insect agency; for I have found that plants carefully protected from insects produce the full number of pods. How, then, comes it that such a vast number of the seedlings are mongrelized? It must arise from the pollen of a distinct *variety* having a prepotent effect over the flower's own pollen; and that this is part of the general law of good being derived from the intercrossing of distinct individuals of the same species. When distinct *species* are crossed the case is reversed, for a plant's own pollen is almost always prepotent over foreign pollen; but to this subject we shall return in a future chapter.

In the case of a large tree covered with innumerable flowers, it may be objected that pollen could seldom be carried from tree to tree, and at most only from flower to flower on the same tree; and flowers on the same tree can be considered as distinct individuals only in a limited sense. I believe this objection to be valid, but that nature has largely provided against it by giving to trees a strong tendency to bear flowers with separated sexes. When the sexes are separated, although the male and female flowers may be produced on the same tree, pollen must be regularly carried from flower to flower; and this will give a better chance of pollen being occasionally carried from tree to tree. That trees belonging to all orders have their sexes more often separated than other plants, I find to be the case in this country; and at my request Dr. Hooker tabulated the trees of New Zealand, and Dr. Asa Gray those of the United States, and the result was as I anticipated. On the other hand, Dr. Hooker informs me that the rule does not hold good in Australia: but if most of the Australian trees are dichogamous, the same result would follow as if they bore flowers with separated sexes. I have made these few remarks on trees simply to call attention to the subject.

Turning for a brief space to animals: various terrestrial species are hermaphrodites, such as the land Mollusca and earthworms; but these all pair. As yet I have not found a single terrestrial animal which can fertilise itself. This remarkable fact, which offers so strong a contrast with terrestrial plants, is intelligible on the view of an occasional cross being indispensable; for owing to the nature of the fertilising element there are no means, analogous to the action of insects and of the wind with plants, by which an occasional cross could be effected with terrestrial animals without the concurrence of two individuals. Of aquatic animals, there are many self-fertilising hermaphrodites; but here the currents of water offer an obvious means for an occasional cross. As in the case of flowers, I have as yet failed, after consultation with one of the highest authorities, namely, Professor Huxley, to discover a single hermaphrodite animal with the organs of reproduction so perfectly enclosed that access from without, and the occasional influence of a distinct individual, can be shown to be physically impossible. Cirripedes long appeared to me to present, under this point of view, a case of great difficulty; but I have been enabled, by a fortunate chance, to prove that two individuals, though both are self-fertilising hermaphrodites, do sometimes cross.

It must have struck most naturalists as a strange anomaly that, both with animals and plants, some species of the same family and even of the same genus, though agreeing closely with each other in their whole organisation, are hermaphrodites, and some unisexual. But if, in fact, all hermaphrodites do occasionally intercross, the difference between them and unisexual species is, as far as function is concerned, very small.

From these several considerations and from the many special facts which I have collected, but which I am unable here to give, it appears that with animals and plants an occasional intercross between distinct individuals is a very general, if not universal, law of nature.

CIRCUMSTANCES FAVOURABLE FOR THE PRODUCTION OF NEW FORMS THROUGH NATURAL SELECTION

This is an extremely intricate subject. A great amount of variability, under which term individual differences are always included, will evidently be favourable. A large number of individuals, by giving a better chance within any given period for the appearance of profitable variations, will compensate for a lesser amount of variability in each individual and is, I believe, a highly important element of success. Though Nature grants long periods of time for the work of natural selection, she does not grant an indefinite period; for as all organic beings are striving to seize on each place in the economy of nature, if any one species does not become modified and improved in a corresponding degree with its competitors, it will be exterminated. Unless favourable variations be inherited by some at least of the offspring, nothing can be effected by natural selection. The tendency to reversion may often check or prevent the work; but as this tendency has not prevented man from forming by selection numerous domestic races, why should it prevail against natural selection?

In the case of methodical selection, a breeder selects for some definite object, and if the individuals be allowed freely to intercross, his work will completely fail. But when many men, without intending to alter the breed, have a nearly common standard of perfection, and all try to procure and breed from the best animals, improvement surely but slowly follows from this unconscious process of selection, notwithstanding that there is no separation of selected individuals. Thus it will be under nature; for within a confined area, with some place in the natural polity not perfectly occupied, all the individuals varying in the right direction, though in different degrees, will tend to be preserved. But if the area be large, its several districts will almost certainly present different conditions of life; and then, if the same species undergoes modification in different districts, the newly-formed varieties will intercross on the confines of each. But we shall see in the sixth chapter that intermediate varieties, inhabiting intermediate districts, will in the long run generally be supplanted by one of the adjoining varieties. Intercrossing will chiefly affect those animals which unite for each birth and wander much, and which do not breed at a very quick rate. Hence with animals of this nature, for instance, birds, varieties will generally be confined to separated countries; and this I find to be the case. With hermaphrodite organisms which cross only occasionally, and likewise with animals which unite for each birth, but which wander little and can increase at a rapid rate, a new and improved variety might be quickly formed on any one spot, and might there maintain itself in a body and afterwards spread, so that the individuals of the new variety would chiefly cross together. On this principle, nurserymen always prefer saving seed from a large body of plants, as the chance of intercrossing is thus lessened.

Even with animals which unite for each birth, and which do not propagate rapidly, we must not assume that free intercrossing would always eliminate the effects of natural selection; for I can bring forward a considerable body of facts showing that within the same area, two varieties of the same animal may long remain distinct, from haunting different stations, from breeding at slightly different seasons, or from the individuals of each variety preferring to pair together.

PRODUCTION OF NEW FORMS

Intercrossing plays a very important part in nature by keeping
the individuals of the same species, or of the same variety, true and
uniform in character. It will obviously thus act far more efficiently
with those animals which unite for each birth; but, as already stated,
we have reason to believe that occasional intercrosses take place with
all animals and plants. Even if these take place only at long intervals
of time, the young thus produced will gain so much in vigour and
fertility over the offspring from long-continued self-fertilisation,
that they will have a better chance of surviving and propagating
their kind; and thus in the long run the influence of crosses, even
at rare intervals, will be great. With respect to organic beings extremely low in the scale, which do not propagate sexually, nor con-
jugate, and which cannot possibly intercross, uniformity of character
can be retained by them under the same conditions of life, only
through the principle of inheritance, and through natural selection
which will destroy any individuals departing from the proper type.
If the conditions of life change and the form undergoes modification,
uniformity of character can be given to the modified offspring, solely
by natural selection preserving similar favourable variations.

Isolation, also, is an important element in the modification of
species through natural selection. In a confined or isolated area, if
not very large, the organic and inorganic conditions of life will
generally be almost uniform; so that natural selection will tend to
modify all the varying individuals of the same species in the same
manner. Intercrossing with the inhabitants of the surrounding districts will, also, be thus prevented. Moritz Wagner has lately published an interesting essay on this subject, and has shown that the
service rendered by isolation in preventing crosses between newly-
formed varieties is probably greater even than I supposed. But from
reasons already assigned I can by no means agree with this naturalist,
that migration and isolation are necessary elements for the formation
of new species. The importance of isolation is likewise great in preventing, after any physical change in the conditions such as of climate, elevation of the land, etc., the immigration of better adapted
organisms; and thus new places in the natural economy of the district will be left open to be filled up by the modification of the old
inhabitants. Lastly, isolation will give time for a new variety to be

improved at a slow rate; and this may sometimes be of much importance. If, however, an isolated area be very small, either from being surrounded by barriers, or from having very peculiar physical conditions, the total number of the inhabitants will be small; and this will retard the production of new species through natural selection, by decreasing the chances of favourable variations arising.

The mere lapse of time by itself does nothing, either for or against natural selection. I state this because it has been erroneously asserted that the element of time has been assumed by me to play an all-important part in modifying species, as if all the forms of life were necessarily undergoing change through some innate law. Lapse of time is only so far important, and its importance in this respect is great, that it gives a better chance of beneficial variations arising and of their being selected, accumulated, and fixed. It likewise tends to increase the direct action of the physical conditions of life, in relation to the constitution of each organism.

If we turn to nature to test the truth of these remarks, and look at any small isolated area, such as an oceanic island, although the number of species inhabiting it is small, as we shall see in our chapter on Geographical Distribution; yet of these species a very large proportion are endemic,—that is, have been produced there and nowhere else in the world. Hence an oceanic island at first sight seems to have been highly favourable for the production of new species. But we may thus deceive ourselves, for to ascertain whether a small isolated area, or a large open area like a continent, has been most favourable for the production of new organic forms, we ought to make the comparison within equal times; and this we are incapable of doing.

Although isolation is of great importance in the production of new species, on the whole I am inclined to believe that largeness of area is still more important, especially for the production of species which shall prove capable of enduring for a long period, and of spreading widely. Throughout a great and open area, not only will there be a better chance of favourable variations, arising from the large number of individuals of the same species there supported, but the conditions of life are much more complex from the large number of already existing species; and if some of these many species become modified and improved, others will have to be improved in a corresponding degree, or they will be exterminated. Each new form, also, as soon as it has been much improved, will be able to spread over the open and continuous area, and will thus come into competition with many other forms. Moreover, great areas, though now continuous, will often, owing to former oscillations of level, have existed in a broken condition; so that the good effects of isolation will generally, to a certain extent, have concurred. Finally, I conclude that, although small isolated areas have been in some respects highly favourable for the production of new species, yet that the course of modification will generally have been more rapid on large areas; and what is more important, that the new forms produced on large areas, which already have been victorious over many competitors, will be those that will spread most widely, and will give rise to the greatest number of new varieties and species. They will thus play a more important part in the changing history of the organic world.

In accordance with this view, we can, perhaps, understand some facts which will be again alluded to in our chapter on Geographical Distribution; for instance, the fact of the productions of the smaller continent of Australia now yielding before those of the larger Europæo-Asiatic area. Thus, also, it is that continental productions have everywhere become so largely naturalised on islands. On a small island, the race for life will have been less severe, and there will have been less modification and less extermination. Hence, we can understand how it is that the flora of Madeira, according to Oswald Heer, resembles to a certain extent the extinct tertiary flora of Europe. All fresh-water basins, taken together, make a small area compared with that of the sea or of the land. Consequently, the competition between fresh-water productions will have been less severe than elsewhere; new forms will have been then more slowly produced, and old forms more slowly exterminated. And it is in fresh-water basins that we find seven genera of Ganoid fishes, remnants of a once preponderant order: and in fresh water we find some of the most anomalous forms now known in the world as the Ornithorhynchus and Lepidosiren, which, like fossils, connect to a certain extent orders at present widely sundered in the natural scale. These anomalous forms may be called living fossils; they have endured to the present day, from having inhabited a confined area, and from having been exposed to less varied, and therefore less severe, competition.

To sum up, as far as the extreme intricacy of the subject permits, the circumstances favourable and unfavourable for the production of new species through natural selection. I conclude that for terrestrial productions a large continental area, which has undergone many oscillations of level, will have been the most favourable for the production of many new forms of life, fitted to endure for a long time and to spread widely. Whilst the area existed as a continent, the inhabitants will have been numerous in individuals and kinds, and will have been subjected to severe competition. When converted by subsidence into large separate islands, there will still have existed many individuals of the same species on each island; intercrossing on the confines of the range of each new species will have been checked; after physical changes of any kind, immigration will have been prevented, so that new places in the polity of each island will have had to be filled up by the modification of the old inhabitants; and time will have been allowed for the varieties in each to become well modified and perfected. When, by renewed elevation, the islands were reconverted into a continental area, there will again have been very severe competition: the most favoured or improved varieties will have been enabled to spread: there will have been much extinction of the less improved forms, and the relative proportional numbers of the various inhabitants of the reunited continent will again have been changed; and again there will have been a fair field for natural selection to improve still further the inhabitants, and thus to produce new species.

That natural selection generally acts with extreme slowness I fully admit. It can act only when there are places in the natural polity of a district which can be better occupied by the modification of some of its existing inhabitants. The occurrence of such places will often depend on physical changes, which generally take place very slowly, and on the immigration of better adapted forms being prevented. As some few of the old inhabitants become modified, the mutual relations of others will often be disturbed; and this will create new places, ready to be filled up by better adapted forms; but all this will take place very slowly. Although all the individuals of the same species differ in some slight degree from each other, it would often be long before differences of the right nature in various parts of the organisation might occur. The result would often be greatly retarded by free intercrossing. Many will exclaim that these several causes are amply sufficient to neutralise the power of natural selection. I do not believe so. But I do believe that natural selection will generally act very slowly, only at long intervals of time, and only on a few of the inhabitants of the same region. I further believe that these slow, intermittent results accord well with what geology tells us of the rate and manner at which the inhabitants of the world have changed.

Slow though the process of selection may be, if feeble man can do much by artificial selection, I can see no limit to the amount of change, to the beauty and complexity of the co-adaptations between all organic beings, one with another and with their physical conditions of life, which may have been affected in the long course of time through nature's power of selection, that is by the survival of the fittest.

EXTINCTION CAUSED BY NATURAL SELECTION

This subject will be more fully discussed in our chapter on Geology; but it must here be alluded to from being intimately connected with natural selection. Natural selection acts solely through the preservation of variations in some way advantageous, which consequently endure. Owing to the high geometrical rate of increase of all organic beings, each area is already fully stocked with inhabitants; and it follows from this, that as the favoured forms increase in number, so, generally, will the less favoured decrease and become rare. Rarity, as geology tells us, is the precursor to extinction. We can see that any form which is represented by few individuals will run a good chance of utter extinction, during great fluctuations in the nature of the seasons, or from a temporary increase in the number of its enemies. But we may go further than this; for, as new forms are produced, unless we admit that specific forms can go on indefinitely increasing in number, many old forms must become extinct. That the number of specific forms has not indefinitely increased, geology plainly tells us; and we shall presently attempt to show why it is that the number of species throughout the world has not become immeasurably great.

We have seen that the species which are most numerous in individuals have the best chance of producing favourable variations within any given period. We have evidence of this, in the facts stated in the second chapter, showing that it is the common and diffused or dominant species which offer the greatest number of recorded varieties. Hence, rare species will be less quickly modified or improved within any given period; they will consequently be beaten in the race for life by the modified and improved descendants of the commoner species.

From these several considerations I think it inevitably follows, that as new species in the course of time are formed through natural selection, others will become rarer and rarer, and finally extinct. The forms which stand in closest competition with those undergoing modification and improvement, will naturally suffer most. And we have seen in the chapter on the Struggle for Existence, that it is the most closely-allied forms,—varieties of the same species, and species of the same genus or of related genera,—which, from having nearly the same structure, constitution, and habits, generally come into the severest competition with each other; consequently, each new variety or species, during the progress of its formation, will generally press hardest on its nearest kindred, and tend to exterminate them. We see the same process of extermination amongst our domesticated productions, through the selection of improved forms by man. Many curious instances could be given showing how quickly new breeds of cattle, sheep, and other animals, and varieties of flowers, take the place of older and inferior kinds. In Yorkshire, it is historically known that the ancient black cattle were displaced by the long-horns, and that these "were swept away by the shorthorns" (I quote the words of an agricultural writer) "as if by some murderous pestilence."

DIVERGENCE OF CHARACTER

The principle, which I have designated by this term, is of high importance, and explains, as I believe, several important facts. In the first place, varieties, even strongly marked ones, though having somewhat of the character of species—as is shown by the hopeless doubts in many cases how to rank them—yet certainly differ far less from each other than do good and distinct species. Nevertheless, according to my view, varieties are species in the process of formation, or are, as I have called them, incipient species. How, then, does the lesser difference between varieties become augmented into the greater difference between species? That this does habitually happen, we must infer from most of the innumerable species throughout nature presenting well-marked differences; whereas varieties, the supposed prototypes and parents of future well-marked species, present slight and ill-defined differences. Mere chance, as we may call it, might cause one variety to differ in some character from its parents, and the offspring of this variety again to differ from its parent in the very same character and in a greater degree; but this alone would never account for so habitual and large a degree of difference as that between the species of the same genus.

As has always been my practice, I have sought light on this head from our domestic productions. We shall here find something analogous. It will be admitted that the production of races so different as shorthorn and Hereford cattle, race and cart horses, the several breeds of pigeons, etc., could never have been effected by the mere chance accumulation of similar variations during many successive generations. In practice, a fancier is, for instance, struck by a pigeon having a slightly shorter beak; another fancier is struck by a pigeon having a rather longer beak; and on the acknowledged principle that "fanciers do not and will not admire a medium standard, but like extremes," they both go on (as has actually occurred with the sub-breeds of the tumbler pigeon) choosing and breeding from birds with longer and longer beaks, or with shorter and shorter beaks. Again, we may suppose that at an early period of history, the men of one nation or district required swifter horses, whilst those of another required stronger and bulkier horses. The early differences would be very slight; but, in the course of time, from the continued selection of swifter horses in the one case, and of stronger ones in the other, the differences would become greater, and would be noted as forming two sub-breeds. Ultimately, after the lapse of centuries, these sub-breeds would become converted into two well-established and distinct breeds. As the differences became greater, the inferior animals with intermediate characters, being neither very swift nor very strong, would not have been used for breeding, and will thus have tended to disappear. Here, then, we see in man's productions the action of what may be called the principle of divergence, causing differences, at first barely appreciable, steadily to increase, and the breeds to diverge in character, both from each other and from their common parent.

But how, it may be asked, can any analogous principle apply in nature? I believe it can and does apply most efficiently (though it was a long time before I saw how), from the simple circumstance that the more diversified the descendants from any one species become in structure, constitution, and habits, by so much will they be better enabled to seize on many and widely diversified places in the polity of nature, and so be enabled to increase in numbers.

We can clearly discern this in the case of animals with simple habits. Take the case of a carnivorous quadruped, of which the number that can be supported in any country has long ago arrived at its full average. If its natural power of increase be allowed to act, it can succeed in increasing (the country not undergoing any change in conditions) only by its varying descendants seizing on places at present occupied by other animals; some of them, for instance, being enabled to feed on new kinds of prey, either dead or alive; some inhabiting new stations, climbing trees, frequenting water, and some perhaps becoming less carnivorous. The more diversified in habits and structure the descendants of our carnivorous animals become the more places they will be enabled to occupy. What applies to one animal will apply throughout all time to all animals—that is, if they vary—for otherwise natural selection can effect nothing. So it will be with plants. It has been experimentally proved, that if a plot of ground be sown with one species of grass, and a similar plot be sown with several distinct genera of grasses, a greater number of plants and a greater weight of dry herbage can be raised in the latter than in the former case. The same has been found to hold good when one variety and several mixed varieties of wheat have been sown on equal spaces of ground. Hence, if any one species of grass were to go on varying, and the varieties were continually selected which differed from each other in the same manner, though in a very slight degree, as do the distinct species and genera of grasses, a greater number of individual plants of this species, including its modified descendants, would succeed in living on the same piece of ground. And we know that each species and each variety of grass is annually sowing almost countless seeds; and is thus striving, as it may be said, to the utmost to increase in number. Consequently, in the course of many thousand generations, the most distinct varieties of any one species of grass would have the best chance of succeeding and of increasing in numbers, and thus of supplanting the less distinct varieties; and varieties, when rendered very distinct from each other, take the rank of species.

The truth of the principle that the greatest amount of life can be supported by great diversification of structure, is seen under many natural circumstances. In an extremely small area, especially if freely open to immigration, and where the contest between individual and individual must be very severe, we always find great diversity in its inhabitants. For instance, I found that a piece of turf, three feet by four in size, which had been exposed for many years to exactly the same conditions, supported twenty species of plants, and these belonged to eighteen genera and to eight orders, which shows how much these plants differed from each other. So it is with the plants and insects on small and uniform islets: also in small ponds of fresh water. Farmers find that they can raise most food by a rotation of plants belonging to the most different orders; nature follows what may be called a simultaneous rotation. Most of the animals and plants which live close round any small piece of ground, could live on it (supposing its nature not to be in any way peculiar), and may be said to be striving to the utmost to live there; but, it is seen, that where they come into the closest competition, the advantages of diversification of structure, with the accompanying differences of habit and constitution, determine that the inhabitants, which thus jostle each other most closely, shall, as a general rule, belong to what we call different genera and orders.

The same principle is seen in the naturalisation of plants through man's agency in foreign lands. It might have been expected that the plants which would succeed in becoming naturalised in any land would generally have been closely allied to the indigenes; for these are commonly looked at as specially created and adapted for their own country. It might also, perhaps, have been expected that naturalised plants would have belonged to a few groups more especially adapted to certain stations in their new homes. But the case is very different; and Alph. de Candolle has well remarked, in his great and admirable work, that floras gain by naturalisation, proportionally with the number of the native genera and species, far more in new genera than in new species. To give a single instance: in the last edition of Dr. Asa Gray's 'Manual of the Flora of the Northern United States,' 260 naturalised plants are enumerated, and these belong to 162 genera. We thus see that these naturalised plants are of a highly diversified nature. They differ, moreover, to a large extent, from the indigenes, for out of the 162 naturalised genera, no less than 100 genera are not there indigenous, and thus a large proportional addition is made to the genera now living in the United States.

By considering the nature of the plants or animals which have in any country struggled successfully with the indigenes, and have there become naturalised, we may gain some crude idea in what manner some of the natives would have to be modified, in order to gain an advantage over their compatriots; and we may at least infer that diversification of structure, amounting to new generic differences, would be profitable to them.

The advantage of diversification of structure in the inhabitants of the same region is, in fact, the same as that of the physiological division of labor in the organs of the same individual body—a subject so well elucidated by Milne Edwards. No physiologist doubts that a stomach adapted to digest vegetable matter alone, or flesh alone, draws most nutriment from these substances. So in the general economy of any land, the more widely and perfectly the animals and plants are diversified for different habits of life, so will a greater number of individuals be capable of there supporting themselves. A set of animals, with their organisation but little diversified, could hardly compete with a set more perfectly diversified in structure. It may be doubted, for instance, whether the Australian marsupials, which are divided into groups differing but little from each other, and feebly representing, as Mr. Waterhouse and others have remarked, our carnivorous, ruminant, and rodent mammals, could successfully compete with these well-developed orders. In the Australian mammals, we see the process of diversification in an early and incomplete stage of development.

THE PROBABLE EFFECTS OF THE ACTION OF NATURAL SELECTION THROUGH DIVERGENCE OF CHARACTER AND EXTINCTION, ON THE DESCENDANTS OF A COMMON ANCESTOR

After the foregoing discussion, which has been much compressed, we may assume that the modified descendants of any one species will succeed so much the better as they become more diversified in structure, and are thus enabled to encroach on places occupied by other beings. Now let us see how this principle of benefit being derived from divergence of character, combined with the principles of natural selection and of extinction, tends to act.

The accompanying diagram will aid us in understanding this rather perplexing subject. Let A to L represent the species of a genus large in its own country; these species are supposed to resemble each other in unequal degrees, as is so generally the case in nature, and as is represented in the diagram by the letters standing at unequal distances. I have said a large genus, because, as we saw in the second chapter, on an average more species vary in large genera than in small genera; and the varying species of the large genera present a greater number of varieties. We have, also, seen that the species, which are the commonest and the most widely diffused, vary more than do the rare and restricted species. Let (A) be a common, widely-diffused, and varying species, belonging to a genus large in its own country. The branching and diverging dotted lines of unequal lengths proceeding from (A), may represent its varying offspring. The variations are supposed to be extremely slight, but of the most diversified nature; they are not supposed all to appear

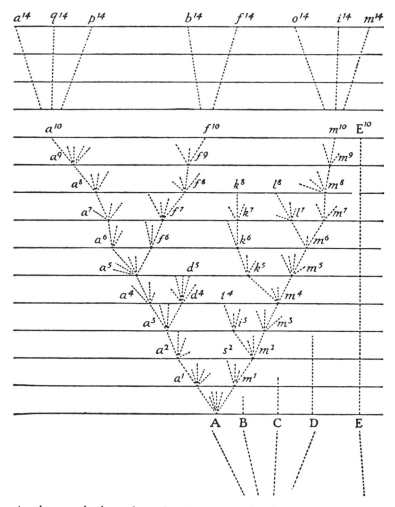

simultaneously, but often after long intervals of time; nor are they all supposed to endure for equal periods. Only those variations which are in some way profitable will be preserved or naturally selected. And here the importance of the principle of benefit derived from divergence of character comes in; for this will generally lead to the most different or divergent variations (represented by the outer

216

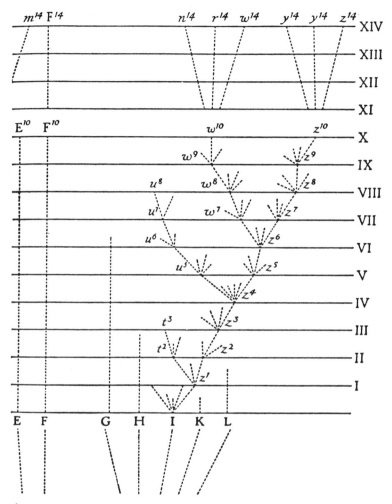

dotted lines) being preserved and accumulated by natural selection. When a dotted line reaches one of the horizontal lines, and is there marked by a small numbered letter, a sufficient amount of variation is supposed to have been accumulated to form it into a fairly well-marked variety, such as would be thought worthy of record in a systematic work.

common parent. If we suppose the amount of change between each horizontal line in our diagram to be excessively small, these three forms may still be only well-marked varieties; but we have only to suppose the steps in the process of modification to be more numerous or greater in amount, to convert these three forms into doubtful or at least into well-defined species. Thus the diagram illustrates the steps by which the small differences distinguishing varieties are increased into the larger differences distinguishing species. By continuing the same process for a greater number of generations (as shown in the diagram in a condensed and simplified manner), we get eight species, marked by the letters between a^{14} and m^{14}, all descended from (A). Thus, as I believe, species are multiplied, and genera are formed.

In a large genus it is probable that more than one species would vary. In the diagram I have assumed that a second species (I) has produced, by analogous steps, after ten thousand generations, either two well-marked varieties (w^{10} and z^{10}) or two species, according to the amount of change supposed to be represented between the horizontal lines. After fourteen thousand generations, six new species, marked by the letters n^{14} to z^{14}, are supposed to have been produced. In any genus, the species which are already very different in character from each other, will generally tend to produce the greatest number of modified descendants; for these will have the best chance of seizing on new and widely different places in the polity of nature: hence in the diagram I have chosen the extreme species (A), and the nearly extreme species (I), as those which have largely varied, and have given rise to new varieties and species. The other nine species (marked by capital letters) of our original genus, may for long but unequal periods continue to transmit unaltered descendants; and this is shown in the diagram by the dotted lines unequally prolonged upwards.

But during the process of modification, represented in the diagram, another of our principles, namely that of extinction, will have played an important part. As in each fully stocked country natural selection necessarily acts by the selected form having some advantage in the struggle for life over other forms, there will be a constant tendency in the improved descendants of any one species to supplant and exterminate in each stage of descent their predecessors and their original progenitor. For it should be remembered that the competition will generally be most severe between those forms which are most nearly related to each other in habits, constitution, and structure. Hence all the intermediate forms between the earlier and later states, that is between the less and more improved states of the same species, as well as the original parent-species itself, will generally tend to become extinct. So it probably will be with many whole collateral lines of descent which will be conquered by later and improved lines. If, however, the modified offspring of a species get into some distinct country, or become quickly adapted to some quite new station, in which offspring and progenitor do not come into competition, both may continue to exist.

If, then, our diagram be assumed to represent a considerable amount of modification, species (A) and all the earlier varieties will have become extinct, being replaced by eight new species (a^{14} to m^{14}); and species (I) will be replaced by six (n^{14} to z^{14}) new species.

But we may go further than this. The original species of our genus were supposed to resemble each other in unequal degrees, as is so generally the case in nature; species (A) being more nearly related to B, C, and D, than to the other species; and species (I) more to G, H, K, L, than to the others. These two species (A) and (I) were also supposed to be very common and widely diffused species, so that they must originally have had some advantage over most of the other species of the genus. Their modified descendants, fourteen in number at the fourteen-thousandth generation, will probably have inherited some of the same advantages; they have also been modified and improved in a diversified manner at each stage of descent, so as to have become adapted to many related places in the natural economy of their country. It seems, therefore, extremely probable that they will have taken the places of, and thus exterminated, not only their parents (A) and (I), but likewise some of the original species which were most nearly related to their parents. Hence very few of the original species will have transmitted offspring to the fourteen-thousandth generation. We may suppose that only one, (F), of the two species (E) and (F) which were least closely related to the other nine original species, has transmitted descendants to this late stage of descent.

The new species in our diagram, descended from the original eleven species, will now be fifteen in number. Owing to the divergent tendency of natural selection, the extreme amount of difference in character between species a^{14} and z^{14} will be much greater than that between the most distinct of the original eleven species. The new species, moreover, will be allied to each other in a widely different manner. Of the eight descendants from (A) the three marked a^{14}, q^{14}, p^{14}, will be nearly related from having recently branched off from a^{10}; b^{14}, and f^{14}, from having diverged at an earlier period from a^5, will be in some degree distinct from the three first-named species; and lastly, o^{14}, i^{14} and m^{14} will be nearly related one to the other, but, from having diverged at the first commencement of the process of modification, will be widely different from the other five species, and may constitute a sub-genus or a distinct genus.

The six descendants from (I) will form two sub-genera or genera. But as the original species (I) differed largely from (A), standing nearly at the extreme end of the original genus, the six descendants from (I) will, owing to inheritance alone, differ considerably from the eight descendants from (A); the two groups, moreover, are supposed to have gone on diverging in different directions. The intermediate species, also (and this is a very important consideration), which connected the original species (A) and (I), have all become, excepting (F), extinct, and have left no descendants. Hence the six new species descended from (I), and the eight descendants from (A), will have to be ranked as very distinct genera, or even as distinct sub-families.

Thus it is, as I believe, that two or more genera are produced by descent with modification, from two or more species of the same genus. And the two or more parent-species are supposed to be descended from some one species of an earlier genus. In our diagram, this is indicated by the broken lines, beneath the capital letters, converging in sub-branches downwards towards a single point; this point represents a species, the supposed progenitor of our several sub-genera and genera.

It is worth while to reflect for a moment on the character of the new species F^{14}, which is supposed not to have diverged much in character, but to have retained the form of (F), either unaltered or altered only in a slight degree. In this case, its affinities to the other fourteen new species will be of a curious and circuitous nature. Being descended from a form which stood between the parent-species (A) and (I), now supposed to be extinct and unknown, it will be in some degree intermediate in character between the two groups descended from these two species. But as these two groups have gone on diverging in character from the type of their parents, the new species (F^{14}) will not be directly intermediate between them, but rather between types of the two groups; and every naturalist will be able to call such cases before his mind.

In the diagram, each horizontal line has hitherto been supposed to represent a thousand generations, but each may represent a million or more generations; it may also represent a section of the successive strata of the earth's crust including extinct remains. We shall, when we come to our chapter on Geology, have to refer again to this subject, and I think we shall then see that the diagram throws light on the affinities of extinct beings, which, though generally belonging to the same orders, families, or genera, with those now living, yet are often, in some degree, intermediate in character between existing groups; and we can understand this fact, for the extinct species lived at various remote epochs when the branching lines of descent had diverged less.

I see no reason to limit the process of modification, as now explained, to the formation of genera alone. If, in the diagram, we suppose the amount of change represented by each successive group of diverging dotted lines to be great, the forms marked a^{14} to p^{14}, those marked b^{14} and f^{14}, and those marked o^{14} to m^{14}, will form three very distinct genera. We shall also have two very distinct genera descended from (I), differing widely from the descendants of (A). Those two groups of genera will thus form two distinct families, or orders, according to the amount of divergent modification supposed to be represented in the diagram. And the two new families, or orders, are descended from two species of the original genus, and these are supposed to be descended from some still more ancient and unknown form.

We have seen that in each country it is the species belonging to the larger genera which oftenest present varieties or incipient species. This, indeed, might have been expected; for, as natural selection acts through one form having some advantage over other forms in the struggle for existence, it will chiefly act on those which already have some advantage; and the largeness of any group shows that its species have inherited from a common ancestor some advantage in common. Hence, the struggle for the production of new and modified descendants will mainly lie between the larger groups which are all trying to increase in number. One large group will slowly conquer another large group, reduce its numbers, and thus lessen its chance of further variation and improvement. Within the same large group, the later and more highly perfected sub-groups, from branching out and seizing on many new places in the polity of Nature, will constantly tend to supplant and destroy the earlier and less improved sub-groups. Small and broken groups and sub-groups will finally disappear. Looking to the future, we can predict that the groups of organic beings which are now large and triumphant, and which are least broken up, that is, which have as yet suffered least extinction, will, for a long period, continue to increase. But which groups will ultimately prevail, no man can predict; for we know that many groups, formerly most extensively developed, have now become extinct. Looking still more remotely to the future, we may predict that, owing to the continued and steady increase of the larger groups, a multitude of smaller groups will become utterly extinct, and leave no modified descendants; and consequently, that, of the species living at any one period extremely few will transmit descendants to a remote futurity. I shall have to return to this subject in the chapter on Classification, but I may add that as, according to this view, extremely few of the more ancient species have transmitted descendants to the present day, and, as all the descendants of the same species form a class, we can understand how it is that there exist so few classes in each main division of the animal and vegetable kingdoms. Although few of the most ancient species have left modified descendants, yet, at remote geological periods, the earth may have been almost as well peopled with species of many genera, families, orders, and classes, as at the present time.

EFFECTS OF NATURAL SELECTION

ON THE DEGREE TO WHICH ORGANISATION TENDS TO ADVANCE

Natural Selection acts exclusively by the preservation and accumulation of variations, which are beneficial under the organic and inorganic conditions to which each creature is exposed at all periods of life. The ultimate result is that each creature tends to become more and more improved in relation to its conditions. This improvement inevitably leads to the gradual advancement of the organisation of the greater number of living beings throughout the world. But here we enter on a very intricate subject, for naturalists have not defined to each other's satisfaction what is meant by an advance in organisation. Amongst the vertebrata the degree of intellect and an approach in structure to man clearly come into play. It might be thought that the amount of change which the various parts and organs pass through in their development from the embryo to maturity would suffice as a standard of comparison; but there are cases, as with certain parasitic crustaceans, in which several parts of the structure become less perfect, so that the mature animal cannot be called higher than its larva. Von Baer's standard seems the most widely applicable and the best, namely, the amount of differentiation of the parts of the same organic being, in the adult state, as I should be inclined to add, and their specialisation for different functions; or, as Milne Edwards would express it, the completeness of the division of physiological labour. But we shall see how obscure this subject is if we look, for instance, to fishes, amongst which some naturalists rank those as highest which, like the sharks, approach nearest to amphibians; whilst other naturalists range the common bony or teleostean fishes as the highest, inasmuch as they are most strictly fish-like, and differ most from the other vertebrate classes. We see still more plainly the obscurity of the subject by turning to plants, amongst which the standard of intellect is of course quite excluded; and here some botanists rank those plants as highest which have every organ, as sepals, petals, stamens, and pistils, fully developed in each flower; whereas other botanists, probably with more truth, look at the plants which have their several organs much modified and reduced in number, as the highest.

If we take as the standard of high organisation, the amount of differentiation and specialisation of the several organs in each being when adult (and this will include the advancement of the brain for intellectual purposes), natural selection clearly leads towards this standard: for all physiologists admit that the specialisation of organs, inasmuch as in this state they perform their functions better, is an advantage to each being; and hence the accumulation of variations tending towards specialisation is within the scope of natural selection. On the other hand, we can see, bearing in mind that all organic beings are striving to increase at a high ratio and to seize on every unoccupied or less well occupied place in the economy of nature, that it is quite possible for natural selection gradually to fit a being to a situation in which several organs would be superfluous or useless: in such cases there would be retrogression in the scale of organisation. Whether organisation on the whole has actually advanced from the remotest geological periods to the present day will be more conveniently discussed in our chapter on Geological Succession.

But it may be objected that if all organic beings thus tend to rise in the scale, how is it that throughout the world a multitude of the lowest forms still exist; and how is it that in each great class some forms are far more highly developed than others? Why have not the more highly developed forms everywhere supplanted and exterminated the lower? Lamarck, who believed in an innate and inevitable tendency towards perfection in all organic beings, seems to have felt this difficulty so strongly, that he was led to suppose that new and simple forms are continually being produced by spontaneous generation. Science has not as yet proved the truth of this belief, whatever the future may reveal. On our theory the continued existence of lowly organisms offers no difficulty; for natural selection or the survival of the fittest, does not necessarily include progressive development—it only takes advantage of such variations as arise and are beneficial to each creature under its complex relations of life. And it may be asked what advantage, as far as we can see, would it be to an infusorian animalcule—to an intestinal worm—or even to an earthworm, to be highly organised. If it were no advantage, these forms would be left, by natural selection, unimproved or but little improved, and might remain for indefinite ages in their present lowly condition. And geology tells us that some of the lowest forms, as the infusoria and rhizopods, have remained for an enormous period in nearly their present state. But to suppose that most of the many now existing low forms have not in the least advanced since the first dawn of life would be extremely rash; for every naturalist who has dissected some of the beings now ranked as very low in the scale, must have been struck with their really wondrous and beautiful organisation.

Nearly the same remarks are applicable if we look to the different grades of organisation within the same great group; for instance, in the Vertebrata, to the co-existence of mammals and fish—amongst Mammalia, to the co-existence of man and the ornithorhynchus—amongst fishes, to the co-existence of the shark and the lancelet (Amphioxus), which latter fish in the extreme simplicity of its structure approaches the invertebrate classes. But mammals and fish hardly come into competition with each other; the advancement of the whole class of mammals, or of certain members in this class, to the highest grade, would not lead to their taking the place of fishes. Physiologists believe that the brain must be bathed by warm blood to be highly active, and this requires aërial respiration; so that warm-blooded mammals when inhabiting the water lie under a disadvantage in having to come continually to the surface to breathe. With fishes, members of the shark family would not tend to supplant the lancelet; for the lancelet, as I hear from Fritz Müller, has as sole companion and competitor on the barren sandy shore of South Brazil, an anomalous annelid. The three lowest orders of mammals, namely, marsupials, edentata, and rodents, co-exist in South America in the same region with numerous monkeys, and probably interfere little with each other. Although organisation, on the whole, may have advanced and be still advancing throughout the world, yet the scale will always present many degrees of perfection; for the high advancement of certain whole classes, or of certain members of each class, does not at all necessarily lead to the extinction of those groups with which they do not enter into close competition. In some cases, as we shall hereafter see, lowly organised forms appear to have been preserved to the present day, from inhabiting confined or peculiar stations, where they have been subjected to less severe competition, and where their scanty numbers have retarded the chance of favorable variations arising.

Finally, I believe that many lowly organised forms now exist throughout the world, from various causes. In some cases variations or individual differences of a favorable nature may never have arisen for natural selection to act on and accumulate. In no case, probably, has time sufficed for the utmost possible amount of development. In some few cases there has been what we must call retrogression of organisation. But the main cause lies in the fact that under very simple conditions of life a high organisation would be of no service, —possibly would be of actual disservice, as being of a more delicate nature, and more liable to be put out of order and injured.

Looking to the first dawn of life, when all organic beings, as we may believe, presented the simplest structure, how, it has been asked, could the first steps in the advancement or differentiation of parts have arisen? Mr. Herbert Spencer would probably answer, that, as soon as simple unicellular organism came by growth or division to be compounded of several cells, or became attached to any supporting surface, his law "that homologous units of any order became differentiated in proportion as their relations to incident forces became different" would come into action. But as we have no facts to guide us, speculation on the subject is almost useless. It is, however, an error to suppose that there would be no struggle for existence, and, consequently, no natural selection, until many forms had been produced: variations in a single species inhabiting an isolated station might be beneficial, and thus the whole mass of individuals might be modified, or two distinct forms might arise. But, as I remarked towards the close of the Introduction, no one ought to feel surprise at much remaining as yet unexplained on the origin of species, if we make due allowance for our profound ignorance on the mutual relations of the inhabitants of the world at the present time, and still more so during past ages.

CONVERGENCE OF CHARACTER

Mr. H. C. Watson thinks that I have overrated the importance of divergence of character (in which, however, he apparently believes), and that convergence, as it may be called, has likewise played a part. If two species, belonging to two distinct though allied genera, had both produced a large number of new and divergent forms, it is conceivable that these might approach each other so closely that they would have all to be classed under the same genus; and thus the descendants of two distinct genera would converge into one. But it would in most cases be extremely rash to attribute to convergence a close and general similarity of structure in the modified descendants of widely distinct forms. The shape of a crystal is determined solely by the molecular forces, and it is not surprising that dissimilar substances should sometimes assume the same form; but with organic beings we should bear in mind that the form of each depends on an infinitude of complex relations, namely on the variations which have arisen, these being due to causes far too intricate to be followed out,— on the nature of the variations which have been preserved or selected, and this depends on the surrounding physical conditions, and in a still higher degree on the surrounding organisms with which each being has come into competition,—and lastly, on inheritance (in itself a fluctuating element) from innumerable progenitors, all of which have had their forms determined through equally complex relations. It is incredible that the descendants of two organisms, which had originally differed in a marked manner, should ever afterwards converge so closely as to lead to a near approach to identity throughout their whole organisation. If this had occurred, we should meet with the same form, independently of genetic connection, recurring in widely separated geological formations; and the balance of evidence is opposed to any such an admission.

Mr. Watson has also objected that the continued action of natural selection, together with divergence of character, would tend to make an indefinite number of specific forms. As far as mere inorganic conditions are concerned, it seems probable that a sufficient number of species would soon become adapted to all considerable diversities of heat, moisture, etc.; but I fully admit that the mutual relations of organic beings are more important; and as the number of species in any country goes on increasing, the organic conditions of life must become more and more complex. Consequently there seems at first sight no limit to the amount of profitable diversification of structure, and therefore no limit to the number of species which might be produced. We do not know that even the most prolific area is fully stocked with specific forms: at the Cape of Good Hope and in Australia, which support such an astonishing number of species, many European plants have become naturalised. But geology shows us, that from an early part of the tertiary period the number of species of shells, and that from the middle part of this same period the number of mammals, has not greatly or at all increased. What then checks an indefinite increase in the number of species? The amount of life (I do not mean the number of specific forms) supported on an area must have a limit, depending so largely as it does on physical conditions; therefore, if an area be inhabited by very many species, each or nearly each species will be represented by few individuals; and such species will be liable to extermination from accidental fluctuations in the nature of the seasons or in the number of their enemies. The process of extermination in such cases would be rapid, whereas the production of new species must always be slow. Imagine the extreme case of as many species as individuals in England, and the first severe winter or very dry summer would exterminate thousands on thousands of species. Rare species, and each species will become rare if the number of species in any country becomes indefinitely increased, will, on the principle often explained, present within a given period few favorable variations; consequently, the process of giving birth to new specific forms would thus be retarded. When any species becomes very rare, close interbreeding will help to exterminate it; authors have thought that this comes into play in accounting for the deterioration of the aurochs in Lithuania, of red deer in Scotland, and of bears in Norway, etc. Lastly, and this I am inclined to think is the most important element, a dominant species, which has already beaten many competitors in its own home, will tend to spread and supplant many others. Alph. de Candolle has shown that those species which spread widely, tend generally to spread *very* widely; consequently, they will tend to supplant and exterminate several species in several areas, and thus check the inordinate increase of specific forms throughout the world. Dr. Hooker has recently shown that in the southeast corner of Australia, where, apparently, there are many invaders from different quarters of the globe, the endemic Australian species have been greatly reduced in number. How much weight to attribute to these several considerations I will not pretend to say; but conjointly they must limit in each country the tendency to an indefinite augmentation of specific forms.

SUMMARY OF CHAPTER

If under changing conditions of life organic beings present individual differences in almost every part of their structure, and this cannot be disputed; if there be, owing to their geometrical rate of increase, a severe struggle for life at some age, season, or year, and this certainly cannot be disputed; then, considering the infinite complexity of the relations of all organic beings to each other and to their conditions of life, causing an infinite diversity in structure, constitution, and habits, to be advantageous to them, it would be a most extraordinary fact if no variations had ever occurred useful to each being's own welfare, in the same manner as so many variations have occurred useful to man. But if variations useful to any organic being ever do occur, assuredly individuals thus characterised will have the best chance of being preserved in the struggle for life; and from the strong principle of inheritance, these will tend to produce offspring similarly characterised. This principle of preservation, or the survival of the fittest, I have called Natural Selection. It leads to the improvement of each creature in relation to its organic and inorganic conditions of life; and consequently, in most cases, to what must be regarded as an advance in organisation. Nevertheless, low and simple forms will long endure if well fitted for their simple conditions of life.

Natural selection, on the principle of qualities being inherited at corresponding ages, can modify the egg, seed, or young, as easily as the adult. Amongst many animals, sexual selection will have given its aid to ordinary selection, by assuring to the most vigorous and best adapted males the greatest number of offspring. Sexual selection will also give characters useful to the males alone, in their struggles or rivalry with other males; and these characters will be transmitted to one sex or to both sexes, according to the form of inheritance which prevails.

Whether natural selection has really thus acted in adapting the various forms of life to their several conditions and stations, must be judged by the general tenor and balance of evidence given in the following chapters. But we have already seen how it entails extinction; and how largely extinction has acted in the world's history, geology plainly declares. Natural selection, also, leads to divergence of character; for the more organic beings diverge in structure, habits, and constitution, by so much the more can a large number be supported on the area,—of which we see proof by looking to the inhabitants of any small spot, and to the productions naturalised in foreign lands. Therefore, during the modification of the descendants of any one species, and during the incessant struggle of all species to increase in numbers, the more diversified the descendants become, the better will be their chance of success in the battle for life. Thus the small differences distinguishing varieties of the same species, steadily tend to increase, till they equal the greater differences between species of the same genus, or even of distinct genera.

We have seen that it is the common, the widely diffused and widely ranging species, belonging to the larger genera within each class, which vary most; and these tend to transmit to their modified offspring that superiority which now makes them dominant in their own countries. Natural selection, as has just been remarked, leads to divergence of character and to much extinction of the less improved and intermediate forms of life. On these principles, the nature of the affinities, and the generally well-defined distinctions between the innumerable organic beings in each class throughout the world, may be explained. It is a truly wonderful fact—the wonder of which we are apt to overlook from familiarity—that all animals and all plants throughout all time and space should be related to each other in groups, subordinate to groups, in the manner which we everywhere behold—namely, varieties of the same specie most closely related, species of the same genus less closely and unequally related, forming sections and sub-genera, species of distinct genera much less closely related, and genera related in different degrees, forming subfamilies, families, orders, sub-classes, and classes. The several subordinate groups in any class cannot be ranked in a single file, but seem clustered round points, and these round other points, and so on in almost endless cycles. If species had been independently created, no explanation would have been possible of this kind of classification;

but it is explained through inheritance and the complex action of natural selection, entailing extinction and divergence of character, as we have seen illustrated in the diagram.

The affinities of all the beings of the same class have sometimes been represented by a great tree. I believe this simile largely speaks the truth. The green and budding twigs may represent existing species; and those produced during former years may represent the long succession of extinct species. At each period of growth all the growing twigs have tried to branch out on all sides, and to overtop and kill the surrounding twigs and branches, in the same manner as species and groups of species have at all times overmastered other species in the great battle for life. The limbs divided into great branches, and these into lesser and lesser branches, were themselves once, when the tree was young, budding twigs; and this connection of the former and present buds, by ramifying branches, may well represent the classification of all extinct and living species in groups subordinate to groups. Of the many twigs which flourished when the tree was a mere bush, only two or three, now grown into great branches, yet survive and bear the other branches; so with the species which lived during long-past geological periods, very few have left living and modified descendants. From the first growth of the tree, many a limb and branch has decayed and dropped off; and these fallen branches of various sizes may represent those whole orders, families, and genera which have now no living representatives, and which are known to us only in a fossil state. As we here and there see a thin straggling branch springing from a fork low down in a tree, and which by some chance has been favoured and is still alive on its summit, so we occasionally see an animal like the Ornithorhynchus or Lepidosiren, which in some small degree connects by its affinities two large branches of life, and which has apparently been saved from fatal competition by having inhabited a protected station. As buds give rise by growth to fresh buds, and these, if vigorous, branch out and overtop on all sides many a feebler branch, so by generation I believe it has been with the great Tree of Life, which fills with its dead and broken branches the crust of the earth, and covers the surface with its ever-branching and beautiful ramifications.

231

CHAPTER XV

RECAPITULATION AND CONCLUSION

Recapitulation of the objections to the theory of Natural Selection—
Recapitulation of the general and special circumstances in its favour
—Causes of the general belief in the immutability of species—How
far the theory of Natural Selection may be extended—Effects of its
adoption on the study of Natural History—Concluding remarks.

AS this whole volume is one long argument, it may be convenient to the reader to have the leading facts and inferences
briefly recapitulated.

That many and serious objections may be advanced against the theory of descent with modification through Variation and Natural Selection, I do not deny. I have endeavoured to give to them their full
force. Nothing at first can appear more difficult to believe than that
the more complex organs and instincts have been perfected, not by
means superior to, though analogous with, human reason, but by the
accumulation of innumerable slight variations, each good for the individual possessor. Nevertheless, this difficulty, though appearing to
our imagination insuperably great, cannot be considered real if we
admit the following propositions, namely, that all parts of the organisation and instincts offer, at least, individual differences—that there
is a struggle for existence leading to the preservation of profitable
deviations of structure or instinct—and, lastly, that gradations in the
state of perfection of each organ may have existed, each good of its
kind. The truth of these propositions cannot, I think, be disputed.

It is, no doubt, extremely difficult even to conjecture by what gradations many structures have been perfected, more especially amongst
broken and failing groups of organic beings, which have suffered
much extinction; but we see so many strange gradations in nature,
that we ought to be extremely cautious in saying that any organ or
instinct, or any whole structure, could not have arrived at its present
state by many graduated steps. There are, it must be admitted, cases
of special difficulty opposed to the theory of Natural Selection; and

one of the most curious of these is the existence in the same community of two or three defined castes of workers or sterile female ants; but I have attempted to show how these difficulties can be mastered.

With respect to the almost universal sterility of species when first crossed, which forms so remarkable a contrast with the almost universal fertility of varieties when crossed, I must refer the reader to the recapitulation of the facts given at the end of the ninth chapter, which seem to me conclusively to show that this sterility is no more a special endowment than is the incapacity of two distinct kinds of trees to be grafted together; but that it is incidental on differences confined to the reproductive systems of the intercrossed species. We see the truth of this conclusion in the vast difference in the results of crossing the same two species reciprocally,—that is, when one species is first used as the father and then as the mother. Analogy from the consideration of dimorphic and trimorphic plants clearly leads to the same conclusion, for when the forms are illegitimately united, they yield few or no seed, and their offspring are more or less sterile: and these forms belong to the same undoubted species, and differ from each other in no respect except in their reproductive organs and functions.

Although the fertility of varieties when intercrossed and of their mongrel offspring has been asserted by so many authors to be universal, this cannot be considered as quite correct after the facts given on the high authority of Gärtner and Kölreuter. Most of the varieties which have been experimented on have been produced under domestication; and as domestication (I do not mean mere confinement) almost certainly tends to eliminate that sterility which, judging from analogy, would have affected the parent-species if intercrossed. we ought not to expect that domestication would likewise induce sterility in their modified descendants when crossed. This elimination of sterility apparently follows from the same cause which allows our domestic animals to breed freely under diversified circumstances: and this again apparently follows from their having been gradually accustomed to frequent changes in their conditions of life.

A double and parallel series of facts seems to throw much light on the sterility of species, when first crossed, and of their hybrid offspring. On the one side, there is good reason to believe that slight changes in the conditions of life give vigour and fertility to all organic beings. We know also that a cross between the distinct individuals of the same variety, and between distinct varieties, increases the number of their offspring, and certainly gives to them increased size and vigour. This is chiefly owing to the forms which are crossed having been exposed to somewhat different conditions of life; for I have ascertained by a laborious series of experiments that if all the individuals of the same variety be subjected during several generations to the same conditions, the good derived from crossing is often much diminished or wholly disappears. This is one side of the case. On the other side, we know that species which have long been exposed to nearly uniform conditions, when they are subjected under confinement to new and greatly changed conditions, either perish, or if they survive, are rendered sterile, though retaining perfect health. This does not occur, or only in a very slight degree, with our domesticated productions, which have long been exposed to fluctuating conditions. Hence when we find that hybrids produced by a cross between two distinct species are few in number, owing to their perishing soon after conception or at a very early age, or if surviving that they are rendered more or less sterile, it seems highly probable that this result is due to their having been in fact subjected to a great change in their conditions of life, from being compounded of two distinct organisations. He who will explain in a definite manner why, for instance, an elephant or a fox will not breed under confinement in its native country, whilst the domestic pig or dog will breed freely under the most diversified conditions, will at the same time be able to give a definite answer to the question why two distinct species, when crossed, as well as their hybrid offspring, are generally rendered more or less sterile, whilst two domesticated varieties when crossed and their mongrel offspring are perfectly fertile.

Turning to geographical distribution, the difficulties encountered on the theory of descent with modification are serious enough. All the individuals of the same species, and all the species of the same genus, or even higher group, are descended from common parents; and therefore, in however distant and isolated parts of the world they may now be found, they must in the course of successive generations have travelled from some one point to all the others. We are often wholly unable even to conjecture how this could have been effected. Yet, as we have reason to believe that some species have retained the same specific form for very long periods of time, immensely long as measured by years, too much stress ought not to be laid on the occasional wide diffusion of the same species; for during very long periods there will always have been a good chance for wide migration by many means. A broken or interrupted range may often be accounted for by the extinction of the species in the intermediate regions. It cannot be denied that we are as yet very ignorant as to the full extent of the various climatal and geographical changes which have affected the earth during modern periods; and such changes will often have facilitated migration. As an example, I have attempted to show how potent has been the influence of the Glacial period on the distribution of the same and of allied species throughout the world. We are as yet profoundly ignorant of the many occasional means of transport. With respect to distinct species of the same genus inhabiting distant and isolated regions, as the process of modification has necessarily been slow, all the means of migration will have been possible during a very long period; and consequently the difficulty of the wide diffusion of the species of the same genus is in some degree lessened.

As according to the theory of natural selection an interminable number of intermediate forms must have existed, linking together all the species in each group by gradations as fine as are our existing varieties, it may be asked, Why do we not see these linking forms all around us? Why are not all organic beings blended together in an inextricable chaos? With respect to existing forms, we should remember that we have no right to expect (excepting in rare cases) to discover *directly* connecting links between them, but only between each and some extinct and supplanted form. Even on a wide area, which has during a long period remained continuous, and of which the climatic and other conditions of life change insensibly in proceeding from a district occupied by one species into another district occupied by a closely allied species, we have no just right to expect often to find intermediate varieties in the intermediate zones. For we have reason to believe that only a few species of a genus ever undergo change; the other species becoming utterly extinct and leaving no modified progeny. Of the species which do change, only a few within the same country change at the same time; and all modifications are slowly effected. I have also shown that the intermediate varieties which probably at first existed in the intermediate zones, would be liable to be supplanted by the allied forms on either hand; for the latter, from existing in greater numbers, would generally be modified and improved at a quicker rate than the intermediate varieties, which existed in lesser numbers; so that the intermediate varieties would, in the long run, be supplanted and exterminated.

On this doctrine of the extermination of an infinitude of connecting links, between the living and extinct inhabitants of the world, and at each successive period between the extinct and still older species, why is not every geological formation charged with such links? Why does not every collection of fossil remains afford plain evidence of the gradation and mutation of the forms of life? Although geological research has undoubtedly revealed the former existence of many links, bringing numerous forms of life much closer together, it does not yield the infinitely many fine gradations between past and present species required on the theory; and this is the most obvious of the many objections which may be urged against it. Why, again, do whole groups of allied species appear, though this appearance is often false, to have come in suddenly on the successive geological stages? Although we now know that organic beings appeared on this globe, at a period incalculably remote, long before the lowest bed of the Cambrian system was deposited, why do we not find beneath this system great piles of strata stored with the remains of the progenitors of the Cambrian fossils? For on the theory, such strata must somewhere have been deposited at these ancient and utterly unknown epochs of the world's history.

I can answer these questions and objections only on the supposition that the geological record is far more imperfect than most geologists believe. The number of specimens in all our museums is absolutely as nothing compared with the countless generations of countless species which have certainly existed. The parent-form of any two or more species would not be in all its characters directly intermediate between its modified offspring, any more than the rock pigeon is directly intermediate in crop and tail between its descendants, the pouter and fantail pigeons. We should not be able to recognise a species as the parent of another and modified species, if we were to examine the two ever so closely, unless we possessed most of the intermediate links; and owing to the imperfection of the geological record, we have no just right to expect to find so many links. If two or three, or even more linking forms were discovered, they would simply be ranked by many naturalists as so many new species, more especially if found in different geological sub-stages, let their differences be ever so slight. Numerous existing doubtful forms could be named which are probably varieties; but who will pretend that in future ages so many fossil links will be discovered, that naturalists will be able to decide whether or not these doubtful forms ought to be called varieties? Only a small portion of the world has been geologically explored. Only organic beings of certain classes can be preserved in a fossil condition, at least in any great number. Many species when once formed never undergo any further change but become extinct without leaving modified descendants; and the periods, during which species have undergone modification, though long as measured by years, have probably been short in comparison with the periods during which they retained the same form. It is the dominant and widely ranging species which vary most frequently and vary most, and varieties are often at first local—both causes rendering the discovery of intermediate links in any one formation less likely. Local varieties will not spread into other and distant regions until they are considerably modified and improved; and when they have spread, and are discovered in a geological formation, they appear as if suddenly created there, and will be simply classed as new species. Most formations have been intermittent in their accumulation; and their duration has probably been shorter than the average duration of specific forms. Successive formations are in most cases separated from each other by blank intervals of time of great length; for fossiliferous formations thick enough to resist future degradation can as a general rule be accumulated only where much sediment is deposited on the subsiding bed of the sea. During the alternate periods of elevation and of stationary level the record will generally be blank. During these latter periods there will probably be more variability in the forms of life; during periods of subsidence, more extinction.

With respect to the absence of strata rich in fossils beneath the Cambrian formation, I can recur only to the hypothesis given in the tenth chapter; namely, that though our continents and oceans have endured for an enormous period in nearly their present relative positions, we have no reason to assume that this has always been the case; consequently formations much older than any now known may lie buried beneath the great oceans. With respect to the lapse of time not having been sufficient since our planet was consolidated for the assumed amount of organic change, and this objection, as urged by Sir William Thompson, is probably one of the gravest as yet advanced, I can only say, firstly, that we do not know at what rate species change as measured by years, and secondly, that many philosophers are not as yet willing to admit that we know enough of the constitution of the universe and of the interior of our globe to speculate with safety on its past duration.

That the geological record is imperfect, all will admit; but that it is imperfect to the degree required by our theory, few will be inclined to admit. If we look to long enough intervals of time, geology plainly declares that species have all changed; and they have changed in the manner required by the theory, for they have changed slowly and in a graduated manner. We clearly see this in the fossil remains from consecutive formations invariably being much more closely related to each other, than are the fossils from widely separated formations.

Such is the sum of the several chief objections and difficulties which may be justly urged against the theory; and I have now briefly recapitulated the answers and explanations which, as far as I can see, may be given. I have felt these difficulties far too heavily during many years to doubt their weight. But it deserves especial notice that the more important objections relate to questions on which we are confessedly ignorant; nor do we know how ignorant we are. We do not know all the possible transitional gradations between the simplest and the most perfect organs; it cannot be pretended that we know all the varied means of Distribution during the long lapse of years, or that we know how imperfect is the Geological Record. Serious as these several objections are, in my judgment they are by no means sufficient to overthrow the theory of descent with subse-quent modification.

Now let us turn to the other side of the argument. Under domesti-cation we see much variability, caused, or at least excited, by changed conditions of life; but often in so obscure a manner, that we are tempted to consider the variations as spontaneous. Variability is governed by many complex laws, by correlated growth, compensa-tion, the increased use and disuse of parts, and the definite action of the surrounding conditions. There is much difficulty in ascertain-ing how largely our domestic productions have been modified; but we may safely infer that the amount has been large, and that modi-fication can be inherited for long periods. As long as the conditions of life remain the same, we have reason to believe that a modification, which has already been inherited for many generations, may continue to be inherited for an almost infinite number of generations. On the other hand, we have evidence that variability when it has once come into play, does not cease under domestication for a very long period; nor do we know that it ever ceases, for new varieties are still occa sionally produced by our oldest domesticated productions.

Variability is not actually caused by man; he only unintentionally exposes organic beings to new conditions of life, and then nature acts on the organisation and causes it to vary. But man can and does select the variations given to him by nature, and thus accumulates them in any desired manner. He thus adapts animals and plants for his own benefit or pleasure. He may do this methodically, or he may do it unconsciously by preserving the individuals most useful or pleasing to him without any intention of altering the breed. It is certain that he can largely influence the character of a breed by selecting, in each successive generation, individual differences so slight as to be inappreciable except by an educated eye. This uncon-scious process of selection has been the great agency in the formation of the most distinct and useful domestic breeds. That many breeds produced by man have to a large extent the character of natural species, is shown by the inextricable doubts whether many of them are varieties or aboriginally distinct species.

There is no reason why the principles which have acted so efficiently under domestication should not have acted under nature. In the survival of favoured individuals and races, during the constantly-recurrent Struggle for Existence, we see a powerful and ever-acting form of Selection. The struggle for existence inevitably follows from the high geometrical ratio of increase which is common to all organic beings. This high rate of increase is proved by calculation,—by the rapid increase of many animals and plants during a succession of peculiar seasons, and when naturalised in new countries. More individuals are born than can possibly survive. A grain in the balance may determine which individuals shall live, and which shall die,—which variety or species shall increase in number, and which shall decrease, or finally become extinct. As the individuals of the same species come in all respects into the closest competition with each other, the struggle will generally be most severe between them; it will be almost equally severe between the varieties of the same species, and next in severity between the species of the same genus. On the other hand the struggle will often be severe between beings remote in the scale of nature. The slightest advantage in certain individuals, at any age or during any season, over those with which they come into competition, or better adaptation in however slight a degree to the surrounding physical conditions, will, in the long run, turn the balance.

With animals having separated sexes, there will be in most cases a struggle between the males for the possession of the females. The most vigorous males, or those which have most successfully struggled with their conditions of life, will generally leave most progeny. But success will often depend on the males having special weapons, or means of defence, or charms; and a slight advantage will lead to victory.

As geology plainly proclaims that each land has undergone great physical changes, we might have expected to find that organic beings have varied under nature, in the same way as they have varied under domestication. And if there has been any variability under nature, it would be an unaccountable fact if natural selection had not come into play. It has often been asserted, but the assertion is incapable of proof, that the amount of variation under nature is a strictly limited quantity. Man, though acting on external characters alone and often capriciously, can produce within a short period a great result by adding up mere individual differences in his domestic productions; and every one admits that species present individual differences. But, besides such differences, all naturalists admit that natural varieties exist, which are considered sufficiently distinct to be worthy of record in systematic works. No one has drawn any clear distinction between individual differences and slight varieties; or between more plainly marked varieties and sub-species and species. On separate continents, and on different parts of the same continent when divided by barriers of any kind, and on outlying islands, what a multitude of forms exist, which some experienced naturalists rank as varieties, others as geographical races or sub-species, and others as distinct, though closely allied species!

If then, animals and plants do vary, let it be ever so slightly or slowly, why should not variations or individual differences, which are in any way beneficial, be preserved and accumulated through natural selection, or the survival of the fittest? If man can by patience select variations useful to him, why, under changing and complex conditions of life, should not variations useful to nature's living products often arise, and be preserved or selected? What limit can be put to this power, acting during long ages and rigidly scrutinising the whole constitution, structure, and habits of each creature, —favouring the good and rejecting the bad? I can see no limit to this power, in slowly and beautifully adapting each form to the most complex relations of life. The theory of natural selection, even if we look no farther than this, seems to be in the highest degree probable. I have already recapitulated, as fairly as I could, the opposed difficulties and objections: now let us turn to the special facts and arguments in favour of the theory.

On the view that species are only strongly marked and permanent varieties, and that each species first existed as a variety, we can see why it is that no line of demarcation can be drawn between species, commonly supposed to have been produced by special acts of creation, and varieties which are acknowledged to have been produced by secondary laws. On this same view we can understand how it is that in a region where many species of a genus have been produced, and where they now flourish, these same species should present many varieties; for where the manufactory of species has been active, we might expect, as a general rule, to find it still in action; and this is the case if varieties be incipient species. Moreover, the species of the larger genera, which afford the greater number of varieties or incipient species, retain to a certain degree the character of varieties; for they differ from each other by a less amount of difference than do the species of smaller genera. The closely allied species also of the larger genera apparently have restricted ranges, and in their affinities they are clustered in little groups round other species—in both respects resembling varieties. These are strange relations on the view that each species was independently created, but are intelligible if each existed first as a variety.

As each species tends by its geometrical rate of reproduction to increase inordinately in number; and as the modified descendants of each species will be enabled to increase by as much as they become more diversified in habits and structure, so as to be able to seize on many and widely different places in the economy of nature, there will be a constant tendency in natural selection to preserve the most divergent offspring of any one species. Hence, during a long-continued course of modification, the slight differences characteristic of varieties of the same species, tend to be augmented into the greater differences characteristic of the species of the same genus. New and improved varieties will inevitably supplant and exterminate the older, less improved, and intermediate varieties; and thus species are rendered to a large extent defined and distinct objects. Dominant species belonging to the larger groups within each class tend to give birth to new and dominant forms; so that each large group tends to become still larger, and at the same time more divergent in character. But as all groups cannot thus go on increasing in size, for the world would not hold them, the more dominant groups beat the less dominant. This tendency in the large groups to go on increasing in size and diverging in character, together with the inevitable contingency of much extinction, explains the arrangement of all the forms of life in groups subordinate to groups, all within a few great classes, which has prevailed throughout all time. This grand fact of the grouping of all organic beings under what is called the Natural System, is utterly inexplicable on the theory of creation.

As Natural Selection acts solely by accumulating slight, successive, favourable variations, it can produce no great or sudden modifications; it can act only by short and slow steps. Hence, the canon of "Natura non facit saltum," which every fresh addition to our knowledge tends to confirm, is on this theory intelligible. We can see why throughout nature the same general end is gained by an almost infinite diversity of means, for every peculiarity when once acquired is long inherited, and structures already modified in many different ways have to be adapted for the same general purpose. We can, in short, see why nature is prodigal in variety, though niggard in innovation. But why this should be a law of nature if each species has been independently created no man can explain.

Many other facts are, as it seems to me, explicable on this theory. How strange it is that a bird, under the form of a woodpecker, should prey on insects on the ground; that upland geese which rarely or never swim, should possess webbed feet; that a thrush-like bird should dive and feed on sub-aquatic insects; and that a petrel should have the habits and structure fitting it for the life of an auk! and so in endless other cases. But on the view of each species constantly trying to increase in number, with natural selection always ready to adapt the slowly varying descendants of each to any unoccupied or ill-occupied place in nature, these facts cease to be strange, or might even have been anticipated.

We can to a certain extent understand how it is that there is so much beauty throughout nature; for this may be largely attributed to the agency of selection. That beauty, according to our sense of it, is not universal, must be admitted by every one who will look at some venomous snakes, at some fishes, and at certain hideous bats with a distorted resemblance to the human face. Sexual selection has given the most brilliant colours, elegant patterns, and other ornaments to the males, and sometimes to both sexes, of many birds, butterflies, and other animals. With birds it has often rendered the voice of the male musical to the female, as well as to our ears. Flowers and fruit have been rendered conspicuous by brilliant colours in contrast with the green foliage, in order that the flowers may be easily seen, visited, and fertilised by insects, and the seeds disseminated by birds. How it comes that certain colours, sounds, and forms should give pleasure to man and the lower animals,—that is, how the sense of beauty in its simplest form was first acquired,— we do not know any more than how certain odours and flavours were first rendered agreeable.

As Natural Selection acts by competition, it adapts and improves the inhabitants of each country only in relation to their co-inhabitants; so that we need feel no surprise at the species of any one country, although on the ordinary view supposed to have been created and specially adapted for that country, being beaten and supplanted by the naturalised productions from another land. Nor ought we to marvel if all the contrivances in nature be not, as far as we can judge, absolutely perfect, as in the case even of the human eye; or if some of them be abhorrent to our ideas of fitness. We need not marvel at the sting of the bee, when used against an enemy, causing the bee's own death; at drones being produced in such great numbers for one single act, and being then slaughtered by their sterile sisters; at the astonishing waste of pollen by our fir trees; at the instinctive hatred of the queen bee for her own fertile daughters; at ichneumonidæ feeding within the living bodies of caterpillars; or at other such cases. The wonder indeed is, on the theory of natural selection, that more cases of the want of absolute perfection have not been detected.

The complex and little known laws governing the production of varieties are the same, as far as we can judge, with the laws which have governed the production of distinct species. In both case physical conditions seem to have produced some direct and definite effect, but how much we cannot say. Thus, when varieties enter an new station, they occasionally assume some of the characters proper to the species of that station. With both varieties and species, use and disuse seem to have produced a considerable effect; for it is impossible to resist this conclusion when we look, for instance, a the loggerheaded duck, which has wings incapable of flight, in nearly the same condition as in the domestic duck; or when we loo at the burrowing tucu tucu, which is occasionally blind, and then certain moles, which are habitually blind and have their eyes covered with skin; or when we look at the blind animals inhabiting the dark caves of America and Europe. With varieties and species, correlated variation seems to have played an important part, so that when one part has been modified other parts have been necessarily modified. With both varieties and species, reversions to long-lost characters occasionally occur. How inexplicable on the theory of creation is the occasional appearance of stripes on the shoulders and legs of the several species of the horse-genus and of their hybrids! How simply is this fact explained if we believe that these species are all descended from a striped progenitor, in the same manner as the several domestic breeds of the pigeon are descended from the blue and barred rock pigeon!

On the ordinary view of each species having been independently created, why should specific characters, or those by which the species of the same genus differ from each other, be more variable than generic characters in which they all agree? Why, for instance, should the colour of a flower be more likely to vary in any one species of a genus, if the other species possess differently coloured flowers, than if all possessed the same coloured flowers? If species are only well-marked varieties, of which the characters have become in a high degree permanent, we can understand this fact; for they have already varied since they branched off from a common progenitor in certain characters, by which they have come to be specifically distinct from each other; therefore these same characters would be more likely again to vary than the generic characters which have been inherited without change for an immense period. It is inexplicable on the theory of creation why a part developed in a very unusual manner in one species alone of a genus, and therefore, as we may naturally infer, of great importance to that species, should be eminently liable to variation; but, on our view, this part has undergone, since the several species branched off from a common progenitor, an unusual amount of variability and modification, and therefore we might expect the part generally to be still variable. But a part may be developed in the most unusual manner, like the wing of a bat, and yet not be more variable than any other structure, if the part be common to many subordinate forms, that is, if it has been inherited for a very long period; for in this case it will have been rendered constant by long-continued natural selection.

Glancing at instincts, marvellous as some are, they offer no greater difficulty than do corporeal structures on the theory of the natural selection of successive, slight, but profitable modifications. We can thus understand why nature moves by graduated steps in endowing different animals of the same class with their several instincts. I have attempted to show how much light the principle of gradation throws on the admirable architectural powers of the hive bee. Habit no doubt often comes into play in modifying instincts; but it certainly is not indispensable, as we see in the case of neuter insects, which leave no progeny to inherit the effects of long-continued habit. On the view of all the species of the same genus having descended from a common parent, and having inherited much in common, we can understand how it is that allied species, when placed under widely different conditions of life, yet follow nearly the same instincts; why the thrushes of tropical and temperate South America, for instance, line their nests with mud like our British species. On the view of instincts having been slowly acquired through natural selection, we need not marvel at some instincts being not perfect and liable to mistakes, and at many instincts causing other animals to suffer.

If species be only well-marked and permanent varieties, we can at once see why their crossed offspring should follow the same complex laws in their degrees and kinds of resemblance to their parents,—in being absorbed into each other by successive crosses, and in other such points,—as do the crossed offspring of acknowledged varieties. This similarity would be a strange fact, if species had been independently created and varieties had been produced through secondary laws.

If we admit that the geological record is imperfect to an extreme degree, then the facts, which the record does give, strongly support the theory of descent with modification. New species have come on the stage slowly and at successive intervals; and the amount of change, after equal intervals of time, is widely different in different groups. The extinction of species and of whole groups of species which has played so conspicuous a part in the history of the organ-

world, almost inevitably follows from the principle of natural selection; for old forms are supplanted by new and improved forms. Neither single species nor groups of species reappear when the chain of ordinary generation is once broken. The gradual diffusion of dominant forms, with the slow modification of their descendants, causes the forms of life, after long intervals of time, to appear as if they had changed simultaneously throughout the world. The fact of the fossil remains of each formation being in some degree intermediate in character between the fossils in the formations above and below, is simply explained by their intermediate position in the chain of descent. The grand fact that all extinct beings can be classed with all recent beings, naturally follows from the living and the extinct being the offspring of common parents. As species have generally diverged in character during their long course of descent and modification, we can understand why it is that the more ancient forms, or early progenitors of each group, so often occupy a position in some degree intermediate between existing groups. Recent forms are generally looked upon as being, on the whole, higher in the scale of organisation than ancient forms; and they must be higher, in so far as the later and more improved forms have conquered the older and less improved forms in the struggle for life; they have also generally had their organs more specialised for different functions. This fact is perfectly compatible with numerous beings still retaining simple and but little improved structures, fitted for simple conditions of life; it is likewise compatible with some forms having retrograded in organisation, by having become at each stage of descent better fitted for new and degraded habits of life. Lastly, the wonderful law of the long endurance of allied forms on the same continent,—of marsupials in Australia, of edentata in America, and other such cases,—is intelligible, for within the same country the existing and the extinct will be closely allied by descent.

Looking to geographical distribution, if we admit that there has been during the long course of ages much migration from one part of the world to another, owing to former climatal and geographical changes and to the many occasional and unknown means of dispersal, then we can understand, on the theory of descent with modification, most of the great leading facts in Distribution. We can see why there should be so striking a parallelism in the distribution of organic beings throughout space, and in their geological succession throughout time; for in both cases the beings have been connected by the bond of ordinary generation, and the means of modification have been the same. We see the full meaning of the wonderful fact, which has struck every traveller, namely, that on the same continent, under the most diverse conditions, under heat and cold, on mountain and lowland, on deserts and marshes, most of the inhabitants within each great class are plainly related; for they are the descendants of the same progenitors and early colonists. On this same principle of former migration, combined in most cases with modification, we can understand, by the aid of the Glacial period, the identity of some few plants, and the close alliance of many others, on the most distant mountains, and in the northern and southern temperate zones; and likewise the close alliance of some of the inhabitants of the sea in the northern and southern temperate latitudes, though separated by the whole intertropical ocean. Although two countries may present physical conditions as closely similar as the same species ever require, we need feel no surprise at their inhabitants being widely different, if they have been for a long period completely sundered from each other; for as the relation of organism to organism is the most important of all relations, and as the two countries will have received colonists at various periods and in different proportions, from some other country or from each other, the course of modification in the two areas will inevitably have been different.

On this view of migration, with subsequent modification, we see why oceanic islands are inhabited by only few species, but of these why many are peculiar or endemic forms. We clearly see why species belonging to those groups of animals which cannot cross wide spaces of the ocean, as frogs and terrestrial mammals, do no inhabit oceanic islands; and why, on the other hand, new and peculiar species of bats, animals which can traverse the ocean, are often found on islands far distant from any continent. Such cases as the presence of peculiar species of bats on oceanic islands and the absence of all other terrestrial mammals, are facts utterly inexplicable on the theory of independent acts of creation.

The existence of closely allied or representative species in any two areas, implies, on the theory of descent with modification, that the same parent-forms formerly inhabited both areas: and we almost invariably find that wherever many closely allied species inhabit two areas, some identical species are still common to both. Wherever many closely allied yet distinct species occur, doubtful forms and varieties belonging to the same groups likewise occur. It is a rule of high generality that the inhabitants of each area are related to the inhabitants of the nearest source whence immigrants might have derived. We see this in the striking relation of nearly all the plants and animals of the Galapagos archipelago, of Juan Fernandez, and of the other American islands, to the plants and animals of the neighbouring American mainland; and of those of the Cape de Verde archipelago, and of the other African islands to the African mainland. It must be admitted that these facts receive no explanation on the theory of creation.

The fact, as we have seen, that all past and present organic beings can be arranged within a few great classes, in groups subordinate to groups, and with the extinct groups often falling in between the recent groups, is intelligible on the theory of natural selection with its contingencies of extinction and divergence of character. On these same principles we see how it is, that the mutual affinities of the forms within each class are so complex and circuitous. We see why certain characters are far more serviceable than others for classification; why adaptive characters, though of paramount importance to the beings, are of hardly any importance in classification; why characters derived from rudimentary parts, though of no service to the beings, are often of high classificatory value; and why embryological characters are often the most valuable of all. The real affinities of all organic beings, in contradistinction to their adaptive resemblances, are due to inheritance or community of descent. The Natural System is a genealogical arrangement, with the acquired grades of difference, marked by the terms, varieties, species, genera, families, etc.; and we have to discover the lines of descent by the most permanent characters whatever they may be and of however slight vital importance.

The similar framework of bones in the hand of a man, wing of a bat, fin of a porpoise, and leg of the horse,—the same number of vertebræ forming the neck of the giraffe and of the elephant, and innumerable other such facts, at once explain themselves on the theory of descent with slow and slight successive modifications. The similarity of pattern in the wing and in the leg of a bat, though used for such different purpose,—in the jaws and legs of a crab,—in the petals, stamens, and pistils of a flower, is likewise, to a large extent, intelligible on the view of the gradual modification of parts or organs, which were aboriginally alike in an early progenitor in each of these classes. On the principle of successive variations not always supervening at an early age, and being inherited at a corresponding not early period of life, we clearly see why the embryos of mammals, birds, reptiles, and fishes should be so closely similar, and so unlike the adult forms. We may cease marvelling at the embryo of an air-breathing mammal or bird having branchial slits and arteries running in loops, like those of a fish which has to breathe the air dissolved in water by the aid of well-developed branchiæ.

Disuse, aided sometimes by natural selection, will often have reduced organs when rendered useless under changed habits or conditions of life; and we can understand on this view the meaning of rudimentary organs. But disuse and selection will generally act on each creature, when it has come to maturity and has to play its full part in the struggle for existence, and will thus have little power on an organ during early life; hence the organ will not be reduced or rendered rudimentary at this early age. The calf, for instance, has inherited teeth, which never cut through the gums of the upper jaw, from an early progenitor having well-developed teeth; and we may believe, that the teeth in the mature animal were formerly reduced by disuse, owing to the tongue and palate, or lips, having become excellently fitted through natural selection to browse without their aid; whereas in the calf, the teeth have been left unaffected, and on the principle of inheritance at corresponding ages have been inherited from a remote period to the present day. On the view of each organism with all its separate parts having been specially created, how utterly inexplicable is it that organs bearing the plain stamp of inutility, such as the teeth in the embryonic calf or the shrivelled wings under the soldered wing-covers of many beetles, should so frequently occur. Nature may be said to have taken pains to reveal her scheme of modification, by means of rudimentary organs, of embryological and homologous structures, but we are too blind to understand her meaning.

I have now recapitulated the facts and considerations which have thoroughly convinced me that species have been modified, during a long course of descent. This has been effected chiefly through the natural selection of numerous successive, slight, favourable variations; aided in an important manner by the inherited effects of the use and disuse of parts; and in an unimportant manner, that is in relation to adaptive structures, whether past or present, by the direct action of external conditions, and by variations which seem to us in our ignorance to arise spontaneously. It appears that I formerly underrated the frequency and value of these latter forms of variation, as leading to permanent modifications of structure independently of natural selection. But as my conclusions have lately been much misrepresented, and it has been stated that I attribute the modification of species exclusively to natural selection, I may be permitted to remark that in the first edition of this work, and subsequently, I placed in a most conspicuous position—namely, at the close of the Introduction—the following words: "I am convinced that natural selection has been the main but not the exclusive means of modification." This has been of no avail. Great is the power of steady misrepresentation; but the history of science shows that fortunately this power does not long endure.

It can hardly be supposed that a false theory would explain, in so satisfactory a manner as does the theory of natural selection, the several large classes of facts above specified. It has recently been objected that this is an unsafe method of arguing; but it is a method used in judging of the common events of life, and has often been used by the greatest natural philosophers. The undulatory theory of light has thus been arrived at; and the belief in the revolution of the earth on its own axis was until lately supported by hardly any direct evidence. It is no valid objection that science as yet throws no light on the far higher problem of the essence or origin of life. Who can explain what is the essence of the attraction of gravity? No one now objects to following out the results consequent on this unknown element of attraction; notwithstanding that Leibnitz formerly accused Newton of introducing "occult qualities and miracles into philosophy."

I see no good reason why the views given in this volume should shock the religious feelings of any one. It is satisfactory, as showing how transient such impressions are, to remember that the greatest discovery ever made by man, namely, the law of the attraction of gravity, was also attacked by Leibnitz, "as subversive of natural, and inferentially of revealed, religion." A celebrated author and divine has written to me that "he has gradually learnt to see that it is just as noble a conception of the Deity to believe that He created a few original forms capable of self-development into other and needful forms, as to believe that He required a fresh act of creation to supply the voids caused by the action of His laws."

Why, it may be asked, until recently did nearly all the most eminent living naturalists and geologists disbelieve in the mutability of species. It cannot be asserted that organic beings in a state of nature are subject to no variation; it cannot be proved that the amount of variation in the course of long ages is a limited quantity; no clear distinction has been, or can be, drawn between species and well-marked varieties. It cannot be maintained that species when intercrossed are invariably sterile, and varieties invariably fertile; or that sterility is a special endowment and sign of creation. The belief that species were immutable productions was almost unavoidable as long as the history of the world was thought to be of short duration; and now that we have acquired some idea of the lapse of time, we are too apt to assume, without proof, that the geological record is so perfect that it would have afforded us plain evidence of the mutation of species, if they had undergone mutation.

But the chief cause of our natural unwillingness to admit that one species has given birth to other and distinct species, is that we are always slow in admitting great changes of which we do not see the steps. The difficulty is the same as that felt by so many geologists when Lyell first insisted that long lines of inland cliffs had been formed, and great valleys excavated, by the agencies which we see still at work. The mind cannot possibly grasp the full meaning of the term of even a million years; it cannot add up and perceive the full effects of many slight variations, accumulated during an almost infinite number of generations.

Although I am fully convinced of the truth of the views given in this volume under the form of an abstract, I by no means expect to convince experienced naturalists whose minds are stocked with a multitude of facts all viewed, during a long course of years, from a point of view directly opposite to mine. It is so easy to hide our ignorance under such expressions as the "plan of creation," "unity of design," etc., and to think that we give an explanation when we only restate a fact. Any one whose disposition leads him to attach more weight to unexplained difficulties than to the explanation of a certain number of facts will certainly reject the theory. A few naturalists, endowed with much flexibility of mind, and who have already begun to doubt the immutability of species, may be influenced by this volume; but I look with confidence to the future, to young and rising naturalists, who will be able to view both sides of the question with impartiality. Whoever is led to believe that species are mutable will do good service by conscientiously expressing his conviction; for thus only can the load of prejudice by which this subject is overwhelmed be removed.

Several eminent naturalists have of late published their belief that a multitude of reputed species in each genus are not real species; but that other species are real, that is, have been independently created. This seems to me a strange conclusion to arrive at. They admit that a multitude of forms, which till lately they themselves thought were special creations, and which are still thus looked at by the majority of naturalists, and which consequently have all the external characteristic features of true species,—they admit that these have been produced by variation, but they refuse to extend the same view to other and slightly different forms. Nevertheless they do not pretend that they can define, or even conjecture, which are the created forms of life, and which are those produced by secondary laws. They admit variation as a *vera causa* in one case, they arbitrarily reject it in another, without assigning any distinction in the two cases. The day will come when this will be given as a curious illustration of the blindness of preconceived opinion. These authors seem no more startled at a miraculous act of creation than at an ordinary birth. But do they really believe that at innumerable periods in the earth's history certain elemental atoms have been commanded suddenly to flash into living tissues? Do they believe that at each supposed act of creation one individual or many were produced? Were all the infinitely numerous kinds of animals and plants created as eggs or seed, or as full grown? and in the case of mammals, were they created bearing the false marks of nourishment from the mother's womb? Undoubtedly some of these same questions cannot be answered by those who believe in the appearance or creation of only a few forms of life, or of some one form alone. It has been maintained by several authors that it is as easy to believe in the creation of a million beings as of one; but Maupertuis' philosophical axiom "of least action" leads the mind more willingly to admit the smaller number; and certainly we ought not to believe that innumerable beings within each great class have been created with plain, but deceptive, marks of descent from a single parent.

As a record of a former state of things, I have retained in the foregoing paragraphs, and elsewhere, several sentences which imply that naturalists believe in the separate creation of each species; and I have been much censured for having thus expressed myself. But undoubtedly this was the general belief when the first edition of the present work appeared. I formerly spoke to very many naturalists on the subject of evolution, and never once met with any sympathetic agreement. It is probable that some did then believe in evolution, but they were either silent, or expressed themselves so ambiguously that it was not easy to understand their meaning. Now, things are wholly changed, and almost every naturalist admits the great principle of evolution. There are, however, some who still think that species have suddenly given birth, through quite unexplained means, to new and totally different forms: but, as I have attempted to show, weighty evidence can be opposed to the admission of great and abrupt modifications. Under a scientific point of view, and as leading to further investigation, but little advantage is gained by believing that new forms are suddenly developed in an inexplicable manner from old and widely different forms, over the old belief in the creation of species from the dust of the earth.

It may be asked how far I extend the doctrine of the modification of species. The question is difficult to answer, because the more distinct the forms are which we consider, by so much the arguments in favour of community of descent become fewer in number and less in force. But some arguments of the greatest weight extend very far. All the members of whole classes are connected together by a chain of affinities, and all can be classed on the same principle, in groups subordinate to groups. Fossil remains sometimes tend to fill up very wide intervals between existing orders.

Organs in a rudimentary condition plainly show that an early progenitor had the organ in a fully developed condition; and this in some cases implies an enormous amount of modification in the descendants. Throughout whole classes various structures are formed on the same pattern, and at a very early age the embryos closely resemble each other. Therefore I cannot doubt that the theory of descent with modification embraces all the members of the same great class or kingdom. I believe that animals are descended from at most only four or five progenitors, and plants from an equal or lesser number.

Analogy would lead me one step farther, namely, to the belief that all animals and plants are descended from some one prototype. But analogy may be a deceitful guide. Nevertheless all living things have much in common, in their chemical composition, their cellular structure, their laws of growth, and their liability to injurious influences. We see this even in so trifling a fact as that the same poison often similarly affects plants and animals; or that the poison secreted by the gallfly produces monstrous growths on the wild rose or oak tree. With all organic beings, excepting perhaps some of the very lowest, sexual reproduction seems to be essentially similar. With all, as far as is at present known, the germinal vesicle is the same; so that all organisms start from a common origin. If we look even to the two main divisions—namely, to the animal and vegetable kingdoms—certain low forms are so far intermediate in character that naturalists have disputed to which kingdom they should be referred. As Professor Asa Gray has remarked, "the spores and other reproductive bodies of many of the lower algæ may claim to have first a characteristically animal, and then an unequivocal vegetable, existence." Therefore, on the principle of natural selection with divergence of character, it does not seem incredible that, from some such low and intermediate form, both animals and plants may have been developed; and, if we admit this, we must likewise admit that all the organic beings which have ever lived on this earth may be descended from some one primordial form. But this inference is chiefly grounded on analogy, and it is immaterial whether or not it be accepted. No doubt it is possible, as Mr. G. H. Lewes has urged, that at the first commencement of life many different forms were evolved; but if so, we may conclude that only a very few have left modified descendants. For, as I have recently remarked in regard to the members of each great kingdom, such as the Vertebrata, Articulata, etc., we have distinct evidence in their embryological, homologous, and rudimentary structures, that within each kingdom all the members are descended from a single progenitor.

When the views advanced by me in this volume, and by Mr. Wallace, or when analogous views on the origin of species are generally admitted, we can dimly foresee that there will be a considerable revolution in natural history. Systematists will be able to pursue their labours as at present; but they will not be incessantly haunted by the shadowy doubt whether this or that form be a true species. This, I feel sure and I speak after experience, will be no slight relief. The endless disputes whether or not some fifty species of British brambles are good species will cease. Systematists will have only to decide (not that this will be easy) whether any form be sufficiently constant and distinct from other forms, to be capable of definition; and if definable, whether the differences be sufficiently important to deserve a specific name. This latter point will become a far more essential consideration than it is at present; for differences, however slight, between any two forms, if not blended by intermediate gradations, are looked at by most naturalists as sufficient to raise both forms to the rank of species.

Hereafter we shall be compelled to acknowledge that the only distinction between species and well-marked varieties is, that the latter are known, or believed, to be connected at the present day by intermediate gradations whereas species were formerly thus connected. Hence, without rejecting the consideration of the present existence of intermediate gradations between any two forms, we shall be led to weigh more carefully and to value higher the actual amount of difference between them. It is quite possible that forms now generally acknowledged to be merely varieties may hereafter be thought worthy of specific names; and in this case scientific and common language will come into accordance. In short, we shall have to treat species in the same manner as those naturalists treat genera, who admit that genera are merely artificial combinations made for convenience. This may not be a cheering prospect; but we shall at least be freed from the vain search for the undiscovered and undiscoverable essence of the term species.

The other and more general departments of natural history will rise greatly in interest. The terms used by naturalists, of affinity, relationship, community of type, paternity, morphology, adaptive characters, rudimentary and aborted organs, etc., will cease to be metaphorical, and will have a plain signification. When we no longer look at an organic being as a savage looks at a ship, as something wholly beyond his comprehension; when we regard every production of nature as one which has had a long history; when we contemplate every complex structure and instinct as the summing up of many contrivances, each useful to the possessor, in the same way as any great mechanical invention is the summing up of the labour, the experience, the reason, and even the blunders of numerous workmen; when we thus view each organic being, how far more interesting—I speak from experience—does the study of natural history become!

A grand and almost untrodden field of inquiry will be opened, on the causes and laws of variation, on correlation, on the effects of use and disuse, on the direct action of external conditions, and so forth. The study of domestic productions will rise immensely in value. A new variety raised by man will be a more important and interesting subject for study than one more species added to the infinitude of already recorded species. Our classifications will come to be, as far as they can be so made, genealogies; and will then truly give what may be called the plan of creation. The rules for classifying will no doubt become simpler when we have a definite object in view. We possess no pedigrees or armorial bearings; and we have to discover and trace the many diverging lines of descent in our natural genealogies, by characters of any kind which have long been inherited. Rudimentary organs will speak infallibly with respect to the nature of long-lost structures. Species and groups of species which are called aberrant, and which may fancifully be called living fossils, will aid us in forming a picture of the ancient forms of life. Embryology will often reveal to us the structure, in some degree obscured, of the prototypes of each great class.

When we can feel assured that all the individuals of the same species, and all the closely allied species of most genera, have, within a not very remote period descended from one parent, and have migrated from some one birth-place; and when we better know the many means of migration, then, by the light which geology now throws, and will continue to throw, on former changes of climate and of the level of the land, we shall surely be enabled to trace in an admirable manner the former migrations of the inhabitants of the whole world. Even at present, by comparing the differences between the inhabitants of the sea on the opposite sides of a continent, and the nature of the various inhabitants on that continent in relation to their apparent means of immigration, some light can be thrown on ancient geography.

The noble science of Geology loses glory from the extreme imperfection of the record. The crust of the earth with its imbedded remains must not be looked at as a well-filled museum, but as a poor collection made at hazard and at rare intervals. The accumulation of each great fossiliferous formation will be recognised as having depended on an unusual concurrence of favourable circumstances, and the blank intervals between the successive stages as having been of vast duration. But we shall be able to gauge with some security the duration of these intervals by a comparison of the preceding and succeeding organic forms. We must be cautious in attempting to correlate as strictly contemporaneous two formations, which do not include many identical species, by the general succession of the forms of life. As species are produced and exterminated by slowly acting and still existing causes, and not by miraculous acts of creation; and as the most important of all causes of organic change is one which is almost independent of altered and perhaps suddenly altered physical conditions, namely, the mutual relation of organism to organism,—the improvement of one organism entailing the improvement or the extermination of others; it follows, that the amount of organic change in the fossils of consecutive formations probably serves as a fair measure of the relative, though not actual lapse of time. A number of species, however, keeping in a body might remain for a long period unchanged, whilst within the same period, several of these species by migrating into new countries and coming into competition with foreign associates, might become modified; so that we must not overrate the accuracy of organic change as a measure of time.

In the future I see open fields for far more important researches. Psychology will be securely based on the foundation already well laid by Mr. Herbert Spencer, that of the necessary acquirement of each mental power and capacity by gradation. Much light will be thrown on the origin of man and his history.

Authors of the highest eminence seem to be fully satisfied with the view that each species has been independently created. To my mind it accords better with what we know of the laws impressed on matter by the Creator, that the production and extinction of the past and present inhabitants of the world should have been due to secondary causes, like those determining the birth and death of the individual. When I view all beings not as special creations, but as the lineal descendants of some few beings which lived long before the first bed of the Cambrian system was deposited, they seem to me to become ennobled. Judging from the past, we may safely infer that not one living species will transmit its unaltered likeness to a distant futurity. And of the species now living very few will transmit progeny of any kind to a far distant futurity; for the manner in which all organic beings are grouped, shows that the greater number of species in each genus, and all the species in many genera, have left no descendants, but have become utterly extinct. We can so far take a prophetic glance into futurity as to foretell that it will be the common and widely spread species, belonging to the larger and dominant groups within each class, which will ultimately prevail and procreate new and dominant species. As all the living forms of life are the lineal descendants of those which lived long before the Cambrian epoch, we may feel certain that the ordinary succession by generation has never once been broken, and that no cataclysm has desolated the whole world. Hence we may look with some confidence to a secure future of great length. And as natural selection works solely by and for the good of each being, all corporeal and mental endowments will tend to progress towards perfection.

It is interesting to contemplate a tangled bank, clothed with many plants of many kinds, with birds singing on the bushes, with various insects flitting about, and with worms crawling through the damp earth, and to reflect that these elaborately constructed forms, so different from each other, and dependent upon each other in so complex a manner, have all been produced by laws acting around us. These laws, taken in the largest sense, being Growth with Reproduction; Inheritance which is almost implied by reproduction; Variability from the indirect and direct action of the conditions of life, and from use and disuse: a Ratio of Increase so high as to lead to a Struggle for Life, and as a consequence to Natural Selection, entailing Divergence of Character and the Extinction of less improved forms. Thus, from the war of nature, from famine and death, the most exalted object which we are capable of conceiving, namely, the production of the higher animals, directly follows. There is grandeur in this view of life, with its several powers, having been originally breathed by the Creator into a few forms or into one; and that, whilst this planet has gone cycling on according to the fixed law of gravity, from so simple a beginning endless forms most beautiful and most wonderful have been, and are being, evolved.

DESCENT OF MAN

Summary of the last two Chapters.—There can be no doubt that the difference between the mind of the lowest man and that of the highest animal is immense. An anthropomorphous ape, if he could take a dispassionate view of his own case, would admit that though he could form an artful plan to plunder a garden—though he could use stones for fighting or for breaking open nuts, yet that the thought of fashioning a stone into a tool was quite beyond his scope. Still less, as he would admit, could he follow out a train of metaphysical reasoning, or solve a mathematical problem, or reflect on God, or admire a grand natural scene. Some apes, however, would probably declare that they could and did admire the beauty of the colored skin and fur of their partners in marriage. They would admit, that though they could make other apes understand by cries some of their perceptions and simpler

The Duke of Argyll ('Primeval Man,' 1869, p. 188) has some good remarks on the contest in man's nature between right and wrong.

wants, the notion of expressing definite ideas by definite
sounds had never crossed their minds. They might insist
that they were ready to aid their fellow-apes of the same
troop in many ways, to risk their lives for them, and to
take charge of their orphans; but they would be forced to
acknowledge that disinterested love for all living creatures,
the most noble attribute of man, was quite beyond their
comprehension.

Nevertheless the difference in mind between man and
the higher animals, great as it is, is certainly one of degree
and not of kind. We have seen that the senses and intui-
tions, the various emotions and faculties, such as love,
memory, attention, curiosity, imitation, reason, etc., of
which man boasts, may be found in an incipient, or even
sometimes in a well-developed condition, in the lower animals. They are also capable of some inherited improvement, as we see in the domestic dog compared with the
wolf or jackal. If it be maintained that certain powers,
such as self-consciousness, abstraction, etc., are peculiar to
man, it may well be that these are the incidental results
of other highly-advanced intellectual faculties; and these
again are mainly the result of the continued use of a
highly-developed language. At what age does the new-
born infant possess the power of abstraction, or become
self-conscious and reflect on its own existence? We cannot answer; nor can we answer in regard to the ascending
organic scale. The half-art and half-instinct of language
still bears the stamp of its gradual evolution. The en-
nobling belief in God is not universal with man; and the
belief in active spiritual agencies naturally follows from
his other mental powers. The moral sense perhaps affords
the best and highest distinction between man and the
lower animals; but I need not say any thing on this head,
as I have so lately endeavored to show that the social
instincts—the prime principle of man's moral consti-

tution[39]—with the aid of active intellectual powers and
the effects of habit, naturally lead to the golden rule, "As
ye would that men should do to you, do ye to them likewise;" and this lies at the foundation of morality.

In a future chapter I shall make some few remarks on
the probable steps and means by which the several mental
and moral faculties of man have been gradually evolved.
That this at least is possible ought not to be denied, when
we daily see their development in every infant; and when
we may trace a perfect gradation from the mind of an
utter idiot, lower than that of the lowest animal, to the
mind of a Newton.

[39] 'The Thoughts of Marcus Aurelius,' etc., p. 139.

CHAPTER IV.

ON THE MANNER OF DEVELOPMENT OF MAN FROM SOME LOWER FORM.

Variability of Body and Mind in Man.—Inheritance.—Causes of Variability.—Laws of Variation the same in Man as in the Lower Animals.
—Direct Action of the Conditions of Life.—Effects of the Increased
Use and Disuse of Parts.—Arrested Development.—Reversion.—Cor-
related Variation.—Rate of Increase.—Checks to Increase.—Natural
Selection.—Man the most Dominant Animal in the World.—Impor-
tance of his Corporeal Structure.—The Causes which have led to his
becoming erect.—Consequent Changes of Structure.—Decrease in
Size of the Canine Teeth.—Increased Size and Altered Shape of the
Skull.—Nakedness.—Absence of a Tail.—Defenceless Condition of
Man.

WE have seen in the first chapter that the homological
structure of man, his embryological development and the
rudiments which he still retains, all declare in the plainest
manner that he is descended from some lower form. The
possession of exalted mental powers is no insuperable objection to this conclusion. In order that an ape-like creature should have been transformed into man, it is necessary that this early form, as well as many successive links,
should all have varied in mind and body. It is impossible
to obtain direct evidence on this head; but if it can be
shown that man now varies—that his variations are induced by the same general causes, and obey the same
general laws, as in the case of the lower animals—there
can be little doubt that the preceding intermediate links

varied in a like manner. The variations at each successive stage of descent must, also, have been in some manner accumulated and fixed.

The facts and conclusions to be given in this chapter
relate almost exclusively to the probable means by which
the transformation of man has been effected, as far as his
bodily structure is concerned. The following chapter will
be devoted to the development of his intellectual and
moral faculties. But the present discussion likewise bears
on the origin of the different races or species of mankind,
whichever term may be preferred.

It is manifest that man is now subject to much variability. No two individuals of the same race are quite
alike. We may compare millions of faces, and each will
be distinct. There is an equally great amount of diversity
in the proportions and dimensions of the various parts of
the body; the length of the legs being one of the most
variable points.[1] Although in some quarters of the world
an elongated skull, and in other quarters a short skull prevails, yet there is great diversity of shape even within the
limits of the same race, as with the aborigines of America
and South Australia—the latter a race "probably as pure
and homogeneous in blood, customs, and language, as any
in existence"—and even with the inhabitants of so confined an area as the Sandwich Islands.[2] An eminent den-
tist assures me that there is nearly as much diversity in
the teeth as in the features. The chief arteries so frequently run in abnormal courses, that it has been found
useful for surgical purposes to calculate from 12,000

[1] 'Investigations in Military and Anthropolog. Statistics of American
Soldiers,' by B. A. Gould, 1869, p. 256.

[2] With respect to the "Cranial forms of the American aborigines,"
see Dr. Aitken Meigs in 'Proc. Acad. Nat. Sci.' Philadelphia, May, 1866.
On the Australians, see Huxley, in Lyell's 'Antiquity of Man,' 1863, p. 87.
On the Sandwich Islanders, Prof. J. Wyman, 'Observations on Crania,'
Boston, 1868, p. 18.

corpses how often each course prevails.' The muscles are
eminently variable; thus those of the foot were found by
Prof. Turner⁴ not to be strictly alike in any two out of
fifty bodies; and in some the deviations were considerable.
Prof. Turner adds that the power of performing the appropriate movements must have been modified in accordance with the several deviations. Mr. J. Wood has re-
corded⁵ the occurrence of 295 muscular variations in
thirty-six subjects, and in another set of the same number
no less than 558 variations, reckoning both sides of the
body as one. In the last set, not one body out of the
thirty-six was "found totally wanting in departures from
the standard descriptions of the muscular system given
in anatomical text-books." A single body presented the
extraordinary number of twenty-five distinct abnormalities. The same muscle sometimes varies in many ways:
thus Prof. Macalister describes⁶ no less than twenty distinct variations in the *palmaris accessorius*.

The famous old anatomist, Wolff,⁷ insists that the internal viscera are more variable than the external parts:
*Nulla particula est quæ non aliter et aliter in aliis se
habeat hominibus.* He has even written a treatise on the
choice of typical examples of the viscera for representation.
A discussion on the beau-ideal of the liver, lungs, kidneys,
etc., as of the human face divine, sounds strange in our
ears.

The variability or diversity of the mental faculties in
men of the same race, not to mention the greater differences between the men of distinct races, is so notorious

---

³ 'Anatomy of the Arteries,' by R. Quain.
⁴ 'Transact. Royal Soc.' Edinburgh, vol. xxiv. pp. 175, 189.
⁵ 'Proc. Royal Soc.' 1867, p. 544; also 1868, pp. 483, 524. There is
a previous paper, 1866, p. 229.
⁶ 'Proc. R. Irish Academy,' vol. x. 1868, p. 141.
⁷ 'Act. Acad.,' St. Petersburg, 1778, part ii. p. 217.

that not a word need here be said. So it is with the lower
animals, as has been illustrated by a few examples in the
last chapter. All who have had charge of menageries
admit this fact, and we see it plainly in our dogs and other
domestic animals. Brehm especially insists that each individual monkey of those which he kept under confinement in Africa had its own peculiar disposition and temper: he mentions one baboon remarkable for its high intelligence; and the keepers in the Zoological Gardens
pointed out to me a monkey, belonging to the New World
division, equally remarkable for intelligence. Rengger,
also, insists on the diversity in the various mental characters of the monkeys of the same species which he kept in
Paraguay; and this diversity, as he adds, is partly innate,
and partly the result of the manner in which they have
been treated or educated.[8]

I have elsewhere[9] so fully discussed the subject of Inheritance that I need here add hardly any thing. A
greater number of facts have been collected with respect
to the transmission of the most trifling, as well as of the
most important characters in man than in any of the lower
animals; though the facts are copious enough with respect
to the latter. So in regard to mental qualities, their transmission is manifest in our dogs, horses, and other domestic animals. Besides special tastes and habits, general intelligence, courage, bad and good temper, etc., are certainly transmitted. With man we see similar facts in almost every family; and we now know through the admirable labors of Mr. Galton[10] that genius, which implies a

[8] Brehm, 'Thierleben,' B. i. s. 58, 87. Rengger, 'Säugethiere von
Paraguay,' s. 57.
[9] 'Variation of Animals and Plants under Domestication,' vol. ii. chap.
xii.
[10] 'Hereditary Genius: an Inquiry into its Laws and Consequences,'
1869.

wonderfully complex combination of high faculties, tends
to be inherited; and, on the other hand, it is too certain
that insanity and deteriorated mental powers likewise run
in the same families.

With respect to the causes of variability we are in all
cases very ignorant; but we can see that in man as in the
lower animals, they stand in some relation with the conditions to which each species has been exposed during
several generations. Domesticated animals vary more
than those in a state of nature; and this is apparently due
to the diversified and changing nature of their conditions.
The different races of man resemble in this respect domesticated animals, and so do the individuals of the same
race when inhabiting a very wide area, like that of
America. We see the influence of diversified conditions
in the more civilized nations, the members of which belong to different grades of rank and follow different occu-
pations, presenting a greater range of character than the
members of barbarous nations. But the uniformity of
savages has often been exaggerated, and in some cases can
hardly be said to exist.[11] It is nevertheless an error to
speak of man, even if we look only to the conditions
to which he has been subjected, as "far more domesticated"[12] than any other animal. Some savage races, such
as the Australians, are not exposed to more diversified
conditions than are many species which have very wide
ranges. In another and much more important respect,
man differs widely from any strictly-domesticated animal;

[11] Mr. Bates remarks ('The Naturalist on the Amazons,' 1863, vol. ii.
p. 159), with respect to the Indians of the same South-American tribe,
"No two of them were at all similar in the shape of the head; one man
had an oval visage with fine features, and another was quite Mongolian
in breadth and prominence of cheek, spread of nostrils, and obliquity of
eyes."

[12] Blumenbach, 'Treatises on Anthropolog.' Eng. translat., 1865, p. 205.

for his breeding has not been controlled, either through
methodical or unconscious selection. No race or body of
men has been so completely subjugated by other men,
that certain individuals have been preserved and thus unconsciously selected, from being in some way more useful
to their masters. Nor have certain male and female individuals been intentionally picked out and matched, except in the well-known case of the Prussian grenadiers;
and in this case man obeyed, as might have been expected, the law of methodical selection; for it is asserted that
many tall men were reared in the villages inhabited by
the grenadiers with their tall wives.

If we consider all the races of man, as forming a single
species, his range is enormous; but some separate races,
as the Americans and Polynesians, have very wide ranges.
It is a well-known law that widely-ranging species are
much more variable than species with restricted ranges;
and the variability of man may with more truth be compared with that of widely-ranging species, than with that
of domesticated animals.

Not only does variability appear to be induced in man
and the lower animals by the same general causes, but in
both the same characters are affected in a closely analogous manner. This has been proved in such full detail
by Godron and Quatrefages, that I need here only refer
to their works.[13] Monstrosities, which graduate into
slight variations, are likewise so similar in man and the
lower animals, that the same classification and the same
terms can be used for both, as may be seen in Isidore
Geoffroy St.-Hilaire's great work.[14] This is a necessary

[13] Godron, ' De l'Espèce,' 1859, tom. ii. livre 3. Quatrefages, ' Unité
de l'Espèce Humaine,' 1861. Also Lectures on Anthropology, given in
the ' Revue des Cours Scientifiques,' 1866–1868.

[14] ' Hist. Gen. et Part. des Anomalies de l'Organisation,' in three vol
umes, tom. i. 1832.

consequence of the same laws of change prevailing throughout the animal kingdom. In my work on the variation of domestic animals, I have attempted to arrange in a rude fashion the laws of variation under the following heads: The direct and definite action of changed conditions, as shown by all or nearly all the individuals of the same species varying in the same manner under the same circumstances. The effects of the long-continued use or disuse of parts. The cohesion of homologous parts. The variability of multiple parts. Compensation of growth; but of this law I have found no good instances in the case of man. The effects of the mechanical pressure of one part on another; as of the pelvis on the cranium of the infant in the womb. Arrests of development, leading to the diminution or suppression of parts. The reappearance of long-lost characters through reversion. And lastly, correlated variation. All these so-called laws apply equally to man and the lower animals; and most of them even to plants. It would be superfluous here to discuss all of them;[16] but several are so important for us, that they must be treated at considerable length.

Conclusion.—In this chapter we have seen that as man at the present day is liable, like every other animal, to multiform individual differences or slight variations, so no doubt were the early progenitors of man; the variations being then as now induced by the same general causes, and governed by the same general and complex laws. As all animals tend to multiply beyond their means of subsistence, so it must have been with the progenitors of man; and this will inevitably have led to a struggle for existence and to natural selection. This latter process will have been greatly aided by the inherited effects of the increased use of parts; these two processes incessantly reacting on each other. It appears, also, as we shall hereafter see, that various unimportant characters have been acquired by man through sexual selection. An unexplained residuum of change, perhaps a large one, must be left to the assumed uniform action of those unknown agencies, which occasionally induce strongly-marked and abrupt deviations of structure in our domestic productions.

Judging from the habits of savages and of the greater number of the Quadrumana, primeval men, and even the ape-like progenitors of man, probably lived in society. With strictly social animals, natural selection sometimes acts indirectly on the individual, through the preservation of variations which are beneficial only to the community. A community including a large number of well-endowed individuals increases in number and is victorious over other and less well-endowed communities; although each separate member may gain no advantage over the other members of the same community. With associated insects many remarkable structures, which are of little or no service to the individual or its own offspring, such as the pollen-collecting apparatus, or the sting of the worker-bee, or the great jaws of soldier-ants, have been thus acquired. With the higher social animals, I am not aware that any structure has been modified solely for the good of the community, though some are of secondary service to it. For instance, the horns of ruminants and the great canine teeth of baboons appear to have been acquired by the males as weapons for sexual strife, but they are used in defence of the herd or troop. In regard to certain mental faculties the case, as we shall see in the following chapter, is wholly different; for these faculties have been chiefly, or even exclusively, gained for the benefit of the community; the individuals composing the community being at the same time indirectly benefited.

It has often been objected to such views as the foregoing, that man is one of the most helpless and defenceless creatures in the world; and that during his early and less well-developed condition he would have been still more helpless. The Duke of Argyll, for instance, insists [81] that "the human frame has diverged from the structure of brutes, in the direction of greater physical helplessness and weakness. That is to say, it is a divergence which of all others it is most impossible to ascribe to mere natural selection." He adduces the naked and unprotected state

[81] 'Primeval Man,' 1869, p. 66.

of the body, the absence of great teeth or claws for defence, the little strength of man, his small speed in running, and his slight power of smell, by which to discover food or to avoid danger. To these deficiencies there might have been added the still more serious loss of the power of quickly climbing trees, so as to escape from enemies. Seeing that the unclothed Fuegians can exist under their wretched climate, the loss of hair would not have been a great injury to primeval man, if he inhabited a warm country. When we compare defenceless man with the apes, many of which are provided with formidable canine teeth, we must remember that these in their fully-developed condition are possessed by the males alone, being chiefly used by them for fighting with their rivals; yet the females, which are not thus provided, are able to survive.

In regard to bodily size or strength, we do not know whether man is descended from some comparatively small species, like the chimpanzee, or from one as powerful as the gorilla; and, therefore, we cannot say whether man has become larger and stronger, or smaller and weaker, in comparison with his progenitors. We should, however, bear in mind that an animal possessing great size, strength, and ferocity, and which, like the gorilla, could defend itself from all enemies, would probably, though not necessarily, have failed to become social; and this would most effectually have checked the acquirement by man of his higher mental qualities, such as sympathy and the love of his fellow-creatures. Hence it might have been an immense advantage to man to have sprung from some comparatively weak creature.

The slight corporeal strength of man, his little speed, his want of natural weapons, etc., are more than counterbalanced, firstly by his intellectual powers, through which he has, while still remaining in a barbarous state, formed for himself weapons, tools, etc., and secondly by his social qualities which lead him to give aid to his fellow-men and to receive it in return. No country in the world abounds in a greater degree with dangerous beasts than Southern Africa; no country presents more fearful physical hardships than the Arctic regions; yet one of the puniest races, namely, the Bushmen, maintain themselves in Southern Africa, as do the dwarfed Esquimaux in the Arctic regions. The early progenitors of man were, no doubt, inferior in intellect, and probably in social disposition, to the lowest existing savages; but it is quite conceivable that they might have existed, or even flourished, if, while they gradually lost their brute-like powers, such as climbing trees, etc., they at the same time advanced in intellect. But granting that the progenitors of man were far more helpless and defenceless than any existing savages, if they had inhabited some warm continent, or large island, such as Australia or New Guinea, or Borneo (the latter island being now tenanted by the orang), they would not have been exposed to any special danger. In an area as large as one of these islands, the competition between tribe and tribe would have been sufficient, under favorable conditions, to have raised man, through the survival of the fittest, combined with the inherited effects of habit, to his present high position in the organic scale.

273

5

Sigmund Freud,   TOTEM AND TABOO   (Trans. by A.A. Brill)

Ralph Waldo Emerson,   "THE OVER-SOUL"

1. What is a totem? What does it represent to the
    clan and what are the clan's obligations to the
    totem?

2. Define exogamy and tell how is it associated with
    the totem. What is meant by the prohibition and
    what are the consequences of trespassing it?

3. Freud connects the compulsion prohibition of neur-
    otics and the taboo. Explain how he unifies these
    two concepts.

4. Explain the meaning of ambivalent behavior and tell
    how such behavior evolved from the taboo. Accord-
    ing to Freud, man has an ambivalent attitude toward
    the impulse to kill. How did Freud arrive at this
    conclusion?

5. According to Freud, what is the nature and origin
    of the human conscience?

6. How does Freud explain the origins of and the pur-
    pose for a god? How is this related to the father
    figure?

7. Freud holds that the Oedipus Complex is the nucleus
    of neuroses. Why?

8. Darwin is said to have had a strong influence on
    Freud's thinking. Can you see examples of this
    influence?

9. What is the Oversoul? How does it relate to our
    own individual souls? What does it have to do with
    human interaction?

10. Why does human nature always remain to some extent
    mysterious and inexplicable according to Emerson?

11. Many people regard Emerson's view as supremely optimistic and Freud's as extremely pessimistic. What do you think? Which view is more realistic? Explain.

12. What is the true nature of man according to Emerson? How does our blindness to this "true nature" cause us to have a jaundiced view of man?

13. How does Emerson say that we can come into contact with our "true nature"? How does the soul grow and develop?

Sigmund Freud (1856-1939) is known as the father of psychoanalysis. Although trained in physiology, he turned to this new field for the care and treatment of the emotionally disturbed. Psychoanalysis is a philosophy of human nature as well as a form of treatment. In the following selections from *Totem and Taboo* in which Freud is comparing the psychic resemblances between savage cultures and neurotics, the origins of some of his most popular and controversial ideas are explained. Among these are explanations for the origins of the incest taboo, the practice of exogamy, the causes of neuroses, the origins of the conscious and the unconscious and many others. Freud's work provides us with a scientific as well as an anthropological point of view of the nature of man.

TOTEM AND TABOO

I *The savage's dread of incest*

Primitive man is known to us by the stages of development through which he has passed: that is, through
the inanimate monuments and implements which he
has left behind for us, through our knowledge of his
art, his religion and his attitude towards life, which
we have received either directly or through the medium of legends, myths and fairy tales; and through
the remnants of his ways of thinking that survive in
our own manners and customs. Moreover, in a certain
sense he is still our contemporary: there are people
whom we still consider more closely related to primitive man than to ourselves, in whom we therefore recognize the direct descendants and representatives of
earlier man. We can thus judge the so-called savage
and semi-savage races; their psychic life assumes a peculiar interest for us, for we can recognize in their
psychic life a well-preserved, early stage of our own
development.

If this assumption is correct, a comparison of the "Psychology of Primitive Races" as taught by folklore, with the psychology of the neurotic as it has become known through psychoanalysis, will reveal numerous points of correspondence and throw new light on subjects that are more or less familiar to us.

For outer as well as for inner reasons, I am choosing for this comparison those tribes which have been described by ethnographists as being most backward and wretched: the aborigines of the youngest continent, namely Australia, whose fauna has also preserved for us so much that is archaic and no longer to be found elsewhere.

The aborigines of Australia are looked upon as a peculiar race which shows neither physical nor linguistic relationship with its nearest neighbours, the Melanesian, Polynesian and Malayan races. They do not build houses or permanent huts; they do not cultivate the soil or keep any domestic animals except dogs; and they do not even know the art of pottery. They live exclusively on the flesh of all sorts of animals which they kill in the chase, and on the roots which they dig. Kings or chieftains are unknown among them, and all communal affairs are decided by the elders in assembly. It is quite doubtful whether they evince any traces of religion in the form of worship of higher beings. The tribes living in the interior who have to contend with the greatest vicissitudes of life owing to a scarcity of water, seem in every way more primitive than those who live near the coast.

We surely would not expect that these poor naked cannibals should be moral in their sex life according to our ideas, or that they should have imposed a high degree of restriction upon their sexual impulses. And yet we learn that they have considered it their duty to exercise the most searching care and the most painful rigour in guarding against incestuous sexual relations. In fact their whole social organization seems to serve this object or to have been brought into relation with its attainment.

Among the Australians the system of *Totemism* takes the place of all religious and social institutions. Australian tribes are divided into smaller *septs* or clans, each taking the name of its *totem*. Now what is a totem? As a rule it is an animal, either edible or harmless, or dangerous and feared; more rarely the totem is a plant or a force of nature (rain, water), which stands in a peculiar relation to the whole clan. The totem is first of all the tribal ancestor of the clan, as well as its tutelary spirit and protector; it sends oracles and, though otherwise dangerous, the totem knows and spares its children. The members of a totem are therefore under a sacred obligation not to kill (destroy) their totem, to abstain from eating its meat or from any other enjoyment of it. Any violation of these prohibitions is automatically punished. The character of a totem is inherent not only in a single animal or a single being but in all the members of the species. From time to time festivals are held at which the members of a totem represent or imitate, in ceremonial dances, the movements and characteristics of their totems.

The totem is hereditary either through the maternal or the paternal line (maternal transmission probably always preceded and was only later supplanted by the paternal). The attachment to a totem is the foundation of all the social obligations of an Australian: it extends on the one hand beyond the tribal relationship, and on the other hand it super-sedes consanguineous relationship.[1]

The totem is not limited to district or to locality; the members of a totem may live separated from one another and on friendly terms with adherents of other totems.[2]

[1] Frazer, *Totemism and Exogamy*, Vol. I, p. 53. "The totem bond is stronger than the bond of blood or family in the modern sense."

[2] This very brief extract of the totemic system cannot be left without some elucidation and without discussing its limitations. The name Totem or Totam was first learned from the North American Indians by the Englishman, J. Long, in 1791. The subject has gradually acquired great scientific interest and has called forth a copious literature. I refer especially to *Totemism and Exogamy* by J. G. Frazer, 4 vols., 1910, and the books and articles of Andrew Lang (*The Secret of Totem*, 1905). The credit for having recognized the significance of totemism for the ancient history of man belongs to the Scotchman, J. Ferguson MacLennan (*Fortnightly Review*, 1869-70). Exterior to Australia, totemic institutions were found and are still observed among North American Indians, as well as among the races of the Polynesian Islands group, in East India, and in a large part of Africa. Many traces and survivals otherwise hard to interpret lead to the conclusion that totemism also once existed among the aboriginal Aryan and Semitic races of Europe, so that many investigators are inclined to recognize in totemism a necessary phase of human development through which every race has passed.

How then did prehistoric man come to acquire a totem; that is, how did he come to make his descent from this or that animal foundation of his social duties and, as we shall hear, of his sexual restrictions as well? Many different theories have been advanced to explain this, a review of which the reader may find in Wundt's *Voelkerpsychologie* (Vol. II: *Mythus und Religion*).

I promise soon to make the problem of totemism a subject of special study in which an effort will be made to solve it by applying the psychoanalytic method. (Cf. The fourth chapter of this work.)

Not only is the theory of totemism controversial, but the very facts concerning it are hardly to be expressed in such general statements as were attempted above. There is hardly an assertion to which one would not have to add exceptions and contradictions. But it must not be forgotten that even the most primitive and conservative races are, in a certain sense, old, and have a long

And now, finally, we must consider that peculiarity of the totemic system which attracts the interest of the psychoanalyst. Almost everywhere the totem prevails there also exists the law that *the members of the same totem are not allowed to enter into sexual relations with each other; that is, that they cannot marry each other.* This represents the *exogamy* which is associated with the totem.

This sternly maintained prohibition is very remarkable. There is nothing to account for it in anything that we have hitherto learned from the conception of the totem or from any of its attributes; that is, we do not understand how it happened to enter the system of totemism. We are therefore not astonished if some investigators simply assume that at first exogamy— both as to its origin and to its meaning—had nothing to do with totemism, but that it was added to it at some time without any deeper association, when marriage restrictions proved necessary. However that may be, the association of totemism and exogamy exists, and proves to be very strong.

Let us elucidate the meaning of this prohibition through further discussion.

(*a*) The violation of the prohibition is not left to what is, so to speak, an automatic punishment, as is the case with other violations of the prohibitions of the totem (e.g., not to kill the totem animal), but is

---

period behind them during which whatsoever was aboriginal with them has undergone much development and distortion. Thus among those races who still evince it, we find totemism to-day in the most manifold states of decay and disintegration; we observe that fragments of it have passed over to other social and religious institutions; or it may exist in fixed forms but far removed from its original nature. The difficulty then consists in the fact that it is not altogether easy to decide what in the actual conditions is to be taken as a faithful copy of the significant past and what is to be considered as a secondary distortion of it.

most energetically avenged by the whole tribe as if it
were a question of warding off a danger that threatens
the community as a whole or a guilt that weighs upon
all. A few sentences from Frazer's book[3] will show
how seriously such trespasses are treated by these savages who, according to our standard, are otherwise
very immoral.

"In Australia the regular penalty for sexual intercourse with a person of a forbidden clan is death. It
matters not whether the woman is of the same local
group or has been captured in war from another
tribe; a man of the wrong clan who uses her as his
wife is hunted down and killed by his clansmen, and
so is the woman; though in some cases, if they succeed
in eluding capture for a certain time, the offence may
be condoned. In the Ta-Ta-thi tribe, New South
Wales, in the rare cases which occur, the man is killed,
but the woman is only beaten or speared, or both,
till she is nearly dead; the reason given for not actually killing her being that she was probably coerced.
Even in casual amours the clan prohibitions are
strictly observed; any violations of these prohibitions
'are regarded with the utmost abhorrence and are
punished by death' (Howitt)."

(b) As the same severe punishment is also meted
out for temporary love affairs which have not resulted
in childbirth, the assumption of other motives, perhaps of a practical nature, becomes improbable.

(c) As the totem is hereditary and is not changed
by marriage, the results of the prohibition, for instance in the case of maternal heredity, are easily perceived. If, for example, the man belongs to a clan
with the totem of the Kangaroo and marries a woman
of the Emu totem, the children, both boys and girls,

[3] Frazer, l.c., p. 54.

are all Emu. According to the totem law incestuous relations with his mother and his sister, who are Emu like himself, are therefore made impossible for a son of this marriage.[4]

(*d*) But we need only a reminder to realize that the exogamy connected with the totem accomplishes more; that is, aims at more than the prevention of incest with the mother or the sisters. It also makes it impossible for the man to have sexual union with all the women of his own group, with a number of females, therefore, who are not consanguineously related to him, by treating all these women like blood relations. The psychological justification for this extraordinary restriction, which far exceeds anything comparable to it among civilized races, is not, at first, evident. All we seem to understand is that the rôle of the totem (the animal) as ancestor is taken very seriously. Everybody descended from the same totem is consanguineous; that is, of one family; and in this family the most distant grades of relationship are recognized as an absolute obstacle to sexual union.

Thus these savages reveal to us an unusually high grade of incest dread or incest sensitiveness, combined with the peculiarity, which we do not very well understand, of substituting the totem relationship for the real blood relationship. But we must not exaggerate this contradiction too much, and let us bear in mind

[4] But the father, who is a Kangaroo, is free—at least under this prohibition—to commit incest with his daughters, who are Emu. In the case of paternal inheritance of the totem the father would be Kangaroo as well as the children; then incest with the daughters would be forbidden to the father and incest with the mother would be left open to the son. These consequences of the totem prohibition seem to indicate that the maternal inheritance is older than the paternal one, for there are grounds for assuming that the totem prohibitions are directed first of all against the incestuous desires of the son.

that the totem prohibitions include real incest as a special case.

In what manner the substitution of the totem group for the actual family has come about remains a riddle, the solution of which is perhaps bound up with the explanation of the totem itself. Of course it must be remembered that with a certain freedom of sexual intercourse, extending beyond the limitations of matrimony, the blood relationship, and with it also the prevention of incest, becomes so uncertain that we cannot dispense with some other basis for the prohibition. It is therefore not superfluous to note that the customs of Australians recognize social conditions and festive occasions at which the exclusive conjugal right of a man to a woman is violated.

The linguistic customs of these tribes, as well as of most totem races, reveals a peculiarity which undoubtedly is pertinent in this connection. For the designations of relationship of which they make use do not take into consideration the relationship between two individuals, but between an individual and his group; they belong, according to the expression of L. H. Morgan, to the "classifying" system. That means that a man calls not only his begetter "father" but also every other man who, according to the tribal regulations, might have married his mother and thus become his father; he calls "mother" not only the woman who bore him but also every other woman who might have become his mother without violation of the tribal laws; he calls "brothers" and "sisters" not only the children of his real parents, but also the children of all the persons named who stand in the parental group relation with him, and so on. The kinship names which two Australians give each other do not, therefore, necessarily point to a blood relationship between them, as they would have to according to the custom of our language; they signify much more the social than the physical relations. An approach to this classifying system is perhaps to be found in our nursery, when the child is induced to greet every male and female friend of the parents as "uncle" and "aunt," or it may be found in a transferred sense when we speak of "Brothers in Apollo," or "Sisters in Christ."

The explanation of this linguistic custom, which seems so strange to us, is simple if looked upon as a remnant and indication of those marriage institutions which the Rev. L. Fison has called "group marriage," characterized by a number of men exercising conjugal rights over a number of women. The children of this group marriage would then rightly look upon each other as brothers and sisters although not born of the same mother, and would take all the men of the group for their fathers.

Although a number of authors, as, for instance, B. Westermarck in his *History of Human Marriage*,[5] oppose the conclusions which others have drawn from the existence of group-relationship names, the best authorities on the Australian savages are agreed that the classificatory relationship names must be considered as survivals from the period of group marriages. And, according to Spencer and Gillen,[6] a certain form of group marriage can be established as still existing to-day among the tribes of the Urabunna and the Dieri. Group marriage therefore preceded individual marriage among these races, and did not disappear without leaving distinct traces in language and custom.

[5] Second edition, 1902.
[6] *The Native Tribes of Central Australia* (London, 1899).

But if we replace individual marriage, we can then grasp the apparent excess of cases of incest shunning which we have met among these same races. The totem exogamy, or prohibition of sexual intercourse between members of the same clan, seemed the most appropriate means for the prevention of group incest; and this totem exogamy then became fixed and long survived its original motivation.

II *Taboo and the ambivalence of emotions*

Taboo is a Polynesian word, the translation of which provides difficulties for us because we no longer possess the idea which it connotes. It was still current with the ancient Romans: their word "sacer" was the same as the taboo of the Polynesians. The ἄγος of the Greeks and the Kodaush of the Hebrews must also have signified the same thing which the Polynesians express through their word taboo and what many races in America, Africa (Madagascar), North and Central Asia express through analogous designations.

For us the meaning of taboo branches off into two opposite directions. On the one hand it means to us, sacred, consecrated: but on the other hand it means, uncanny, dangerous, forbidden, and unclean. The opposite for taboo is designated in Polynesian by the word *noa* and signifies something ordinary and generally accessible. Thus something like the concept of reserve inheres in taboo; taboo expresses itself essentially in prohibitions and restrictions. Our combination of "holy dred" would often express the meaning of taboo.

The taboo restrictions are different from religious or moral prohibitions. They are not traced to a commandment of a god but really they themselves impose their own prohibitions; they are differentiated from moral prohibitions by failing to be included in a system which declares abstinences in general to be necessary and gives reasons for this necessity. The taboo prohibitions lack all justification and are of unknown origin. Though incomprehensible to us they are taken as a matter of course by those who are under their dominance.

Wundt[1] calls taboo the oldest unwritten code of law of humanity. It is generally assumed that taboo is older than the gods and goes back to the pre-religious age.

As we are in need of an impartial presentation of the subject of taboo before subjecting it to psychoanalytic consideration I shall now cite an excerpt from the article *Taboo* in the *Encyclopædia Britannica* written by the anthropologist Northcote W. Thomas:[2]

"Properly speaking taboo includes only (a) the sacred (or unclean) character of persons or things, (b) the kind of prohibition which results from this character, and (c) the sanctity (or uncleanliness) which results from a violation of the prohibition. The converse of taboo in Polynesia is 'noa' and allied forms which mean 'general' or 'common' . . .

"Various classes of taboo in the wider sense may be

[1] *Voelkerpsychologie*, II. Band: *Mythus und Religion*, 1906, II. p. 308.
[2] Eleventh Edition; this article also gives the most important references.

distinguished: 1. natural or direct, the result of 'mana' mysterious (power) inherent in a person or thing; 2. communicated or indirect, equally the result of 'mana' but (a) acquired or (b) imposed by a priest, chief or other person; 3. intermediate, where both factors are present, as in the appropriation of a wife to her husband. The term taboo is also applied to ritual prohibitions of a different nature; but its use in these senses is better avoided. It might be argued that the term should be extended to embrace cases in which the sanction of the prohibition is the creation of a god or spirit, i.e., to religious interdictions as distinguished from magical, but there is neither automatic action nor contagion in such a case, and a better term for it is religious interdiction.

"The objects of the taboo are many: 1. direct taboos aim at (a) protection of important persons—chiefs, priests, etc.—and things against harm; (b) safeguarding of the weak—women, children and common people generally—from the powerful mana (magical influence) of chiefs and priests; (c) providing against the dangers incurred by handling or coming in contact with corpses, by eating certain food, etc.; (d) guarding the chief acts of life—births, initiation, marriage and sexual functions—against interference; (e) securing human beings against the wrath or power of gods and spirits;[3] (f) securing unborn infants and young children who stand in a specially sympathetic relation with their parents, from the consequence of certain actions, and more especially from the communication of qualities supposed to be derived from certain foods. 2. Taboos are imposed in

[3] This application of the taboo can be omitted as not originally belonging in this connection.

order to secure against thieves the property of an individual, his fields, tools, etc."

Other parts of the article may be summarized as follows. Originally the punishment for the violation of a taboo was probably left to an inner, automatic arrangement. The violated taboo avenged itself. Wherever the taboo was related to ideas of gods and demons an automatic punishment was expected from the power of the god-head. In other cases, probably as a result of a further development of the idea, society took over the punishment of the offender, whose action has endangered his companions. Thus man's first systems of punishment are also connected with taboo.

"The violation of a taboo makes the offender himself taboo." The author goes on to say that certain dangers resulting from the violation of a taboo may be exorcised through acts of penance and ceremonies of purification.

A peculiar power inherent in persons and ghosts, which can be transmitted from them to inanimate objects, is regarded as a source of the taboo. This part of the article reads as follows: "Persons or things which are regarded as taboo may be compared to objects charged with electricity; they are the seat of tremendous power which is transmissible by contact, and may be liberated with destructive effect if the organisms which provoke its discharge are too weak to resist it; the result of a violation of a taboo depends partly on the strength of the magical influence inherent in the taboo object or person, partly on the strength of the opposing mana of the violator of the taboo. Thus, kings and chiefs are possessed of great power, and it is death for their subjects to address them directly;

but a minister or other person of greater *mana* than common, can approach them unharmed, and can in turn be approached by their inferiors without risk. . . . So, too, indirect taboos depend for their strength on the mana of him who opposes them; if it is a chief or a priest, they are more powerful than those imposed by a common person."

The fact that a taboo is transmissible has surely given rise to the effort of removing it through expiatory ceremonies.

The author states that there are permanent and temporary taboos. The former comprise priests and chiefs as well as the dead and everything that has belonged to them. Temporary taboos attach themselves to certain conditions such as menstruation and childbed, the status of the warrior before and after the expedition, the activities of fishing and of the chase, and similar activities. A general taboo may also be imposed upon a large district like an ecclesiastical interdict, and may then last for years.

If I judge my readers' impressions correctly, I dare say that after hearing all that was said about taboo they are far from knowing what to understand by it and where to store it in their minds. This is surely due to the insufficient information I have given and to the omission of all discussions concerning the relation of taboo to superstition, to belief in the soul, and to religion. On the other hand I fear that a more detailed description of what is known about taboo would be still more confusing; I can therefore assure the reader that the state of affairs is really far from clear. We may say, however, that we deal with a series of restrictions which these primitive races impose upon themselves; this and that is forbidden without any apparent reason; nor does it occur to them to question this matter, for they subject themselves to these restrictions as a matter of course and are convinced that any transgression will be punished automatically in the most severe manner. There are reliable reports that innocent transgressions of such prohibitions have actually been punished automatically. For instance, the innocent offender who had eaten from a forbidden animal became deeply depressed, expected his death and then actually died. The prohibitions mostly concern matters which are capable of enjoyment, such as freedom of movement and unrestrained intercourse; in some cases they appear very ingenious, evidently representing abstinences and renunciations; in other cases their content is quite incomprehensible: they seem to concern themselves with trifles and give the impression of ceremonials. Something like a theory seems to underlie all these prohibitions; it seems as if these prohibitions are necessary because some persons and objects possess a dangerous power which is transmitted by contact with the object so charged, almost like a contagion. The quantity of this dangerous property is also taken into consideration. Some persons or things have more of it than others and the danger is precisely in accordance with the charge. The most peculiar part of it is that any one who has violated such a prohibition assumes the nature of the forbidden object as if he had absorbed the whole dangerous charge. This power is inherent in all persons who are more or less prominent, such as kings, priests and the newly born; in all exceptional physical states, such as menstruation, puberty and birth; in everything sinister, like illness and death, and in everything connected with these conditions by virtue of contagion or dissemination.

However, the term "taboo" includes all persons,

localities, objects and temporary conditions which are carriers or sources of this mysterious attribute. The prohibition derived from this attribute is also designated as taboo, and lastly taboo, in the literal sense, includes everything that is sacred, above the ordinary, and at the same time dangerous, unclean and mysterious.

Both this word and the system corresponding to it express a fragment of psychic life which really is not comprehensible to us. And indeed it would seem that no understanding of it could be possible without entering into the study of the beliefs in spirits and demons which is so characteristic of these low grades of culture.

2

He who approaches the problem of taboo from the field of psychoanalysis, which is concerned with the study of the unconscious part of the individual's psychic life, needs but a moment's reflection to realize that these phenomena are by no means foreign to him. He knows people who have individually created such taboo prohibitions for themselves, which they follow as strictly as savages observe the taboos common to their tribe or society. If he were not accustomed to call these individuals "compulsion neurotics" he would find the term "taboo disease" quite appropriate for their mal-

[8] *l.c.*, p. 313.

ady. Psychoanalytic investigation has taught him the clinical etiology and the essential part of the psychological mechanism of this compulsion disease, so that he cannot resist applying what he has learnt there to explain corresponding manifestations in folk psychology.

There is one warning to which we shall have to give heed in making this attempt. The similarity between taboo and compulsion disease may be purely superficial, holding good only for the manifestations of both without extending into their deeper characteristics. Nature loves to use identical forms in the most widely different biological connections as, for instance, for coral stems and plants and even for certain crystals or for the formation of certain chemical precipitates. It would certainly be both premature and unprofitable to base conclusions relating to inner relationships upon the correspondence of merely mechanical conditions. We shall bear this warning in mind without, however, giving up our intended comparison on account of the possibility of such confusions.

The first and most striking correspondence between the compulsion prohibitions of neurotics and taboo lies in the fact that the origin of these prohibitions is just as unmotivated and enigmatic. They have appeared at some time or other and must now be retained on account of an unconquerable anxiety. An external threat of punishment is superfluous, because an inner certainty (a conscience) exists that violation will be followed by unbearable disaster. The very most that compulsion patients can tell us is the vague premonition that some person of their environment will suffer harm if they should violate the prohibition. Of what the harm is to consist is not known, and this inadequate information is more likely to be obtained during the later discussions of the expiatory and defensive actions than when the prohibitions themselves are being discussed.

As in the case of taboo the nucleus of the neurotic prohibition is the act of touching, whence we derive the name "touching phobia" or *délire de toucher*. The prohibition extends not only to direct contact with the body but also to the figurative use of the phrase as "to come into contact" or "be in touch with some one or some thing." Anything that leads the thoughts to what is prohibited and thus calls forth mental contact is just as much prohibited as immediate bodily contact; this same extension is also found in taboo.

Some prohibitions are easily understood from their purpose but others strike us as incomprehensible, foolish and senseless. We designate such commands as "ceremonials" and we find that taboo customs show the same variations.

Obsessive prohibitions possess an extraordinary capacity for displacement; they make use of almost any form of connection to extend from one object to another and then in turn make this new object "impossible," as one of my patients aptly puts it. This impossibility finally lays an embargo upon the whole world. The compulsion neurotics act as if the "impossible" persons and things were the carriers of a dangerous contagion which is ready to displace itself through contact to all neighbouring things. We have already emphasized the same characteristics of contagion and transference in the description of taboo prohibitions. We also know that any one who has violated a taboo by touching something which is taboo becomes taboo himself, and no one may come into contact with him.

I shall put side by side two examples of transference or, to use a better term, displacement, one from the life of the Maori, and the other from my observation of a woman suffering from a compulsion neurosis:

"For a similar reason a Maori chief would not blow on a fire with his mouth; for his sacred breath would communicate its sanctity to the fire, which would pass it on to the meat in the pot, which would pass it on to the man who ate the meat which was in the pot, which stood on the fire, which was breathed on by the chief; so that the eater, infected by the chief's breath conveyed through these intermediaries, would surely die." [9]

My patient demanded that a utensil which her husband had purchased and brought home should be removed lest it make the place where she lives impossible. For she has heard that this object was bought in a store which is situated, let us say, in Stag Street. But as the word "stag" is the name of a friend now in a distant city, whom she has known in her youth under her maiden name and whom she now finds "impossible," that is taboo; the object bought in Vienna is just as taboo as this friend with whom she does not want to come into contact.

Compulsion prohibitions, like taboo prohibitions, entail the most extraordinary renunciations and restrictions of life, but a part of these can be removed by carrying out certain acts which now also must be done because they have acquired a compulsive character (obsessive acts); there is no doubt that these acts are in the nature of penances, expiations, defence reactions, and purifications. The most common of these

[9] Frazer, *The Golden Bough*, II: *Taboo and the Perils of the Soul*, 1911, p. 136.

obsessive acts is washing with water (washing obses-
sion). A part of the taboo prohibitions can also be
replaced in this way, that is to say, their violation
can be made good through such a "ceremonial," and
here too lustration through water is the preferred
way.

Let us now summarize the points in which the correspondence between taboo customs and the symptoms
of compulsion neurosis are most clearly manifested:
1. In the lack of motivation of the commandments, 2.
in their enforcement through an inner need, 3. in
their capacity of displacement and in the danger of
contagion from what is prohibited, 4. and in the causation of ceremonial actions and commandments which
emanate from the forbidden.

However, psychoanalysis has made us familiar with
the clinical history as well as the psychic mechanism
of compulsion neurosis. Thus the history of a typical
case of touching phobia reads as follows: In the very
beginning, during the early period of childhood, the
person manifested a strong pleasure in touching himself, the object of which was much more specialized
than one would be inclined to suspect. Presently the
carrying out of this very pleasurable act of touching
was opposed by a prohibition from without.[10] The
prohibition was accepted because it was supported by
strong inner forces;[11] it proved to be stronger than the
impulse which wanted to manifest itself through this
act of touching. But due to the primitive psychic constitution of the child this prohibition did not succeed
in abolishing the impulse. Its only success lay in repressing the impulse (the pleasure of touching) and

[10] Both the pleasure and the prohibition referred to touching
one's own genitals.
[11] The relation to beloved persons who impose the prohibition.

banishing it into the unconscious. Both the prohibition and the impulse remained; the impulse because it had only been repressed and not abolished, the prohibition, because if it had ceased the impulse would have broken through into consciousness and would have been carried out. An unsolved situation, a psychic fixation, had thus been created and now everything else emanated from the continued conflict between prohibition and impulse.

The main characteristic of the psychic constellation which has thus gone under fixation lies in what one might call the ambivalent behaviour[12] of the individual to the object, or rather to an action regarding it. The individual constantly wants to carry out this action (the act of touching), he sees in it the highest pleasure, but he may not carry it out, and he even abominates it. The opposition between these two streams cannot be easily adjusted because—there is no other way to express it—they are so localized in the psychic life that they cannot meet. The prohibition becomes fully conscious, while the surviving pleasure of touching remains unconscious, the person knowing nothing about it. If this psychological factor did not exist the ambivalence could neither maintain itself so long nor lead to such subsequent manifestations.

In the clinical history of the case we have emphasized the appearance of the prohibition in early childhood as the determining factor; but for the further elaboration of the neurosis this rôle is played by the repression which appears at this age. On account of the repression which has taken place, which is connected with forgetting (amnesia), the motivation of the prohibition that has become conscious remains unknown, and all attempts to unravel it intellectually

12 To use an excellent term coined by Bleuler.

must fail, as the point of attack cannot be found. The prohibition owes its strength—its compulsive character—to its association with its unknown counterpart, the hidden and unabated pleasure, that is to say, to an inner need into which conscious insight is lacking. The transferability and reproductive power of the prohibition reflect a process which harmonizes with the unconscious pleasure and is very much facilitated through the psychological determinants of the unconscious. The pleasure of the impulse constantly undergoes displacement in order to escape the blocking which it encounters and seeks to acquire surrogates for the forbidden in the form of substitutive objects and actions. For the same reason the prohibition also wanders and spreads to the new aims of the proscribed impulse. Every new advance of the repressed libido is answered by the prohibition with a new severity. The mutual inhibition of these two contending forces creates a need for discharge and for lessening the existing tension, in which we may recognize the motivation for the compulsive acts. In the neurosis there are distinctly acts of compromise which on the one hand may be regarded as proofs of remorse and efforts to expiate and similiar actions; but on the other hand they are at the same time substitutive actions which recompense the impulse for what has been forbidden. It is a law of neurotic diseases that these obsessive acts serve the impulse more and more and come nearer and nearer to the original and forbidden act.

We may now make the attempt to study taboo as if it were of the same nature as the compulsive prohibitions of our patients. It must naturally be clearly understood that many of the taboo prohibitions which we shall study are already secondary, displaced and distorted, so that we shall have to be satisfied if we can shed some light upon the earliest and most important taboo prohibitions. We must also remember that the differences in the situation of the savage and of the neurotic may be important enough to exclude complete correspondence and prevent a point by point transfer from one to the other, such as would be possible if we were dealing with exact copies.

First of all it must be said that it is useless to question savages as to the real motivation of their prohibitions or as to the genesis of taboo. According to our assumption they must be incapable of telling us anything about it since this motivation is "unconscious" to them. But following the model of the compulsive prohibition we shall construct the history of taboo as follows: Taboos are very ancient prohibitions which at one time were forced upon a generation of primitive people from without, that is, they probably were forcibly impressed upon them by an earlier generation. These prohibitions concerned actions for which there existed a strong desire. The prohibitions maintained themselves from generation to generation, perhaps only as the result of a tradition set up by paternal and social authority. But in later generations they have perhaps already become "organized" as a piece of inherited psychic property. Whether there are such "innate ideas" or whether these have brought about the fixation of the taboo by themselves or by co-operating with education no one could decide in the particular case in question. The persistence of taboo teaches, however, one thing, namely, that the original pleasure to do the forbidden still continues among taboo races. They therefore assume an *ambivalent attitude* toward their taboo prohibitions; in their unconscious they would like nothing better than to transgress them but they are also afraid to do it; they are afraid just because they would like to transgress, and the fear is stronger than the pleasure. But in every individual of the race the desire for it is unconscious, just as in the neurotic.

The oldest and most important taboo prohibitions are the two basic laws of *totemism:* namely not to kill the totem animal, and to avoid sexual intercourse with totem companions of the other sex.

It would therefore seem that these must have been the oldest and strongest desires of mankind. We cannot understand this and therefore we cannot use these examples to test our assumptions as long as the meaning and the origin of the totemic system is so wholly unknown to us. But the very wording of these taboos and the fact that they occur together will remind any one who knows the results of the psychoanalytic investigation of individuals of something quite definite which psychoanalysts call the central point of the infantile wish life and the nucleus of the later neurosis.[13]

All other varieties of taboo phenomena which have led to the attempted classifications noted above become unified if we sum them up in the following sentence: The basis of taboo is a forbidden action for which there exists a strong inclination in the unconscious.

We know, without understanding it, that whoever does what is prohibited and violates the taboo, becomes himself taboo. But how can we connect this fact with the other, namely that the taboo adheres not only to persons who have done what is prohibited but also to persons who are in exceptional circumstances, to these circumstances themselves, and to im-

[13] See Chapter IV: *Totemism, etc.*

personal things? What can this dangerous attribute be which always remains the same under all these different conditions? Only one thing, namely, the propensity to arouse the ambivalence of man and to tempt him to violate the prohibition.

An individual who has violated a taboo becomes himself taboo because he has the dangerous property of tempting others to follow his example. He arouses envy; why should he be allowed to do what is prohibited to others? He is therefore really *contagious,* in so far as every example incites to imitation, and therefore he himself must be avoided.

But a person may become permanently or temporarily taboo without having violated any taboos, for the simple reason that he is in a condition which has the property of inciting the forbidden desires of others and of awakening the ambivalent conflict in them. Most of the exceptional positions and conditions have this character and possess this dangerous power. The king or chieftain rouses envy of his prerogatives: everybody would perhaps like to be king. The dead, the newly born and women when they are incapacitated all act as incitements on account of their peculiar helplessness, while the individual who has just reached sexual maturity tempts through the promise of a new pleasure. Therefore all these persons and all these conditions are taboo, for one must not yield to the temptations which they offer.

Now, too, we understand why the forces inherent in the "mana" of various persons can neutralize one another so that the mana of one individual can partly cancel that of the other. The taboo of a king is too strong for his subject because the social difference between them is too great. But a minister, for example, can become the harmless mediator between them.

Translated from the language of taboo into the language of normal psychology this means: the subject who shrinks from the tremendous temptation which contact with the king creates for him can brook the intercourse of an official, whom he does not have to envy so much and whose position perhaps seems attainable to him. The minister, on his part, can moderate his envy of the king by taking into consideration the power that has been granted to him. Thus smaller differences in the magic power that lead to temptation are less to be feared than exceptionally big differences.

It is equally clear how the violation of certain taboo prohibitions becomes a social danger which must be punished or expiated by all the members of society lest it harm them all. This danger really exists if we substitute the known impulses for the unconscious desires. It consists in the possibility of imitation, as a result of which society would soon be dissolved. If the others did not punish the violation they would perforce become aware that they want to imitate the evil doer.

Though the secret meaning of a taboo prohibition cannot possibly be of so special a nature as in the case of a neurosis, we must not be astonished to find that touching plays a similar role in taboo prohibition as in the *délire de toucher*. To touch is the beginning of every act of possession, of every attempt to make use of a person or thing.

We have interpreted the power of contagion which inheres in the taboo as the property of leading into temptation, and of inciting to imitation. This does not seem to be in accord with the fact that the contagiousness of the taboo is above all manifested in the transference to objects which thus themselves become carriers of the taboo.

This transferability of the taboo reflects what is found in the neurosis, namely, the constant tendency of the unconscious impulse to become displaced through associative channels upon new objects. Our attention is thus drawn to the fact that the dangerous magic power of the mana corresponds to two real faculties, the capacity of reminding man of his forbidden wishes, and the apparently more important one of tempting him to violate the prohibition in the service of these wishes. Both functions reunite into one, however, if we assume it to be in accord with a primitive psychic life that with the awakening of a memory of a forbidden action there should also be combined the awakening of the tendency to carry out the action. Memory and temptation then again coincide. We must also admit that if the example of a person who has violated a prohibition leads another to the same action, the disobedience of the prohibition has been transmitted like a contagion, just as the taboo is tranferred from a person to an object, and from this to another.

If the violation of a taboo can be condoned through expiation or penance, which means, of course, a *renunciation* of a possession or a liberty, we have the proof that the observance of a taboo regulation was itself a renunciation of something really wished for. The omission of one renunciation is cancelled through a renunciation at some other point. This would lead us to conclude that, as far as taboo ceremonials are concerned, penance is more primitive than purification.

Let us now summarize what understanding we have

gained of taboo through its comparison with the compulsive prohibition of the neurotic. Taboo is a very primitive prohibition imposed from without (by an authority) and directed against the strongest desires of man. The desire to violate it continues in the unconscious; persons who obey the taboo have an ambivalent feeling toward what is affected by the taboo. The magic power attributed to taboo goes back to its ability to lead man into temptation; it behaves like a contagion, because the example is contagious, and because the prohibited desire becomes displaced in the unconscious upon something else. The expiation for the violation of a taboo through a renunciation proves that a renunciation is at the basis of the observance of the taboo.

4

Having thus explained the basis on which the very instructive taboo of the dead has grown up, we must not miss the opportunity of adding a few observations which may become important for the understanding of taboo in general.

The projection of unconscious hostility upon demons in the taboo of the dead is only a single example from a whole series of processes to which we must grant the greatest influence in the formation of primitive psychic life. In the foregoing case the mechanism of projection is used to settle an emotional conflict; it serves the same purpose in a large number of psychic situations which lead to neuroses. But projection is not specially created for the purpose of defence, it also comes into being where there are no conflicts. The projection of inner perceptions to the outside is a primitive mechanism which, for instance, also influences our sense perceptions, so that it normally has the greatest share in shaping our outer world. Under conditions that have not yet been sufficiently determined even inner perceptions of ideational and emotional processes are projected outwardly, like sense perceptions, and are used to shape the outer world, whereas they ought to remain in the inner world. This is perhaps genetically connected with the fact that the function of attention was originally directed not towards the inner world, but to the stimuli streaming in from the outer world, and only received reports of pleasure and pain from the endopsychic processes. Only with the development of the language of abstract thought through the association of sensory remnants of word representations with inner processes, did the latter gradually become capable of perception. Before this took place primitive man had developed a picture of the outer world through the outward projection of inner perceptions, which we, with our reinforced conscious perception, must now translate back into psychology.

The projection of their own evil impulses upon demons is only a part of what has become the world system ("Weltanschauung") of primitive man which we shall discuss later as "animalism." We shall then have to ascertain the psychological nature of such a system formation and the points of support which we shall find in the analysis of these system formations will again bring us face to face with the neurosis. For the present we merely wish to suggest that the "secondary elaboration" of the dream content is the prototype of all these system formations.[53] And let us not forget that beginning at the stage of system formation there are two origins for every act judged by consciousness, namely the systematic, and the real but unconscious origin.[54]

Wundt[55] remarks that "among the influences which myth everywhere ascribes to demons the evil ones preponderate, so that according to the religions of races evil demons are evidently older than good demons." Now it is quite possible that the whole conception of demons was derived from the extremely important relation to the dead. In the further course of human development the ambivalence inherent in this relation then manifested itself by allowing two altogether contrary psychic formations to issue from the

[53] Freud, *The Interpretation of Dreams.*
[54] The projection creations of primitive man resemble the personifications through which the poet projects his warring impulses out of himself, as separated individuals.
[55] *Myth and Religion,* p. 129.

same root, namely, the fear of demons and of *ghosts*, and the reverence for ancestors.[56] Nothing testifies so much to the influence of mourning on the origin of belief in demons as the fact that demons were always taken to be the spirits of persons not long dead. Mourning has a very distinct psychic task to perform, namely, to detach the memories and expectations of the survivors from the dead. When this work is accomplished the grief, and with it the remorse and reproach, lessens, and therefore also the fear of the demon. But the very spirits which at first were feared as demons now serve a friendlier purpose; they are revered as ancestors and appealed to for help in times of distress.

If we survey the relation of survivors to the dead through the course of the ages, it is very evident that the ambivalent feeling has extraordinarily abated. We now find it easy to suppress whatever unconscious hostility towards the dead there may still exist without any special psychic effort on our part. Where formerly satisfied hate and painful tenderness struggled with each other, we now find piety, which appears like a cicatrice and demands: *De mortuis nil nisi bene.* Only neurotics still blur the mourning for the loss of their dear ones with attacks of compulsive reproaches which psychoanalysis reveals as the old ambivalent emotional feeling. How this change was brought about, and to what extent constitutional changes and real improvement of familiar relations

[56] In the psychoanalysis of neurotic persons who suffer, or have suffered, in their childhood from the fear of ghosts, it is often not difficult to expose these ghosts as the parents. Compare also in this connection the communication of P. Haeberlin, *Sexual Ghosts (Sexual Problems*, Feb. 1912), where it is a question of another erotically accentuated person, but where the father was dead.

share in causing the abatement of the ambivalent feeling, need not be discussed here. But this example would lead us to assume *that the psychic impulses of primitive man possessed a higher degree of ambivalence than is found at present among civilized human beings. With the decline of this ambivalence the taboo, as the compromise symptom of the ambivalent conflict, also slowly disappeared.* Neurotics who are compelled to reproduce this conflict, together with the taboo resulting from it, may be said to have brought with them an atavistic remnant in the form of an archaic constitution the compensation of which in the interest of cultural demands entails the most prodigious psychic efforts on their part.

At this point we may recall the confusing information which Wundt offered us about the double meaning of the word taboo, namely, holy and unclean (see above). It was supposed that originally the word taboo did not yet mean holy and unclean but signified something demonic, something which may not be touched, thus emphasizing a characteristic common to both extremes of the later conception; this persistent common trait proves, however, that an original correspondence existed between what was holy and what was unclean, which only later became differentiated.

In contrast to this, our discussion readily shows that the double meaning in question belonged to the word taboo from the very beginning and that it serves to designate a definite ambivalence as well as everything which has come into existence on the basis of this ambivalence. Taboo is itself an ambivalent word and by way of supplement we may add that the established meaning of this word might of itself have allowed us to guess what we have found as the result of extensive investigation, namely, that the taboo prohibition is to be explained as the result of an emotional ambivalence. A study of the oldest languages has taught us that at one time there were many such words which included their own contrasts so that they were in a certain sense ambivalent, though perhaps not exactly in the same sense as the word taboo.[57] Slight vocal modifications of this primitive word containing two opposite meanings later served to create a separate linguistic expression for the two opposites originally united in one word.

The word taboo has had a different fate; with the diminished importance of the ambivalence which it connotes it has itself disappeared, or rather, the words analogous to it have vanished from the vocabulary. In a later connection I hope to be able to show that a tangible historic change is probably concealed behind the fate of this conception; that the word at first was associated with definite human relations which were characterized by great emotional ambivalence from which it expanded to other analogous relations.

Unless we are mistaken, the understanding of taboo also throws light upon the nature and origin of *conscience*. Without stretching ideas we can speak of a taboo conscience and a taboo sense of guilt after the violation of a taboo. Taboo conscience is probably the oldest form in which we meet the phenomenon of conscience.

For what is "conscience"? According to linguistic testimony it belongs to what we know most surely; in some languages its meaning is hardly to be distinguished from consciousness.

[57] Compare my article on Abel's *Gegensinn der Urwort* in the *Jahrbuch für Psychoanalytische und Psychopathologische Forschungen*, Bd. II, 1910.

Conscience is the inner perception of objections to definite wish impulses that exist in us; but the emphasis is put upon the fact that this rejection does not have to depend on anything else, that it is sure of itself. This becomes even plainer in the case of a guilty conscience, where we become aware of the inner condemnation of such acts which realized some of our definite wish impulses. Confirmation seems superfluous here; whoever has a conscience must feel in himself the justification of the condemnation, and the reproach for the accomplished action. But this same character is evinced by the attitude of savages towards taboo. Taboo is a command of conscience, the violation of which causes a terrible sense of guilt which is as self-evident as its origin is unknown.[58]

It is therefore probable that conscience also originates on the basis of an ambivalent feeling from quite definite human relations which contain this ambivalence. It probably originates under conditions which are in force both for taboo and the compulsion neurosis, that is, one component of the two contrasting feelings is unconscious and is kept repressed by the compulsive domination of the other component. This is confirmed by many things which we have learned from our analysis of neurosis. In the first place the character of compulsion neurotics shows a predominant trait of painful conscientiousness which is a symptom of reaction against the temptation which lurks in the unconscious, and which develops into the highest degrees of guilty conscience as their illness

[58] It is an interesting parallel that the sense of guilt resulting from the violation of a taboo is in no way diminished if the violation took place unwittingly (see examples above), and that even in the Greek myth the guilt of Oedipus is not cancelled by the fact that it was incurred without his knowledge and will and even against them.

grows worse. Indeed, one may venture the assertion that if the origin of guilty conscience could not be discovered through compulsion neurotic patients, there would be no prospect of ever discovering it. This task is successfully solved in the case of the individual neurotic, and we are confident of finding a similar solution in the case of races.

In the second place we cannot help noticing that the sense of guilt contains much of the nature of anxiety; without hesitation it may be described as "conscience phobia." But fear points to unconscious sources. The psychology of the neuroses taught us that when wish feelings undergo repression their libido becomes transformed into anxiety. In addition we must bear in mind that the sense of guilt also contains something unknown and unconscious, namely the motivation for the rejection. The character of anxiety in the sense of guilt corresponds to this unknown quantity.

If taboo expresses itself mainly in prohibitions it may well be considered self-evident, without remote proof from the analogy with neurosis, that it is based on a positive, desireful impulse. For what nobody desires to do does not have to be forbidden, and certainly whatever is expressly forbidden must be an object of desire. If we applied this plausible theory to primitive races we would have to conclude that among their strongest temptations were desires to kill their kings and priests, to commit incest, to abuse their dead and the like. That is not very probable. And if we should apply the same theory to those cases in which we ourselves seem to hear the voice of conscience most clearly we would arouse the greatest contradiction. For there we would assert with the utmost certainty that we did not feel the slightest temptation to violate any of these commandments, as for example, the commandment: Thou shalt not kill, and that we felt nothing but repugnance at the very idea.

But if we grant the testimony of our conscience the importance it claims, then the prohibition—the taboo as well as our moral prohibitions—becomes superfluous, while the existence of a conscience, in turn, remains unexplained and the connection between conscience, taboo and neurosis disappears. The net result of this would then be our present state of understanding unless we view the problem psychoanalytically.

But if we take into account the following results of psychoanalysis, our understanding of the problem is greatly advanced. The analysis of dreams of normal individuals has shown that our own temptation to kill others is stronger and more frequent than we had suspected and that it produces psychic effects even where it does not reveal itself to our consciousness. And when we have learnt that the obsessive rules of certain neurotics are nothing but measures of self-reassurance and self-punishment erected against the reinforced impulse to commit murder, we can return with fresh appreciation to our previous hypothesis that every prohibition must conceal a desire. We can then assume that this desire to murder actually exists and that the taboo as well as the moral prohibition are psychologically by no means superfluous but are, on the contrary, explained and justified through our ambivalent attitude towards the impulse to slay.

The nature of this ambivalent relation so often emphasized as fundamental, namely, that the positive underlying desire is unconscious, opens the possibility of showing further connections and explaining further problems. The psychic processes in the unconscious are not entirely identical with those known to us from our conscious psychic life, but have the benefit of certain notable liberties of which the latter are deprived. An unconscious impulse need not have originated where we find it expressed, it can spring from an entirely different place and may originally have referred to other persons and relations, but through the mechanism of *displacement,* it reaches the point where it comes to our notice. Thanks to the indestructibility of unconscious processes and their inaccessibility to correction, the impulse may be saved over from earlier times to which it was adapted to later periods and conditions in which its manifestations must necessarily seem foreign. These are all only hints, but a careful elaboration of them would show how important they may become for the understanding of the development of civilization.

In closing these discussions we do not want to neglect to make an observation that will be of use for later investigations. Even if we insist upon the essential similarity between taboo and moral prohibitions we do not dispute that a psychological difference must exist between them. A change in the relations of the fundamental ambivalence can be the only reason why the prohibition no longer appears in the form of a taboo.

In the analytical consideration of taboo phenomena we have hitherto allowed ourselves to be guided by their demonstrable agreements with compulsion neurosis; but as taboo is not a neurosis but a social creation we are also confronted with the task of showing wherein lies the essential difference between the neurosis and a product of culture like the taboo.

Here again I will take a single fact as my starting point. Primitive races fear a punishment for the violation of a taboo, usually a serious disease or death.

This punishment threatens only him who has been guilty of the violation. It is different with the compulsion neurosis. If the patient wants to do something that is forbidden to him he does not fear punishment for himself, but for another person. The person is usually indefinite, but, by means of analysis, is easily recognized as some one very near and dear to the patient. The neurotic therefore acts as if he were altruistic, while primitive man seems egotistical. Only if retribution fails to overtake the taboo violator spontaneously does a collective feeling awaken among savages that they are all threatened through the sacrilege, and they hasten to inflict the omitted punishment themselves. It is easy for us to explain the mechanism of this solidarity. It is a question of fear of the contagious example, the temptation to imitate, that is to say, of the capacity of the taboo to infect. If some one has succeeded in satisfying the repressed desire, the same desire must manifest itself in all his companions; hence, in order to keep down this temptation, this envied individual must be despoiled of the fruit of his daring. Not infrequently the punishment gives the executors themselves an opportunity to commit the same sacrilegious act by justifying it as an expiation. This is really one of the fundamentals of the human code of punishment which rightly presumes the same forbidden impulses in the criminal and in the members of society who avenge his offence.

Psychoanalysis here confirms what the pious were wont to say, that we are all miserable sinners. How then shall we explain the unexpected nobility of the neurosis which fears nothing for itself and everything for the beloved person?

Psychoanalytic investigation shows that this nobility is not primary. Originally, that is to say at the begin-

ning of the disease, the threat of punishment per-
tained to one's own person; in every case the fear was
for one's own life; the fear of death being only later
displaced upon another beloved person. The process
is somewhat complicated but we have a complete
grasp of it. An evil impulse—a death wish—towards
the beloved person is always at the basis of the formation of a prohibition. This is repressed through a
prohibition, and the prohibition is connected with a
certain act which by displacement usually substitutes
the hostile for the beloved person, and the execution
of this act is threatened with the penalty of death. But
the process goes further and the original wish for the
death of the beloved other person is then replaced by
fear for his death. The tender altruistic trait of the
neurosis therefore merely *compensates* for the opposite attitude of brutal egotism which is at the basis of
it. If we designate as social these emotional impulses
which are determined through regard for another
person who is not taken as a sexual object, we can
emphasize the withdrawal of these social factors as an
essential feature of the neurosis, which is later disguised through over-compensation.

Without lingering over the origin of these social
impulses and their relation to other fundamental impulses of man, we will bring out the second main
characteristic of the neurosis by means of another example. The form in which taboo manifests itself has
the greatest similarity to the touching phobia of neurotics, the *délire de toucher*. As a matter of fact this
neurosis is regularly concerned with the prohibition of
sexual touching and psychoanalysis has quite generally shown that the motive power which is deflected
and displaced in the neurosis is of sexual origin. In
taboo the forbidden contact has evidently not only

sexual significance but rather the more general one of attack, of acquisition and of personal assertion. If it is prohibited to touch the chief or something that was in contact with him it means that an inhibition should be imposed upon the same impulse which on other occasions expresses itself in suspicious surveillance of the chief and even in physical ill-treatment of him before his coronation (see above). *Thus the preponderance of sexual components of the impulse over the social components is the determining factor of the neurosis.* But the social impulses themselves came into being through the union of egotistical and erotic components into special entities.

From this single example of a comparison between taboo and compulsion neurosis it is already possible to guess the relation between individual forms of the neurosis and the creations of culture, and in what respect the study of the psychology of the neurosis is important for the understanding of the development of culture.

In one way the neuroses show a striking and far-reaching correspondence with the great social productions of art, religion and philosophy, while again they seem like distortions of them. We may say that hysteria is a caricature of an artistic creation, a compulsion neurosis a caricature of a religion, and a paranoiac delusion a caricature of a philosophic system. In the last analysis this deviation goes back to the fact that the neuroses are asocial formations; they seek to accomplish by private means what arose in society through collective labour. In analysing the impulse of the neuroses one learns that motive powers of sexual origin exercise the determining influence in them, while the corresponding cultural creations rest upon social impulses and on such as have issued from the combination of egotistical and sexual components. It seems that the sexual need is not capable of uniting men in the same way as the demands of self-preservation; sexual satisfaction is in the first place the private concern of the individual.

Genetically the asocial nature of the neurosis springs from its original tendency to flee from a dissatisfying reality to a more pleasurable world of phantasy. This real world which neurotics shun is dominated by the society of human beings and by the institutions created by them; the estrangement from reality is at the same time a withdrawal from human companionship.

6

I am under the influence of many strong motives which restrain me from the attempt to discuss the further development of religions from their beginning in totemism up to their present state. I shall follow out only two threads as I see them appearing in the weft with especial distinctness: the motive of the totem sacrifice and the relation of the son to the father.[81]

Robertson Smith has shown us that the old totem feast returns in the original form of sacrifice. The meaning of the rite is the same: sanctification through participation in the common meal. The sense of guilt, which can only be allayed through the solidarity of all the participants, has also been retained. In addition to this there is the tribal deity in whose supposed presence the sacrifice takes place, who takes part in the meal like a member of the tribe, and with whom identification is effected by the act of eating the sacrifice. How does the god come into this situation which originally was foreign to him?

The answer might be that the idea of god had meanwhile appeared,—no one knows whence—and

[81] Compare *Transformations and Symbols of the Libido,* by C. G. Jung, in which some dissenting points of view are represented.

had dominated the whole religious life, and that the totem feast, like everything else that wished to survive, had been forced to fit itself into the new system. However, psychoanalytic investigation of the individual teaches with especial emphasis that god is in every case modelled after the father and that our personal relation to god is dependent upon our relation to our physical father, fluctuating and changing with him, and that god at bottom is nothing but an exalted father. Here also, as in the case of totemism, psychoanalysis advises us to believe the faithful, who call god father just as they called the totem their ancestor. If psychoanalysis deserves any consideration at all, then the share of the father in the idea of a god must be very important, quite aside from all the other origins and meanings of god upon which psychoanalysis can throw no light. But then the father would be represented twice in primitive sacrifice, first as god, and secondly as the totem-animal-sacrifice, and we must ask, with all due regard for the limited number of solutions which psychoanalysis offers, whether this is possible and what the meaning of it may be.

We know that there are a number of relations of the god to the holy animal (the totem and the sacrificial animal): 1. Usually one animal is sacred to every god, sometimes even several animals. 2. In certain, especially holy, sacrifices, the so-called "mystical" sacrifices, the very animal which had been sanctified through the god was sacrificed to him.[82] 3. The god was often revered in the form of an animal, or from another point of view, animals enjoyed a godlike reverence long after the period of totemism. 4. In myths the god is frequently transformed into an animal, often into the animal that is sacred to him. From

[82] Robertson Smith, *Religion of the Semites*, Second Edition, 1907.

this the assumption was obvious that the god himself was the animal, and that he had evolved from the totem animal at a later stage of religious feeling. But the reflection that the totem itself is nothing but a substitute for the father relieves us of all further discussion. Thus the totem may have been the first form of the father substitute and the god a later one in which the father regained his human form. Such a new creation from the root of all religious evolution, namely, the longing for the father, might become possible if in the course of time an essential change had taken place in the relation to the father and perhaps also to the animal.

Such changes are easily divined even if we disregard the beginning of a psychic estrangement from the animal as well as the disintegration of totemism through animal domestication.[83] The situation created by the removal of the father contained an element which in the course of time must have brought about an extraordinary increase of longing for the father. For the brothers who had joined forces to kill the father had each been animated by the wish to become like the father and had given expression to this wish by incorporating parts of the substitute for him in the totem feast. In consequence of the pressure which the bonds of the brother clan exercised upon each member, this wish had to remain unfulfilled. No one could or was allowed to attain the father's perfection of power, which was the thing they had all sought. Thus the bitter feeling against the father which had incited to the deed could subside in the course of time, while the longing for him grew, and an ideal could arise having as a content the fullness of power and the freedom from restriction of the

[83] See above, p. 177.

conquered primal father, as well as the willingness to subject themselves to him. The original democratic equality of each member of the tribe could no longer be retained on account of the interference of cultural changes; in consequence of which there arose a tendency to revive the old father ideal in the creation of gods through the veneration of those individuals who had distinguished themselves above the rest. That a man should become a god and that a god should die, which to-day seems to us an outrageous presumption, was still by no means offensive to the conceptions of classical antiquity.[84] But the deification of the murdered father from whom the tribe now derived its origin was a much more serious attempt at expiation than the former covenant with the totem.

In this evolution I am at a loss to indicate the place of the great maternal deities who perhaps everywhere preceded the paternal deities. But it seems certain that the change in the relation to the father was not restricted to religion but logically extended to the other side of human life influenced by the removal of the father, namely, the social organization. With the institution of paternal deities the fatherless society gradually changed into a patriarchal one. The family was a reconstruction of the former primal horde and also restored a great part of their former rights to the fathers. Now there were patriarchs again but the social achievements of the brother clan had

[84] "To us moderns, for whom the breach which divides the human and divine has deepened into an impassable gulf, such mimicry may appear impious, but it was otherwise with the ancients. To their thinking gods and men were akin, for many families traced their descent from a divinity, and the deification of a man probably seemed as little extraordinary to them as the canonization of a saint seems to a modern Catholic." Frazer, *The Golden Bough*, I; *The Magic Art and the Evolution of Kings*, II, p. 177.

not been given up and the actual difference between the new family patriarchs and the unrestricted primal father was great enough to ensure the continuation of the religious need, the preservation of the unsatisfied longing for the father.

The father therefore really appears twice in the scene of sacrifice before the tribal god, once as the god and again as the totem-sacrificial-animal. But in attempting to understand this situation we must beware of interpretations which superficially seek to translate it as an allegory, and which forget the historical stages in the process. The twofold presence of the father corresponds to the two successive meanings of the scene. The ambivalent attitude towards the father as well as the victory of the son's tender emotional feelings over his hostile ones, have here found plastic expression. The scene of vanquishing the father, his greatest degradation, furnishes here the material to represent his highest triumph. The meaning which sacrifice has quite generally acquired is found in the fact that in the very same action which continues the memory of this misdeed it offers satisfaction to the father for the ignominy put upon him.

In the further development the animal loses its sacredness and the sacrifice its relation to the celebration of the totem; the rite becomes a simple offering to the deity, a self-deprivation in favour of the god. God himself is now so exalted above man that he can be communicated with only through a priest as intermediary. At the same time the social order produces godlike kings who transfer the patriarchal system to the state. It must be said that the revenge of the deposed and reinstated father has been very cruel; it culminated in the dominance of authority. The subjugated sons have used the new relation to disburden themselves still more of their sense of guilt. Sacrifice, as it is now constituted, is entirely beyond their responsibility. God himself has demanded and ordained it. Myths in which the god himself kills the animal that is sacred to him, which he himself really is, belong to this phase. This is the greatest possible denial of the great misdeed with which society and the sense of guilt began. There is an unmistakable second meaning in this sacrificial demonstration. It expresses satisfaction at the fact that the earlier father substitute has been abandoned in favour of the higher conception of god. The superficial allegorical translation of the scene here roughly corresponds with its psychoanalytic interpretation by saying that the god is represented as overcoming the animal part of his nature.[85]

But it would be erroneous to believe that in this period of renewed patriarchal authority the hostile impulses which belong to the father complex had entirely subsided. On the contrary, the first phases in the domination of the two new substitutive formations for the father, those of gods and kings, plainly show the most energetic expression of that ambivalence which is characteristic of religion.

In his great work, *The Golden Bough*, Frazer has expressed the conjecture that the first kings of the

[85] It is known that the overcoming of one generation of gods by another in mythology represents the historical process of the substitution of one religious system by another, either as the result of conquest by a strange race or by means of a psychological development. In the latter case the myth approaches the "functional phenomena" in H. Silberer's sense. That the god who kills the animal is a symbol of the libido, as asserted by C. G. Jung (*l.c.*), presupposes a different conception of the libido from that hitherto held, and at any rate seems to me questionable.

Latin tribes were strangers who played the part of a deity and were solemnly sacrificed in this rôle on specified holidays. The yearly sacrifice (self-sacrifice is a variant) of a god seems to have been an important feature of Semitic religions. The ceremony of human sacrifice in various parts of the inhabited world makes it certain that these human beings ended their lives as representatives of the deity. This sacrificial custom can still be traced in later times in the substitution of an inanimate imitation (doll) for the living person. The theanthropic god sacrifice into which unfortunately I cannot enter with the same thoroughness with which the animal sacrifice has been treated throws the clearest light upon the meaning of the older forms of sacrifice. It acknowledges with unsurpassable candour that the object of the sacrificial action has always been the same, being identical with what is now revered as a god, namely with the father. The question as to the relation of animal to human sacrifice can now be easily solved. The original animal sacrifice was already a substitute for a human sacrifice, for the solemn killing of the father, and when the father substitute regained its human form, the animal substitute could also be retransformed into a human sacrifice.

Thus the memory of that first great act of sacrifice had proved to be indestructible despite all attempts to forget it, and just at the moment when men strove to get as far away as possible from its motives, the undistorted repetition of it had to appear in the form of the god sacrifice. I need not fully indicate here the developments of religious thought which made this return possible in the form of rationalizations. Robertson Smith who is, of course, far removed

from the idea of tracing sacrifice back to this great
event of man's primal history, says that the ceremony
of the festivals in which the old Semites celebrated
the death of a deity were interpreted as "a commem-
oration of a mythical tragedy" and that the attend-
ant lament was not characterized by spontaneous sympathy, but displayed a compulsive character, something that was imposed by the fear of a divine wrath.[86]
We are in a position to acknowledge that this interpretation was correct, the feelings of the celebrants
being well explained by the basic situation.

We may now accept it as a fact that in the further
development of religions these two inciting factors,
the son's sense of guilt and his defiance, were never
again extinguished. Every attempted solution of the
religious problem and every kind of reconciliation of
the two opposing psychic forces gradually falls to the
ground, probably under the combined influence of
cultural changes, historical events, and inner psychic
transformations.

The endeavour of the son to put himself in place of
the father god, appeared with greater and greater distinctness. With the introduction of agriculture the
importance of the son in the patriarchal family increased. He was emboldened to give new expression
to his incestuous libido which found symbolic satisfaction in labouring over mother earth. There came
into existence figures of gods like Attis, Adonis, Tam-
muz, and others, spirits of vegetation as well as youth-

[86] *Religion of the Semites*, pp. 412-413. "The mourning is not a
spontaneous expression of sympathy with the divine tragedy, but
obligatory and enforced by fear of supernatural anger. And a
chief object of the mourners is *to disclaim responsibility for the
god's death*—a point which has already come before us in connexion with theanthropic sacrifices, such as the 'ox-murder at
Athens.' "

ful divinities who enjoyed the favours of maternal deities and committed incest with the mother in defiance of the father. But the sense of guilt which was not allayed through these creations, was expressed in myths which visited these youthful lovers of the maternal goddesses with short life and punishment through castration or through the wrath of the father god appearing in animal form. Adonis was killed by the boar, the sacred animal of Aphrodite; Attis, the lover of Kybele, died of castration.[87] The lamentation for these gods and the joy at their resurrection have gone over into the ritual of another son which divinity was destined to survive long.

When Christianity began its entry into the ancient world it met with the competition of the religion of Mithras and for a long time it was doubtful which deity was to be the victor.

The bright figure of the youthful Persian god has eluded our understanding. Perhaps we may conclude from the illustrations of Mithras slaying the steers that he represented the son who carried out the sacrifice of the father by himself and thus released the

[87] The fear of castration plays an extraordinarily big rôle in disturbing the relations to the father in the case of our youthful neurotics. In Ferenczi's excellent study we have seen how the boy recognized his totem in the animal which snaps at his little penis. When children learn about ritual circumcision they identify it with castration. To my knowledge the parallel in the psychology of races to this attitude of our children has not yet been drawn. The circumcision which was so frequent in primordial times among primitive races belongs to the period of initiation in which its meaning is to be found; it has only secondarily been relegated to an earlier time of life. It is very interesting that among primitive men circumcision is combined with or replaced by the cutting off of the hair and the drawing of teeth, and that our children, who cannot know anything about this, really treat these two operations as equivalents to castration when they display their fear of them.

brothers from their oppressing complicity in the deed. There was another way of allaying this sense of guilt and this is the one that Christ took. He sacrificed his own life and thereby redeemed the brothers from primal sin.

The theory of primal sin is of Orphic origin; it was preserved in the mysteries and thence penetrated into the philosophic schools of Greek antiquity.[88] Men were the descendents of Titans, who had killed and dismembered the young Dionysos-Zagreus; the weight of this crime oppressed them. A fragment of Anaximander says that the unity of the world was destroyed by a primordial crime and everything that issued from it must carry on the punishment for this crime.[89] Although the features of banding together, killing, and dismembering as expressed in the deed of the Titans very clearly recall the totem sacrifice described by St. Nilus—as also many other myths of antiquity, for example, the death of Orpheus himself—we are nevertheless disturbed here by the variation according to which a youthful god was murdered.

In the Christian myth man's original sin is undoubtedly an offence against God the Father, and if Christ redeems mankind from the weight of original sin by sacrificing his own life, he forces us to the conclusion that this sin was murder. According to the law of retaliation which is deeply rooted in human feeling, a murder can be atoned only by the sacrifice of another life; the self-sacrifice points to a blood-guilt.[90]

[88] Reinach, *Cultes, Mythes, et Religions,* II, p. 75.
[89] "Une sorte de péche proethnique," *l.c.,* p. 76.
[90] The suicidal impulses of our neurotics regularly prove to be self-punishments for death wishes directed against others.

And if this sacrifice of one's own life brings about a reconciliation with god, the father, then the crime which must be expiated can only have been the murder of the father.

Thus in the Christian doctrine mankind most unreservedly acknowledges the guilty deed of primordial times because it now has found the most complete expiation for this deed in the sacrificial death of the son. The reconciliation with the father is the more thorough because simultaneously with this sacrifice there follows the complete renunciation of women, for whose sake mankind rebelled against the father. But now also the psychological fatality of ambivalence demands its rights. In the same deed which offers the greatest possible expiation to the father, the son also attains the goal of his wishes against the father. He becomes a god himself beside or rather in place of his father. The religion of the son succeeds the religion of the father. As a sign of this substitution the old totem feast is revived again in the form of communion in which the band of brothers now eats the flesh and blood of the son and no longer that of the father, the sons thereby identifying themselves with him and becoming holy themselves. Thus through the ages we see the identity of the totem feast with the animal sacrifice, the theanthropic human sacrifice, and the Christian eucharist, and in all these solemn occasions we recognize the after-effects of that crime which so oppressed men but of which they must have been so proud. At bottom, however, the Christian communion is a new setting aside of the father, a repetition of the crime that must be expiated. We see how well justified is Frazer's dictum that "the Christian communion has absorbed within itself a sacrament which is doubtless far older than Christianity." [91]

7

A process like the removal of the primal father by the band of brothers must have left ineradicable traces in the history of mankind and must have expressed itself the more frequently in numerous substitutive formations the less it itself was to be remembered.[92] I am avoiding the temptation of pointing out these traces in mythology, where they are not hard to find, and am turning to another field in following a hint of S. Reinach in his suggestive treatment of the death of Orpheus.[93]

There is a situation in the history of Greek art which is strikingly familiar even if profoundly divergent, to the scene of a totem feast discovered by Robertson Smith. It is the situation of the oldest Greek tragedy. A group of persons, all of the same name and dressed in the same way, surround a single figure upon whose words and actions they are dependent, to represent the chorus and the original single impersonator of the hero. Later developments created a second and a third actor in order to repre-

---

[91] *Eating the God*, p. 51. . . . Nobody familiar with the literature on this subject will assume that the tracing back of the Christian communion to the totem feast is an idea of the author of this book.

[92] Ariel in *The Tempest:*

> Full fathom five thy father lies:
> Of his bones are coral made;
> Those are pearls that were his eyes;
> Nothing of him that doth fade
> But doth suffer a sea-change
> Into something rich and strange. . . .

[93] La Mort d'Orphée, *Cultes, Mythes, et Religions*, Vol. II, p. 100.

sent opponents in playing, and off-shoots of the hero, but the character of the hero as well as his relation to the chorus remains unchanged. The hero of the tragedy had to suffer; this is to-day still the essential content of a tragedy. He had taken upon himself the so-called "tragic guilt," which is not always easy to explain; it is often not a guilt in the ordinary sense. Almost always it consisted of a rebellion against a divine or human authority and the chorus accompanied the hero with their sympathies, trying to restrain and warn him, and lamented his fate after he had met with what was considered fitting punishment for his daring attempt.

But why did the hero of the tragedy have to suffer, and what was the meaning of his "tragic" guilt? We will cut short the discussion by a prompt answer. He had to suffer because he was the primal father, the hero of that primordial tragedy the repetition of which here serves a certain tendency, and the tragic guilt is the guilt which he had to take upon himself in order to free the chorus of theirs. The scene upon the stage came into being through purposive distortion of the historical scene or, one is tempted to say, it was the result of refined hypocrisy. Actually, in the old situation, it was the members of the chorus themselves who had caused the suffering of the hero; here, on the other hand, they exhaust themselves in sympathy and regret, and the hero himself is to blame for his suffering. The crime foisted upon him, namely, presumption and rebellion against a great authority, is the same as that which in the past oppressed the colleagues of the chorus, namely, the band of brothers. Thus the tragic hero, though still against his will, is made the redeemer of the chorus.

When one bears in mind the suffering of the divine goat Dionysos in the performance of the Greek tragedy and the lament of the retinue of goats who identified themselves with him, one can easily understand how the almost extinct drama was reviewed in the Middle Ages in the Passion of Christ.

In closing this study, which has been carried out in extremely condensed form, I want to state the conclusion that the beginnings of religion, ethics, society, and art meet in the Œdipus complex. This is in entire accord with the findings of psychoanalysis, namely, that the nucleus of all neuroses as far as our present knowledge of them goes is the Œdipus complex. It comes as a great surprise to me that these problems of racial psychology can also be solved through a single concrete instance, such as the relation to the father. Perhaps another psychological problem must be included here. We have so frequently had occasion to show the ambivalence of emotions in its real sense, that is to say the coincidence of love and hate towards the same object, at the root of important cultural formations. We know nothing about the origin of this ambivalence. It may be assumed to be a fundamental phenomenon of our emotional life. But the other possibility seems to me also worthy of consideration: that ambivalence, originally foreign to our emotional life, was acquired by mankind from the father complex,[94] where psychoanalytic investigation of the individual to-day still reveals the strongest expression of it.[95]

[94] That is to say, the parent complex.
[95] I am used to being misunderstood and therefore do not think it superfluous to state clearly that in giving these deductions I am by no means oblivious of the complex nature of the phenomena which give rise to them; the only claim made is that a new factor has been added to the already known or still unrecog-

Before closing we must take into account that the remarkable convergence reached in these illustrations, pointing to a single inclusive relation, ought not to blind us to the uncertainties of our assumptions and to the difficulties of our conclusions. Of these difficulties I will point out only two which must have forced themselves upon many readers.

In the first place it can hardly have escaped any one that we base everything upon the assumption of a psyche of the mass in which psychic processes occur as in the psychic life of the individual. Moreover, we let the sense of guilt for a deed survive for thousands of years, remaining effective in generations which could not have known anything of this deed. We allow an emotional process such as might have arisen among generations of sons that had been ill-treated by their fathers, to continue to new generations which had escaped such treatment by the very removal of the father. These seem indeed to be weighty objections and any other explanation which can avoid such assumptions would seem to merit preference.

But further consideration shows that we ourselves do not have to carry the whole responsibility for such daring. Without the assumption of a mass psyche, or a continuity in the emotional life of mankind which permits us to disregard the interruptions of psychic acts through the transgression of individuals, social psychology could not exist at all. If psychic processes of one generation did not continue in the next, if each

---

nized origins of religion, morality, and society, which was furnished through psychoanalytic experience. The synthesis of the whole explanation must be left to another. But it is in the nature of this new contribution that it could play none other than the central rôle in such a synthesis, although it will be necessary to overcome great affective resistances before such importance will be conceded to it.

had to acquire its attitude towards life afresh, there would be no progress in this field and almost no development. We are now confronted by two new questions: how much can be attributed to this psychic continuity within the series of generations, and what ways and means does a generation use to transfer its psychic states to the next generation? I do not claim that these problems have been sufficiently explained or that direct communication and tradition, of which one immediately thinks, are adequate for the task. Social psychology is in general little concerned with the manner in which the required continuity in the psychic life of succeeding generations is established. A part of the task seems to be performed by the inheritance of psychic dispositions which, however, need certain incentives in the individual life in order to become effective. This may be the meaning of the poet's words: Strive to possess yourself of what you have inherited from your ancestors. The problem would appear more difficult if we could admit that there are psychic impulses which can be so completely suppressed that they leave no traces whatsoever behind them. But that does not exist. The greatest suppression must leave room for distorted substitutions and their resulting reactions. But in that case we may assume that no generation is capable of concealing its more important psychic processes from the next. For psychoanalysis has taught us that in his unconscious psychic activity every person possesses an apparatus which enables him to interpret the reactions of others, that is to say, to straighten out the distortions which the other person has affected in the expression of his feelings. By this method of unconscious understanding of all customs, ceremonies, and laws which the original relation to the primal father had left behind, later generations may also have succeeded in taking over this legacy of feelings.

There is another objection which the analytic method of thought itself might raise.

We have interpreted the first rules of morality and moral restrictions of primitive society as reactions to a deed which gave the authors of it the conception of crime. They regretted this deed and decided that it should not be repeated and that its execution must bring no gain. This creative sense of guilt has not become extinct with us. We find its asocial effects in neurotics producing new rules of morality and continued restrictions, in expiation for misdeeds committed, or as precautions against misdeeds to be committed.[96] But when we examine these neurotics for the deeds which have called forth such reactions, we are disappointed. We do not find deeds, but only impulses and feelings which sought evil but which were restrained from carrying it out. Only psychic realities and not actual ones are at the basis of the neurotics' sense of guilt. It is characteristic of the neurosis to put a psychic reality above an actual one and to react as seriously to thoughts as the normal person reacts only towards realities.

May it not be true that the case was somewhat the same with primitive men? We are justified in ascribing to them an extraordinary over-valuation of their psychic acts as a partial manifestation of their narcistic organization.[97] According to this the mere impulses of hostility towards the father and the existence of the wish phantasy to kill and devour him may have sufficed to bring about the moral reaction which has created totemism and taboo. We should thus escape

[96] Compare Chapter II.
[97] See Chapter III.

the necessity of tracing back the beginning of our cultural possession, of which we rightly are so proud, to a horrible crime which wounds all our feelings. The causal connexion, which stretches from that beginning to the present time, would not be impaired, for the psychic reality would be of sufficient importance to account for all those consequences. It may be agreed that a change has really taken place in the form of society from the father horde to the brother clan. This is a strong argument, but it is not conclusive. The change might have been accomplished in a less violent manner and still have conditioned the appearance of the moral reaction. As long as the pressure of the primal father was felt the hostile feelings against him were justified and repentance at these feelings had to wait for another opportunity. Of as little validity is the second objection, that everything derived from the ambivalent relation to the father, namely taboos, and rules of sacrifice, is characterized by the highest seriousness and by complete reality The ceremonials and inhibitions of compulsion neurotics exhibit this characteristic too and yet they go back to a merely psychic reality, to resolution and not to execution. We must beware of introducing the contempt for what is merely thought or wished which characterizes our sober world where there are only material values, into the world of primitive man and the neurotic, which is full of inner riches only.

We face a decision here which is really not easy. But let us begin by acknowledging that the difference which may seem fundamental to others does not, in our judgment, touch the most important part of the subject. If wishes and impulses have the full value of fact for primitive man, it is for us to follow such a conception intelligently instead of correcting it according to our standard. But in that case we must scrutinize more closely the prototype of the neurosis itself which is responsible for having raised this doubt. It is not true that compulsion neurotics, who to-day are under the pressure of over-morality, defend themselves only against the psychic reality of temptations and punish themselves for impulses which they have only felt. A piece of historic reality is also involved; in their childhood these persons had nothing but evil impulses and as far as their childish impotence permitted they put them into action. Each of these over-good persons had a period of badness in his childhood, and a perverse phase as a fore-runner and a premise of the latter over-morality. The analogy between primitive men and neurotics is therefore much more fundamentally established if we assume that with the former, too, the psychic reality, concerning whose structure there is no doubt, originally coincided with the actual reality, and that primitive men really did what according to all testimony they intended to do.

But we must not let our judgment about primitive men be influenced too far by the analogy with neurotics. Differences must also be taken into account. Of course the sharp division between thinking and doing as we draw it does not exist either with savages or with neurotics. But the neurotic is above all inhibited in his actions; with him the thought is a complete substitute for the deed. Primitive man is not inhibited, the thought is directly converted into the deed, the deed is for him so to speak rather a substitute for the thought, and for that reason I think we may well assume in the case we are discussing, though without vouching for the absolute certainty of the decision, that "In the beginning was the deed."

Although the son of a New England parson and a minister himself, Ralph Waldo Emerson (1803-1882) preferred the life of public lecturer and essayist to that of a clergyman. An immensely popular speaker, he was also an important philosopher and moralist. His philosophy, which he called Idealism, but which is generally known as Transcendentalism was expounded in his first book of essays, of which *The Oversoul* is the cornerstone.

THE OVER-SOUL

"But souls that of his own good life partake,
He loves as his own self; dear as his eye
They are to Him: He'll never them forsake:
When they shall die, then God hmself shall die:
They live, they live in blest eternity."

Henry More,

Space is ample, east and west,
But two cannot go abreast,
Cannot travel in it two:
Yonder masterful cuckoo
Crowds every egg out of the nest,
Quick or dead, except its own;
A spell is laid on sod and stone,
Night and Day 've been tampered with,
Every quality and pith
Surcharged and sultry with a power
That works its will on age and hour.

THERE is a difference between one and another hour of life in their authority and subsequent effect. Our faith comes in moments; our vice is habitual. Yet there is a depth in those brief moments which constrains us to ascribe more reality to them than to all other experiences. For this reason the argument which is always forthcoming to silence those who conceive extraordinary hopes of man, namely the appeal to experience, is for ever invalid and vain. We give up the past to the objector, and yet we hope. He must explain this hope. We grant that human life is mean, but how did we find out that it was mean? What is the ground of this uneasiness of ours; of this old discontent? What is the universal sense of want and ignorance, but the fine innuendo by which the soul makes its enormous claim? Why do men feel that the natural history of man has never been written, but he is always leaving behind what you have said of him, and it becomes old, and books of metaphysics worth less? The philosophy of six thousand years has not searched the chambers and magazines of the soul. In its experiments there has always remained, in the last analysis, a residuum it could not resolve. Man is a stream whose source is hidden. Our being is descending into us from we know not whence. The most exact calculator has no prescience that somewhat incalculable may not balk the very next moment. I am constrained every moment to acknowledge a higher origin for events than the will I call mine.

As with events, so is it with thoughts. When I watch that flowing river, which, out of regions I see not, pours for a season its streams into me, I see that I am a pensioner; not a cause but a surprised spectator of this ethereal water; that I desire and look up and put myself in the attitude of reception, but from some alien energy the visions come.

The Supreme Critic on the errors of the past and the present, and the only prophet of that which must be, is that great nature in which we rest as the earth lies in the soft arms of the atmosphere; that Unity, that Over-Soul, within which every man's particular being is contained and made one with all other; that common heart of which all sincere conversation is the worship, to which all right action is submission; that overpowering reality which confutes our tricks and talents, and constrains every one to pass for what he is, and to speak from his character and not from his tongue, and which evermore tends to pass into our thought and hand and become wisdom and virtue and power and beauty. We live in succession, in division, in parts, in particles. Meantime within man is the soul of the whole; the wise silence; the universal beauty, to which every part and particle is equally related; the eternal ONE. And this deep power in which we exist and whose beatitude is all accessible to us, is not only self-sufficing and perfect in every hour, but the act of seeing and the thing seen, the seer and the spectacle, the subject and the object, are one. We see the world piece by piece, as the sun, the moon, the animal, the tree; but the whole, of which these are the shining parts, is the soul. Only by the vision of that Wisdom can the horoscope of the ages be read, and by falling back on our better thoughts, by yielding to the spirit of prophecy which is innate in every man, we can know what it saith. Every man's words who speaks from that life must sound vain to those who do not dwell in the same thought on their own part. I dare not speak for it. My words do not carry its august sense; they fall short and cold. Only itself can inspire whom it will, and behold! their speech shall be lyrical, and sweet, and universal as the rising of the wind. Yet I desire, even by profane words, if I may not use sacred, to indicate the heaven of this deity and to report what hints I have collected of the transcendent simplicity and energy of the Highest Law.

If we consider what happens in conversation, in reveries, in remorse, in times of passion, in surprises, in the instructions of dreams, wherein often we see ourselves in masquerade—the droll disguises only magnifying and enhancing a real element and forcing it on our distant notice—we shall catch many hints that will broaden and lighten into knowledge of the secret of nature. All goes to show that the soul in man is not an organ, but animates and exercises all the organs; is not a function, like the power of memory, of calculation, of comparison, but uses these as hands and feet; is not a faculty, but a light; is not the intellect or the will, but the master of the intellect and the will; is the background of our being, in which they lie—an immensity not possessed and that cannot be possessed. From within or from behind, a light shines through us upon things and makes us aware that we are nothing, but the light is all. A man is the façade of a temple wherein all wisdom and all good abide. What we commonly call man, the eating, drinking, planting, counting man, does not, as we know him, represent himself, but misrepresents himself. Him we do not respect, but the soul, whose organ he is, would he let it appear through his action, would make our knees bend. When it breathes through his intellect, it is genius; when it breathes through his will, it is virtue; when it flows through his affection, it is love. And the blindness of the intellect begins when it would be something of itself. The weakness of the will begins when the individual would be something of himself. All reform aims in some one particular to let the soul have its way through us; in other words, to engage us to obey.

Of this pure nature every man is at some time sensible. Language cannot paint it with his colors. It is too subtile. It is undefinable, unmeasurable; but we know that it pervades and contains us. We know that all spiritual being is in man. A wise old proverb says, "God comes to see us without bell;" that is, as there is no screen or ceiling between our heads and the infinite heavens, so is there no bar or wall in the soul, where man, the effect, ceases, and God, the cause, begins. The walls are taken away. We lie open on one side to the deeps of spiritual nature, to the attributes of God. Justice we see and know, Love, Freedom, Power. These natures no man ever got above, but they tower over us, and most in the moment when our interests tempt us to wound them.

The sovereignty of this nature whereof we speak is made known by its independency of those limitations which circumscribe us on every hand. The soul circumscribes all things. As I have said, it contradicts all experience. In like manner it abolishes time and space. The influence of the senses has in most men overpowered the mind to that degree that the walls of time and space have come to look real and insurmountable; and to speak with levity of these limits is, in the world, the sign of insanity. Yet time and space are but inverse measures of the force of the soul. The spirit sports with time—

"Can crowd eternity into an hour,
Or stretch an hour to eternity."

We are often made to feel that there is another youth and age than that which is measured from the year of our natural birth. Some thoughts always find us young, and keep us so. Such a thought is the love of the universal and eternal beauty. Every man parts from that contemplation with the feeling that it rather belongs to ages than to mortal life. The least activity of the intellectual powers redeems us in a degree from the conditions of time. In sickness, in languor, give us a strain of

poetry or a profound sentence, and we are refreshed; or produce a volume of Plato or Shakspeare, or remind us of their
names, and instantly we come into a feeling of longevity. See
how the deep divine thought reduces centuries and millenniums,
and makes itself present through all ages. Is the teaching of
Christ less effective now than it was when first his mouth was
opened? The emphasis of facts and persons in my thought has
nothing to do with time. And so always the soul's scale is one,
the scale of the senses and the understanding is another. Before
the revelations of the soul, Time, Space and Nature shrink away.
In common speech we refer all things to time, as we habitually
refer the immensely sundered stars to one concave sphere. And
so we say that the Judgment is distant or near, that the Millen-
nium approaches, that a day of certain political, moral, social
reforms is at hand, and the like, when we mean that in the
nature of things one of the facts we contemplate is external
and fugitive, and the other is permanent and connate with the
soul. The things we now esteem fixed shall, one by one, detach
themselves like ripe fruit from our experience, and fall. The
wind shall blow them none knows whither. The landscape, the
figures, Boston, London, are facts as fugitive as any institution
past, or any whiff of mist or smoke, and so is society, and so is
the world. The soul looketh steadily forwards, creating a world
before her, leaving worlds behind her. She has no dates, nor
rites, nor persons, nor specialties, nor men. The soul knows
only the soul; the web of events is the flowing robe in which
she is clothed.

After its own law and not by arithmetic is the rate of its progress to be computed. The soul's advances are not made by gradation, such as can be represented by motion in a straight line, but
rather by ascension of state, such as can be represented by
metamorphosis—from the egg to the worm, from the worm to
the fly. The growths of genius are of a certain *total* character,
that does not advance the elect individual first over John, then
Adam, then Richard, and give to each the pain of discovered in-
feriority—but by every throe of growth the man expands there
where he works, passing, at each pulsation, classes, populations.

of men. With each divine impulse the mind rends the thin rinds of the visible and finite, and comes out into eternity, and inspires and expires its air. It converses with truths that have always been spoken in the world, and becomes conscious of a closer sympathy with Zeno and Arrian than with persons in the house.

This is the law of moral and of mental gain. The simple rise as by specific levity not into a particular virtue, but into the region of all the virtues. They are in the spirit which contains them all. The soul requires purity, but purity is not it; requires justice, but justice is not that; requires beneficence, but is somewhat better; so that there is a kind of descent and accommodation felt when we leave speaking of moral nature to urge a virtue which it enjoins. To the well-born child all the virtues are natural, and not painfully acquired. Speak to his heart, and the man becomes suddenly virtuous.

Within the same sentiment is the germ of intellectual growth, which obeys the same law. Those who are capable of humility, of justice, of love, of aspiration, stand already on a platform that commands the sciences and arts, speech and poetry, action and grace. For whoso dwells in this moral beatitude already anticipates those special powers which men prize so highly. The lover has no talent, no skill, which passes for quite nothing with his enamored maiden, however little she may possess of related faculty; and the heart which abandons itself to the Supreme Mind finds itself related to all its works, and will travel a royal road to particular knowledges and powers. In ascending to this primary and aboriginal sentiment we have come from our remote station on the circumference instantaneously to the centre of the world, where, as in the closet of God, we see causes, and anticipate the universe, which is but a slow effect.

One mode of the divine teaching is the incarnation of the spirit in a form—in forms, like my own. I live in society; with persons who answer to thoughts in my own mind, or express a certain obedience to the great instincts to which I live. I see its presence to them. I am certified of a common nature; and these other souls, these separated selves, draw me as nothing else can. They stir in me the new emotions we call passion; of love, hatred, fear, admiration, pity; thence come conversation, competition, persuasion, cities and war. Persons are supplementary to the primary teaching of the soul. In youth we are mad for persons. Childhood and youth see all the world in them. But the larger experience of man discovers the identical nature appearing through them all. Persons themselves acquaint us with the impersonal. In all conversation between two persons tacit reference is made, as to a third party, to a common nature. That third party or common nature is not social; it is impersonal; is God. And so in groups where debate is earnest, and especially on high questions, the company become aware that the thought rises to an equal level in all bosoms, that all have a spiritual property in what was said, as well as the sayer. They all become wiser than they were. It arches over them like a temple, this unity of thought in which every heart beats with nobler sense of power and duty, and thinks and acts with unusual solemnity. All are conscious of attaining to a higher self-possession. It shines for all. There is a certain wisdom of humanity which is common to the greatest men with the lowest, and which our ordinary education often labors to silence and obstruct. The mind is one, and the best minds, who love truth for its own sake, think much less of property in truth. They accept it thankfully everywhere, and do not label or stamp it with any man's name, for it is theirs long beforehand, and from eternity. The learned and the studious of thought have no monopoly of wisdom. Their violence of direction in some degree disqualifies them to think truly. We owe many valuable observations to people who are not very acute or profound, and who say the thing without effort which we want and have long been hunting in vain. The action of the soul is oftener in that which is felt and left unsaid than in that which is said in any conversation. It broods over every society, and they unconsciously seek for it in each other. We know better than we do. We do not yet possess ourselves, and we know at the same time that we are much more. I feel the same truth how often in my trivial conversation with my neighbors, that somewhat higher in each of us overlooks this by-play, and Jove nods to Jove from behind each of us.

Men descend to meet. In their habitual and mean service to the world, for which they forsake their native nobleness, they resemble those Arabian sheiks who dwell in mean houses and affect an external poverty, to escape the rapacity of the Pacha, and reserve all their display of wealth for their interior and guarded retirements.

As it is present in all persons, so it is in every period of life. It is adult already in the infant man. In my dealing with my child, my Latin and Greek, my accomplishments and my money stead me nothing; but as much soul as I have avails. If I am wilful, he sets his will against mine, one for one, and leaves me, if I please, the degradation of beating him by my superiority of strength. But if I renounce my will and act for the soul, setting that up as umpire between us two, out of his young eyes looks the same soul; he reveres and loves with me.

The soul is the perceiver and revealer of truth. We know truth when he see it, let sceptic and scoffer say what they choose. Foolish people ask you, when you have spoken what they do not wish to hear, 'How do you know it is truth, and not an error of your own?' We know truth when we see it, from opinion, as we know when we are awake that we are awake. It was a grand sentence of Emanuel Swedenborg, which would alone indicate the greatness of that man's perception—"It is no proof of a man's understanding to be able to affirm whatever he pleases; but to be able to discern that what is true is true, and that what is false is false—this is the mark and character of intelligence." In the book I read, the good thought returns to me, as every truth will, the image of the whole soul. To the bad thought which I find in it, the same soul becomes a discerning, separating sword, and lops it away. We are wiser than we know. If we will not interfere with our thought, but will act entirely, or see how the thing stands in God, we know the particular thing, and every thing, and every man. For the Maker of all things and all persons stands behind us and casts his dread omniscience through us over things.

But beyond this recognition of its own in particular passages of the individual's experience, it also reveals truth. And
here we should seek to reinforce ourselves by its very presence,
and to speak with a worthier, loftier strain of that advent. For
the soul's communication of truth is the highest event in nature, since it then does not give somewhat from itself, but it
gives itself, or passes into and becomes that man whom it en-
lightens; or in proportion to that truth he receives, it takes him
to itself.

We distinguish the announcements of the soul, its manifestations of its own nature, by the term *Revelation*. These are
always attended by the emotion of the sublime. For this communication is an influx of the Divine mind into our mind. It is
an ebb of the individual rivulet before the flowing surges of the
sea of life. Every distinct apprehension of this central commandment agitates men with awe and delight. A thrill passes
through all men at the reception of new truth, or at the performance of a great action, which comes out of the heart of
nature. In these communications the power to see is not separated from the will to do, but the insight proceeds from
obedience, and the obedience proceeds from a joyful perception. Every moment when the individual feels himself in-
vaded by it is memorable. By the necessity of our constitution
a certain enthusiasm attends the individual's consciousness of
that divine presence. The character and duration of this enthusiasm vary with the state of the individual, from an ecstasy and
trance and prophetic inspiration—which is its rarer appearance
—to the faintest glow of virtuous emotion, in which form it
warms, like our household fires, all the families and associations of men, and makes society possible. A certain tendency to
insanity has always attended the opening of the religious sense
in men, as if they had been "blasted with excess of light."
The trances of Socrates, the "union" of Plotinus, the vision of
Porphyry, the conversion of Paul, the aurora of Behmen, the
convulsions of George Fox and his Quakers, the illumination of
Swedenborg, are of this kind. What was in the case of these
remarkable persons a ravishment, has, in innumerable instances

in common life, been exhibited in less striking manner. Every-where the history of religion betrays a tendency to enthusiasm. The rapture of the Moravian and Quietist; the opening of the eternal sense of the Word, in the language of the New Jerusalem Church; the *revival* of the Calvinistic churches; the *experiences* of the Methodists, are varying forms of that shudder of awe and delight with which the individual soul always mingles with the universal soul.

The nature of these revelations is the same; they are per-ceptions of the absolute law. They are solutions of the soul's own questions. They do not answer the questions which the understanding asks. The soul answers never by words, but by the thing itself that is inquired after.

Revelation is the disclosure of the soul. The popular notion of a revelation is that it is a telling of fortunes. In past oracles of the soul the understanding seeks to find answers to sensual ques-tions, and undertakes to tell from God how long men shall exist, what their hands shall do and who shall be their company, adding names and dates and places. But we must pick no locks. We must check this low curiosity. An answer in words is delusive; it is really no answer to the questions you ask. Do not require a description of the countries towards which you sail. The description does not describe them to you, and to-morrow you arrive there and know them by inhabiting them. Men ask concerning the immortality of the soul, the employ-ments of heaven, the state of the sinner, and so forth. They even dream that Jesus has left replies to precisely these inter-rogatories. Never a moment did that sublime spirit speak in their *patois*. To truth, justice, love, the attributes of the soul, the idea of immutableness is essentially associated. Jesus, living in these moral sentiments, heedless of sensual fortunes, heeding only the manifestations of these, never made the separation of the idea of duration from the essence of these attributes, nor uttered a syllable concerning the duration of the soul. It was left to his disciples to sever duration from the moral elements, and to teach the immortality of the soul as a doctrine, and main-tain it by evidences. The moment the doctrine of the immortality is separately taught, man is already fallen. In the flowing of love, in the adoration of humility, there is no question of continuance. No inspired man ever asks this question or condescends to these evidences. For the soul is true to itself, and the man in whom it is shed abroad cannot wander from the present, which is infinite, to a future which would be finite.

These questions which we lust to ask about the future are a confession of sin. God has no answer for them. No answer in words can reply to a question of things. It is not in an arbitrary "decree of God," but in the nature of man, that a veil shuts down on the facts of to-morrow; for the soul will not have us read any other cipher than that of cause and effect. By this veil which curtains events it instructs the children of men to live in to-day. The only mode of obtaining an answer to these questions of the senses is to forego all low curiosity, and, accepting the tide of being which floats us into the secret of nature, work and live, work and live, and all unawares the advancing soul has built and forged for itself a new condition, and the question and the answer are one.

By the same fire, vital, consecrating, celestial, which burns until it shall dissolve all things into the waves and surges of an ocean of light, we see and know each other, and what spirit each is of. Who can tell the grounds of his knowledge of the character of the several individuals in his circle of friends? No man. Yet their acts and words do not disappoint him. In that man, though he knew no ill of him, he put no trust. In that other, though they had seldom met, authentic signs had yet passed, to signify that he might be trusted as one who had an interest in his own character. We know each other very well—which of us has been just to himself and whether that which we teach or behold is only an inspiration or is our honest effort also.

We are all discerners of spirits. That diagnosis lies aloft in our life or unconscious power. The intercourse of society, its trade, its religion, its friendships, its quarrels, is one wide judicial investigation of character. In full court, or in small committee, or confronted face to face, accuser and accused, men offer themselves to be judged. Against their will they exhibit those decisive trifles by which character is read. But who judges? and what? Not our understanding. We do not read them by learning or craft. No; the wisdom of the wise man consists herein, that he does not judge them; he lets them judge themselves and merely reads and records their own verdict.

By virtue of this inevitable nature, private will is overpowered, and, maugre our efforts or our imperfections, your genius will speak from you, and mine from me. That which we are, we shall teach, not voluntarily but involuntarily. Thoughts come into our minds by avenues which we never left open, and thoughts go out of our minds through avenues which we never voluntarily opened. Character teaches over our head. The infallible index of true progress is found in the tone the man takes. Neither his age, nor his breeding, nor company, nor books, nor actions, nor talents, nor all together can hinder him from being deferential to a higher spirit than his own. If he have not found his home in God, his manners, his forms of speech, the turn of his sentences, the build, shall I say, of all his opinions will involuntarily confess it, let him brave it out how he will. If we have found his centre, the Deity will shine through him, through all the disguises of ignorance, of ungenial temperament, of unfavorable circumstance. The tone of seeking is one, and the tone of having is another.

The great distinction between teachers sacred or literary— between poets like Herbert, and poets like Pope—between philosophers like Spinoza, Kant and Coleridge, and philosophers like Locke, Paley, Mackintosh and Stewart—between men of the world who are reckoned accomplished talkers, and here and there a fervent mystic, prophesying half insane under the infinitude of his thought—is that one class speak *from within*, or from experience, as parties and possessors of the fact; and the other class *from without*, as spectators merely, or perhaps as acquainted with the fact on the evidence of third persons. It is of no use to preach to me from without. I can do that too easily myself. Jesus speaks always from within, and in a degree that transcends all others. In that is the miracle. I believe beforehand that it ought so to be. All men stand continually in the expectation of the appearance of such a teacher. But if a man do not speak from within the veil, where the word is one with that it tells of, let him lowly confess it.

The same Omniscience flows into the intellect and makes what we call genius. Much of the wisdom of the world is not wisdom, and the most illuminated class of men are no doubt superior to literary fame, and are not writers. Among the multitude of scholars and authors we feel no hallowing presence; we are sensible of a knack and skill rather than of inspiration; they have a light and know not whence it comes and call it their own; their talent is some exaggerated faculty, some overgrown member, so that their strength is a disease. In these instances the intellectual gifts do not make the impression of virtue, but almost of vice; and we feel that a man's talents stand in the way of his advancement in truth. But genius is religious. It is a larger imbibing of the common heart. It is not anomalous, but more like and not less like other men. There is in all great poets a wisdom of humanity which is superior to any talents they exercise. The author, the wit, the partisan, the fine gentleman, does not take place of the man. Humanity shines in Homer, in Chaucer, in Spenser, in Shakspeare, in Milton. They are content with truth. They use the positive degree. They seem frigid and phlegmatic to those who have been spiced with the frantic passion and violent coloring of inferior but popular writers. For they are poets by the free course which they allow to the informing soul, which through their eyes beholds again and blesses the things which it hath made. The soul is superior to its knowledge, wiser than any of its works. The great poet makes us feel our own wealth, and then we think less of his compositions. His best communication to our mind is to teach us to despise all he has done. Shakspeare carries us to such a lofty strain of intelligent activity as to suggest a wealth which beggars his own; and we then feel that the splendid works which he has created, and which in other hours we extol as a sort of self-existent poetry, take no stronger hold of real nature than the shadow of a passing traveller on the rock. The inspiration which uttered itself in Hamlet and Lear could utter things as good from day to day for ever. Why then should I make account of Hamlet and Lear, as if we had not the soul from which they fell as syllables from the tongue?

This energy does not descend into individual life on any other condition than entire possession. It comes to the lowly and simple; it comes to whomsoever will put off what is foreign and proud; it comes as insight; it comes as serenity and grandeur. When we see those whom it inhabits, we are apprised of new degrees of greatness. From that inspiration the man comes back with a changed tone. He does not talk with men with an eye to their opinion. He tries them. It requires of us to be plain and true. The vain traveller attempts to embellish his life by quoting my lord and the prince and the countess, who thus said or did to *him*. The ambitious vulgar show you their spoons and brooches and rings, and preserve their cards and compliments. The more cultivated, in their account of their own experience, cull out the pleasing, poetic circumstance—the visit to Rome, the man of genius they saw, the brilliant friend they know; still further on perhaps the gorgeous landscape, the mountain lights, the mountain thoughts they enjoyed yesterday —and so seek to throw a romantic color over their life. But the soul that ascends to worship the great God is plain and true; has no rose-color, no fine friends, no chivalry, no adventures; does not want admiration; dwells in the hour that now is, in the earnest experience of the common day—by reason of the present moment and the mere trifle having become porous to thought and bibulous of the sea of light.

Converse with a mind that is grandly simple, and literature looks like word-catching. The simplest utterances are worthiest to be written, yet are they so cheap and so things of course, that in the infinite riches of the soul it is like gathering a few pebbles off the ground, or bottling a little air in a phial, when the whole earth and the whole atmosphere are ours. Nothing can pass there, or make you one of the circle, but the casting aside your trappings and dealing man to man in naked truth, plain confession and omniscient affirmation.

Souls such as these treat you as gods would, walk as gods in the earth, accepting without any admiration your wit, your bounty, your virtue even—say rather your act of duty, for your virtue they own as their proper blood, royal as themselves, and over-royal, and the father of the gods. But what rebuke their plain fraternal bearing casts on the mutual flattery with which authors solace each other and wound themselves! These flatter not. I do not wonder that these men go to see Cromwell and Christina and Charles the Second and James the First and the Grand Turk. For they are, in their own elevation, the fellows of kings, and must feel the servile tone of conversation in the world. They must always be a godsend to princes, for they confront them, a king to a king, without ducking or concession, and give a high nature the refreshment and satisfaction of resistance, of plain humanity, of even companionship and of new ideas. They leave them wiser and superior men. Souls like these make us feel that sincerity is more excellent than flattery. Deal so plainly with man and woman as to constrain the utmost sincerity and destroy all hope of trifling with you. It is the highest compliment you can pay. Their "highest praising," said Milton, "is not flattery, and their plainest advice is a kind of praising."

Ineffable is the union of man and God in every act of the soul. The simplest person who in his integrity worships God, becomes God; yet for ever and ever the influx of this better and universal self is new and unsearchable. It inspires awe and astonishment. How dear, how soothing to man, arises the idea of God, peopling the lonely place, effacing the scars of our mistakes and disappointments! When we have broken our god of tradition and ceased from our god of rhetoric, then may God fire the heart with his presence. It is the doubling of the heart itself, nay, the infinite enlargement of the heart with a power of growth to a new infinity on every side. It inspires in man an infallible trust. He has not the conviction, but the sight, that the best is the true, and may in that thought easily dismiss all particular uncertainties and fears, and adjourn to the sure revelation of time the solution of his private riddles. He is sure that his welfare is dear to the heart of being. In the presence of law to his mind he is overflowed with a reliance so universal that it sweeps away all cherished hopes and the most stable projects of mortal condition in its flood. He believes that he cannot escape from his good. The things that are really for thee gravitate to thee. You are running to seek your friend. Let your feet run, but your mind need not. If you do not find him, will you not acquiesce that it is best you should not find him? for there is a power, which, as it is in you, is in him also, and could therefore very well bring you together, if it were for the best. You are preparing with eagerness to go and render a service to which your talent and your taste invite you, the love of men and the hope of fame. Has it not occurred to you that you have no right to go, unless you are equally willing to be prevented from going? O, believe, as thou livest, that every sound that is spoken over the round world, which thou oughtest to hear, will vibrate on thine ear! Every proverb, every book, every byword that belongs to thee for aid or comfort, shall surely come home through open or winding passages. Every friend whom not thy fantastic will but the great and tender heart in thee craveth, shall lock thee in his embrace. And this because the heart in thee is the heart of all; not a valve, not a wall, not an intersection is there anywhere in nature, but one blood rolls uninterruptedly an endless circulation through all men, as the water of the globe is all one sea, and, truly seen, its tide is one.

Let man then learn the revelation of all nature and all thought to his heart; this, namely; that the Highest dwells with him; that the sources of nature are in his own mind, if the sentiment of duty is there. But if he would know what the great God speaketh, he must 'go into his closet and shut the door,' as Jesus said. God will not make himself manifest to cowards. He must greatly listen to himself, withdrawing himself from all the accents of other men's devotion. Even their prayers are hurtful to him, until he have made his own. Our religion vulgarly stands on numbers of believers. Whenever the appeal is made—no matter how indirectly—to numbers, proclamation is then and there made that religion is not. He that finds God a sweet enveloping thought to him never counts his company. When I sit in that presence, who shall dare to come in? When I rest in perfect humility, when I burn with pure love, what can Calvin or Swedenborg say?

It makes no difference whether the appeal is to numbers or to one. The faith that stands on authority is not faith. The reliance on authority measures the decline of religion, the withdrawal of the soul. The position men have given to Jesus, now for many centuries of history, is a position of authority. It characterizes themselves. It cannot alter the eternal facts. Great is the soul, and plain. It is no flatterer, it is no follower; it never appeals from itself. It believes in itself. Before the immense possibilities of man all mere experience, all past biography, however spotless and sainted, shrinks away. Before that heaven which our presentiments foreshow us, we cannot easily praise any form of life we have seen or read of. We not only affirm that we have few great men, but, absolutely speaking, that we have none; that we have no history, no record of any character or mode of living that entirely contents us. The saints and demigods whom history worships we are constrained to accept with a grain of allowance. Though in our lonely hours we draw a new strength out of their memory, yet, pressed on our attention, as they are by the thoughtless and customary, they fatigue and invade. The soul gives itself, alone, original and pure, to the Lonely, Original and Pure, who, on that condition, gladly inhabits, leads and speaks through it. Then is it glad, young and nimble. It is not wise, but it sees through all things. It is not called religious, but it is innocent. It calls the light its own, and feels that the grass grows and the stone falls by a law inferior to, and dependent on, its nature. Behold, it saith, I am born into the great, the universal mind. I, the imperfect, adore my own Perfect. I am somehow receptive of the great soul, and thereby I do overlook the sun and the stars and feel them to be the fair accidents and effects which change and pass. More and more the surges of everlasting nature enter into me, and I become public and human in my regards and actions. So come I to live in thoughts and act with energies which are immortal

Thus revering the soul, and learning, as the ancient said, that "its beauty is immense," man will come to see that the world is the perennial miracle which the soul worketh, and be less astonished at particular wonders; he will learn that there is no profane history; that all history is sacred; that the universe is represented in an atom, in a moment of time. He will weave no longer a spotted life of shreds and patches, but he will live with a divine unity. He will cease from what is base and frivolous in his life and be content with all places and with any service he can render. He will calmly front the morrow in the negligency of that trust which carries God with it and so hath already the whole future in the bottom of the heart.

Sigmund Freud,   THE ORIGIN AND DEVELOPMENT OF
                  PSYCHOANALYSIS

1. How does Freud distinguish between illness which
    is the result of organic disease of the brain and
    that which is the result of "hysteria"?

2. Explain Freud's statement, "Our hysterical patients
    suffer from reminiscences."

3. How does Freud differ from Janet in explaining
    hysteria?

4. Why did Freud give up hypnotism in his treatment of
    patients? What was his alternative?

5. Explain Freud's statement, "It is on this idea of
    resistance that I based my theory of the psychic
    process of hystericals."

6. What is the significance of the "unconscious" in
    Freud's theory?

7. What is the importance of dreams for Freud?

8. If dreams are wish-fulfillments, how does Freud
    account for anxiety dreams?

9. What is the significance of the bungling of acts
    ("Freudian slips")?

10. Do you agree with Freud's emphasis on sexuality in
    the factors which lead to neurosis? Is there an
    infant sexuality?

11. What is Freud's idea of transfer?

12. What possible positive effects does Freud see in
    sublimation? What are the limits of sublimation?

In this series of lectures, first published in the *American Journal of Psychology* in 1910, Freud outlines the bases for his theory of psychoanalysis which has had such a profound influence on interpretations of man ever since. Some would suggest that Freud stands with Galileo, Darwin, and Einstein in revolutionizing ideas about man's place in the universe. Poet W. H. Auden wrote of him: "...A world he changed simply by looking back with no false regrets; All that he did was to remember like the old and be honest like children... To us he is no more a person, now but a whole climate of opinion... ."

THE ORIGIN AND DEVELOPMENT OF PSYCHOANALYSIS

First Lecture

Ladies and Gentlemen: It is a new and somewhat embarrassing experience for me to appear as lecturer before students of the New World. I assume that I owe this honor to the association of my name with the theme of psychoanalysis, and consequently it is of psychoanalysis that I shall aim to speak. I shall attempt to give you in very brief form an historical survey of the origin and further development of this new method of research and cure.

Granted that it is a merit to have created psychoanalysis, it is not my merit. I was a student, busy with the passing of my last examinations, when another physician of Vienna, Dr. Joseph Breuer, made the first application of this method to the case of an hysterical girl (1880-82). We must now examine the history of this case and its treatment, which can be found in detail in "Studien über Hysterie," later published by Dr. Breuer and myself.

But first one word. I have noticed, with considerable satisfaction, that the majority of my hearers do not belong to the medical profession. Now do not fear that a medical education is necessary to follow what I shall have to say. We shall now accompany the doctors a little way,

357

but soon we shall take leave of them and follow Dr. Breuer on a way which is quite his own.

Dr. Breuer's patient was a girl of twenty-one, of a high degree of intelligence. She had developed in the course of her two years' illness a series of physical and mental disturbances which well deserved to be taken seriously. She had a severe paralysis of both right extremities, with anæsthesia, and at times the same affection of the members of the left side of the body; disturbance of eye-movements, and much impairment of vision; difficulty in maintaining the position of the head, an intense *Tussis nervosa,* nausea when she attempted to take nourishment, and at one time for several weeks a loss of the power to drink, in spite of tormenting thirst. Her power of speech was also diminished, and this progressed so far that she could neither speak nor understand her mother tongue; and, finally, she was subject to states of "absence," of confusion, delirium, alteration of her whole personality. These states will later claim our attention.

When one hears of such a case, one does not need to be a physician to incline to the opinion that we are concerned here with a serious injury, probably of the brain, for which there is little hope of cure and which will probably lead to the early death of the patient. The doctors will tell us, however, that in one type of cases with just as unfavorable symptoms, another, far more favorable, opinion is justified. When one finds such a series of symptoms in the case of a young girl whose vital organs (heart, kidneys) are shown by objective tests to be normal, but who has suffered from strong emotional disturbances, and when the symptoms differ in certain finer characteristics from what one might logically expect, in a case like this the doctors are not too much disturbed. They consider that there is present no organic lesion of the brain, but that enigmatical state, known since the time of the Greek physicians as hysteria, which can simulate a whole series of symptoms of various diseases. They consider in such a case that the life of the patient is not in danger and that a restoration to health will probably come about of itself. The differentiation of such an hysteria from a severe organic lesion is not always very easy. But we do not need to know how a differential diagnosis of this kind is made; you may be sure that the case of Breuer's patient was such that no skillful physician could fail to diagnose an hysteria. We may also add a word here from the history of the case. The illness first appeared while the patient was caring for her father, whom she tenderly loved, during the severe illness which led to his death, a task which she was compelled to abandon because she herself fell ill.

So far it has seemed best to go with the doctors, but we shall soon part company with them. You must not think that the outlook of a patient with regard to medical aid is essentially bettered when the diagnosis points to hysteria rather than organic disease of the brain. Against the serious brain diseases medical skill is in most cases powerless, but also in the case of hysterical affections the doctor can do nothing. He must leave it to benign nature, when and how his hopeful prognosis will be realized.* Accordingly, with the recognition of the disease as hys-

---

* I know that this view no longer holds today, but in the lecture I take myself and my hearers back to the time before 1880. If things have become different since that time it has been largely due to the work the history of which I am sketching.

teria, little is changed in the situation of the patient, but there is a great change in the attitude of the doctor. We can observe that he acts quite differently toward hystericals than toward patients suffering from organic diseases. He will not bring the same interests to the former as to the latter, since their suffering is much less serious and yet seems to set up the claim to be valued just as seriously.

But there is another motive in this action. The physician, who through his studies has learned so much that is hidden from the laity, can realize in his thought the causes and alterations of the brain disorders in patients suffering from apoplexy or dementia, a representation which must be right up to a certain point, for by it he is enabled to understand the nature of each symptom. But before the details of hysterical symptoms, all his knowledge, his anatomical-physiological and pathological education, desert him. He cannot understand hysteria. He is in the same position before it as the layman. And that is not agreeable to anyone who is in the habit of setting such a high valuation upon his knowledge. Hystericals, accordingly, tend to lose his sympathy; he considers them persons who overstep the laws of his science, as the orthodox regard heretics; he ascribes to them all possible evils, blames them for exaggeration and intentional deceit, "simulation," and he punishes them by withdrawing his interest.

Now Dr. Breuer did not deserve this reproach in this case; he gave his patient sympathy and interest, although at first he did not understand how to help her. Probably this was easier for him on account of those superior qualities of the patient's mind and character, to which he bears witness in his account of the case.

His sympathetic observation soon found the means which made the first help possible. It had been noticed that the patient, in her states of "absence," of psychic alteration, usually mumbled over several words to herself. These seemed to spring from associations with which her thoughts were busy. The doctor, who was able to get these words, put her in a sort of hypnosis and repeated them to her over and over, in order to bring up any associations that they might have. The patient yielded to his suggestion and reproduced for him those psychic creations which controlled her thoughts during her "absences," and which betrayed themselves in these single spoken words. These were fancies, deeply sad, often poetically beautiful, day dreams, we might call them, which commonly took as their starting point the situation of a girl beside the sick-bed of her father. Whenever she had related a number of such fancies, she was, as it were, freed and restored to her normal mental life. This state of health could last for several hours, and then give place on the next day to a new "absence," which was removed in the same way by relating the newly created fancies. It was impossible not to get the impression that the psychic alteration which was expressed in the "absence" was a consequence of the excitations originating from these intensely emotional fancy-images. The patient herself, who at this time of her illness strangely enough understood and spoke only English, gave this new kind of treatment the name "talking cure," or jokingly designated it as "chimney-sweeping."

The doctor soon hit upon the fact that through such cleansing of the soul more could be accomplished than a temporary removal of the constantly recurring mental "clouds." Symptoms of the disease would disappear when in hypnosis the patient could be made to remember the situation and the associative connections under which they first appeared, provided free vent was given to the emotions which they aroused. "There was in the summer a time of intense heat, and the patient had suffered very much from thirst; for, without any apparent reason, she had suddenly become unable to drink. She would take a glass of water in her hand, but as soon as it touched her lips she would push it away as though suffering from hydrophobia. Obviously for these few seconds she was in her absent state. She ate only fruit, melons and the like, in order to relieve this tormenting thirst. When this had been going on about six weeks, she was talking one day in hypnosis about her English governess, whom she disliked, and finally told, with every sign of disgust, how she had come into the room of the governess, and how that lady's little dog, that she abhorred, had drunk out of a glass. Out of respect for the conventions the patient had remained silent. Now, after she had given energetic expression to her restrained anger, she asked for a drink, drank a large quantity of water without trouble, and woke from hypnosis with the glass at her lips. The symptom thereupon vanished permanently."

Permit me to dwell for a moment on this experience. No one had ever cured an hysterical symptom by such means before, or had come so near understanding its cause. This would be a pregnant discovery if the expectation could be confirmed that still other, perhaps the

majority of symptoms, originated in this way and could
be removed by the same method. Breuer spared no pains
to convince himself of this and investigated the patho-
genesis of the other more serious symptoms in a more
orderly way. Such was indeed the case; almost all the
symptoms originated in exactly this way, as remnants, as
precipitates, if you like, of affectively toned experiences,
which for that reason we later called "psychic traumata."
The nature of the symptoms became clear through their
relation to the scene which caused them. They were, to
use the technical term, "determined" (*determiniert*) by
the scene whose memory traces they embodied, and so
could no longer be described as arbitrary or enigmatical
functions of the neurosis.

Only one variation from what might be expected must
be mentioned. It was not always a single experience
which occasioned the symptom, but usually several,
perhaps many similar, repeated traumata cooperated in
this effect. It was necessary to repeat the whole series of
pathogenic memories in chronological sequence, and
of course in reverse order, the last first and the first last.
It was quite impossible to reach the first and often most
essential trauma directly, without first clearing away
those coming later.

You will of course want to hear me speak of other
examples of the causation of hysterical symptoms beside
this of inability to drink on account of the disgust caused
by the dog drinking from the glass. I must, however, if
I hold to my program, limit myself to very few examples.
Breuer relates, for instance, that his patient's visual
disturbances could be traced back to external causes, in
the following way: "The patient, with tears in her eyes,

was sitting by the sick-bed when her father suddenly asked her what time it was. She could not see distinctly, strained her eyes to see, brought the watch near her eyes so that the dial seemed very large (macropia and strabismus conv.), or else she tried hard to suppress her tears, so that the sick man might not see them."

All the pathogenic impressions sprang from the time when she shared in the care of her sick father. "Once she was watching at night in the greatest anxiety for the patient, who was in a high fever, and in suspense, for a surgeon was expected from Vienna, to operate on the patient. Her mother had gone out for a little while, and Anna sat by the sick-bed, her right arm hanging over the back of her chair. She fell into a revery and saw a black snake emerge, as it were, from the wall and approach the sick man as though to bite him. (It is very probable that several snakes had actually been seen in the meadow behind the house, that she had already been frightened by them, and that these former experiences furnished the material for the hallucination.) She tried to drive off the creature, but was as though paralyzed. Her right arm, which was hanging over the back of the chair, had "gone to sleep," become anæsthetic and paretic, and as she was looking at it, the fingers changed into little snakes with death's-heads. (The nails.) Probably she attempted to drive away the snake with her paralyzed right hand, and so the anæsthesia and paralysis of this member formed associations with the snake hallucination. When this had vanished, she tried in her anguish to speak, but could not. She could not express herself in any language, until finally she thought of the words of an English nursery song, and thereafter she could think and speak only in this language." When the memory of this scene was revived in hypnosis the paralysis of the right arm, which had existed since the beginning of the illness, was cured and the treatment ended.

When, a number of years later, I began to use Breuer's researches and treatment on my own patients, my experiences completely coincided with his. In the case of a woman of about fory, there was a tic, a peculiar smacking noise which manifested itself whenever she was laboring under any excitement, without any obvious cause. It had its origin in two experiences which had this common element, that she attempted to make no noise, but that by a sort of counter-will this noise broke the stillness. On the first occasion, she had finally after much trouble put her sick child to sleep, and she tried to be very quiet so as not to awaken it. On the second occasion, during a ride with both her children in a thunderstorm the horses took fright, and she carefully avoided any noise for fear of frightening them still more. I give this example instead of many others which are cited in the *Studien über Hysterie.*

Ladies and gentlemen, if you will permit me to generalize, as is indispensable in so brief a presentation, we may express our results up to this point in the formula: *Our hysterical patients suffer from reminiscences.* Their symptoms are the remnants and the memory symbols of certain (traumatic) experiences.

A comparison with other memory symbols from other sources will perhaps enable us better to understand this symbolism. The memorials and monuments with which we adorn our great cities, are also such memory symbols. If you walk through London you will find before one of the greatest railway stations of the city a richly decorated

Gothic pillar—"Charing Cross." One of the old Plantagenet kings, in the thirteenth century, caused the body of his beloved queen Eleanor to be borne to Westminster, and had Gothic crosses erected at each of the stations where the coffin was set down. Charing Cross is the last of these monuments, which preserve the memory of this sad journey. In another part of the city, you will see a high pillar of more modern construction, which is merely called "the Monument." This is in memory of the great fire which broke out in the neighborhood in the year 1666, and destroyed a great part of the city. These monuments are memory symbols like the hysterical symptoms; so far the comparison seems justified. But what would you say to a Londoner who today stood sadly before the monument to the funeral of Queen Eleanor, instead of going about his business with the haste engendered by modern industrial conditions, or rejoicing with the young queen of his own heart? Or to another, who before "the Monument" bemoaned the burning of his loved native city, which long since has arisen again so much more splendid than before?

Now hystericals and all neurotics behave like these two unpractical Londoners, not only in that they remember the painful experiences of the distant past, but because they are still strongly affected by them. They cannot escape from the past and neglect present reality in its favor. This fixation of the mental life on the pathogenic traumata is an essential, and practically a most significant characteristic of the neurosis. I will willingly concede the objection which you are probably formulating, as you think over the history of Breuer's patient. All her traumata originated at the time when she was caring for her sick father, and her symptoms could only be regarded as memory symbols of his sickness and death. They corresponded to mourning, and a fixation on thoughts of the dead so short a time after death is certainly not pathological, but rather corresponds to normal emotional behavior. I concede this: there is nothing abnormal in the fixation of feeling on the trauma shown by Breuer's patient. But in other cases, like that of the tic that I have mentioned, the occasions for which lay ten and fifteen years back, the characteristic of this abnormal clinging to the past is very clear, and Breuer's patient would probably have developed it, if she had not come under the "cathartic treatment" such a short time after the traumatic experiences and the beginning of the disease.

We have so far only explained the relation of the hysterical symptoms to the life history of the patient; now by considering two further factors which Breuer observed, we may get a hint as to the processes of the beginning of the illness and those of the cure. With regard to the first, it is especially to be noted that Breuer's patient in almost all pathogenic situations had to suppress a strong excitement, instead of giving vent to it by appropriate words and deeds. In the little experience with her governess' dog, she suppressed, through regard for the conventions, all manifestations of her very intense disgust. While she was seated by her father's sick bed, she was careful to betray nothing of her anxiety and her painful depression to the patient. When, later, she reproduced the same scene before the physician, the emotion which she had suppressed on the occurrence of the scene burst out with especial strength, as though it had been pent up all along. The symptom which had been caused by that scene reached its greatest intensity while the doctor was striving to revive the memory of the scene, and vanished after it had been fully laid bare. On the other hand, experience shows that if the patient is reproducing the traumatic scene to the physician, the process has no curative effect if, by some peculiar chance, there is no development of emotion. It is apparently these emotional processes upon which the illness of the patient and the restoration to health are dependent. We feel justified in regarding "emotion" as a quantity which may become increased, derived and displaced. So we are forced to the conclusion that the patient fell ill because the emotion developed in the pathogenic situation was prevented from escaping normally, and that the essence of the sickness lies in the fact that these "imprisoned" *(eingeklemmt)* emotions undergo a series of abnormal changes. In part they are preserved as a lasting charge and as a source of constant disturbance in psychical life; in part they undergo a change into unusual bodily innervations and inhibitions, which present themselves as the physical symptoms of the case. We have coined the name "hysterical conversion" for the latter process. Part of our mental energy is, under normal conditions, conducted off by way of physical innervation and gives what we call "the expression of emotions." Hysterical conversion exaggerates this part of the course of a mental process which is emotionally colored; it corresponds to a far more intense emotional expression, which finds outlet by new paths. If a stream flows in two channels, an overflow of one will take place as soon as the current in the other meets with an obstacle.

You see that we are in a fair way to arrive at a purely psychological theory of hysteria, in which we assign the first rank to the affective processes. A second observation of Breuer compels us to ascribe to the altered condition of consciousness a great part in determining the characteristics of the disease. His patient showed many sorts of mental states, conditions of "absence," confusion and alteration of character, besides her normal state. In her normal state she was entirely ignorant of the pathogenic scenes and of their connection with her symptoms. She had forgotten those scenes, or at any rate had dissociated them from their pathogenic connection. When the patient was hypnotized, it was possible, after considerable difficulty, to recall those scenes to her memory, and by this means of recall the symptoms were removed. It would have been extremely perplexing to know how to interpret this fact, if hypnotic practice and experiments had not pointed out the way. Through the study of hypnotic phenomena, the conception, strange though it was at first, has become familiar, that in one and the same individual several mental groupings are possible, which may remain relatively independent of each other, "know nothing" of each other, and which may cause a splitting of consciousness along lines which they lay down. Cases of such a sort, known as "double personality" (*"double conscience"*), occasionally appear spontaneously. If in such a division of personality consciousness remains constantly bound up with one of the two states, this is called the *conscious* mental state, and the other the *unconscious*. In the well-known phenomena of so-called post hypnotic suggestion, in which a command given in hypnosis is later executed in the normal state as though by an imperative suggestion, we have an excellent basis for understanding how the unconscious state can influence the conscious, although the latter is ignorant of the existence of the former. In the same way it is quite possible to explain the facts in hysterical cases. Breuer came to the conclusion that the hysterical symptoms originated in such peculiar mental states, which he called "hypnoidal states" (*hypnoide Zustande*). Experiences of an emotional nature, which occur during such hypnoidal states easily become pathogenic, since such states do not present the conditions for a normal draining off of the emotion of the exciting processes. And as a result there arises a peculiar product of this exciting process, that is, the symptom, and this is projected like a foreign body into the normal state. The latter has, then, no conception of the hypnoidal pathogenic situation. Where a symptom arises, we also find an amnesia, a memory gap, and the filling of this gap includes the removal of the conditions under which the symptom originated.

I am afraid that this portion of my treatment will not seem very clear, but you must remember that we are dealing here with new and difficult views, which perhaps could not be made much clearer. This all goes to show that our knowledge in this field is not yet far advanced. Breuer's idea of the hypnoidal states has, moreover, been shown to be superfluous and a hindrance to further investigation, and has been dropped from present conceptions of psychoanalysis. Later I shall at least suggest what other influences and processes have been disclosed besides that of the hypnoidal states, to which Breuer limited the causal moment.

You have probably also felt, and rightly, that Breuer's investigations gave you only a very incomplete theory and insufficient explanation of the phenomena which we have observed. But complete theories do not fall from Heaven, and you would have had still greater reason to be distrustful, had any one offered you at the beginning of his observations a well-rounded theory, without any gaps; such a theory could only be the child of his speculations and not the fruit of an unprejudiced investigation of the facts.

Second Lecture

Ladies and Gentlemen: At about the same time that Breuer was using the "talking-cure" with his patient, M. Charcot began in Paris, with the hystericals of the Salpetrière, those researches which were to lead to a new understanding of the disease. These results were, however, not yet known in Vienna. But when about ten years later Breuer and I published our preliminary communication on the psychic mechanism of hysterical phenomena, which grew out of the cathartic treatment of Breuer's first patient, we were both of us under the spell of Charcot's investigations. We made the pathogenic experiences of our patients, which acted as psychic traumata, equivalent to those physical traumata whose influence on hysterical paralyses Charcot had determined; and Breuer's hypothesis of hypnoidal states is itself only an echo of the fact that Charcot had artificially reproduced those traumata paralyses in hypnosis.

The great French observer, whose student I was during the years 1885-86, had no natural bent for creating psychological theories. His student, P. Janet, was the first to attempt to penetrate more deeply into the psychic processes of hysteria, and we followed his example, when we made the mental splitting and the dissociation of personality the central points of our theory. Janet propounds a theory of hysteria which draws upon the principal theories of heredity and degeneration which are current in France. According to his view hysteria is a form of degenerative alteration of the nervous system, manifesting itself in a congenital "weakness" of the function of psychic synthesis. The hysterical patient is from the start incapable of correlating and unifying the manifold of his mental processes, and so there arises the tendency to mental dissociation. If you will permit me to use a banal but clear illustration, Janet's hysterical reminds one of a weak woman who has been shopping, and is now on her way home, laden with packages and bundles of every description. She cannot manage the whole lot with her two arms and her ten fingers, and soon she drops one. When she stoops to pick this up, another breaks loose, and so it goes on.

Now it does not agree very well with this assumed mental weakness of hystericals, that there can be observed in hysterical cases, besides the phenomena of lessened functioning, examples of a partial increase of functional capacity, as a sort of compensation. At the time when Breuer's patient had forgotten her mother-tongue and all other languages save English, her control of English attained such a level that if a German book was put before her she could give a fluent, perfect translation of its contents at sight. When later I undertook to continue on my own account the investigations begun by Breuer, I soon came to another view of the origin of hysterical dissociation (or splitting of consciousness). It was inevitable that my views should diverge widely and radically, for my point of departure was not, like that of Janet, laboratory researches, but attempts at therapy. Above everything else, it was practical needs that urged me on. The cathartic treatment, as Breuer had made use of it, presupposed that the patient should be put in deep hypnosis, for only in hypnosis was available the knowledge of his pathogenic associations, which were unknown to him in his normal state. Now hypnosis, as a fanciful, and so to speak, mystical, aid, I soon came to dislike; and when I discovered that, in spite of all my efforts, I could not hypnotize by any means all of my patients, I resolved to give up hypnotism and to make the cathartic method independent of it.

Since I could not alter the psychic state of most of my patients at my wish, I directed my efforts to working with them in their normal state. This seems at first sight to be a particularly senseless and aimless undertaking. The problem was this: to find out something from the patient that the doctor did not know and the patient himself did not know. How could one hope to make such a method succeed? The memory of a very noteworthy and instructive proceeding came to my aid, which I had seen in Bernheim's clinic at Nancy. Bernheim showed us that persons put in a condition of hypnotic somnambulism, and subjected to all sorts of experiences, had only apparently lost the memory of those somnambulic experiences, and that their memory of them could be awakened even in the normal state. If he asked them about their experiences during somnambulism, they said at first that they did not remember, but if he persisted, urged, assured them that they did know, then every time the forgotten memory came back.

Accordingly I did this with my patients. When I had reached in my procedure with them a point at which they declared that they knew nothing more, I would assure them that they did know, that they must just tell it out, and I would venture the assertion that the memory which would emerge at the moment that I laid my hand on the patient's forehead would be the right one. In this way I succeeded, without hypnosis, in learning from the patient all that was necessary for a construction of the connection between the forgotten pathogenic scenes and the symptoms which they had left behind. This was a troublesome and in its length an exhausting proceeding, and did not lend itself to a finished technique. But I did not give it up without drawing definite conclusions from the data which I had gained. I had substantiated the fact that the forgotten memories were not lost. They were in the possession of the patient, ready to emerge and form associations with his other mental content, but hindered from becoming conscious, and forced to remain in the unconscious by some sort of a force. The existence of this force could be assumed with certainty, for in attempting to drag up the unconscious memories into the consciousness of the patient, in opposition to this force, one got the sensation of his own personal effort striving to overcome it. One could get an idea of this force, which maintained the pathological situation, from the resistance of the patient.

It is on this idea of *resistance* that I based my theory of the psychic processes of hystericals. It had been found that in order to cure the patient it was necessary that this force should be overcome. Now with the mechanism of the cure as a starting point, quite a definite theory could be constructed. These same forces, which in the present situation as resistances opposed the emergence of the forgotten ideas into consciousness, must themselves have caused the forgetting, and repressed from consciousness the pathogenic experiences. I called this hypothetical process "repression" (*Verdrangung*), and considered that it was proved by the undeniable existence of resistance.

But now the question arose: what were those forces, and what were the conditions of this repression, in which we were now able to recognize the pathogenic mechanism of hysteria? A comparative study of the pathogenic situations, which the cathartic treatment has made possible, allows us to answer this question. In all those experiences, it had happened that a wish had been aroused, which was in sharp opposition to the other desires of the individual, and was not capable of being reconciled with the ethical, æsthetic and personal pretensions of the patient's personality. There had been a short conflict, and the end of this inner struggle was the repression of the idea which presented itself to consciousness as the bearer of this irreconcilable wish. This was, then, repressed from consciousness and forgotten. The incompatibility of the idea in question with the "ego" of the patient was the motive of the repression, the ethical and other pretensions of the individual were the repressing forces. The presence of the incompatible wish, or the duration of the conflict, had given rise to a high degree of mental pain; this pain was avoided by the repression. This latter process is evidently in such a case a device for the protection of the personality.

I will not multiply examples, but will give you the history of a single one of my cases, in which the conditions and the utility of the repression process stand out clearly enough. Of course for my purpose I must abridge the history of the case and omit many valuable theoretical considerations. It is that of a young girl, who was deeply attached to her father, who had died a short time before, and in whose care she had shared—a situation analogous to that of Breuer's patient. When her older sister married, the girl grew to feel a peculiar sympathy for her new brother-in-law, which easily passed with her for family tenderness. This sister soon fell ill and died, while the patient and her mother were away. The absent ones were hastily recalled, without being told fully of the painful situation. As the girl stood by the bedside of her dead sister, for one short moment there surged up in her mind an idea, which might be framed in these words: "Now he is free and can marry me." We may be sure that this idea, which betrayed to her consciousness her intense love for her brother-in-law, of which she had not been conscious, was the next moment consigned to repression by her revolted feelings. The girl fell ill with severe hysterical symptoms, and, when I came to treat the case, it appeared that she had entirely forgotten that scene at her sister's bedside and the unnatural, egoistic desire which had arisen in her. She remembered it during the treatment, reproduced the pathogenic moment with every sign of intense emotional excitement, and was cured by this treatment.

Perhaps I can make the process of repression and its

necessary relation to the resistance of the patient, more concrete by a rough illustration, which I will derive from our present situation.

Suppose that here in this hall and in this audience, whose exemplary stillness and attention I cannot sufficiently commend, there is an individual who is creating a disturbance, and, by his ill-bred laughing, talking, by scraping his feet, distracts my attention from my task. I explain that I cannot go on with my lecture under these conditions, and thereupon several strong men among you get up, and, after a short struggle, eject the disturber of the peace from the hall. He is now "repressed," and I can continue my lecture. But in order that the disturbance may not be repeated, in case the man who has just been thrown out attempts to force his way back into the room, the gentlemen who have executed my suggestion take their chairs to the door and establish themselves there as a "resistance," to keep up the repression. Now, if you transfer both locations to the psyche, calling this "consciousness," and the outside the "unconscious," you have a tolerably good illustration of the process of repression.

We can see now the difference between our theory and that of Janet. We do not derive the psychic fission from a congenital lack of capacity on the part of the mental apparatus to synthesize its experiences, but we explain it dynamically by the conflict of opposing mental forces, we recognize in it the result of an active striving of each mental complex against the other.

New questions at once arise in great number from our theory. The situation of psychic conflict is a very frequent one; an attempt of the ego to defend itself from painful memories can be observed everywhere, and yet the result is not a mental fission. We cannot avoid the assumption that still other conditions are necessary, if the conflict is to result in dissociation. I willingly concede that with the assumption of "repression" we stand, not at the end, but at the very beginning of a psychological theory. But we can advance only one step at a time, and the completion of our knowledge must await further and more thorough work.

Now do not attempt to bring the case of Breuer's patient under the point of view of repression. This history cannot be subjected to such an attempt, for it was gained with the help of hypnotic influence. Only when hypnosis is excluded can you see the resistances and repressions and get a correct idea of the pathogenic process. Hypnosis conceals the resistances and so makes a certain part of the mental field freely accessible. By this same process the resistances on the borders of this field are heaped up into a rampart, which makes all beyond inaccessible.

The most valuable things that we have learned from Breuer's observations were his conclusions as to the connection of the symptoms with the pathogenic experiences or psychic traumata, and we must not neglect to evaluate this result properly from the standpoint of the repression-theory. It is not at first evident how we can get from the repression to the creation of the symptoms. Instead of giving a complicated theoretical derivation, I will return at this point to the illustration which I used to typify repression.

Remember that with the ejection of the rowdy and the establishment of the watchers before the door, the affair is not necessarily ended. It may very well happen that the ejected man, now embittered and quite careless of consequences, gives us more to do. He is no longer among us, we are free from his presence, his scornful laugh, his half-audible remarks, but in a certain sense the repression has miscarried, for he makes a terrible uproar outside, and by his outcries and by hammering on the door with his fists interferes with my lecture more than before. Under these circumstances it would be hailed with delight if possibly our honored president, Dr. Stanley Hall, should take upon himself the rôle of peacemaker and mediator. He would speak with the rowdy on the outside, and then turn to us with the recommendation that we let him in again, provided he would guarantee to behave himself better. On Dr. Hall's authority we decide to stop the repression, and now quiet and peace reign again. This is in fact a fairly good presentation of the task devolving upon the physician in the psychoanalytic therapy of neuroses. To say the same thing more directly: we come to the conclusion, from working with hysterical patients and other neurotics, that they have not fully succeeded in repressing the idea to which the incompatible wish is attached. They have, indeed, driven it out of consciousness and out of memory, and apparently saved themselves a great amount of psychic pain, *but in the unconscious the suppressed wish still exists,* only waiting for its chance to become active, and finally succeeds in sending into consciousness, instead of the repressed idea, a disguised and unrecognizable surrogate-creation *(Ersatzbildung),* to which the same painful sensations associate themselves that the patient thought he was rid of through his repression. This surrogate of the suppressed idea—the symptom—is secure against further attacks from the defenses of the ego, and instead of a short conflict there originates now a permanent suffering. We can observe in the symptom, besides the tokens of its disguise, a remnant of traceable similarity with the originally repressed idea; the way in which the surrogate is built up can be discovered during the psychoanalytic treatment of the patient, and for his cure the symptom must be traced back over the same route to the repressed idea. If this repressed material is once more made part of the conscious mental functions— a process which supposes the overcoming of considerable resistance—the psychic conflict which then arises, the same which the patient wished to avoid, is made capable of a happier termination, under the guidance of the physician, than is offered by repression. There are several possible suitable decisions which can bring conflict and neurosis to a happy end; in particular cases the attempt may be made to combine several of these. Either the personality of the patient may be convinced that he has been wrong in rejecting the pathogenic wish, and he may be made to accept it either wholly or in part; or this wish may itself be directed to a higher goal which is free from objection, by what is called sublimation (*Sublimierung*); or the rejection may be recognized as rightly motivated, and the automatic and therefore insufficient mechanism of repression be reinforced by the higher, more characteristically human mental faculties: one succeeds in mastering his wishes by conscious thought.

Forgive me if I have not been able to present more clearly these main points of the treatment which is today known as "psychoanalysis." The difficulties do not lie merely in the newness of the subject.

Regarding the nature of the unacceptable wishes, which succeed in making their influence felt out of the unconscious, in spite of repression; and regarding the question of what subjective and constitutional factors must be present for such a failure of repression and such a surrogate or symptom creation to take place, we will speak in later remarks.

Third Lecture

Ladies and Gentlemen: It is not always easy to tell the truth, especially when one must be brief, and so today I must correct an incorrect statement that I made in my last lecture.

I told you how when I gave up using hypnosis I pressed my patients to tell me what came into their minds that had to do with the problem we were working on, I told them that they would remember what they had apparently forgotten, and that the thought which irrupted into consciousness (*Einfall*) would surely embody the memory for which we were seeking. I claimed that I substantiated the fact that the first idea of my patients brought the right clew and could be shown to be the forgotten continuation of the memory. Now this is not always so; I represented it as being so simple only for purposes of abbreviation. In fact, it would only happen the first time that the right forgotten material would emerge through simple pressure on my part. If the experience was continued, ideas emerged in every case which could not be the right ones, for they were not to the purpose, and the patients themselves rejected them as incorrect. Pressure was of no further service here, and one could only regret again having given up hypnosis. In this state of perplexity I clung to a prejudice which years later was proved by my friend C. G. Jung of the University of Zürich and his pupils to have a scientific justification. I must confess that it is often of great advantage to have prejudices. I put a high value on the strength of the determination of mental processes, and I could not believe that any idea which occurred to the patient, which originated in a state of concentrated attention, could be quite arbitrary and out of all relation to the forgotten idea that we were seeking. That it was not identical with the latter, could be satisfactorily explained by the hypothetical psychological situation. In the patients whom I treated there were two opposing forces: on the one hand the conscious striving to drag up into consciousness the forgotten experience which was present in the unconscious; and on the other hand the resistance which we have seen, which set itself against the emergence of the suppressed idea or its associates into consciousness. In case this resistance was nonexistent or very slight, the forgotten material could become conscious without disguise (*Enstellung*). It was then a natural supposition that the disguise would be more complete, the greater the resistance to the emergence of the idea. Thoughts which broke into the patient's consciousness instead of the ideas sought for, were accordingly made up just like symptoms; they were new, artificial, ephemeral surrogates for the repressed ideas, and differed from these just in proportion as they had been more completely disguised under the influence of the resistances. These surrogates must, however, show a certain similarity with the ideas which are the object of our search, by virtue of their nature as symptoms; and when the resistance is not too intensive it is possible from the nature of these irruptions to discover the hidden object of our search. This must be related to the repressed thought as a sort of allusion, as a statement of the same thing in *indirect* terms.

We know cases in normal psychology in which analogous situations to the one which we have assumed give rise to similar experiences. Such a case is that of wit. By my study of psychoanalytic technique I was necessarily led to a consideration of the problem of the nature of wit. I will give one example of this sort, which, too, is a story that originally appeared in English.

The anecdote runs: Two unscrupulous business men had succeeded by fortunate speculations in accumulating a large fortune, and then directed their efforts to breaking into good society. Among other means they thought it would be of advantage to be painted by the most famous and expensive artist of the city, a man whose paintings were considered as events. The costly paintings were first shown at a great soirée and both hosts led the most influential connoisseur and art critic to the wall of the salon on which the portraits were hung, to elicit his admiring judgment. The critic looked for a long time, looked about as though in search of something, and then merely asked, pointing out the vacant space between the two pictures: "And where is the Saviour?"

I see that you are all laughing over this good example of wit, which we will now attempt to analyze. We understand that the critic means to say: "You are a couple of malefactors, like those between whom the Saviour was crucified." But he does not say this, he expresses himself instead in a way that at first seems not to the purpose and not related to the matter in hand, but which at the next moment we recognize as an *allusion* to the insult at which he aims, and as a perfect surrogate for it. We cannot expect to find in the case of wit all those relations that our theory supposes for the origin of the irruptive ideas of our patients, but it is my desire to lay stress on the similar motivation of wit and irruptive idea. Why does not the critic say directly what he has to say to the two rogues? Because, in addition to his desire to say it straight out, he is actuated by strong opposite motives. It is a proceeding which is liable to be dangerous to offend people who are one's hosts, and who can call to their aid the strong arms of numerous servants. One might easily suffer the same fate that I used in the previous lecture to illustrate repression. On this ground, the critic does not express the particular insult directly, but in a disguised form, as an allusion with omission. The same constellation comes into play, according to our hypothesis, when our patient produces the irruptive idea as a surrogate for the forgotten idea which is the object of the quest.

Ladies and Gentlemen, it is very useful to designate a group of ideas which belong together and have a common emotive tone, according to the custom of the Zürich school (Bleuler, Jung and others), as a "complex." So we can say that if we set out from the last memories of the patient to look for a repressed complex, we have every prospect of discovering it, if only the patient will communicate to us a sufficient number of the ideas which come into his head. So we let the patient speak along any line that he desires, and cling to the hypothesis that nothing can occur to him except what has some indirect bearing on the complex that we are seeking. If this method of discovering the repressed complexes seems too circumstantial, I can at least assure you that it is the only available one.

In practicing this technique, one is further bothered by the fact that the patient often stops, is at a standstill, and considers that he has nothing to say; nothing occurs to him. If this were really the case and the patient were right, our procedure would again be proven inapplicable. Closer observation shows that such an absence of ideas never really occurs, and that it only appears to when the patient holds back or rejects the idea which he perceives, under the influence of the resistance, which disguises itself as critical judgment of the value of the idea. The patient can be protected from this if he is warned in advance of this circumstance, and told to take no account of the critical attitude. He must say anything that comes into his mind, fully laying aside such critical choice, even though he may think it unessential, irrelevant, nonsensical, especially when the idea is one which is unpleasant to dwell on. By following this prescription we secure the material which sets us on the track of the repressed complex.

These irruptive ideas, which the patient himself values little, if he is under the influence of the resistance and not that of the physician, are for the psychologist like the ore, which by simple methods of interpretation he reduces from its crude state to valuable metal. If one desires to gain in a short time a preliminary knowledge of the patient's repressed complexes, without going into the question of their arrangement and association, this examination may be conducted with the help of the association experiments, as Jung and his pupils have perfected them. This procedure is to the psychologist what qualitative analysis is to the chemist; it may be dispensed with in the therapy of neurotic patients, but is indispensable in the investigations of the psychoses, which have been begun by the Zürich school with such valuable results.

This method of work with whatever comes into the patient's head when he submits to psychoanalytic treatment, is not the only technical means at our disposal for the widening of consciousness. Two other methods of procedure serve the same purpose, the interpretation of his dreams and the evaluation of acts which he bungles or does without intending to *(Fehl- und Zufallshandlungen).*

I might say, esteemed hearers, that for a long time I hesitated whether instead of this hurried survey of the whole field of psychoanalysis, I should not rather offer you a thorough consideration of the analysis of dreams; a purely subjective and apparently secondary motive decided me against this. It seemed rather an impropriety that in this country, so devoted to practical pursuits, I should pose as "interpreter of dreams," before you had a chance to discover what significance the old and despised art can claim.

Interpretation of dreams is in fact the *via regia* to the interpretation of the unconscious, the surest ground of psychoanalysis and a field in which every worker must win his convictions and gain his education. If I were asked how one could become a psychoanalyst, I should answer, through the study of his own dreams. With great tact all opponents of the psychoanalytic theory have so far either evaded any criticism of the *Traumdeutung* or have attempted to pass over it with the most superficial objections. If, on the contrary, you will undertake the solution of the problems of dream life, the novelties which psychoanalysis present to your thoughts will no longer be difficulties.

You must remember that our nightly dream productions show the greatest outer similarity and inner relationship to the creations of the insane, but on the other hand are compatible with full health during waking life. It does not sound at all absurd to say that whoever regards these normal sense illusions, these delusions and alterations of character as matter for amazement instead of understanding, has not the least prospect of understanding the abnormal creations of diseased mental states in any other than the lay sense. You may with confidence place in this lay group all the psychiatrists of today. Follow me now on a brief excursion through the field of dream problems.

In our waking state we usually treat dreams with as little consideration as the patient treats the irruptive ideas which the psychoanalyst demands from him. It is evident that we reject them, for we forget them quickly and completely. The slight valuation which we place on them is based, with those dreams that are not confused and nonsensical, on the feeling that they are foreign to our personality, and, with other dreams on their evident **absurdity and senselessness. Our rejection derives support** from the unrestrained shamelessness and the immoral longings which are obvious in many dreams. Antiquity, as we know, did not share this light valuation of dreams. The lower classes of our people today stick close to the value which they set on dreams; they, however, expect from them, as did the ancients, the revelation of the future. I confess that I see no need to adopt mystical hypotheses to fill out the gaps in our present knowledge, and so I have never been able to find anything that supported the hyopothesis of the prophetic nature of dreams. Many other things, which are wonderful enough, can be said about them.

And first, not all dreams are so foreign to the character of the dreamer, are incomprehensible and confused. If you will undertake to consider the dreams of young children from the age of a year and a half on, you will find them quite simple and easy to interpret. The young child always dreams of the fulfillment of wishes which were aroused in him the day before and were not satisfied. You need no art of interpretation to discover this simple solution, you only need to inquire into the experiences of the child on the day before (the "dream day"). Now it would certainly be a most satisfactory solution of the dream-riddle, if the dreams of adults, too, were the same as those of children, fulfillments of wishes which had been aroused in them during the dream day. This is actually the fact; the difficulties which stand in the way of this solution can be removed step by step by a thorough analysis of the dream.

There is, first of all, the most weighty objection, that the dreams of adults generally have an incomprehensible content, which shows wish-fulfillment least of anything. The answer is this: these dreams have undergone a process of disguise, the psychic content which underlies them was originally meant for quite different verbal expression. You must differentiate between the *manifest dream-content,* which we remember in the morning only confusedly, and with difficulty clothe in words which seem arbitrary, and the *latent dream-thoughts,* whose presence in the unconscious we must assume. This distortion of the dream (*Traumentstellung*) is the same process which has been revealed to you in the investigations of the creations (*symptoms*) of hysterical subjects; it points to the fact that the same opposition of psychic forces has its share in the creation of dreams as in the creation of symptoms.

The manifest dream-content is the disguised surrogate for the unconscious dream thoughts, and this disguising is the work of the defensive forces of the ego, of the resistances. These prevent the repressed wishes from entering consciousness during the waking life, and even in the relaxation of sleep they are still strong enough to force them to hide themselves by a sort of masquerading. The dreamer, then, knows just as little the sense of his dream as the hysterical knows the relation and significance of his symptoms. That there are latent dream-thoughts and that between them and the manifest dream-content there exists the relation just described—of this you may convince yourselves by the analysis of dreams, a procedure the technique of which is exactly that of psychoanalysis. You must abstract entirely from the apparent connection of the elements in the manifest dream and seek for the irruptive ideas which arise through free association, according to the psychoanalytic laws, from each separate dream element. From this material the latent dream thoughts may be discovered, exactly as one divines the concealed complexes of the patient from the fancies connected with his symptoms and memories. From the latent dream thoughts which you will find in this way, you will see at once how thoroughly justified one is in interpreting the dreams of adults by the same rubrics as those of children. What is now substituted for the manifest dream-content is the real sense of the dream, is always clearly comprehensible, associated with the impressions of the day before, and appears as the fulfilling of an unsatisfied wish. The manifest dream, which we remember after waking, may then be described as a *disguised* fulfillment of *repressed* wishes.

It is also possible by a sort of synthesis to get some insight into the process which has brought about the disguise of the unconscious dream thoughts as the manifest dream-content. We call this process "dream-work" (*Traumarbeit*). This deserves our fullest theoretical interest, since here as nowhere else can we study the unsuspected psychic processes which are existent in the unconscious, or, to express it more exactly, *between* two such separate systems as the conscious and the unconscious. Among these newly discovered psychic processes, two, condensation (*Verdichtung*) and displacement or transvaluation, change of psychic accent (*Verschiebung*), stand out most prominently. Dream work is a special case of the reaction of different mental groupings on each other, and as such is the consequence of psychic fission. In all essential points it seems identical with the work of disguise, which changes the repressed complex in the case of failing repression into symptoms.

You will furthermore discover by the analysis of dreams, most convincingly your own, the unsuspected importance of the rôle which impressions and experiences from early childhood exert on the development of men.

In the dream life the child, as it were, continues his existence in the man, with a retention of all his traits and wishes, including those which he was obliged to allow to fall into disuse in his later years. With irresistible might it will be impressed on you by what processes of development, of repression, sublimation and reaction there arises out of the child, with its peculiar gifts and tendencies, the so-called normal man, the bearer and partly the victim of our painfully acquired civilization. I will also direct your attention to the fact that we have discovered from the analysis of dreams that the unconscious makes use of a sort of symbolism, especially in the presentation of sexual complexes. This symbolism in part varies with the individual, but in part is of a typical nature, and seems to be identical with the symbolism which we suppose to lie behind our myths and legends. It is not impossible that these later creations of the people may find their explanation from the study of dreams.

Finally, I must remind you that you must not be led astray by the objection that the occurrence of anxiety-dreams (*Angsttraüme*), contradicts our idea of the dream as a wish-fulfillment. Apart from the consideration that anxiety-dreams also require interpretation before judgment can be passed on them, one can say quite generally that the anxiety does not depend in such a simple way on the dream content as one might suppose without more knowledge of the facts, and more attention to the conditions of neurotic anxiety. Anxiety is one of the ways in which the ego relieves itself of repressed wishes which have become too strong and so is easy to explain in the dream, if the dream has gone too far towards the fulfilling of the objectionable wish.

You see that the investigation of dreams was justified

by the conclusions which it has given us concerning things otherwise hard to understand. But we came to it in connection with the psychoanalytic treatment of neurotics. From what has been said you can easily understand how the interpretation of dreams, if it is not made too difficult by the resistance of the patient, can lead to a knowledge of the patient's concealed and repressed wishes and the complexes which he is nourishing. I may now pass to that group of everyday mental phenomena whose study has become a technical help for psychoanalysis.

These are the bungling of acts (*Fehlhandlungen*) a-mong normal men as well as among neurotics, to which no significance is ordinarily attached; the forgetting of things which one is supposed to know and at other times really does know (for example the temporary forgetting of proper names); mistakes in speaking (*Versprechen*), which occur so frequently; analogous mistakes in writing (*Verschreiben*) and in reading (*Verlesen*), the automatic execution of purposive acts in wrong situations (*Vergreifen*) and the loss or breaking of objects, etc. These are trifles, for which no one has ever sought a psychological determination, which have passed unchallenged as chance experiences, as consequences of absent-mindedness, inattention and similar conditions. Here, too, are included the acts and gestures executed without being noticed by the subject, to say nothing of the fact that he attaches no psychic importance to them; as playing and trifling with objects, humming melodies, handling one's person and clothing and the like.

These little things, the bungling of acts, like the symptomatic and chance acts (*Symptom- und Zufallshandlungen*) are not so entirely without meaning as is generally supposed by a sort of tacit agreement. They have a meaning, generally easy and sure to interpret from the situation in which they occur, and it can be demonstrated that they either express impulses and purposes which are repressed, hidden if possible from the consciousness of the individual, or that they spring from exactly the same sort of repressed wishes and complexes which we have learned to know already as the creators of symptoms and dreams.

It follows that they deserve the rank of symptoms, and their observation, like that of dreams, can lead to the discovery of the hidden complexes of the psychic life. With their help one will usually betray the most intimate of his secrets. If these occur so easily and commonly among people in health, with whom repression has on the whole succeeded fairly well, this is due to their insignificance and their inconspicuous nature. But they can lay claim to high theoretic value, for they prove the existence of repression and surrogate creations even under the conditions of health. You have already noticed that the psychoanalyst is distinguished by an especially strong belief in the determination of the psychic life. For him there is in the expressions of the psyche nothing trifling, nothing arbitrary and lawless, he expects everywhere a widespread motivation, where customarily such claims are not made; more than that, he is even prepared to find a manifold motivation of these psychic expressions, while our supposedly inborn causal need is satisfied with a single psychic cause.

Now keeping in mind the means which we possess for the discovery of the hidden, forgotten, repressed things in the soul life: the study of the irruptive ideas called up by free association, the patient's dreams, and his bungled and symptomatic acts; and adding to these the evaluation of other phenomena which emerge during the psychoanalytic treatment, on which I shall later make a few remarks under the heading of "transfer" (*Uebertragung*), you will come with me to the conclusion that our technique is already sufficiently efficacious for the solution of the problem of how to introduce the pathogenic psychic material into consciousness, and so to do away with the suffering brought on by the creation of surrogate symptoms.

The fact that by such therapeutic endeavors our knowledge of the mental life of the normal and the abnormal is widened and deepened, can of course only be regarded as an especial attraction and superiority of this method.

I do not know whether you have gained the impression that the technique through whose arsenal I have led you is a peculiarly difficult one. I consider that on the contrary, for one who has mastered it, it is quite adapted for use. But so much is sure, that it is not obvious, that it must be learned no less than the histological or the surgical technique.

You may be surprised to learn that in Europe we have heard very frequently judgments passed on psychoanalysis by persons who knew nothing of its technique and had never practised it, but who demanded scornfully that we show the correctness of our results. There are among these people some who are not in other things unacquainted with scientific methods of thought, who for example would not reject the result of a microscopical research because it cannot be confirmed with the naked eye in anatomical preparations, and who would not pass judgment until they had used the microscope. But in matters of psychoanalysis circumstances are really more unfavorable for gaining recognition. Psychoanalysis will bring the repressed in mental life to conscious acknowledgment, and every one who judges it is himself a man who has such repressions, perhaps maintained only with difficulty. It will consequently call forth the same resistances from him as from the patient, and this resistance can easily succeed in disguising itself as intellectual rejection, and bring forward arguments similar to those from which we protect our patients by the basic principles of psychoanalysis. It is not difficult to substantiate in our opponents the same impairment of intelligence produced by emotivity which we may observe every day with our patients. The arrogance of consciousness which for example rejects dreams so lightly, belongs—quite generally—to the strongest protective apparatus which guards us against the breaking through of the unconscious complexes, and as a result it is hard to convince people of the reality of the unconscious, and to teach them anew what their conscious knowledge contradicts.

Fouth Lecture

Ladies and Gentlemen: At this point you will be asking what the technique which I have described has taught us of the nature of the pathogenic complexes and repressed wishes of neurotics.

One thing in particular: psychoanalytic investigations trace back the symptoms of disease with really surprising regularity to impressions from the sexual life, show us that the pathogenic wishes are of the nature of erotic

impulse-components (*Triebkomponente*), and neces-
sitate the assumption that to disturbances of the erotic
sphere must be ascribed the greatest significance among
the etiological factors of the disease. This holds of both
sexes.

I know that this assertion will not willingly be credited.
Even those investigators who gladly follow my psychological labors, are inclined to think that I overestimate
the etiological share of the sexual moments. They ask me
why other mental excitations should not lead to the
phenomena of repression and surrogate-creation which I
have described. I can give them this answer; that I do not
know why they should not do this, I have no objection to
their doing it, but experience shows that they do not
possess such a significance, and that they merely support
the effect of the sexual moments, without being able to
supplant them. This conclusion was not a theoretical
postulate; in the *Studien über Hysterie,* published in 1895
with Dr. Breuer, I did not stand on this ground. I was
converted to it when my experience was richer and had
led me deeper into the nature of the case. Gentlemen,
there are among you some of my closest friends and adherents, who have traveled to Worcester with me. Ask them,
and they will tell you that they all were at first completely
skeptical of the assertion of the determinative significance
of the sexual etiology, until they were compelled by their
own analytic labors to come to the same conclusion.

The conduct of the patients does not make it any easier
to convince one's self of the correctness of the view which
I have expressed. Instead of willingly giving us information concerning their sexual life, they try to conceal it
by every means in their power. Men generally are not

candid in sexual matters. They do not show their sexuality freely, but they wear a thick overcoat—a fabric of lies—to conceal it, as though it were bad weather in the world of sex. And they are not wrong; sun and wind are not favorable in our civilized society to any demonstration of sex life. In truth no one can freely disclose his erotic life to his neighbor. But when your patients see that in your treatment they may disregard the conventional restraints, they lay aside this veil of lies, and then only are you in a position to formulate a judgment of the question in dispute. Unfortunately physicians are not favored above the rest of the children of men in their personal relationship to the questions of the sex life. Many of them are under the ban of that mixture of prudery and lasciviousness which determines the behavior of most *Kulturmenschen* in affairs of sex.

Now to proceed with the communication of our results. It is true that in another series of cases psychoanalysis at first traces the symptoms back not to the sexual, but to banal traumatic experiences. But the distintion loses its significance through other circumstances. The work of analysis which is necessary for the thorough explanation and complete cure of a case of sickness does not stop in any case with the experience of the time of onset of the disease, but in every case it goes back to the adolescence and the early childhood of the patient. Here only do we hit upon the impressions and circumstances which determine the later sickness. Only the childhood experiences can give the explanation for the sensitivity to later traumata and only when these memory traces, which almost always are forgotten, are discovered and made conscious, is the power developed to banish the symptoms. We arrive here at the same conclusion as in the investigation of dreams—that it is the incompatible, repressed wishes of childhood which lend their power to the creation of symptoms. Without these the reactions upon later traumata discharge normally. But we must consider these mighty wishes of childhood very generally as sexual in nature.

Now I can at any rate be sure of your astonishment. Is there an infantile sexuality? you will ask. Is childhood not rather that period of life which is distinguished by the lack of the sexual impulse? No, gentlemen, it is not at all true that the sexual impulse enters into the child at puberty, as the devils in the gospel entered into the swine. The child has his sexual impulses and activities from the beginning, he brings them with him into the world, and from these the so-called normal sexuality of adults emerges by a significant development through manifold stages. It is not very difficult to observe the expressions of this childish sexual activity; it needs rather a certain art to overlook them or to fail to interpret them.

As fate would have it, I am in a position to call a witness for my assertions from your own midst. I show you here the work of one, Dr. Sanford Bell, published in 1902 in the *American Journal of Psychology*. The author was a fellow of Clark University, the same institution within whose walls we now stand. In this thesis, entitled A Preliminary Study of the Emotion of Love between the Sexes, which appeared three years before my "Drei Abhandlungen zur Sexualtheorie," the author says just what I have been saying to you: "The emotion of sex love . . . does not make its appearance for the first time at the period of adolescence as has been thought." He has, as we should say in Europe, worked by the American method, and has gathered not less than 2,500 positive observations in the course of fifteen years, among them 800 of his own. He says of the signs by which this amorous condition manifests itself: "The unprejudiced mind, in observing these manifestations in hundreds of couples of children, cannot escape referring them to sex origin. The most exacting mind is satisfied when to these observations are added the confessions of those who have as children experienced the emotion to a marked degree of intensity, and whose memories of childhood are relatively distinct." Those of you who are unwilling to believe in infantile sexuality will be most astonished to hear that among those children who fell in love so early not a few are of the tender ages of three, four, and five years.

It would not be surprising if you should believe the observations of a fellow-countryman rather than my own. Fortunately a short time ago from the analysis of a five-year-old boy who was suffering from anxiety, an analysis undertaken with correct technique by his own father, I succeeded in getting a fairly complete picture of the bodily expressions of the impulse and the mental productions of an early stage of childish sexual life. And I must remind you that my friend, Dr. C. G. Jung, read you a few hours ago in this room an observation on a still younger girl who from the same cause as my patient— the birth of a little child in the family—betrayed certainly almost the same secret excitement, wish and complex-creation. Accordingly I am not without hope that you may feel friendly toward this idea of infantile sexuality that was so strange at first. I might also quote the remarkable example of the Zürich psychiatist, E. Bleuler, who said a few years ago openly that he faced my sexual theories incredulous and bewildered, and since that time by his own observations had substantiated them in their whole scope. If it is true that most men, medical observers and others, do not want to know anything about the sexual life of the child, the fact is capable of explanation only too easily. They have forgotten their own infantile sexual activity under the pressure of education for civilization and do not care to be reminded now of the repressed material. You will be convinced otherwise if you begin the investigation by a self-analysis, by an interpretation of your own childhood memories.

Lay aside your doubts and let us evaluate the infantile sexuality of the earliest years. The sexual impulse of the child manifests itself as a very complex one, it permits of an analysis into many components, which spring from different sources. It is entirely disconnected from the function of reproduction which it is later to serve. It permits the child to gain different sorts of pleasure sensations, which we include, by the analogues and connections which they show, under the term sexual pleasures. The great source of infantile sexual pleasure is the auto-excitation of certain particularly sensitive parts of the body; besides the genitals are included the rectum and the opening of the urinary canal, and also the skin and other sensory surfaces. Since in this first phase of child sexual life the satisfaction is found on the child's own body and has nothing to do with any other object, we call this phase after a word coined by Havelock Ellis, that of "auto-eroticism." The parts of the body significant in giving sexual pleasure we call "erogenous zones." The thumb-sucking (*Ludeln*) or passionate sucking (*Wonnesaugen*) of very young children is a good example of such an auto-erotic satisfaction of an erogenous zone. The first scientific observer of this phenomenon, a specialist in children's diseases in Budapest by the name of Lindner, interpreted these rightly as sexual satisfaction and described exhaustively their transformation into other and higher forms of sexual gratification. Another sexual satisfaction of this time of life is the excitation of the genitals by masturbation, which has such a great significance for later life and, in the case of many individuals, is never fully overcome. Besides this and other auto-erotic manifestations we see very early in the child the impulse-components of *sexual pleasure,* or, as we may say, of the *libido,* which presupposes a second person as its object. These impulses appear in opposed pairs, as active and passive. The most important representatives of this group are the pleasure in inflicting pain (sadism) with its passive exhibition-pleasure *(Schaulust).* From the first of these later pairs splits off the curiosity for knowledge, as from the latter impulse toward artistic and theatrical representation. Other sexual manifestations of the child can already be regarded from the viewpoint of object-choice, in which the second person plays the prominent part. The significance of this was primarily based upon motives of the impulse of self-preservation. The difference between the sexes plays, however, in the child no very great rôle. One may attribute to every child, without wronging him, a bit of the homosexual disposition.

The sexual life of the child, rich, but dissociated, in which each single impulse goes about the business of arousing pleasure independently of every other, is later correlated and organized in two general directions, so that by the close of puberty the definite sexual character of the individual is practically finally determined. The single impulses subordinate themselves to the overlord* ship of the genital zone, so that the whole sexual life is taken over into the service of procreation, and their gratification is now significant only so far as they help to prepare and promote the true sexual act. On the other hand, object-choice prevails over auto-eroticism, so that now in the sexual life all components of the sexual impulse are satisfied in the loved person. But not all the original impulse-components are given a share in the final shaping of the sexual life. Even before the advent of puberty certain impulses have undergone the most energetic repression under the impulse of education, and mental forces like shame, disgust and morality are developed, which, like sentinels, keep the repressed wishes in subjection. When there comes, in puberty, the high tide of sexual desire it finds dams in this creation of reactions and resistances. These guide the outflow into the so-called normal channels, and make it impossible to revivify the impulses which have undergone repression.

The most important of these repressed impulses are coprophilism, that is, the pleasure in children connected with the excrements; and, further, the tendencies attaching themselves to the persons of the primitive object-choice.

Gentlemen, a sentence of general pathology says that every process of development brings with it the germ of pathological dispositions in so far as it may be inhibited, delayed, or incompletely carried out. This holds for the development of the sexual function, with its many complications. It is not smoothly completed in all individuals, and may leave behind either abnormalities or disposition to later diseases by the way of later falling back or *regression*. It may happen that not all the partial impulses subordinate themselves to the rule of the genital zone. Such an impulse which has remained disconnected brings about what we call a perversion, which may replace the normal sexual goal by one of its own. It may happen, as has been said before, that the auto-eroticism is not fully overcome, as many sorts of disturbances testify. The originally equal value of both sexes as sexual objects may be maintained and an inclination to homosexual activities in adult life result from this, which, under suitable conditions, rises to the level of exclusive homosexuality. This series of disturbances corresponds to the direct inhibition of development of the sexual function, it includes the perversions and the general *infantilism* of the sex life that are not seldom met with.

The disposition to neuroses is to be derived in another way from an injury to the development of the sex life. The neuroses are related to the perversions as the negative to the positive; in them we find the same impulse-components as in perversions, as bearers of the complexes and as creators of the symptoms; but here they work from out the unconscious. They have undergone a repression, but in spite of this they maintain themselves in the unconscious. Psychoanalysis teaches us that overstrong expression of the impulse in very early life leads to a sort of fixation (*Fixirung*), which then offers a weak point in the articulation of the sexual function. If the exercise of the normal sexual function meets with hindrances in later life, this repression, dating from the time of development, is broken through at just that point at which the infantile fixation took place.

You will now perhaps make the objection: "But all that is not sexuality." I have used the word in a very much wider sense than you are accustomed to understand it. This I willingly concede. But it is a question whether you do not rather use the word in much too narrow a sense when you restrict it to the realm of procreation. You sacrifice by that the understanding of perversions; of the connection between perversion, neurosis, and normal sexual life; and have no means of recognizing, in its true significance, the easily observable beginning of the somatic and mental sexual life of the child. But however you decide about the use of the word, remember that the psychoanalyst understands sexuality in that full sense to which he is led by the evalutation of infantile sexuality.

Now we turn again to the sexual development of the child. We still have much to say here, since we have given more attention to the somatic than to the mental expressions of the sexual life. The primitive object-choice of the child, which is derived from his need of help, demands our further interest. It first attaches to all persons to whom he is accustomed, but soon these give way in favor of his parents. The relation of the child to his parents is, as both direct observation of the child and later analytic investigation of adults agree, not at all free from elements of sexual accessory-excitation (*Miterregung*). The child takes both parents, and especially one, as an object of his erotic wishes. Usually he follows in this the stimulus given by his parents, whose tenderness has very clearly the character of a sex manifestation, though inhibited so far as its goal is concerned. As a rule, the father prefers the daughter, the mother the son; the child reacts to this situation, since, as son, he wishes himself in the place of his father, as daughter, in the place of the mother. The feelings awakened in these relations between parents and children, and, as a resultant of them, those among the children in relation to each other, are not only positively of a tender, but negatively of an inimical sort. The complex built up in this way is destined to quick repression, but it still exerts a great and lasting effect from the unconscious. We must express the opinion that this with its ramifications presents the *nuclear complex* of every neurosis, and so we are prepared to meet with it in a not less effectual way in the other fields of mental life. The myth of King Oedipus, who kills his father and wins his mother as a wife is only the slightly altered presentation of the infantile wish, rejected later by the opposing barriers of incest. Shakespeare's tale of Hamlet rests on the same basis of an incest complex, though better concealed. At the time when the child is still ruled by the still unrepressed nuclear complex, there begins a very significant part of his mental activity which serves sexual interest. He begins to investigate the question of where children come from and guesses more than adults imagine of the true relations by deduction from the signs which he sees. Usually his interest in this investigation is awakened by the threat to his welfare through the birth of another child in the family, in whom at first he sees only a rival. Under the influence of the partial impulses which are active in him he arrives at a number of "infantile sexual theories," as that the same male genitals belong to both sexes, that children are conceived by eating and born through the opening of the intestine, and that sexual intercourse is to be regarded as an inimical act, a sort of overpowering.

But just the unfinished nature of his sexual constitution and the gaps in his knowledge brought about by the hidden condition of the feminine sexual canal, cause the infant investigator to discontinue his work as a failure. The facts of this childish investigation itself as well as the infant sex theories created by it are of determinative significance in the building of the child's character, and in the content of his later neuroses.

It is unavoidable and quite normal that the child should make his parents the objects of his first object-choice. But his *libido* must not remain fixed on these first chosen objects, but must take them merely as a prototype and transfer from these to other persons in the time of definite object-choice. The breaking loose (*Ablösung*) of the child from his parents is thus a problem impossible to escape if the social virtue of the young individual is not to be impaired. During the time that the repressive activity is making its choice among the partial sexual impulses and later, when the influence of the parents, which in the most essential way has furnished the material for these repressions, is lessened, great problems fall to the work of education, which at present certainly does not always solve them in the most intelligent and economic way.

Gentlemen, do not think that with these explanations of the sexual life and the sexual development of the child we have too far departed from psychoanalysis and the cure of neurotic disturbances. If you like, you may regard the psychoanalytic treatment only as a continued education for the overcoming of childhood-remnants (*Kindheitsresten*).

Fifth Lecture

Ladies and Gentlemen: With the discovery of infantile sexuality and the tracing back of the neurotic symptoms to erotic impulse-components we have arrived at several unexpected formulæ for expressing the nature and tendencies of neurotic diseases. We see that the individual falls ill when in consequence of outer hindrances or inner lack of adaptability the satisfaction of the erotic needs in the sphere of reality is denied. We see that he then flees to sickness, in order to find with its help a surrogate satisfaction for that denied him. We recognize that the symptoms of illness contain fractions of the sexual activity of the individual, or his whole sexual life, and we find in the turning away from reality the chief tendency and also the chief injury of the sickness. We may guess that the resistance of our patients against the cure is not a simple one, but is composed of many motives. Not only does the ego of the patient strive against the giving up of the repression by which it has changed itself from its original constitution into its present form, but also the sexual impulses may not renounce their surrogate satisfaction so long as it is not certain that they can be offered anything better in the sphere of reality.

The flight from the unsatisfying reality into what we call, on account of its biologically injurious nature, disease, but which is never without an individual gain in pleasure for the patient, takes place over the path of regression, the return to earlier phases of the sexual life, when satisfaction was not lacking. This regression is seemingly a twofold one, a *temporal,* in so far as the *libido* or erotic need falls back to a temporally earlier stage of development, and a *formal,* since the original and primitive psychic means of expression are applied to the expression of this need. Both sorts of regression focus in childhood and have their common point in the production of an infantile condition of sexual life.

The deeper you penetrate into the pathogenic of neurotic diseases, the more the connection of neuroses with other products of human mentality, even the most valuable, will be revealed to you. You will be reminded that we men, with the high claims of our civilization and under the pressure of our repressions, find reality generally quite unsatisfactory and so keep up a life of fancy in which we love to compensate for what is lacking in the sphere of reality by the production of wish-fulfillments. In these phantasies is often contained very much of the particular constitutional essence of personality and of its tendencies, repressed in real life. The energetic and successful man is he who succeeds by dint of labor in transforming his wish fancies into reality. Where this is not successful in consequence of the resistance of the outer world and the weakness of the individual, there begins the turning away from reality. The individual takes refuge in his satisfying world of fancy. Under certain conditions it still remains possible for him to find another connecting link between these fancies and reality, instead of permanently becoming a stranger to it through the regression into the infantile. If the individual who is displeased with reality is in possession of that *artistic talent* which is still a psychological riddle, he can transform his fancies into artistic creations. So he escapes the fate of a neurosis and wins back his connection with reality by this round-about way. Where this opposition to the real world exists, but this valuable talent fails or proves insufficient, it is unavoidable that the *libido,* following the origin of the fancies, succeeds by means of regression in revivifying the infantile wishes and so producing a neurosis. The neurosis takes, in our time, the place of the cloister, in which were accustomed to take refuge all those whom life had undeceived or who felt themselves too weak for life. Let me give at this point the main result at which we have arrived by the psychoanalytic investigation of neurotics, namely, that neuroses have no peculiar psychic content of their own, which is not also to be found in healthy states; or, as C. G. Jung has expressed it, neurotics fall ill of the same complexes with which we sound people struggle. It depends on quantitative relationships, on the relations of the forces wrestling with each other, whether the struggle leads to health, to a neurosis, or to compensatory over-functioning (*Ueberleistung*).

Ladies and Gentlemen, I have still withheld from you the most remarkable experience which corroborates our assumptions of the sexual impulse-forces of neurotics. Every time that we treat a neurotic psychoanalytically, there occurs in him the so-called phenomenon of *transfer* (*Uebertragung*), that is, he applies to the person of the physician a great amount of tender emotion, often mixed with enmity, which has no foundation in any real relation, and must be derived in every respect from the old wish-fancies of the patient which have become unconscious. Every fragment of his emotive life, which can no longer be called back into memory, is accordingly lived over by the patient in his relations to the physician, and only by such a living of them over in the "transfer" is he convinced of the existence and the power of these unconscious sexual excitations. The symptoms, which, to use a simile from chemistry, are the precipitates of earlier love experiences (in the widest sense), can only be dissolved in the higher temperature of the experience of transfer and transformed into other psychic products. The physician plays in this reaction, to use an excellent expression of S. Ferenczi, the rôle of a *catalytic ferment,* which temporarily attracts to itself the affect which has become free in the course of the process.

The study of transfer can also give you the key to the understanding of hypnotic suggestion, which we at first used with our patients as a technical means of investigation of the unconscious. Hypnosis showed itself at that time to be a therapeutic help, but a hindrance to the scientific knowledge of the real nature of the case, since it cleared away the psychic resistances from a certain field, only to pile them up in an unscalable wall at the boundaries of this field. You must not think that the phenomenon of transfer, about which I can unfortunately say only too little here, is created by the influence of the psychoanalytic treatment. The transfer arises spontaneously in all human relations and in the relations of the patient to the physician; it is everywhere the especial bearer of therapeutic influences, and it works the stronger the less one knows of its presence. Accordingly psychoanalysis does not create it, it merely discloses it to consciousness, and avails itself of it, in order to direct the psychic processes to the wished-for goal. But I cannot leave the theme of transfer without stressing the fact that this phenomenon is of decisive importance to convince not only the patient, but also the physician. I know that all my adherents were first convinced of the correctness of my views through their experience with transfer, and I can very well conceive that one may not win such a surety of judgment so long as he makes no psychoanalysis, and so has not himself observed the effects of transfer.

Ladies and Gentlemen, I am of the opinion that there are, on the intellectual side, two hindrances to acknowledging the value of the psychoanalytic viewpoint: first, the fact that we are not accustomed to reckon with a strict determination of mental life, which holds without exception, and, second, the lack of knowledge of the peculiarities through which unconscious mental processes differ from these conscious ones with which we are familiar. One of the most widespread resistances against the work of psychoanalysis with patients as with persons in health reduces to the latter of the two moments. One is afraid of doing harm by psychoanalysis, one is anxious about calling up into consciousness the repressed sexual impulses of the patient, as though there were danger that they could overpower the higher ethical strivings and rob him of his cultural acquisitions. One can see that the patient has sore places in his soul life, but one is afraid to touch them, lest his suffering be increased. We may use this analogy. It is, of course, better not to touch diseased places when one can only cause pain. Be we know that the suregon does not refrain from the investigation and reinvestigation of the seat of illness, if his invasion has as its aim the restoration of lasting health. Nobody thinks of blaming him for the unavoidable difficulties of the investigation or the phenomena of reaction from the operation, if these only accomplish their purpose, and gain for the patient a final cure by temporarily making his condition worse. The case is similar in psychoanalysis; it can lay claim to the same things as surgery; the increase of pain which takes place in the patient during the treatment is very much less than that which the surgeon imposes upon him, and especially negligible in comparison with the pains of serious illness. But the consequence which is feared, that of a disturbance of the cultural character by the impulse which has been freed from repression, is wholly impossible. In relation to this anxiety we must consider what our experiences have taught us with certainty, that the somatic and mental power of a wish, if once its repression has not succeeded, is incomparably stronger when it is unconscious than when it is conscious, so that by being made conscious it can only be weakened. The unconscious wish cannot be influenced, is free from all strivings in the contrary direction, while the conscious is inhibited by those wishes which are also conscious and which strive against it. The work of psychoanalysis accordingly presents a better substitute, in the service of the highest and most valuable cultural strivings, for the repression which has failed.

Now what is the fate of the wishes which have become free by psychoanalysis, by what means shall they be made harmless for the life of the individual? There are several ways. The general consequence is, that the wish is consumed during the work by the correct mental activity of those better tendencies which are opposed to it. The repression is supplanted by a condemnation carried through with the best means at one's disposal. This is possible, since for the most part we have to abolish only the effects of earlier development stages of the ego. The individual for his part only repressed the useless impulse, because at that time he was himself still incompletely organized and weak; in his present maturity and strength he can, perhaps, conquer without injury to himself that which is inimical to him. A second issue of the work of psychoanalysis may be that the revealed unconscious impulses can now arrive at those useful applications which, in the case of undisturbed developments, they would have found earlier. The extirpation of the infantile wishes is not at all the ideal aim of development. The neurotic has lost, by his repressions, many sources of mental energy whose contingents would have been very valuable for his character building and his life activities. We know a far more purposive process of development, to so-called *sublimation* (*Sublimirung*), by which the energy of infantile wish-excitations is not secluded, but remains capable of application, while for the particular excitations, instead of becoming useless, a higher, eventually no longer sexual, goal is set up. The components of the sexual instinct are especially distinguished by such a capacity for the sublimation and exchange of their sexual goal for one more remote and socially more valuable. To the contributions of the energy won in such a way for the functions of our mental life we probably owe the highest cultural consequences. A repression taking place at an early period excludes the sublimation of the repressed impulse; after the removal of the repression the way to sublimation is again free.

We must not neglect, also, to glance at the third of the

possible issues. A certain part of the suppressed libidinous excitation has a right to direct satisfaction and ought to find it in life. The claims of our civilization make life too hard for the greater part of humanity, and so further the aversion to reality and the origin of neuroses, without producing an excess of cultural gain by this excess of sexual repression. We ought not to go so far as to fully neglect the original animal part of our nature, we ought not to forget that the happiness of individuals cannot be dispensed with as one of the aims of our culture. The plasticity of the sexual-components, manifest in their capacity for sublimation, may cause a great temptation to accomplish greater culture-effects by a more and more far reaching sublimation. But just as little as with our machines we expect to change more than a certain fraction of the applied heat into useful mechanical work, just as little ought we to strive to separate the sexual impulse in its whole extent of energy from its peculiar goal. This cannot succeed, and if the narrowing of sexuality is pushed too far it will have all the evil effects of a robbery.

I do not know whether you will regard the exhortation with which I close as a presumptuous one. I only venture the indirect presentation of my conviction, if I relate an old tale, whose application you may make yourselves. German literature knows a town called Schilda, to whose inhabitants were attributed all sorts of clever pranks. The wiseacres, so the story goes, had a horse, with whose powers of work they were well satisfied, and against whom they had only one grudge, that he consumed so much expensive oats. They concluded that by good management they would break him of this bad habit, by cutting down his rations by several stalks each day, until he had learned to do without them altogether. Things went finely for a while, the horse was weaned to one stalk a day, and on the next day he would at last work without fodder. On the morning of this day the malicious horse was found dead; the citizens of Schilda could not understand why he had died. We should be inclined to believe that the horse had starved, and that without a certain ration of oats no work could be expected from an animal.

7

Jean-Paul Sartre,   EXISTENTIALISM
         (Trans. by Bernard Frechtman)

Laotse, BOOK OF TAO
and Chuangtse, Commentaries
         (Trans. & Ed. by Lin Yutang)

1. Explain the word "existentialism" and tell what Sartre means by "existence precedes essence."

2. How does Sartre define and explain "anguish," "forlornness," and "despair"?

3. "Man is nothing else but what he makes of himself." This, Sartre says, is the first principle of existentialism. Explain this statement and its ramifications for man's responsibility to man and to choices between good and evil.

4. What does Sartre mean by the statement, "In choosing myself, I choose man"?

5. How does Sartre meet the accusation of quietism?

6. Explain Sartre's argument on the question of optimism versus pessimism in existentialism.

7. Compare Sartre's argument that man makes himself -- regardless of the circumstances of his life -- and is wholly responsible for his actions to the positions of Freud and Darwin.

8. The deterministic theories of Freud and Darwin can be contrasted with Sartre's theory of freedom as complete existential openness. Contrast these with Aquinas' understanding of freedom as the ability to act in accordance with one's nature.

9. Do you feel that there is a fundamental difference between Eastern and Western views of human nature? How well do you think Laotse's advice would apply to modern Western man?

10. What is the relationship between character and human nature? How can we know the character of someone?

11. What similarities do you see between the views of
     Laotse and Cicero?

12. Compare and contrast the views of Laotse and
     Sartre on human passivity?

13. What kind of person would Laotse's "best of men"
     be? Would he be a pleasant person to know? Would
     he be aggressive? Strong? Effective?

Jean-Paul Sartre (1905-1980) was a leading expo-
nent of Existentialism, the philosophy which emphasizes
man's freedom and responsibility as well as the individuality of all persons. In *Existentialism is a
Humanism*, Sartre defends existentialism against the
charges of its critics while succinctly presenting the
major points of this philosophy.

EXISTENTIALISM

Man is nothing else but what he makes of himself. Such is the first principle of existentialism. It is also what is called subjectivity,
the name we are labeled with when charges are
brought against us. But what do we mean

by this, if not that man has a greater dignity than a stone or table? For we mean that man first exists, that is, that man first of all is the being who hurls himself toward a future and who is conscious of imagining himself as being in the future. Man is at the start a plan which is aware of itself, rather than a patch of moss, a piece of garbage, or a cauliflower; nothing exists prior to this plan; there is nothing in heaven; man will be what he will have planned to be. Not what he will want to be. Because by the word "will" we generally mean a conscious decision, which is subsequent to what we have already made of ourselves. I may want to belong to a political party, write a book, get married; but all that is only a manifestation of an earlier, more spontaneous choice that is called "will." But if existence really does precede essence, man is responsible for what he is. Thus, existentialism's first move is to make every man aware of what he is and to make the full responsibility of his existence rest on him. And when we say that a man is responsible for himself, we do not only mean that he is responsible for his own individuality, but that he is responsible for all men.

The word subjectivism has two meanings, and our opponents play on the two. Subjectivism means, on the one hand, that an individual chooses and makes himself; and, on the other, that it is impossible for man to transcend human subjectivity. The second of these is the essential meaning of existentialism. When we say that man chooses his own self, we mean that every one of us does likewise; but we also mean by that that in making this choice he also chooses all men. In fact, in creating the man that we want to be, there is not a single one of our acts which does not at the same time create an image of man as we think he ought to be. To choose to be this or that is to affirm at the same time the value of what we choose, because we can never choose evil. We always choose the good, and nothing can be good for us without being good for all.

If, on the other hand, existence precedes essence, and if we grant that we exist and fashion our image at one and the same time, the image is valid for everybody and for our whole age. Thus, our responsibility is much greater than we might have supposed, because it involves all mankind. If I am a workingman and choose to join a Christian trade-union rather than be a communist, and if by being a member I want to show that the best thing for man is resignation, that the kingdom of man is not of this world, I am not only involving my own case—I want to be resigned for everyone. As a result, my action has involved all humanity. To take a more individual matter, if I want to marry, to have children; even if this marriage depends solely on my own circumstances or passion or wish, I am involving all humanity in monogamy and not merely myself. Therefore, I am responsible for myself and for everyone else. I am creating a certain image of man of my own choosing. In choosing myself, I choose man.

This helps us understand what the actual content is of such rather grandiloquent words as anguish, forlornness, despair. As you will see, it's all quite simple.

First, what is meant by anguish? The existentialists say at once that man is anguish. What that means is this: the man who involves himself and who realizes that he is not only the person he chooses to be, but also a lawmaker who is, at the same time, choosing all mankind as well as himself, can not help escape the feeling of his total and deep responsibility. Of course, there are many people who are not anxious; but we claim that they are hiding their anxiety, that they are fleeing from it. Certainly, many people believe that when they do something, they themselves are the only ones involved, and when someone says to them, "What if everyone acted that way?" they shrug their shoulders and answer, "Everyone doesn't act that way." But really, one should always ask himself, "What would happen if everybody looked at things that way?" There is no escaping this disturbing thought except by a kind of double-dealing. A man who lies and makes excuses for himself by saying "not everybody does that," is someone with an uneasy conscience, because the act of lying implies that a universal value is conferred upon the lie.

Anguish is evident even when it conceals itself. This is the anguish that Kierkegaard called the anguish of Abraham. You know the story: an angel has ordered Abraham to sacrifice his son; if it really were an angel who has come and said, "You are Abraham, you shall sacrifice your son," everything would be all right. But everyone might first wonder, "Is it really an angel, and am I really Abraham? What proof do I have?"

There was a madwoman who had hallucinations; someone used to speak to her on the telephone and give her orders. Her doctor asked her, "Who is it who talks to you?" She answered, "He says it's God." What proof did she really have that it was God? If an angel comes to me, what proof is there that it's an angel? And if I hear voices, what proof is there that they come from heaven and not from hell, or from the subconscious, or a pathological condition? What proves that they are addressed to me? What proof is there that I have been appointed to impose my choice and my conception of man on humanity? I'll never find any proof or sign to convince me of that. If a voice addresses me, it is always for me to decide that this is the angel's voice; if I consider that such an act is a good one, it is I who will choose to say that it is good rather than bad.

Now, I'm not being singled out as an Abraham, and yet at every moment I'm obliged to perform exemplary acts. For every man, everything happens as if all mankind had its eyes fixed on him and were guiding itself by what he does. And every man ought to say to himself, "Am I really the kind of man who has the right to act in such a way that humanity might guide itself by my actions?" And if he does not say that to himself, he is masking his anguish.

There is no question here of the kind of anguish which would lead to quietism, to inaction. It is a matter of a simple sort of anguish that anybody who has had responsibilities is familiar with. For example, when a military officer takes the responsibility for an attack and sends a certain number of men to death, he chooses to do so, and in the main he alone makes the choice. Doubtless, orders come from above, but they are too broad; he interprets them, and on this interpretation depend the lives of ten or fourteen or twenty men. In mak-

Existentialism

ing a decision he can not help having a certain anguish. All leaders know this anguish. That doesn't keep them from acting; on the contrary, it is the very condition of their action. For it implies that they envisage a number of possibilities, and when they choose one, they realize that it has value only because it is chosen. We shall see that this kind of anguish, which is the kind that existentialism describes, is explained, in addition, by a direct responsibility to the other men whom it involves. It is not a curtain separating us from action, but is part of action itself.

When we speak of forlornness, a term Heidegger was fond of, we mean only that God does not exist and that we have to face all the consequences of this. The existentialist is strongly opposed to a certain kind of secular ethics which would like to abolish God with the least possible expense. About 1880, some French teachers tried to set up a secular ethics which went something like this: God is a useless and costly hypothesis; we are discarding it; but, meanwhile, in order for there to be an ethics, a society, a civilization, it is essential that certain values be taken seriously and that they be considered as having an *a priori* existence. It must be obligatory, *a priori*, to be honest, not to lie, not to beat your wife, to have children, etc., etc. So we're going to try a little device which will make it possible to show that values exist all the same, inscribed in a heaven of ideas, though otherwise God does not exist. In other words—and this, I believe, is the tendency of everything called reformism in France—nothing will be changed if God does not exist. We shall find ourselves with the same norms of honesty, progress, and humanism, and we shall have made of God an outdated hypothesis which will peacefully die off by itself.

The existentialist, on the contrary, thinks it very distressing that God does not exist, because all possibility of finding values in a heaven of ideas disappears along with Him; there can no longer be an *a priori* Good, since there is no infinite and perfect consciousness to think it. Nowhere is it written that the Good exists, that we must be honest, that we must not lie; because the fact is we are on a plane where there are only men. Dostoievsky said, "If God didn't exist, everything would be possible." That is the very starting point of existentialism. Indeed, everything is permissible if God does not exist, and as a result man is forlorn, because neither within him nor without does he find anything to cling to. He can't start making excuses for himself.

If existence really does precede essence, there is no explaining things away by reference to a fixed and given human nature. In other words, there is no determinism, man is free, man is freedom. On the other hand, if God does not exist, we find no values or commands to turn to which legitimize our conduct. So, in the bright realm of values, we have no excuse behind us, nor justification before us. We are alone, with no excuses.

That is the idea I shall try to convey when I say that man is condemned to be free. Condemned, because he did not create himself, yet, in other respects is free; because, once thrown into the world, he is responsible for everything he does. The existentialist does not believe in the power of passion. He will never agree that a sweeping passion is a ravaging torrent which fatally leads a man to certain acts and is therefore an excuse. He thinks that man is responsible for his passion.

The existentialist does not think that man is going to help himself by finding in the world some omen by which to orient himself. Because he thinks that man will interpret the omen to suit himself. Therefore, he thinks that man, with no support and no aid, is condemned every moment to invent man. Ponge, in a very fine article, has said, "Man is the future of man." That's exactly it. But if it is taken to mean that this future is recorded in heaven, that God sees it, then it is false, because it would really no longer be a future. If it is taken to mean that, whatever a man may be, there is a future to be forged, a virgin future before him, then this remark is sound. But then we are forlorn.

As for despair, the term has a very simple meaning. It means that we shall confine ourselves to reckoning only with what depends upon our will, or on the ensemble of probabilities which make our action possible. When we want something, we always have to reckon with probabilities. I may be counting on the arrival of a friend. The friend is coming by rail or street-car; this supposes that the train will arrive on schedule, or that the street-car will not jump the track. I am left in the realm of possibility; but possibilities are to be reckoned with only to the point where my action comports with the ensemble of these possibilities, and no further. The moment the possibilities I am considering are not rigorously involved by my action, I ought to disengage myself from them, because no God, no scheme, can adapt the world and its possibilities to my will. When Descartes said, "Conquer yourself rather than the world," he meant essentially the same thing.

When all is said and done, what we are accused of, at bottom, is not our pessimism, but an optimistic toughness. If people throw up to us our works of fiction in which we write about people who are soft, weak, cowardly, and sometimes even downright bad, it's not because these people are soft, weak, cowardly, or bad; because if we were to say, as Zola did, that they are that way because of heredity, the workings of environment, society, because of biological or psychological determinism, people would be reassured. They would say, "Well, that's what we're like, no one can do anything about it." But when the existentialist writes about a coward, he says that this coward is responsible for his cowardice. He's not like that because he has a cowardly heart or lung or brain; he's not like that on account of his physiological make-up; but he's like that because he has made himself a coward by his acts. There's no such thing as a cowardly constitution; there are nervous constitutions; there is poor blood, as the common people say, or strong constitutions. But the man whose blood is poor is not a coward on that account, for what makes cowardice is the act of renouncing or yielding. A constitution is not an act; the coward is defined on the basis of the acts he performs. People feel, in a vague sort of way, that this coward we're talking about is guilty of being a coward, and the thought frightens them, What people would like is that a coward or a hero be born that way.

Laotse (571-c.500 B.C.), the founder of one of the two great schools of classical Chinese philosophy, Taoism from the Chinese *tao* meaning "the way", lived about half a century before Confucius, the founder of the other great school, Confucianism. In contrast with Confucius' learned and formal skepticism, Laotse's teaching was religious and even mystical. The excerpts given below in most cases include not only Laotse's original teachings (the verse portions of the text) but also modern explanatory comments followed by the commentary of Chuangtse (d.c.275 B.C.), Laotse's greatest disciple.

BOOK OF TAO
and Commentaries

8. WATER

The best of men is like water;
　Water benefits all things
　And does not compete with them.
It dwells in (the lowly) places that all disdain—
　Wherein it comes near to the Tao.

In his dwelling, (the Sage) loves the (lowly) earth;
In his heart, he loves what is profound;
In his relations with others, he loves kindness;
In his words, he loves sincerity;
In government, he loves peace;
In business affairs, he loves ability;
In his actions, he loves choosing the right time.
　It is because he does not contend
　That he is without reproach.

In a comparative study of Laotse and Chuangtse, prob-
ably the most marked difference is that regarding the
subject of non-contention. As has been pointed out in
the preface, the most important and characteristic teach-
ing of Laotse is on non-contention, humility, gentility and
seeking the lowly position, of which water is the symbol.
Laotse had more passages on teachings of this kind than
on any other topic. But it is difficult, and almost impos-
sible, to find parallel sayings of Chuangtse on the same

subject. This leads one to think that Chuangtse was probably a stronger and harder spirit than the mellow master, who emphasized the spirit of the female. Whereas water became for Laotse a symbol of the strength of gentleness and the wisdom of lying low, in Chuangtse, it became the symbol rather of tranquillity of spirit. See the preface.

8.1. WATER AS THE SYMBOL OF HEAVENLY VIRTUE. When the body is kept bustling about without stop, it becomes fatigued. When the mind is overworked without stop, it becomes worried, and worry causes exhaustion. The nature of water is that it becomes clear when left alone and becomes still when undisturbed. When it is bottled up and cannot flow, it also cannot remain clear. It is the symbol of heavenly virtue. (4:9)

Calm represents the nature of water at its best. In that it may serve as our model, for its power is preserved and is not dispersed through agitation. (2:3)

Chuangtse distinguished between living on the spiritual and the material level. Although his most characteristic teaching was to allow the human spirit to roam about in the immaterial world, he recognized the necessity of living in this world as we find it and meeting the daily problems of life. The daily problems of living were "something which could not be helped, and the cannot-be-helped attitude is the attitude of the Sage." This attitude may be described as one of patient condescension.

8.2. THE TAO OF GOD AND THE TAO OF MAN. That which is low, but must be let alone, is matter. That which is humble, but still must be followed, is the people. That which is always there but still has to be attended to, is affairs. That which is inadequate, but still has to be set forth, is the law. That which is remote from Tao, but still claims our attention, is duty. That which is biased, but must be broadened, is charity. Trivial, but requiring to be strengthened from within, that is ceremony. Contained within, but requiring to be uplifted, that is character. One, but not to be without modification, that is Tao. Spiritual, yet not to be devoid of action, that is God.

Therefore the Sage looks up to God, but does not offer to aid. He perfects his character, but does not involve himself. He guides himself by Tao, but makes no plans. He identifies himself with charity, but does not rely on it. He performs his duties towards his neighbors, but does not set store by them. He responds to ceremony, without avoiding it. He undertakes affairs without declining them, and metes out law without confusion. He relies on the people and does not make light of them. He accommodates himself to the material world and does not ignore it. Things are not worth attending to, yet they have to be attended to. He who does not understand God will not be pure in character. He who has not clear apprehension of Tao will not know where to begin. And he who is not enlightened by Tao—alas indeed for him!

13. PRAISE AND BLAME

"Favor and disgrace cause one dismay;
What we value and what we fear are within our Self.¹

What does this mean:
"Favor and disgrace cause one dismay?"
Those who receive a favor from above
　Are dismayed when they receive it,
　And dismayed when they lose it.

What does this mean:
"What we value and what we fear⁹ are within our
　Self?"
We have fears because we have a self.¹⁰
When we do not regard that self as self,
What have we to fear?

Therefore he who values the world as his self
　May then be entrusted with the government of the
　world;
And he who loves the world as his self—
　The world may then be entrusted to his care.

⁹ Interpreted as life and death. The text of Chuangtse
confirms this interpretation.
¹⁰ Lit. "body."

Man's loss of his original nature comes from the distractions of the material world acting through the five senses. His emancipation of the spirit comes from the doctrine of selflessness which appears to be the common ideal of sainthood in all religions. In Taoist philosophy, this emancipation through selflessness comes through the realization that the individual self is nothing and the great unity of the universe is everything. From this selfless point of view it is therefore natural to regard all the accidents of fortune and misfortune, of honor and disgrace, as things that are entirely superficial and unimportant.

The entire line "Therefore he who values the world as his self may then be entrusted with the government of the world; and he who loves the world as his self—the world may then be entrusted to his care" *appears in Chuangtse in identical wording in selection 3.4, where the context makes the meaning clear.*

13.1. DEFINITION OF HONOR AND HAPPINESS. When one is strong in the knowledge of Tao, one disregards the petty problems of life; when one is strong in the knowledge of character, one ignores the petty problems of knowledge. Petty knowledge is injurious to one's character, and petty conduct is injurious to Tao. Therefore, it is said, "All that one needs to do is to return to the norm himself."

Perfect happiness is described as success. When the ancients spoke of success, they did not mean the symbols of rank and honor; they meant by success the state wherein one's happiness was complete. The modern man means by success the badges of rank and honor. But the badges of rank and honor on a man's body have nothing to do with his original self. They are things that are accidentally loaned to him for a period. You cannot refuse them when they are loaned to you, nor can you keep them when they are taken away from you. Therefore, one should not forget oneself over such insignia of authority, nor should one do what the world is doing because of failure and poverty. He is happy in failure as well as in success, and, therefore, he is without sorrow. If a man is unhappy because things loaned to him have been taken away from him, then it is clear that when he was happy, he had lost his true self. Therefore, it is said, "Those who lose their selves in material things and lose their original nature in the material world may be compared to people who stand on their heads." (4:10)

13.2. OWNERSHIP.

"Can one obtain Tao and possess it?" asked Emperor Shun of Ch'en.

"You don't even own your self. How can you possess Tao?"

"If I don't possess my self, who possesses it?"

"Your self," replied Ch'en, "is a body lent to you by the universe. Your life is not possessed by you; it is a harmony lent to you by the universe. Your nature is not possessed by you; it is a natural evolution lent to you by the universe. Your children and grandchildren are not possessed by you; they are the thrown-off skins (as of snakes or cicadas) lent to you by the universe. Therefore, one goes about without knowing where he is going, stops without knowing what he is holding on to, and eats without knowing how the food tastes. Such activities are merely the working of the *yang* principle of the universe when it is in dominance. How can you ever possess (Tao)?" (6:2)

From this general point of view, the Taoist develops the teachings that "the perfect man is selfless," that instead of seeking security in a special corner of one's home and family, one should rather "entrust that which belongs to the universe to the whole universe," and, therefore, "men should lose themselves in Tao as fish lose themselves in water."

13.3. THE PERFECT MAN IS SELFLESS.

"And a lake sparrow laughed, and said: Pray, what may that creature be going to do? I rise but a few yards in the air and settle down again, after flying around among the reeds. That is as much as anyone would want to fly. Now, wherever can this creature be going to?"

Such, indeed, is the difference between small and great. Take, for instance, a man who creditably fills some small office, or whose influence spreads over a village, or whose character pleases a certain prince. His opinion of himself will be much the same as that lake sparrow's. The philosopher Yung of Sung[11] would laugh at such a one. If the whole world flattered him, he would not be affected thereby, nor if the whole world blamed him would he be dissuaded from what he was doing. For Yung can distinguish between essence and superficialities, and understand what is true honor and shame. Such men are rare in their generation. But even he has not established himself.

Now Liehtse[12] could ride upon the wind. Sailing happily in the cool breeze, he would go on for fifteen days before his return. Among mortals who attain

[11] See Prolegomena, Section 2.
[12] Philosopher about whose life nothing is known. The book *Liehtse* is considered a later compilation.

happiness, such a man is rare. Yet although Liehtse could dispense with walking, he would still have to depend upon something.[13] As for one who is charioted upon the eternal fitness of Heaven and Earth, driving before him the changing elements as his team to roam through the realms of the Infinite, upon what, then, would such a one have need to depend?

Thus it is said, "The perfect man ignores self; the divine man ignores achievement; the true Sage ignores reputation." (1:2)

The doctrine of the great man is (fluid) as shadow to form, as echo to sound. Ask and it responds, fulfilling its abilities as the help-mate of humanity. Noiseless in repose, objectless in motion, he brings you out of the confusion of your coming and going to wander in the Infinite. Formless in his movements, he is eternal with the sun. In respect of his bodily existence, he conforms to the universal standards. Through conformance to the universal standards, he forgets his own individuality. But if he forgets his individuality, how can he regard his possessions as possessions? Those who see possessions in possessions were the wise men of old. Those who regard not possessions as possessions are the friends of Heaven and Earth. (3:9)

13.4. "ENTRUSTING THAT WHICH BELONGS TO THE UNI-VERSE TO THE WHOLE UNIVERSE." A boat may be hidden in a creek, or concealed in a bog, which is generally considered safe. But at midnight a strong man may come and carry it away on his back. Those dull of understanding do not perceive that however you conceal small things in larger ones, there will always be a chance of losing them. But if you entrust that which belongs to the

[13] The wind.

universe to the whole universe, from it there will be no escape. For this is the great law of things.

To have been cast in this human form is to us already a source of joy. How much greater joy beyond our conception to know that that which is now in human form may undergo countless transitions, with only the infinite to look forward to? Therefore it is that the Sage rejoices in that which can never be lost, but endures always. For if we emulate those who can accept graciously long age or short life and the vicissitudes of events, how much more that which informs all creation on which all changing phenomena depend? (2:6)

33. KNOWING ONESELF

He who knows others is learned;
   He who knows himself is wise.
He who conquers others has power of muscles;
   He who conquers himself is strong.
He who is contented is rich.
   He who is determined has strength of will.
He who does not lose his center endures,
He who dies yet (his power) remains has long life.

16. KNOWING THE ETERNAL LAW

Attain the utmost in Passivity,
Hold firm to the basis of Quietude.

The myriad things take shape and rise to activity,
  But I watch them fall back to their repose.
Like vegetation that luxuriantly grows
  But returns to the root (soil) from which it springs.

To return to the root is Repose;
  It is called going back to one's Destiny.
Going back to one's Destiny is to find the Eternal
    Law.
  To know the Eternal Law is Enlightenment.
And not to know the Eternal Law
  Is to court disaster.

He who knows the Eternal Law is tolerant;
Being tolerant, he is impartial;
Being impartial, he is kingly;
Being kingly, he is in accord with Nature;
Being in accord with Nature, he is in accord with Tao;
Being in accord with Tao, he is eternal,
And his whole life is preserved from harm.

8

Paul Tillich,   THE COURAGE TO BE

1. What does Tillich mean by "the courage of despair"?

2. Compare Tillich with Freud on the sources of anxiety.

3. Compare Tillich with Freud on the role of the theater in interpreting human nature.

4. In what sense does Tillich refer to the proposition that "the essence of man is his existence" as "the most despairing and the most courageous sentence in all Existentialist literature"?

5. What is Tillich's basic difference with Sartre?

6. Explain Tillich's statement, "Accepting acceptance though being unacceptable is the basis for the courage of confidence."

7. How does Tillich approach the problems of meaninglessness and doubt?

8. What does Tillich see as the key to "being-itself"?

9. What does Tillich mean by "absolute faith" and "God beyond God"?

A leading theologian of the twentieth century, Paul Tillich (1886-1965) was born in Germany, and had his theological education at the University of Halle. He had taught at the universities of Berlin, Marburg, Dresden, Leipzig, and Frankfurt before being barred from German univerisities in 1933 on account of his criticism of Hitler and the Nazi movement.

Thereupon he came to the United States where he served on the faculties of Union Theological Seminary in New York, Harvard, and the University of Chicago.

His works provided something of a bridge between the old, traditional thought, and the contemporary, modern. Some referred to him as an "apostle to the skeptics".

The Courage to Be (1952) was one of his most popular books.

THE COURAGE TO BE

Existential philosophy gives the theoretical formulation of what we have found as the courage of despair in art and literature. Heidegger in *Sein und Zeit* (which has its independent philosophical standing whatever Heidegger may say about it in criticism and retraction) describes the courage of despair in philosophically exact terms. He carefully elaborates the concepts of non-being, finitude, anxiety, care, having to die, guilt, conscience, self, participation, and so on. After this he analyses a phenomenon which he calls "resolve." The German word for it, *Entschlossenheit*, points to the symbol of unlocking what anxiety, subjection to conformity, and self-seclusion have locked. Once it is unlocked, one can act, but not according to norms given by anybody or anything. Nobody can give directions for the actions of the "resolute" individual—no God, no conventions, no laws of reason, no norms or principles. *We* must be ourselves, *we* must decide where to go. Our conscience is the call to ourselves. It does not tell anything concrete, it is neither the voice of God nor the awareness of eternal principles. It calls us to ourselves out of the behavior of the average man, out of daily talk, the daily routine, out of the adjustment which is the main principle of the conformist courage to be as a part. But if we follow this call

441

we become inescapably guilty, not through moral weakness but through our existential situation. Having the courage to be as ourselves we become guilty, and we are asked to take this existential guilt upon ourselves. Meaninglessness in all its aspects can be faced only by those who resolutely take the anxiety of finitude and guilt upon themselves. There is no norm, no criterion for what is right and wrong. Resoluteness makes right what shall be right. One of Heidegger's historical functions was to carry through the Existentialist analysis of the courage to be as oneself more fully than anyone else and, historically speaking, more destructively.

Sartre draws consequences from the earlier Heidegger which the later Heidegger did not accept. But it remains doubtful whether Sartre was historically right in drawing these consequences. It was easier for Sartre to draw them than for Heidegger, for in the background of Heidegger's ontology lies the mystical concept of being which is without significance for Sartre. Sartre carried through the consequences of Heidegger's Existentialist analyses without mystical restrictions. This is the reason he has become the symbol of present-day Existentialism, a position which is deserved not so much by the originality of his basic concepts as by the radicalism, consistency, and psychological adequacy with which he has carried them through. I refer above all to his proposition that "the essence of man is his existence." This sentence is like a flash of light which illuminates the whole Existentialist scene. One could call it the most despairing and the most courageous sentence in all Existentialist literature. What it says is that there is no essential nature of man, except in the one point that he can make of himself what he wants Man creates what he is. Nothing is given to him to determine his creativity. The essence of his being—the "should-be," "the ought-to-be,"—is not something which he finds; he makes it. Man is what he makes of himself And the courage to be as oneself is the courage to make of oneself what one wants to be.

There are Existentialists of a less radical point of view. Karl Jaspers recommends a new conformity in terms of an all-embracing "philosophical faith"; others speak of a *philosophia perennis;* while Gabriel Marcel moves from an Existentialist radicalism to a position based on the semi-collectivism of medieval thought. Existentialism in philosophy is represented more by Heidegger and Sartre than by anybody else.

THE COURAGE OF DESPAIR IN THE NON-CREATIVE EXISTENTIALIST ATTITUDE

I have dealt in the last sections with people whose creative courage enables them to express existential despair. Not many people are creative. But there is a noncreative Existentialist attitude called cynicism. A cynic today is not the same person the Greeks meant by the term. For the Greeks the cynic was a critic of contemporary culture on the basis of reason and natural law; he was a revolutionary rationalist, a follower of Socrates. Modern cynics are not ready to follow anybody. They have no belief in reason, no criterion of truth, no set of values, no answer to the question of meaning. They try to undermine every norm put before them. Their courage is expressed not creatively but in their form of life. They courageously reject any solution which would deprive them of their freedom of rejecting whatever they want to reject. The cynics are lonely although they need company in order to show their loneliness. They are empty of both preliminary meanings and an ultimate meaning, and therefore easy victims of neurotic anxiety. Much compulsive self-affirmation and much fanatical self-surrender are expressions of the noncreative courage to be as oneself.

THE LIMITS OF THE COURAGE TO BE AS ONESELF

This leads to the question of the limits of the courage to be as oneself in its creative as well as its uncreative forms. Courage is self-affirmation "in spite of," and the courage to be as oneself is self-affirmation of the self as itself. But one must ask: What is this self that affirms itself? Radical Existentialism answers: What it makes of itself. This is all it can say, because anything more would restrict the absolute freedom of the self. The self, cut off from participation in its world, is an empty shell, a mere possibility. It must act because it lives, but it must redo every action because acting involves him who acts in that upon which he acts. It gives content and for this reason it restricts his freedom to make of himself what he wants. In classical theology, both Catholic and Protestant, only

God has this prerogative: He is *ā sē* (from himself) or absolute freedom. Nothing is in him which is not by him. Existentialism, on the basis of the message that God is dead, gives man the divine "a-se-ity." Nothing shall be in man which is not by man. But man is finite, he is given to himself as what he is. He has received his being and with it the structure of his being, including the structure of finite freedom. And finite freedom is not aseity. Man can affirm himself only if he affirms not an empty shell, a mere possibility, but the structure of being in which he finds himself before action and nonaction. Finite freedom has a definite structure, and if the self tries to trespass on this structure it ends in the loss of itself. The nonparticipating hero in Sartre's *The Age of Reason* is caught in a net of contingencies, coming partly from the subconscious levels of his own self, partly from the environment from which he cannot withdraw. The assuredly empty self is filled with contents which enslave it just because it does not know or accept them as contents. This is true too of the cynic, as was said before. He cannot escape the forces of his self which may drive him into complete loss of the freedom that he wants to preserve.

This dialectical self-destruction of the radical forms of the courage to be as oneself has happened on a world-wide scale in the totalitarian reaction of the 20th century against the revolutionary Existentialism of the 19th century. The Existentialist protest against dehumanization and objectivation, together with its courage to be as oneself, have turned into the most elaborate and oppressive forms of collectivism that have appeared in history. It is the great tragedy of our time that Marxism, which had been conceived as a movement for the liberation of everyone, has been transformed into a system of enslavement of everyone, even of those who enslave the others. It is hard to imagine the immensity of this tragedy in terms of psychological destruction, especially within the intelligentsia. The courage to be was undermined in innumerable people because it was the courage to be in the sense of the revolutionary movements of the 19th century. When it broke down, these people turned either to the neocollectivist system, in a fanatic-neurotic reaction against the cause of their tragic disappointment, or to a cynical-neurotic indifference to all systems and every content.

It is obvious that similar observations can be made on the transformation of the Nietzschean type of the courage to be as oneself into the Fascist-Nazi forms of neocollectivism. The totalitarian machines which these movements produced embodied almost everything against which the courage to be as oneself stands. They used all possible means in order to make such courage impossible. Although, in distinction to communism, this system fell down, its aftermath is confusion, indifference, cynicism. And this is the soil on which the longing for authority and for a new collectivism grows.

The last two chapters, that on the courage to be as a part and that on the courage to be as oneself, have shown that the former, if carried through radically, leads to the loss of the self in collectivism and the latter to the loss of the world in Existentialism. This brings us to the question of our last chapter: Is there a courage to be which unites both forms by transcending them?

THE DIVINE-HUMAN ENCOUNTER AND THE COURAGE TO BE

The pole of individualization expresses itself in the religious experience as a personal encounter with God. And the courage derived from it is the courage of confidence in the personal reality which is manifest in the religious experience. In contradistinction to the mystical union one can call this relation a personal communion with the source of courage. Although the two types are in contrast they do not exclude each other. For they are united by the polar interdependence of individualization and participation. The courage of confidence has often, especially in Protestantism, been identified with the courage of faith. But this is not adequate, because confidence is only one element in faith. Faith embraces both mystical participation and personal confidence. Most parts of the Bible describe the religious encounter in strongly personalist terms. Biblicism, notably that of the Reformers, follows this emphasis. Luther directed his attack against the objective, quantitative, and impersonal elements in the Roman system. He fought for an immediate person-to-person relationship between God and man. In him the courage of confidence reached its highest point in the history of Christian thought. Every work of Luther, especially in his earlier years, is filled with such courage. Again and again he uses the word *trotz*, "in spite of." In spite of all the negativities which he had experienced, in spite of the anxiety which dominated that period, he derived the power of self-affirmation from his unshakable confidence in God and from the personal encounter with him. According to the expressions of anxiety in his period, the negativity his courage had to conquer were symbolized in the figures of death and the devil. It has rightly been said that Albrecht Dürer's engraving, "Knight, Death, and the Devil," is a classic expression of the spirit of the Lutheran Reformation and—it might be added—of Luther's courage of confidence, of his form of the courage to be. A knight in full armor is riding through a valley, accompanied by the figure of death on one side, the devil on the other. Fearlessly, concentrated, confident he looks ahead. He is alone but he is not lonely. In his solitude he participates in the power which gives him the courage to affirm himself in spite of the presence of the negativities of existence. His courage is certainly not the courage to be as a part. The Reformation broke away from the semicollectivism of the Middle Ages. Luther's courage of confidence is personal confidence, derived from a person-to-person encounter with God. Neither popes nor councils could give him this confidence. Therefore he had to reject them just because they relied on a doctrine which blocked off the courage of confidence. They sanctioned a system in which the anxiety of death and guilt never was completely conquered. There were many assurances but no certainty, many supports for the courage of confidence but no unquestionable foundation. The collective offered different ways of resisting anxiety but no way in which the individual could take his anxiety upon himself. He never was certain; he never could affirm his being with unconditional confidence. For he never could encounter the unconditional directly with his total being, in an immediate personal relation. There was, except in mysticism, always mediation through the Church, an indirect and partial meeting between God and the soul. When the Reformation removed the mediation and opened up a direct, total, and personal approach to God, a new nonmystical courage to be was possible. It is manifest in the heroic representatives of fighting Protestantism, in the Calvinist as well as in the Lutheran Reformation, and in Calvinism even more conspicuously. It is not the heroism of risking martyrdom, of resisting the authorities, of transforming the structure of Church and society, but it is the courage of confidence which makes these men heroic and which is the basis of the other expressions of their courage. One could say—and liberal Protantism often has said—that the courage of the Reformers is the beginning of the individualistic type of the courage to be as oneself. But such an interpretation confuses a possible historical effect with the matter itself. In the courage of the Reformers the courage to be as oneself is both affirmed and transcended. In comparison with the mystical form of courageous self-affirmation the Protestant courage of confidence affirms the individual self as an individual self in its encounter with God as person. This radically distinguishes the personalism of the Reformation from all the later forms of individualism and Existentialism. The courage of the Reformers is not the courage to be oneself—as it is not the courage to be as a part. It transcends and unites both of them. For the courage of confidence is not rooted in confidence about oneself. The Reformation pronounces the opposite: one can become confident about one's existence only after ceasing to base one's confidence on oneself. On the other hand the courage of confidence is in no way based on anything finite besides oneself, not even on the Church. It is based on God and solely on God, who is experienced in a unique and personal encounter. The courage of the Reformation transcends both the courage to be as a part and the courage to be as oneself. It is threatened neither by the loss of oneself nor by the loss of one's world.

GUILT AND THE COURAGE TO ACCEPT ACCEPTANCE

In the center of the Protestant courage of confidence stands the courage to accept acceptance in spite of the consciousness of guilt. Luther, and in fact the whole period, experienced the anxiety of guilt and condemnation as the main form of their anxiety. The courage to affirm oneself in spite of this anxiety is the courage which we have called the courage of confidence. It is rooted in the personal, total, and immediate certainty of divine forgiveness. There is belief in forgiveness in all forms of man's courage to be, even in neocollectivism. But there is no interpretation of human existence in which it is so predominant as in genuine Protestantism. And there is no movement in history in which it is equally profound and equally paradoxical. In the Lutheran formula that "he who is unjust is just" (in the view of the divine forgiveness) or in the more modern phrasing that "he who is unacceptable is accepted" the victory over the anxiety of guilt and condemnation is sharply expressed. One could say that the courage to be is the courage to accept oneself as accepted in spite of being unacceptable. One does not need to remind the theologians of the fact that this is the genuine meaning of the Pauline-Lutheran doctrine of "justification by faith" (a doctrine which in its original phrasing has become incomprehensible even for students of theology). But one must remind theologians and ministers that in the fight against the anxiety of guilt by psychotherapy the idea of acceptance has received the attention and gained the significance which in the Reformation period was to be seen in phrases like "forgiveness of sins" or "justification through faith." Accepting acceptance though being unacceptable is the basis for the courage of confidence.

Decisive for this self-affirmation is its being independent of any moral, intellectual, or religious precondition: it is not the good or the wise or the pious who are entitled to the courage to accept acceptance but those who are lacking in all these qualities and are aware of being unacceptable. This, however, does not mean acceptance by oneself as oneself. It is not a justification of one's accidental individuality. It is not the Existentialist courage to be as oneself. It is the paradoxical act in which one is accepted by that which infinitely transcends one's individual self. It is in the experience of the Reformers the acceptance of the unacceptable sinner into judging and transforming communion with God.

The courage to be in this respect is the courage to accept the forgiveness of sins, not as an abstract assertion but as the fundamental experience in the encounter with God. Self-affirmation in spite of the anxiety of guilt and condemnation presupposes participation in something which transcends the self. In the communion of healing, for example the psychoanalytic situation, the patient participates in the healing power of the helper by whom he is accepted although he feels himself unacceptable. The healer, in this relationship, does not stand for himself as an individual but represents the objective power of acceptance and self-affirmation. This objective power works through the healer in the patient. Of course, it must be embodied in a person who can realize guilt, who can judge, and who can accept in spite of the judgment. Acceptance by something which is less than personal could never overcome personal self-rejection. A wall to which I confess cannot forgive me. No self-acceptance is possible if one is not accepted in a person-to-person relation. But even if one is personally accepted it needs a self-transcending courage to accept this acceptance, it needs the courage of confidence. For being accepted does not mean that guilt is denied. The healing helper who tried to convince his patient that he was not really guilty would do him a great disservice. He would prevent him from taking his guilt into his self-affirmation. He may help him to transform displaced, neurotic guilt feelings into genuine ones which are, so to speak, put on the right place, but he cannot tell him that there is no guilt in him. He accepts the patient into his communion without condemning anything and without covering up anything.

Here, however, is the point where the religious "acceptance as being accepted" transcends medical healing. Religion asks for the ultimate source of the power which heals by accepting the unacceptable, it asks for God. The acceptance by God, his forgiving or justifying act, is the only and ultimate source of a courage to be which is able to take the anxiety of guilt and condemnation into itself. For the ultimate power of self-affirmation can only be the power of being-itself. Everything less than this, one's own or anybody else's finite power of being, cannot overcome the radical, infinite threat of nonbe-

ing which is experienced in the despair of self-condemna-
tion. This is why the courage of confidence, as it is
expressed in a man like Luther, emphasizes unceasingly exclusive trust in God and rejects any other foundation for
his courage to be, not only as insufficient but as driving
him into more guilt and deeper anxiety. The immense liberation brought to the people of the 16th century by the
message of the Reformers and the creation of their indomitable courage to accept acceptance was due to the *sola
fide* doctrine, namely to the message that the courage of
confidence is conditioned not by anything finite but solely
by that which is unconditional itself and which we experience as unconditional in a person-to-person encounter.

THEISM TRANSCENDED

The courage to take meaninglessness into itself presupposes a relation to the ground of being which we have called "absolute faith." It is without a *special* content, yet it is not without content. The content of absolute faith is the "God above God." Absolute faith and its consequence, the courage that takes the radical doubt, the doubt about God, into itself, transcends the theistic idea of God.

Theism can mean the unspecified affirmation of God. Theism in this sense does not say what it means if it uses the name of God. Because of the traditional and psychological connotations of the word God such an empty theism can produce a reverent mood if it speaks of God. Politicians, dictators, and other people who wish to use rhetoric to make an impression on their audience like to use the word God in this sense. It produces the feeling in their listeners that the speaker is serious and morally trustworthy. This is especially successful if they can brand their foes as atheistic. On a higher level people without a definite religious commitment like to call themselves theistic, not for special purposes but because they cannot stand a world without God, whatever this God may be. They need some of the connotations of the word God and they are afraid of what they call atheism. On the highest level of this kind of theism the name of God is used as a poetic or practical symbol, expressing a profound emotional state or the highest ethical idea. It is a theism which stands on the boundary line between the second type of theism and what we call "theism transcended." But it is still too indefinite to cross this boundary line. The atheistic negation of this whole type of theism is as vague as the theism itself. It may produce an irreverent mood and angry reaction of those who take their theistic affirmation seriously. It may even be felt as justified against the rhetorical-political abuse of the name God, but it is ultimately as irrelevant as the theism which it negates. It cannot reach the state of despair any more than the theism against which it fights can reach the state of faith.

Theism can have another meaning, quite contrary to the first one: it can be the name of what we have called the divine-human encounter. In this case it points to those elements in the Jewish-Christian tradition which emphasize the person-to-person relationship with God. Theism in this sense emphasizes the personalistic passages in the Bible and the Protestant creeds, the personalistic image of God, the word as the tool of creation and revelation, the ethical and social character of the kingdom of God, the personal nature of human faith and divine forgiveness, the historical vision of the universe, the idea of a divine purpose, the infinite distance between creator and creature, the absolute separation between God and the world, the conflict between holy God and sinful man, the person-to-person character of prayer and practical devotion. Theism in this sense is the nonmystical side of biblical religion and historical Christianity. Atheism from the point of view of this theism is the human attempt to escape the divine-human encounter. It is an existential—not a theoretical—problem.

Theism has a third meaning, a strictly theological one. Theological theism is, like every theology, dependent on the religious substance which it conceptualizes. It is dependent on theism in the first sense insofar as it tries to prove the necessity of affirming God in some way; it usually develops the so-called arguments for the "existence" of God. But it is more dependent on theism in the second sense insofar as it tries to establish a doctrine of God which transforms the person-to-person encounter with God into a doctrine about two persons who may or may not meet but who have a reality independent of each other.

Now theism in the first sense must be transcended because it is irrelevant, and theism in the second sense must be transcended because it is one-sided. But theism in the third sense must be transcended because it is wrong. It is bad theology. This can be shown by a more penetrating analysis. The God of theological theism is a being beside others and as such a part of the whole of reality. He certainly is considered its most important part, but as a part and therefore as subjected to the structure of the whole. He is supposed to be beyond the ontological elements and categories which constitute reality. But every statement subjects him to them. He is seen as a self which has a world, as an ego which is related to a thou, as a cause which is separated from its effect, as having a definite space and an endless time. He is a being, not being-itself.

As such he is bound to the subject-object structure of reality, he is an object for us as subjects. At the same time we are objects for him as a subject. And this is decisive for the necessity of transcending theological theism. For God as a subject makes me into an object which is nothing more than an object. He deprives me of my subjectivity because he is all-powerful and all-knowing. I revolt and try to make *him* into an object, but the revolt fails and becomes desperate. God appears as the invincible tyrant, the being in contrast with whom all other beings are without freedom and subjectivity. He is equated with the recent tyrants who with the help of terror try to transform everything into a mere object, a thing among things, a cog in the machine they control. He becomes the model of everything against which Existentialism revolted. This is the God Nietzsche said had to be killed because nobody can tolerate being made into a mere object of absolute knowledge and absolute control. This is the deepest root of atheism. It is an atheism which is justified as the reaction against theological theism and its disturbing implications. It is also the deepest root of the Existentialist despair and the widespread anxiety of meaninglessness in our period.

Theism in all its forms is transcended in the experience we have called absolute faith. It is the accepting of the acceptance without somebody or something that accepts. It is the power of being-itself that accepts and gives the courage to be. This is the highest point to which our analysis has brought us. It cannot be described in the way the

God of all forms of theism can be described. It cannot be described in mystical terms either. It transcends both mysticism and personal encounter, as it transcends both the courage to be as a part and the courage to be as oneself.

THE GOD ABOVE GOD AND THE COURAGE TO BE

The ultimate source of the courage to be is the "God above God"; this is the result of our demand to transcend theism. Only if the God of theism is transcended can the anxiety of doubt and meaninglessness be taken into the courage to be. The God above God is the object of all mystical longing, but mysticism also must be transcended in order to reach him. Mysticism does not take seriously the concrete and the doubt concerning the concrete. It plunges directly into the ground of being and meaning, and leaves the concrete, the world of finite values and meanings, behind. Therefore it does not solve the problem of meaninglessness. In terms of the present religious situation this means that Eastern mysticism is not the solution of the problems of Western Existentialism, although many people attempt this solution. The God above the God of theism is not the devaluation of the meanings which doubt has thrown into the abyss of meaninglessness; he is their potential restitution. Nevertheless absolute faith agrees with the faith implied in mysticism in that both transcend the theistic objectivation of a God who is a being. For mysticism such a God is not more real than any finite being, for the courage to be such a God has disappeared in the abyss of meaninglessness with every other value and meaning.

The God above the God of theism is present, although hidden, in every divine-human encounter. Biblical religion as well as Protestant theology are aware of the paradoxical character of this encounter. They are aware that if God encounters man God is neither object nor subject and is therefore above the scheme into which theism has forced him. They are aware that personalism with respect to God is balanced by a transpersonal presence of the divine. They are aware that forgiveness can be accepted only if the power of acceptance is effective in man—biblically speaking, if the power of grace is effective in man. They are aware of the paradoxical character of every prayer, of speaking to somebody to whom you cannot speak because he is not "somebody," of asking somebody of whom you cannot ask anything because he gives or gives not before you ask, of saying "thou" to somebody who is nearer to the I than the I is to itself. Each of these paradoxes drives the religious consciousness toward a God above the God of theism.

The courage to be which is rooted in the experience of the God above the God of theism unites and transcends the courage to be as a part and the courage to be as oneself. It avoids both the loss of oneself by participation and the loss of one's world by individualization. The acceptance of the God above the God of theism makes us a part of that which is not also a part but is the ground of the whole.

Therefore our self is not lost in a larger whole, which submerges it in the life of a limited group. If the self participates in the power of being-itself it receives itself back. For the power of being acts through the power of the individual selves. It does not swallow them as every limited whole, every collectivism, and every conformism does. This is why the Church, which stands for the power of being-itself or for the God who transcends the God of the religions, claims to be the mediator of the courage to be. A church which is based on the authority of the God of theism cannot make such a claim. It inescapably develops into a collectivist or semicollectivist system itself.

But a church which raises itself in its message and its devotion to the God above the God of theism without sacrificing its concrete symbols can mediate a courage which takes doubt and meaninglessness into itself. It is the Church under the Cross which alone can do this, the Church which preaches the Crucified who cried to God who remained his God after the God of confidence had left him in the darkness of doubt and meaninglessness. To be as a part in such a church is to receive a courage to be in which one cannot lose one's self and in which one receives one's world.

Absolute faith, or the state of being grasped by the God beyond God, is not a state which appears beside other states of the mind. It never is something separated and definite, an event which could be isolated and described. It is always a movement in, with, and under other states of the mind. It is the situation on the boundary of man's possibilities. It *is* this boundary. Therefore it is both the courage of despair and the courage in and above every courage. It is not a place where one can live, it is without the safety of words and concepts, it is without a name, a church, a cult, a theology. But it is moving in the depth of all of them. It is the power of being, in which they participate and of which they are fragmentary expressions.

One can become aware of it in the anxiety of fate and death when the traditional symbols, which enable men to stand the vicissitudes of fate and the horror of death have lost their power. When "providence" has become a superstition and "immortality" something imaginary that which once was the power in these symbols can still be present and create the courage to be in spite of the experience of a chaotic world and a finite existence. The Stoic courage returns but not as the faith in universal reason. It returns as the absolute faith which says Yes to being without seeing anything concrete which could conquer the nonbeing in fate and death.

And one can become aware of the God above the God of theism in the anxiety of guilt and condemnation when the traditional symbols that enable men to withstand the anxiety of guilt and condemnation have lost their power. When "divine judgment" is interpreted as a psychological complex and forgiveness as a remnant of the "father-image," what once was the power in those symbols can still be present and create the courage to be in spite of the experience of an infinite gap between what we are and what we ought to be. The Lutheran courage returns but not supported by the faith in a judging and forgiving God. It returns in terms of the absolute faith which says Yes although there is no special power that conquers guilt. The courage to take the anxiety of meaninglessness upon oneself is the boundary line up to which the courage to be can go. Beyond it is mere non-being. Within it all forms of courage are re-established in the power of the God above the God of theism. *The courage to be is rooted in the God who appears when God has disappeared in the anxiety of doubt.*